advance prai
Kilimanjaro Uncovered

"A fun, informative and inspiring story that follows Alex's journey to the summit of Kilimanjaro on the little known and under appreciated Northern Circuit. Although not a guide, Kilimanjaro Uncovered is full of brilliant little nuggets of information that will help you prepare for the Roof of Africa!"

—Mark Whitman, Author of *Mount Kilimanjaro: Trekkers Guide to the Summit*

"Intriguing, informative, inspirational - A must read for anyone wanting to climb Kilimanjaro and learn more about Tanzania and its people!"

—Mehul Aggarwal, Director Bristol Cottages

"Alex's description of the final push to the summit is some of the best writing I have seen in ages. Her real-time view of experiences is gripping, with clear, honest descriptions of her own thoughts and feelings, and her interpretation of others' reactions to this challenge. Whether you are an adventurer with plans to tackle Kilimanjaro yourself, or are merely attracted to the idea of the challenge, this book will have you reading well into the night. It was a pleasure to edit this book."

—Raewyn Sills, Editor of *Kilimanjaro Uncovered*

"A must read for any mountain trekker either prior to your climb or to just relish the memory of your past climbs. Alex's study of the human interaction and natures of climbers is very telling of the requirements to succeed in summitting not only Mount Kilimanjaro but any high altitude mountain with a team of climbers. Her insights and preparation chapter may save prospective climbers thousands of dollars and will make the adventure as safe and comfortable as possible. I read the book cover to cover in only two sittings. Thank you for memorializing the memories that will last forever Alex!"

—Stewart Juneau, Chairman leTriomphe Property Group, Developer/Owner Ritz Carlton Hotel New Orleans LA USA

"Whether you're the proverbial mountain goat or a tortoise planning to hike Kili's slopes I'd recommend this book. If you're no hiker and have no interest whatsoever in walking anywhere I'd recommend this book. If only for the entertainment of sharing in the experiences of what it means to be human and 'proud to be wild' for nine days, I'd say, read *Kilimanjaro Uncovered* by Alex Tanbai."

—Jeannette Gravett, Author of *Kilimanjaro Uncovered Foreword*

Kilimanjaro
uncovered

An Alternative Path to Bliss

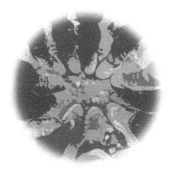

ALEXANDRA TANBAI

With a Foreword by Jeannette Gravett

ISBN: 1539081745
ISBN-13: 978-1539081746
CreateSpace

$1 of every book purchased will be donated to KPAP, the Kilimanjaro Porters Assistance Project, committed to improving the working conditions of the porters on Kilimanjaro.

To Chris

because you made my hike so special.

You are the hero of my story.

To all my fellow hikers

because you made my hike so enjoyable.

You are the heroes of this book.

To all our guides, cooks, waiters and porters

because you made our hike possible.

You are the heroes of Kilimanjaro.

Contents

FOREWORD xii

PREFACE xv

INTRODUCTION xviii

CHAPTER I – BEFORE THE HIKE   1

GETTING SERIOUS 3

BOOKING CONSIDERATIONS 9

  When?   9

  Which route?   11

  Whith whom? Or reasons not to book   21

    Financial considerations   21

    Acute mountain sickness (AMS)   22

    Feeling cold, really cold   24

    Plenty of nicer mountains   25

    No vacation time   27

  Which operator?   31

    Porter treatment   33

    Experienced guides   35

    Equipment – sleeping comfort   37

    Equipment – oxygen and safety   40

    Equipment – dining and post-dining comforts   43

    Food and water   45

    Group size   46

    Group tour offering   47

    My operator choice   47

    Operator selection shortcut for future hikers   48

CONTENTS

SO MANY MORE THINGS TO PREPARE 51

Hiking boots 51

Keeping up the momentum 55

Sorting out my medical preparations 60

A month of shopping 65

No time to take it easy 77

My workout program 81

CHAPTER II – TRAVEL EPISODES **83**

On my way to Tanzania 85

On local grounds 91

Meeting KPAP to learn about porters treatment 97

CHAPTER III – THE HIKE **105**

Day 0: Killing my Diamox rebel 107

Day 1: Shifting my bathroom paradigm 117

Day 2: Pole pole to the land of dust 147

Day 3: Learning Swahili and making friends 171

Day 4: Feeling so alive, yet alone 197

Day 5: Into the wild away from popular routes 221

Day 6: Getting bored of fog, soup and pole pole 243

Day 7: Into thin air 261

Summit Night: Fighting alone and together 283

Day 8 – all the way up: What's the point? 315

Day 8 – half way down: It's not about me 327

Day 9: It's all about us 347

EPILOGUE 381

APPENDIX | 383

Expectations management | 385

Basic Kilimanjaro Swahili | 388

Quotes that made us laugh | 390

Unexpected things to expect on Kilimanjaro | 391

ACKNOWLEDGEMENTS | 393

ABOUT THE AUTHOR | 397

NOTES AND REFERENCES | 399

Foreword

Alex Tanbai tells her story, of a nine-day trek up and down the mighty slopes of Mount Kilimanjaro, with honesty, brutal at times, with self-deprecating humour, real passion and a zest for life. All this, as she hiked on that mountain with a generous portion of high energy. I wonder now, as I did then, whether she shares the same advantageous genetics as the former Olympic Finnish skier, Eero Mäntyranta. That is, that she possibly possesses a greater quantity of red blood cells than most people, a medical condition known as polycythaemia. This would give her an increased oxygen supply in her bloodstream and would thus fuel her lungs and muscles in her beautiful legs! Or maybe she's on steroids? Is she one of the scarily fit guides or porters incognito; put there by them to find out what we truly think about them when they aren't around? Or is she just in the best possible shape?

Whatever the truth, be prepared for a rollicking canter up and down the steep slopes of Kilimanjaro as you read this tale, through her eyes, in the pages that follow. I can still see her white hat bobbing up and down on her head like the fringe on a wild filly from the Camargue as she heads off into the distance. In easy-to-read conversational style she bares her heart with descriptions of what it means to feel vulnerable on such a trek, not least her own vulnerability, and how strength prevails when one feels most exposed. Many books written on Kilimanjaro hikes are full of boasting and authors patting themselves on the back. This isn't one of them.

We were a group of twelve hikers and gelled pretty well – the veritable Motley Crew – each different from the other and from varying situations in life. There is no doubt that should each of us write a book about this trek there would be twelve different versions.

Add to the mix each guide's and porter's viewpoint and one would have another forty-something stories, each from his own, unique perspective. We'd even disagree on certain aspects perceived as fact by one or other of us. It is one of those fascinating human traits that each has his/her own world view.

Alex maintains she knew she'd summit. I hoped and prayed I would. For me the trek was tough and a slog yet an enjoyable experience you may be surprised to know. Not once did I wish that the nine days be in any way reduced. I savoured each energy-sapping *pole pole* moment. My own relatively minor medical ailments slowing me down somewhat incongruously reminded me that she who persists will win in the end. Tenacious Irish genes came into play urging me to *just do it*. It was also a great relief not to succumb to Acute Mountain Sickness (AMS). Once at the summit I felt euphoric, a feeling which lasted about three days afterwards. I cried as I started back down from Uhuru Peak – at the sheer wonder of being there; seeing the receding glaciers; the experience at large; the humans I'd met and the animals who entertained us on the way. Each of us had his/her own summit experience.

You may be tempted to do a solo hike so that you can proceed at your own pace and not annoy the herd. Yet the camaraderie experienced in a group effort is something stimulating even though it be a two-edged sword at times. It isn't even necessarily about liking one another. It's more about the bond that forms between strangers – people so different one from the other, coming together for an intensive period of time, sharing much, getting to know one another to some extent and becoming fairly close because of just that. The adrenaline junkies have to bear with the slowpokes and they in turn need to have patience with the energetic – those impatient *rebels*. That in itself partly makes up the group dynamic. Now, that we're back, Eva calls us "The Mountain Family". She's not talking about an inbred hillbilly mix-up when she says that! At least I don't think she is. Rather, she's talking about that bond we've formed. I think.

Alex writes about all these shared experiences and explores her own personal growth. A mere hike becomes a journey of self-discovery and reflection. Surprisingly, a love story develops. She sees her own preconceptions turned on their heads. The issue of porter welfare is taken up and is being acted upon even as this book goes to print. At a time when political correctness is killing the truth, the honest language here makes for a refreshing read. *Kilimanjaro Uncovered* is also, at times, laugh-out-loud funny – just like life. This makes it real.

It is often the small things that challenge us the most even when our needs are drastically reduced. Issues common to all. The following pages are peppered with just such insights. Not only is it a story of a personal adventure but it's also interspersed with tips on hiking, descriptions of terrain and the actual route taken, the Northern Circuit.

Whether you're the proverbial mountain goat or a tortoise planning to hike Kili's slopes, I'd recommend this book. If you're no hiker and have no interest whatsoever in walking anywhere, I'd recommend this book. If only for the entertainment of sharing in the experiences of what it means to be human and "proud to be wild" for nine days, I'd say, read *Kilimanjaro Uncovered* by Alex Tanbai.

Jeannette Gravett, Sweden, May 2016

Jeannette
(after a steep ascent on our first morning in the jungle)

Preface

Kilimanjaro Uncovered started with a simple idea – to review a little-known hiking route. It ended with a truly life-changing experience – written in real time while I was unconscious of being the subject of transformation.

I expected a difficult climb bringing me close to my physical limits; an uncomfortable week making me dream of my shower and bed; and an achievement that would make me feel proud for weeks to come. None of that came true. Instead, I found what no book could have prepared me for: myself.

Kilimanjaro challenged and changed my thinking so deeply that it would turn my life upside down. I do not believe in good or bad, yet I feel that my journey has made me a better person.

Now I invite you to join me once more on my journey, devoid of beautification and exaggeration, and to look deeper behind the facades. Hopefully my story will help you find happiness in your own adventures, be it on Kilimanjaro or elsewhere.

▲ ▲ ▲

As per my initial idea, *Kilimanjaro Uncovered* remains the first book set on the so-called Northern Circuit route, a path away from mass tourism and truly in the wild. For readers interested in scaling the mountain themselves, it also attempts to provide helpful guidance to prepare for such an adventure. However, *Kilimanjaro Uncovered* has become so much more than a practical review.

Asked at the outset what form this book would need to take to reach a broader audience beyond hiking aficionados, the answer was straightforward: a love story. Obsessed as I was with authentic storytelling, this was not an option.

Little did I expect that my hike would actually turn out to be more about love than anything else. It would be about brotherly love of the people around me, about learning from them, appreciating their uniqueness and our diversity, and forming connections.

As with everything in life, our perception of events is shaped by our interconnections with people around us. Hiking Kilimanjaro was no exception. I was fortunate to share my hiking experience with a wonderful group of fellow hikers and guides, each with their own unique character and strengths that contributed to make our adventure truly enjoyable.

Amongst our hiking group, I met a very special person – a proverbial soul mate. Throughout our nine days together, we would form a unique connection stronger than I would ever have thought possible. Despite our different backgrounds, we shared the same humor; the same enthusiasm about our adventure; the same desire to feel alive by making use of our every last bit of energy; the same joy of giving; and the same longing to feel connected and share our experience with each other. It so happened that this book also became a totally true love story.

Consequently, this book is as much about my individual encounters with each member of our group and this special person, as it is a practical review and investigation. It is as much an emotionally enriching exploration as it is a physically challenging adventure.

What started with a group of strangers became a group of friends. What started with two group members became two soul mates. What started with me became us. Reaching the summit alone meant nothing to me, sharing my journey with others meant everything.

▲ ▲ ▲

Finally, by tragic coincidence, my trip to Kilimanjaro made me aware of the Live Your Legend community. Their founder Scott Dinsmore fell victim to a lethal rockfall one week before I started my hike. He was only 33 years old – just like me, but left a wonderful legacy. Scott believed that the world would be a better place if we all did work that we truly cared about. He created the Live Your Legend community to help people find their own passion and purpose, and make a unique impact on the world.

While my Kilimanjaro journey is coming to its end, another one is just about to start. I have found my passion and a purpose. Hopefully, many of us will live our legends just as Scott wanted all of us to do. As Eva from our hiking group would say: "This year we climbed Mount Kilimanjaro, next year anything is possible".

Alexandra Tanbai, Zurich, November 2015

Yours truly
(at base camp excited about summit night)

Introduction

Kilimanjaro Uncovered spans the greater part of my year, 2015. Chapter I summarizes basic facts and my own conclusions about organizing a Kilimanjaro hike. While I over-researched and over-prepared my own hike, I found a lack of concise, trustworthy information in other literature. Hence, Chapter I is my attempt to provide helpful guidance as part of my own story. However, I do not claim this to be a complete travel guide.

If you are not interested in preparatory and background information, you may wish to skip parts of Chapter I. I have indicated the most technical sections so you can jump straight ahead. Alternatively, you may wish to start directly with my travel story in Chapter II or only my hiking story in Chapter III.

The entire book was mostly written in real time. It therefore captures my impressions, emotions and interactions as accurately as possible. However, while staying true to my own memories, I can only describe my subjective perception. In an effort to provide a more objective and complete account, I have taken two measures.

Firstly, I did not inform our tour operator or my fellow hikers about my intentions to write this book until after our hike. My hope was to provide an unbiased account especially regarding the performance of our tour operator and guides. Now I can safely praise them without leaving you wondering whether their behavior was authentic or influenced by my publication. Similarly, the overwhelming kindness, humor and positive energy of each and every one in our hiking group were authentic and real. This only leaves me wondering how much I may have been influenced by my own writing. At a minimum, certainly it made me look deeper and not accept simple answers, in my search for truth.

Secondly, I have sent a draft for review to each of our group members as well as our operator, soliciting their comments, corrections, different viewpoints or deletions of private details. Their input is reflected herein with a view to providing a more accurate and complete picture, but without sacrificing authenticity. If each of our group members had written a book, certainly each story would have been very different. Some of their names have been changed for privacy reasons and are the only fictitious information in this book.

Finally, I've realized how my expectations about Kilimanjaro were influenced by other books I had read, and how these expectations influenced my feelings about what I actually experienced. To help you enjoy your own hiking experience as much as possible, I have included some expectations management recommendations for you in the Appendix.

Furthermore, I have summarized all the Swahili key words and phrases that we learned while hiking. Surely locals appreciate any effort to speak even just a few words in their language.

On a more humorous note, I conclude with a collection of quotes that made us laugh, as well as all the unexpected things that may happen on Kilimanjaro.

For more information about Kilimanjaro, including photos, useful preparatory information as well as a live blog on related topics, traveler reviews and recommendations, please visit www.kilimanjaro-uncovered.com. For latest news and updates, please follow @KiliUncovered on Facebook or Twitter. To contact me privately, I look forward to your feedback, comments or other thoughts at alexandra.tanbai@kilimanjaro-uncovered.com.

Now let me send you off into your own Kilimanjaro reading exploration – enjoy!

CHAPTER I

BEFORE THE HIKE

▲ ▲ ▲

"Luck is where opportunity meets preparation."

—Seneca

Getting serious

21 APRIL 2015

Click. Send. Relax. WAHOO! After more than three months of researching different options to death, I have finally booked my Mount Kilimanjaro hike. There are two things I don't know yet. First, these three months have only been the beginning of the beginning of the beginning. Second, I have just changed the course of my life BIG TIME. If I knew what I will know a year from now, I would doubt my sanity. Thankfully, I have no psychic talents, and the journey will be the reward for my ignorance.

So let's start with the basics: Why would I spend three months to research my vacation? Because I am a freak – I like to do my research; a perfectionist – I like to get it right; and a dreamer – I declared long time ago that I would live to 120 years of age. Dying on Kilimanjaro would kind of ruin that life goal, wouldn't it? I mean Mount Kilimanjaro is the freaking highest mountain in Africa – rising almost 6,000 meters above sea level (5,895m/19,341ft to be exact)! There are a lot of things that could kill you up there – altitude sickness, rockfall, freezing to death, falling off a cliff . . . or in Africa – malaria, rabies, typhus, sleeping sickness . . . . I am certainly no suicidal adventurer, and only about as adventurous as your average banker. In other words, I like to gamble, but I only take calculated risks when my own fortune is at stake. True to my analytical and investigative character, I *ran the numbers* and conducted my research. Conclusion: There's nothing (abnormally) dangerous about hiking Kilimanjaro (for us tourists).

You don't believe me? Well, let me introduce you to some statistics, or rather crude estimates because there are no official statistics. So one year hence, despite being warned from all insiders and experts that the Kilimanjaro National Park would not give official data, I will feel obliged as an author of a book to verify that assumption. Thus, I will bombard the Kilimanjaro National Park, the Tanzania National Park as well as the Tanzania Tourist Board with contact requests including by e-mail, phone and Twitter. Their lack of response will only confirm what I already suspect − they are trying to hide some unpleasant truths. It could also be pure incompetence, but they do a good job marketing Tanzania as a tourist destination, so I give them the benefit of the doubt. Furthermore, their own regulations require every guide to report immediately to the park authority any "bodily injury to the climber" or "climber's death", and the definition of climber covers tourists, guides and porters. Thus, I am pretty sure they know exactly what's going on, and it's the second part of their climber definition that might reveal some inconvenient truths.

Anecdotally, there is a Twitter account called @TanzaniaRetweet which supposedly is "retweeting all things #Tanzania . . . also . . . #Kilimanjaro". For the sake of awareness building and transparency, I will drop my pseudo-religious *no-social-media* stance one year from now. True to their mission, @TanzaniaRetweet would unfailingly retweet even the very first tweet of my entire life, because it mentions *#Kilimanjaro*. Wahoo, that feels good! But not for long, because soon I will realize that they simply retweet every single tweet about Kilimanjaro, even my retweets. After a week of tweeting practice, I will gain in confidence and tweet my first posts mentioning both *#Kilimanjaro* and *#porters*. Guess what − no retweets! They would ban me for the coming month; even my most innocent tweets about their greatest of all mountains shall not be retweeted. Welcome to the world of social media and mass market manipulation!

Unfortunately, without any official data as of publication, I am unable to verify my assumptions. So for now we are restricted to widely quoted but unconfirmed information: With its increasing popularity, already ca. 60,0000[1] tourist hikers attempt to summit Kilimanjaro every year. Amongst these hikers, fatality estimates range from 1 to 15 deaths per year, while 8 to 10[2] seem to be most frequently quoted. I assume that these numbers are over-stated. On the one hand, they all refer to outdated sources. As of booking, I cannot find any recent online news reports about those deaths. Surely, in the age of Internet and social media, that would go viral? Two widely reported lethal incidents in September 2015 and July 2016 would tragically confirm my logic. On the other hand, I think operators have a bias to over-state the danger, so they can exploit our fears and charge extra for useless safety equipment and marketing.

The latest estimate from a credible source as at publication refers to 3 to 4 deaths per year.[3] However, for sake of illustration, let's take a very conservative view and assume 10 hikers die on Kilimanjaro every year. Based on a total number of 60,000 hikers, this implies a death rate of 0.02% – not a bad record. In Switzerland, where I live, the crude annual death rate is around 0.13% of those younger than 65 years.[4] How does that compare to the 0.02%? Of course this is not an apples-to-apples comparison, but it puts the numbers into perspective. Not convinced yet? Let me give you another data point. The Swiss Alpine Club will record 213 people dying on Swiss mountains in 2015. This includes snow avalanches and skiing accidents, but a total of 61 people will die falling off a cliff while hiking in the Swiss mountains![5] Now how does that compare to the numbers on Kilimanjaro? I might be safer climbing Africa's tallest mountain than hiking in my own neighborhood! No one ever told me not to go hiking in Switzerland because I might die; yet people tend to associate Kilimanjaro with danger.

Being a complete novice to extreme hiking, I was no exception to that unfounded perception. Despite the analytical part of my brain telling me not to worry, I wanted to know exactly what precautions I would need to take in order not to become part of this year's statistical 0.02%, or the roughly 1,000 evacuations taking place every year.[6] Furthermore, I wanted to maximize my chances of reaching the summit and to make sure that this trip would not only be about *ticking the box* but an enjoyable experience along the way. That's why it took me three months of research to finally book my hike!

I found most information to be available online, but for one important consideration – my hiking route. There are different ways to reach the summit and I've opted for a hiking route that is supposed to be *off the beaten track* and relatively new (more about this later). Unsurprisingly, I couldn't find any information about that particular route. Hence, I've just decided today, the very same day that I've booked my hike, that it might be a good idea to record both my conclusions from obsessive research as well as what I will find on that new route, for the benefit of future hikers.

Now you know why I start writing this book, but hey – isn't there a way more important WHY? Such as why have I decided to hike Kili – short for Mount Kilimanjaro – in the first place? To be honest, I don't even know myself. I am not an experienced hiker, I have never done any extreme sports, and I would consider my physical condition just about average. While I am well-traveled, I have never been to Africa, I have never gone on a proper backpacking trip, and I have never slept in a tent (childhood aside). The whole trip is probably going to cost me more than the price of a car. I will definitely feel cold and uncomfortable for a significant part of it, and there are heaps of things that could go wrong and kill me. Here is an extract from my operator's waiver form that I've just signed:

> *"I am aware that, during the trip or activity, I may be subjecting myself to dangers and hazards, which could result in* **physical or emotional trauma, illness, injury, paralysis, death or damage to myself**, *property and/or third-parties. I acknowledge that high-altitude mountain hiking entails known and unanticipated risks including, among other things: the hazards of traveling in uneven mountainous terrain and slips and falls;* **being struck by rock fall, ice fall or other objects dislodged or thrown from above**; *the forces of nature, including* **lightning**, *weather changes; the risk of* **falling off the rock**, *mountain; the risk of exposure to insect bites or* **animal attacks**; *the risk of altitude and cold including* **hypothermia, frostbite, acute mountain sickness, cerebral and pulmonary edema**; *my own physical condition; and the* **physical exertion** *associated with this activity. Additional dangers may include the* **hazards of traveling in the Third World**; *risks associated with viewing wild animals; accident or illness in remote places without access to emergency medical facilities; war,* **terrorism** *and other forces. I understand that this* **description of risks is not complete** *and that other unanticipated inherent risks may occur. I recognize that such risks, dangers and hazards may be present at any time during the trip. I also am aware that* **medical services or facilities may not be readily available** *or accessible during some or all of the time in which I am participating in the trip."*

Not for the faint-hearted, huh? They did a good job making it pretty comprehensive, and because they cannot possibly anticipate hikers committing suicide, as I may do if I can't wash my hair for over a week, they make sure to acknowledge that their description of risks is not complete. Well done!

Luckily, as expected, my obsessive research convinced me that all the risks they explicitly mention are no real risks, if prepared for correctly. My only potential *deal breaker* consideration to start with was: Would I cope without a shower for over a week? That puts me into the *freak* category. Others typically care mostly about excessive cost, danger, altitude sickness or lack of fitness. Not me. My number one worry is my hair. Dealing with an itchy, smelly, greasy scalp for over a week will be my real litmus test – to summit or not to summit? And the thought of anyone seeing me without make-up scares me almost as much. Physically, I don't have the slightest doubt that I can do it. Psychologically, this will push my boundaries more than anything else I have ever done.

So back to the real question: Why, why, why? The idea planted itself into my brain some time mid-2014, when my partner and I were pondering new travel destinations. We both loved traveling, and with busy schedules and the need to coordinate vacations, we wanted to make sure not to miss out on any *must see* destinations. So, being well organized, we made a bucket list of travel priorities for the coming 2-3 years. While browsing for *must see* destinations, I came across Tanzania and immediately got excited by its variety of unique tourist attractions: Hiking up the world's tallest free-standing mountain (Kilimanjaro), going on safari in one of the world's most abundant and diverse game reserves (Serengeti), and enjoying white beaches and fantastic diving at the world's spice island (Zanzibar). What a compelling and diverse mix of attractions, all in one country! Once aware of Tanzania as a great travel destination, my ambitious character took over. I like extremes, and hiking Kili sounded like the perfect challenge, with Serengeti and Zanzibar as perfect rewards.

Except for one little problem: My partner didn't share my enthusiasm. "Are you serious? You don't even know how to climb!"

"Yes, but it seems that no technical skills are required. That's why it's so popular. It's the highest mountain worldwide that you can literally just hike up. Not even any ropes required like we had on Kinabalu", the highest mountain in South East Asia and at just over 4,000 meters (13,400ft) my only higher altitude hiking experience to date.

"O . . . kay," as an experienced camper and outdoors person he was open to the idea. "Why don't you find out a bit more?" he proposed.

And so I did.

"I've looked into it, takes about a week."

"You mean a week in a tent, without a shower? Forget it!"

"Please!!!"

"No way."

Because there are no shortcuts to the top, at least not for us ordinary human beings. No persuasion on my end would do the trick, but I wouldn't give up so easily. We were thinking of going on a joint vacation with friends. Patrik and Stella had also mentioned Tanzania previously, and I was sure they would be able to manage without a shower. If I could get them on board, then surely they could help me convince my partner.

"Yes, we'd like to go to Tanzania, to Zanzibar, but not to Kilimanjaro," Stella knew all about it. "Why would you want to go up there?!" Expensive, tedious, uncomfortable and not even that beautiful!

"It's such a typical investment banker *must do*", Patrik recalled the early days of our career when we initially met, "to show off, boost one's ego and tick the box."

We liked making fun of our former slave years in investment banking, both of us equally happy to have found an exit and made our way back into the real world.

I hadn't thought about Kilimanjaro as a *tick-the-box* adventure, but now I remembered that indeed some of our colleagues in investment banking had been talking about Kilimanjaro ten years ago. Back then, it didn't appeal to me at all and seemed completely out of my league. Many things have changed since. For example, I no longer believe in *mission impossible*. Just that convincing my partner to hike Kilimanjaro had indeed become such a *mission impossible*. As all the concerns about Kilimanjaro mentioned by our friends were true, I was left without arguments to get my way. Why did Kili nevertheless still appeal so much to me? Was there still a little competitive investment banker left deep inside me who simply wanted to tick the box and prove that I could do it?

It didn't matter anymore, because vacation separate from my partner was not on the agenda. With still many other destinations left to explore together, we moved on to other parts of this world. However, Kilimanjaro became a constant shadow in the back of my mind. The more I realized I might NEVER in my life be able to tick that box, the more I wanted it. Forbidden adventures become a mental addiction, don't they?

So what changed? In a nutshell, my relationship unexpectedly went down the drain in autumn 2014. Two months later around New Year, I found myself wondering what to do with my new single life and what plans to make for 2015. The answer was obvious, I had no more excuses: If I really wanted to reach the top of Africa, then there was no better time than now, 2015. And that's how it all started.

BOOKING CONSIDERATIONS

When?

The first question to get my head around, and perhaps the easiest to solve, was when to go. As a perfectionist, I pinned down my summit hike for 28 September 2015, the single best day of the entire year. Why exactly that day? I consulted my astrologer . . . just joking. I am a freak, but on the opposite extreme – it's pure statistics. Let's go step by step.

While theoretically hard-core hikers could go any time, practically I am too wussy for extreme hiking. Kilimanjaro has its seasons with vast differences in expected temperatures, sunshine, clouds, rain and snow on the summit. For me, choosing the season with the least expected discomfort was a no-brainer.

The online community seemed in agreement about the weather question: January, February and September are most recommended. These three months have the unique combination of not being too cold while at the same time showing low levels of cloudiness. After all, what's the point of reaching the top if all we can see are clouds? Even worse than that, clouds not only obstruct our view, they may also translate into moisture that seeps into our clothes and makes us feel cold. Brrr, not for wussies.

September is somewhat colder than January and February, but also has a lower chance of precipitation. Getting wet was the evil to be avoided, so September clearly seemed to be the single best month: No clouds, no rain and not too cold. It also worked well for me because I wanted to complete my adventure in 2015 yet with sufficient time to prepare.

However, I made a mistake in my analysis, allowing myself to be misled by the online community. Most websites refer to temperature measures taken downhill at Moshi. Have they never considered that hikers worry more about temperatures ON the mountain rather than DOWN in the rainforest? To the contrary, lower temperatures in tropical climates may even be a plus rather than a negative for tourists! The truth – as I eventually discovered – is that temperatures are far more stable at higher altitudes on Kilimanjaro throughout the year.[7] Thus in hindsight, I would recommend that the entire dry and least cloudy season from July to September are the best months to go for, avoiding the hot tropical temperatures at the beginning of the year.

Thinking of when to go, there is one more detail to consider: The final hike up to the summit takes place overnight, usually leaving before midnight and arriving for sunset or early morning. Wouldn't it be good if it was not pitch-black, but to enjoy the light of a full moon during that big night? At least that's what several operators recommended. Of course I had to make sure to plan my hike for exactly the best possible time of the year – full moon in September. That special day happened to be September 28 in 2015. Here you go – science beats ignorance.

I should mention that my logic has its drawback – welcome to the crowds! But hey – there is no reasonable alternative. Would you rather be wet and cold yet have the mountain to yourself (how miserable), or dry and warm yet in bad company (how somewhat less miserable)? Even as a self-proclaimed introvert who doesn't want to be seen without make-up, I prefer the latter. The weather will not only dictate my physical comfort, but also my odds of staying healthy and energetic. Logically, this will then again impact my chance of reaching the summit. So we are back to priority number one – always with the end in mind.

BOOKING CONSIDERATIONS

Which route?

WARNING: THIS CHAPTER IS ONLY FOR FUTURE HIKERS OR THE MOST CURIOUS OF READERS. IF YOU ARE NOT INTERESTED IN HIKING YOURSELF OR THE EXTENT OF PREPARATION INVOLVED, PLEASE CONTINUE WITH THE NEXT CHAPTER ON PAGE 21.

The second question to get your head around is which route to take. There are six common routes as well as a few less popular ones, all leading to the summit. By stated order of popularity, the traditional routes include the Machame, Marangu, Lemosho, Shira, Rongai and Umbwe routes.[8] Choice is good, but that much choice made me feel like a teenager asked to choose a career path. Um, how to even start?

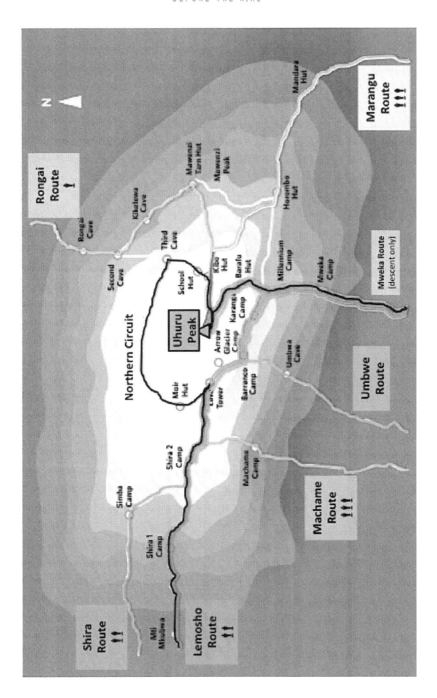

Kilimanjaro hiking routes

Luckily, I knew what to optimize for: Minimize my days without a shower! Makes sense, no? I bet 99% of hikers have that same ingenious idea – keep it short. For ordinary humans, that still means a minimum of five days. What an eternity! There also is an option for the superhuman – speed climbing. Karl Egloff, the record holder as of writing, made it up and down in no more than 6 hours 42 minutes. But hey, let's be realistic. I'm no superhuman, and if you are reading this book, then most likely you aren't either.

So if I would have to spend a minimum of five days on that mountain, then at least I wanted to have some basic comfort. Google "Kilimanjaro accommodation" and your heart will warm: The Marangu route offers huts, no need to sleep in tents! Yippee! I could do it! Could I even have my own hut? And do they provide showers? No, and no. My heart sank again. Memories of a miserable sleepless night in a cold and uncomfortable dorm room on Mount Kinabalu brought me back to my senses. Why would I want to share such a hut with strangers, if I could have a tent by myself? And worse than that, the Marangu route is nicknamed *Coca Cola* route. That sounds so mass touristy. And I don't even like coke or soft drinks in general, which they sell at those huts. Would I want to be such a typical tourist myself? My hair stood on end, and I willingly chose unfiltered water and tents.

As I kept reading, I realized that optimizing for a minimum number of days would be a really stupid thing to do. Why? Because the shorter the hike, the lower your chance of acclimatizing to the high altitude, the higher the chances of developing severe AMS (acute mountain sickness) and not making it to the top. AMS is a serious matter and can kill you. More about that later. For now, suffice to say the best preventive remedy against AMS is to take your time and gain altitude slowly. Why is this not a problem for the superhuman? Apparently, if one is quick enough, appropriately conditioned and with the right anatomical make-up, than AMS symptoms may be suppressed.[9] One thing for sure – I won't be quick enough.

Other than acclimatizing slowly, there is a second reason why taking a short route may not be a good idea: Given everyone tends to follow my initial logic, the shorter routes are also the most popular ones. This means if you go up either the Marangu or Machame routes, you will be doomed to hike with an entire village (unless you choose a cloudy rainy season which doesn't sound like a good idea either). Just to put this into perspective: With 60,000 hikers on Kilimanjaro every year, five months of rainy season (March to May and mid-October to mid-December) and three supposedly very cold months (June to August), I would assume that at least 30,000 hikers (i.e. 50%) will plan their trip during the same 3-4 best months. That means on average more than 200 hikers would start to hike every single day. Add their entourage of porters (usually 3 per person) and guides; you'll quickly count a small village of around 1,000 people, exploding probably to the size of a small town around full moon. Some hikers might like the thought of company and be totally OK with that, willing to accept the associated unpleasantries of mass tourism. Not me – just thinking of 1,000 people peeing and pooping along the same path every single day . . . yuck! I wanted to have a more authentic nature experience without the crowds.

In case you still consider minimizing your time on the mountain but concur with me in terms of avoiding the crowds – why not follow the Umbwe route? It is short and has very low traffic. Sounds a bit too good to be true, and indeed there is a reason for the low traffic. The Umbwe route is very difficult. It goes pretty much straight uphill and doesn't allow for acclimatization; hence it also has the lowest summit success rate. This route is only for strong hikers who are also confident of their ability to acclimatize, [10] like Karl Egloff, but definitely not us ordinary humans.

Upon further research for the best possible route, I learnt about Crater Camp. At an altitude of 5,750 meters (18,800ft), this is the highest camp on Kilimanjaro, right inside the crater and only a few hundred meters from the summit.[11] Why would anyone want to stay that high up? Because it allows you to sleep right beside one of Kilimanjaro's last remaining glaciers, the Furtwängler glacier; and from there you could go to the inner Reusch Crater and look down the 350m (1,150ft) deep Ash Pit,[12] neither of which you get to see otherwise; and because few people have been there, so it adds an extra edge to the trip. Cool, isn't it? Or rather cold, freezing cold when staying overnight, but that's part of the added thrill and challenge. The photos looked fantastic and the reviews by hikers who had been there were very encouraging. It sounded like the absolutely best thing to do for fit people looking for extremes. Oh yes, just right for me! Here comes my over-confidence bias again. Although I don't have any real high altitude hiking experience, I'm a fan of extremes. The added challenge stirs my excitement and makes my heart go wild. Adding such a fascinating and rather unique experience that not many hikers opt for, and thus also having the mountain a bit more to myself, seemed like the perfect choice. I found several tour operators offering the Crater Camp route in combination with the

Lemosho route. Lemosho approaches from the west. It has the advantage of being less busy and a bit longer, thus allowing for more acclimatization time. Perfect! And so I set out to find the best Lemosho / Crater Camp offer.

Meanwhile, I started excitedly spreading my plans among family and friends. "I'm going to hike Kilimanjaro," I announced without the slightest doubt that I could do it.

"Really?" "Why?" "I wouldn't," my friends concurred.

"That's dangerous! Please don't go," my parents pleaded.

"No, it's not. Don't worry. I've looked into it. It's not dangerous," I protested and so would cause them much worry for most of the year.

Was I really sure about the zero risk factor? I felt as if I owed it to my parents to double-check, to make extra sure I would come back safely. And so I did, because I had already seen – yet ignored – sparse comments by some tour operators that they don't offer Crater Camp because of its risks. Of course I didn't mention any of that to my family. I hadn't even taken those comments seriously myself. Anyone trying to book a Kilimanjaro operator will soon find that they are the most contrary of all people. Every single one of them seemed to recommend something else, just to distinguish themselves from each other. Whom to trust? That required a LOT of research. Luckily, I was willing to go the extra mile – all for my parents! And so for a week I did nothing but read pretty much every piece of information that I could find about Cater Camp. I concluded that it presents two dangers.

First, in order to hike up there, most operators would first cross the so-called infamous Western Breach, a strenuous ascent prone to rockfall. In 2006, three hikers were killed by such a rockfall and the Western Breach was subsequently closed. They reopened it in 2007 with an optimized path that minimizes the exposure to rockfall to short sections that can be crossed within a few minutes, but nevertheless the risk remains. The problem lies in the gradual melting of the glacier. As ice becomes soft, the glacier releases rocks in an unpredictable way. An expert investigation concluded that the risk of rockfall would always be there, even though there hadn't been any reported incidents since reopening in 2007.[13] That will change this year and another life will tragically succumb to these uncontrollable forces, but I won't know that until I eventually start my adventure.

The second risk is related to sleeping at such high altitude. Usually, if severe AMS symptoms arise, the immediate treatment is descent. However, evacuation from near the top of Kilimanjaro is a burdensome task. Especially if symptoms arise overnight, I concluded that I might be in trouble.

Both the threat of rockfall and the difficulty of evacuation if problems arise made me realize that Crater Camp wasn't a risk I would want to take. For hikers who really want to go there, it's advisable to first hike up to Uhuru Peak via a safer path and then descend to Crater Camp from there, adding the overnight stay after summiting. This would also be advisable from an acclimatization point of view, following the logic of always sleeping at a lower altitude than the elevation reached during the day.

However, this sounded a bit too extreme even for me. After reaching the peak, surely I would just want to get back down again as soon as possible rather than spending another night up there? And what about my fingers and toes? Surely they will freeze during the long ascent to Uhuru Peak – my initial worry number one, even ahead of greasy hair. Will I get frostbite if I cannot descend to a lower and warmer altitude? Had I done my research properly, I would have realized that Crater Camp is only a few hundred meters from Uhuru Peak, so with regard to temperature it really doesn't matter which one you go to first. But hey – getting all the facts right immediately is close to impossible. Information overload.

Finally, my deliberations were settled by the simple fact that I couldn't find any group tour offering this safer Crater Camp option. I assume this is partly driven by lack of demand, and partly by the additional strain such a route would put on the porters and staff. Typically, porters would not ascend all the way to the summit but wait at base camp. Having them go all the way up to the summit with the weight of all your equipment is very strenuous and risky also for them. Thus, such tours are typically arranged as private tours and also much more expensive than other routes.[14]

With my initial Crater Camp option turning into a no-go, my next best was to consider the normal Lemosho route without the Crater Camp. "Fewer crowds," most operators claimed. "Became busy in recent years," others contradicted. "All nonsense," I concluded. A simple glance at the map reveals the truth: Lemosho route joins with the very busy Machame route on the fourth day. Thus, even if the beginning might still be less crowded, for most of the hike I would actually be on the very route with the highest traffic that I was trying to avoid. It didn't require much brainwork to figure that out. Do operators think we are all idiots? Or do most tourists blindly follow what their operators recommend?

Not me, on to the next option: the Rongai route. This is the only route that ascends from the north, which generally attracts more rainfall than the southern slopes. No surprise that it's less busy than the other routes! Furthermore, its scenery is said to be not that beautiful. Most importantly, it is no longer than the Machame route. That brought me back to brutal statistics: The shorter the route, the lower my chances of success. I had meanwhile figured out the number one success factor to making it to the top: number of days without shower. You don't believe me? Here are the official statistics:[15] On a five-day route, only 27% of hikers make it to the summit. This increases to 44% on a six-day route, like Rongai or Machame. Still awfully low, don't you think? Luckily, that percentage increases to 85% for eight-day routes. Some people cope with high altitude better than others, and even one and the same person may handle altitude differently at different times. There's really no way to predict how you will cope with it. The single best thing you can do to maximize your chances of summit success is to take your time. Even your fitness level is only secondary; and athletes have not been found to perform any better. Rather to the contrary, they tend to ascend too fast jeopardizing their own success exactly because of their high fitness level.[16]

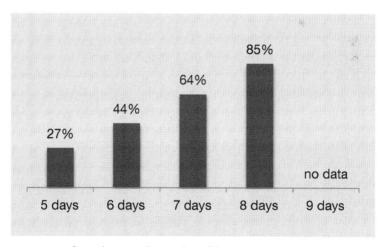

Summit success by number of days on the mountain

As the whole trip costs a considerable amount of money and I am certainly not one of those admirably tenacious travelers who attempt the hike two or three times until they finally make it to the top, I am determined to do everything I can to make it up there the first time round. In my mind, this is a once in a lifetime experience and I would be seriously disappointed with myself if I failed – I can't allow this to happen.

If you still wish to go for a shorter route, here is the good news: You can simply add in one or two extra days staying overnight twice at the same camp(s). Most operators already offer such extended group tours. If you are concerned about your fitness level and prefer to have some rest days in between, that sounds like the best way to do it. As for myself, however, I was looking for a physical challenge and wanted to maximize my hiking time on the mountain. Staying overnight twice at the same camp didn't appeal to me.

So what should I do? Take a big risk or bear with the crowds? Fortunately, there was one more option left – the Northern Circuit route. According to the Ultimate Kilimanjaro website, it is the newest route on Kilimanjaro.[17] Indeed, I couldn't find it offered by any other operator (though that will change quickly and as of publication you will have more choice).

The Northern Circuit route starts at the Western Londorossi gate and follows the Lemosho Route for three nights. On the fourth day, it briefly intersects with the busy Machame route. Thereafter, however, it goes off into complete wilderness while circumventing the peak on the northern side, the only route to do so.[18] Only the final summit ascent would have to be shared with the busy Marangu route and the less busy Rongai route, but there was no other choice anyway. The only option not the share the summit hike with other groups would be via the Western Breach, which I already discarded as too dangerous. Furthermore, I concluded that even though Marangu might be busy at the start, it also has a low success rate; thus most hikers would not even make it up to where our routes would join. In a nutshell, the Northern Circuit route should offer the most authentic experience away from the crowds.

So if that route is so good, why does no one go there? Because it's also the longest route. Not in terms of distance – on average less than 10 kilometers (6mi) a day. No big deal, right? But in real terms – nine days! BIG deal! Nine days means eight nights sleeping in a tent, eight days without shower, eight days without washing my hair, and nine entire days without a proper toilet! Could I do that?

I tried to put this into perspective. Ultimate Kilimanjaro also recommended eight days for the Lemosho route and seven days for the Machame and Rongai routes to allow for acclimatization. Therefore, the Northern Circuit was really only 1-2 days longer than its alternatives. What's 1-2 days in exchange for a more authentic wilderness experience and the highest chances of reaching the summit due to the longer acclimatization time? After weighing all options, it seemed like a very reasonable trade-off. The more I read about the Northern Circuit – from the limited information available – the more excited I got.

In summary, just as I had determined September 28 to be the single best day of the entire year for my summit hike, I felt confident that the Northern Circuit would be the single best route on the entire mountain. Tick – second big question sorted! Do you still wonder why it took me over three months to book my hike? Then I've got more in store for you.

BOOKING CONSIDERATIONS

With whom?
Or reasons not to book

Call me upright, but the thought of me alone with a guide and three porters off in the wild on an African mountain didn't appeal to me. So as soon as the idea of Kilimanjaro lodged itself firmly into my brain, I set off to find a partner in crime. That was the hardest of all undertakings. As I asked every single person I knew and could possibly imagine being stuck with for over a week, I got a long list of very valid reasons against hiking Kili in response. Let me give you some examples. If you survive this chapter, then you are good to go!

Financial considerations

Rachael was one of my top two bets. She is the most experienced hiker I know and doesn't shy away from rain or cold. Surely she could manage without a shower for a week. Hence, I shouldn't have been surprised that she knew all about Kili already.

"Oh yes, I looked into it in the past. How much is it again? A few thousand, right?"

"Yes, all in probably around US$5,000."

"How ludicrous! Just to hike a mountain! If I win a big deal, sure, but don't count on it."

Smash, within seconds she brought me back to reality. Money is a very valid consideration. Even if you choose one of the shorter and lower price options (not recommended) and already own all the equipment or manage to borrow whatever you need for free, hiking Kilimanjaro will definitely not be a bargain. Add the costs of your flight, visa, insurance, medical preventions, customary tipping and other miscellaneous expenditures – you probably won't make it under 3,500 to 4,000 US dollars, even on a very low budget version. The only exception might be for travelers living in the region who don't need a long-distance flight, additional medical preventions or insurance coverage. Assuming you prefer a more mid-budget version and to buy some new gear, you will be lucky to make it under 5,000 US dollars. On top of that, most travelers wouldn't want to return home straight after the hike. Once in Tanzania, adding on at least a few days of safari, or Zanzibar, or both, lures us into further digging that hole in our budget. None of these temptations come cheap either. Tanzania is an insanely expensive country to visit! To make matters worse, a new 18% value added tax on tourism services to be implemented from July 2016 will make it even more expensive for you. Some quotes may not yet reflect that change – better check that you won't be charged on top.

I regard my trip as an investment for life and consider myself very fortunate to be able to afford such an adventure – a luxury that will remain unattainable for the majority of people. Rachael is living a comfortable life in a very wealthy country and would be able to afford the trip. However, to her as well as to many others, in light of the limitless other options available to spend our vacation or part with our money, hiking Kili simply is not a sufficiently compelling attraction on a cost-benefit scale. I cannot argue with that. Financial considerations surely are the single most important factor for outdoors and hiking fans to opt against Kilimanjaro in favor of a more reasonably priced (or free) adventure.

Acute mountain sickness (AMS)

On to my friend Nicole, the second of my top two bets. She loves the outdoors, and her past extreme travels would have been far outside my own comfort zone. As she was always looking for new adventures, I reckoned she would be the most likely to join. This time, my hopes survived a bit longer.

"Sounds great! Just give me a few days to read up about it," she sounded excited at first.

Eagerly, I sent her all the information I had researched. While I was waiting for her confirmation, Nicole internalized the harsh reality of sleeping in a tent without running water at high altitudes for over a week.

"I'm not sure that would be fun," she concluded. "I have felt the altitude before, even at around 4,000 meters." Headache, nausea, "I wouldn't want to feel like that again, especially not for an entire week."

Smash, this time it took days rather than seconds, but with the same result. Nicole's reasoning was very understandable, and again I was left without arguments.

"Here is the thing with AMS," – short for acute mountain sickness, also known as altitude sickness – "almost every climber experiences some signs of AMS," my operator replied to my question regarding the number of cases of AMS they've had so far on the Northern Circuit route. "Most climbers experience headaches, dizziness, loss of appetite and fatigue. Most climbers can push on while feeling these effects and proceed on the climb. It's very rare for climbers to experience the more serious side effect such as inability to walk, fluid buildup in the lungs and shortness of breath while resting. Climbers know when they aren't adjusting to the altitude and most of them want to send themselves down the mountain."

That means even if we do everything right, acclimatize as much as possible and take a slow route up the mountain, we're still likely to experience AMS. The symptoms read to me awfully lot like a bad hangover after a late party night, which feels so bad I voluntarily dropped delicious cocktails years ago. Why does it not bother me now? Because I've never experienced any disturbing altitude symptoms, thus I keep indulging in the illusion that it won't happen to me. Never mind that my own higher altitude experience is close to nonexistent. I'm just human – give me two data points and my brain will draw stereotypical convictions for eternity.

Data point number 1: I recently went on a short skiing excursion to Klein Matterhorn in Switzerland (the highest cable car station in Europe at 3,883m/12,740ft of altitude). Due to the relatively rapid ascent via cable cars, it is common for people to feel headaches by the time they reach the final stop. Not me – it wasn't my head but my frozen nose and fingers that made me ski down as fast as I could.

Data point number 2: When I hiked up Mount Kinabalu on Borneo many years ago, I only experienced the obvious shortness of breath forcing me to slow down my pace. After reaching the peak, I remember feeling overly euphoric and invincible, so much so that I started running downhill with arms stretched to both sides as if I could fly. I only came back to reason when I found myself on the ground sliding down a stony slope on my face, nicely alternating between left and right cheek. Ouch, I can't fly! There was no way hiding my stupidity – unsightly crusts covering half my face would tell the truth. I had a close shave, literally indeed, and would learn my lesson.

So for now, I'm holding on to my illusion that my AMS symptoms will remain limited to some light-headedness and perhaps loss of appetite, both symptoms that seem more appealing than frightening to me. Which woman wouldn't like to come back from vacation three kilos lighter for a change? And who wouldn't like to experience a *high* without taking drugs? Well, perhaps high altitude hiking will turn into an addiction for me, but not an unhealthy one I'd like to think. But that's just me.

Feeling cold, really cold

Nicole also discussed the hike with someone who had already been to Kilimanjaro. Her recollection was that she felt cold and miserable all the time, especially during the night, but at higher altitudes even during the day. The problem is that once you are cold, you don't warm up again easily without a hot shower or other heating amenities. I guess there are two sides to that.

On the one hand, I am also scared of getting cold fingers and toes. When skiing in freezing temperatures, I often have to descend to lower slopes or stop for a hot drink in order to avoid getting frostbite. I know it will require buying the best of the best equipment in order to avoid getting cold during the summit ascent. Even with the best equipment, I'm not yet fully convinced that I will be able to manage. The thought of hiking throughout a freezing cold and windy night in the middle of nowhere terrifies me.

On the other hand, being cold throughout all nights seems avoidable by making sure your operator provides good rental sleeping bags suitable for very low temperatures. I've read in various reviews that this really makes a big difference and none of the hikers with adequate equipment felt cold overnight. So to me, despite my chronically cold fingers and toes, I don't consider fear of cold strong enough a reason to back off.

I've also read reviews that eating hot food for lunch and not only for dinner makes a big difference, and indeed I will see for myself that a hot soup makes all the difference on a cold cloudy day.

Finally, choosing the right season is crucial in order to avoid feeling too cold. What I already assume today will prove to be right – never

ever would I want to be up there when it's too cloudy and rainy. I really mean it: Don't even think about it – never ever!

Plenty of nicer mountains

With my two best bets turning into a no-go, I continued my search for a hiking companion. My date at the time seemed like the next best choice: Fit – motivating me to keep up; strong – making me feel safe; entertaining – killing any onset of boredom; a natural *oven* – allowing me to warm up my frozen fingers on his unfailingly warm hands; and of course a little bit of romance during vacation wouldn't hurt either. Sounds too good to be true?

My date, let's call him Steve, kept his cool about the trip, but he felt sufficiently intrigued to make some inquiries. By chance, he met an experienced hiker who had already been to Kili, so Steve used the opportunity to learn more about it.

"An experience to live through once but never again," that hiker commented. If we wanted to hike a beautiful mountain, there would be plenty of better choices literally just on our doorstep in Switzerland and neighboring countries. Mountains in Europe don't charge hiking fees, so why would we want to pay so much to hike Kili instead? In that hiker's conclusion, Kilimanjaro is for people who want to tick the box, but not for those looking for a truly enjoyable hiking experience.

It's true that living in Switzerland we are spoilt with beautiful mountains. So why would I want to fly all the way to Africa and pay a lot of money to hike just an average mountain in terms of beauty? Even in Tanzania, Mount Meru, the country's second highest mountain situated right next to Kilimanjaro, is said to boast amazing scenery and wildlife, beating its big brother by far, without the tourist crowds.[19]

Smash, once again I found myself left without reasons why it had to be the highest of all mountains that I would ever be able to climb as an amateur.

To my own astonishment, despite all the many arguments against Kili, I have remained unwavering. All these no-goes have stirred my initial spark of interest into a raging fire of excitement. Perhaps I am a *box ticker* and simply want to say that I have done it. However, I like to believe there is more to it. I simply love the challenge, the idea of going somewhere more exotic, having a personal pet project with all the required preparations and research that I have to (and love to) do.

Call me naïve, but I even truly believe that I will be enjoying my trip. I realize my attitude is very personal and there's no point trying to convince someone who doesn't feel that excitement. On the one hand, they may not make it to the top without good motivation to keep them going; on the other hand, they'll probably make your trip a nightmare with all their complaining and *I-told-you-so*.

As for my date, we had a lovely weekend in Italy. Heading back to Zurich on a mountain shortcut that I proposed for a change of scenery and following the car's navigation system, we drove up the most serpentine, tedious and forlorn road I'd ever been on.

"What if the mountain pass up there is still closed over winter?" Steve wondered.

"Might be, I have no mobile reception to double-check. Only one way to find out."

So we kept driving for one of the longest hours of my entire life, just to find out that the mountain pass was closed indeed.

"I told you so!" An angry voice shouted at me. "Why didn't you check that properly?"

All of a sudden I had caused Armageddon by my entire irresponsibility and stupidity; and would spend the next five minutes listening to an angry explosion of accusations, culminating in Kilimanjaro:

"Tsk, you really think I would climb a 5,000-meter mountain with you, if you don't even find the way home!?"

Fortunately, our interests were aligned – I no longer wanted him to come with me to Africa either, or anywhere else for that matter. Unfortunately, I still fail to understand the connection between following a usually very trustworthy navigation system and hiking Kilimanjaro. Let's see whether I will become any wiser on that close to 6,000-meter mountain.

▲ ▲ ▲

As Steve became history, I was close to giving up hope of finding a travel companion. However, I was too hooked onto my plans to let go easily. Here was the good news: Kilimanjaro had plenty of group tour offers, no need to go on a private tour. But what if I would end up with a bunch of weirdoes? Well, that thought didn't cross my mind, perhaps because I am a weirdo myself. I like the thought of meeting new people – that might be half the fun! Given the significant cost involved and rather exotic location, surely most hikers would have a lot of travel experience before they dare to scale such a mountain. In my experience, the more well-traveled a person, the more likely they are to be open-minded, interesting to talk to and easy to get along with. And hey, even if I end up with some grumpy nuisances, no one forces me to talk to them.

The more I thought about it, the less being alone in a group seemed like an issue, and the more excited I got about the prospect of meeting interesting people along the way.

The only thing that keeps worrying me is not having someone to share the experience. How will I feel on the summit, when I've finally made it but find myself all alone? Not literally of course, because there will be hundreds of others up there, but no one who I care much about. How will it feel standing next to couples and groups of friends who will have each other to celebrate and take photos together? I have no choice. The alternative of not going at all is definitely not a good alternative. So what the heck – I will survive! Even if I need to have my summit picture taken alone.

No vacation time

As of writing, hope has returned. I may have found a travel companion! A friend introduced me to Jana, who also wanted to hike Kilimanjaro last year.

"I couldn't find anyone to join, so I went to Machu Picchu instead. I would be interested. It's just that I'm about to start a new job and don't know yet whether I will get my vacation approved."

It was a good start, but I was keen to move quickly. "Interested" felt like such a non-committal word. I had meanwhile learned that there was only one group tour for the Northern Circuit route at the time that I had concluded to be the single best date of the entire year. That tour started to fill up with available spaces becoming fewer and fewer each week. Being a perfectionist, of course I didn't want to miss out on that chance and was anxious to book in order to secure my place. While it would have been easy to arrange a private tour for Jana and myself for little more money, I didn't want to run the risk of hiking alone if she couldn't join. So we agreed that I would book first, and she would join later once she had her vacation approved.

Finally everything seemed to be settled and I was ready to book my trip. However, I didn't want to *dictate* the route and tour operator I had chosen onto Jana. So I sent her all the information I had researched, and she kindly invited me to her place for dinner to discuss. That evening, I met Jana's boyfriend Diego for the first time, and got to know Jana a lot better. To my surprise, she was not only an experienced hiker but also a skilled technical mountaineer. She knew perfectly everything about the right equipment, and the *dos and don'ts* of high altitude hiking. I was impressed. Even more importantly, we seemed to get along very well and I could easily see myself spending my hiking vacation with her – what a perfect travel companion!

"So how certain are you that you want join?" I was keen to assess her commitment.

"I've already made up my mind; I want to come for sure. It's really just my formal vacation approval that I need to wait for, and Diego is still deciding whether he also wants to come."

Her definite answer, and that even Diego might, join came as a big surprise to me. I was exhilarated. Finally I wouldn't need to go alone!

"The only problem is timing. It would be easier for us if we could delay it a little bit. It seems the weather is still good in October, only a bit cloudier but therefore also less crowded. Couldn't we postpone it by a month?"

"Yes sure!" If that gives me a confirmed travel companion in return!

With that, all seemed to be in place, and I was ready to book. However, the delay into October kept bothering me. If it was equally good, why had I not considered it previously? I couldn't find an immediate reason. As I kept digging for information, some websites indicated that the rainy season may already start mid-October, not only in November as suggested on most websites. I double-checked with the tour operator.

"The chance of rain is higher end October. We would advise you to go latest early October if possible," they confirmed.

Huh, that didn't sound too good. In my mind, rain had to be avoided for two reasons:

First, I didn't want to get wet on the mountain. According to everything I had read, once clothes became wet up there, they wouldn't dry anymore. Of course I could use ponchos and other rain protection, but that still sounded like an unnecessary hassle to me. Worse than that, rain would turn the paths muddy and slippery, increasing the risk of falls and injuries.

Second, rain goes hand in hand with more mosquitoes. I had meanwhile learnt that the local type of malaria could be lethal. To make matters worse, even with appropriate medication, there would be no 100% guarantee of immunization. [20] Lifelong experience warned me that mosquitoes always find me, no matter what precaution I take. The thought of getting bitten incessantly during my vacation didn't appeal to me. Of course there wouldn't be any mosquitoes on Kilimanjaro at higher altitudes, but even the first and last days would be enough to risk an infection. Furthermore, I didn't plan to return home straight afterwards but add a safari or a trip to Zanzibar. That wouldn't be any fun during the rainy, mosquito-prone season?!

I informed Jana about my timing considerations, worried that she would back out. However, she understood and agreed to stick to September, even though it would make it harder for her to join. How wonderful! Finally it was all set so that I could eventually book my trip, keeping my fingers crossed that Jana can make it.

BOOKING CONSIDERATIONS

Which operator?

WARNING: THIS CHAPTER IS ONLY FOR FUTURE HIKERS OR THE MOST CURIOUS OF READERS. IF YOU ARE NOT INTERESTED IN HIKING YOURSELF OR THE EXTENT OF PREPARATION INVOLVED, PLEASE CONTINUE WITH THE NEXT CHAPTER ON PAGE 51.

Good news first – reaching the top of Africa is relatively easy. You will have porters carrying all your stuff (except your daypack, but you could even pay a small extra fee to have that carried as well), setting up your tent, fetching and boiling water, even carrying and cleaning a portable toilet. You will have a cook and waiter serving you breakfast, lunch, dinner and snacks. You will have a lead guide and at least one assistant guide to lead you up the mountain, watch out for any AMS symptoms and take care of you in case of any emergencies. You may have people bring you hot water to wash your face in the morning and evening. I've even read about hikers literally being carried up to the top by their guides because they couldn't have made it on their own. I don't think this is good practice, neither on the part of the hiker (doesn't it feel like cheating?) nor on the part of the guide (wouldn't it be better to send their client down the mountain as quickly as possible if they can't handle it anymore?), but it seems to happen nevertheless. The point being, hiking Kilimanjaro is not comparable to real trekking where you actually have to carry all your stuff and take care of yourself.

Of course, if you are extremely experienced and fit, you may consider doing it all by yourself. I've read about such rare exceptions, but that's definitely not me. Should you belong to that superhuman category, let me mention two considerations. First, by park regulations you need to be accompanied by a guide from a registered tour operator at all times. Like it or not, you will have some company and you will have to pay for that. Second, bear in mind that you will need to drink a lot. While your guide may help you locate the water sources, there are simply NO water sources in the so-called Alpine Desert zone and further up (i.e. for your last almost 2,000m/6,000ft of altitude gain). That means you will have to carry a LOT of water up to base camp in order to stay sufficiently hydrated for your summit hike. Should you manage to accomplish such a feat and do it all by yourself, I would love to hear your success story!

Here comes the bad news for us ordinary humans: Selecting a tour operator is the most difficult of tasks. We are spoilt for choice, and that very choice turns into a nightmare. No two operators seem to agree on the best approach in terms of route, number of acclimatization days, equipment, safety procedures and so forth. To make matters worse, you will find positive and negative reviews for almost every operator, and you cannot know which of those reviews are sincere and which are manipulative. Travelers have complained about significant pressure from certain operators to write good reviews, as well as bribery to have their bad reviews upgraded or removed.[21]

In a nutshell: Transparency is poor, and the information you will read on different websites couldn't be any more contradictory. Obviously, at least half of the information must be marketing gimmicks or outright lies. Whom to trust?

You have two choices: The easy option would be to simply follow someone else's recommendation or any first operator that appears reasonable. Never mind that they may be biased or simply good at marketing but nothing else. Obviously, this means taking a risk. The second option would be safer and more likely to lead you to your dream vacation, but it has a significant drawback: Spending an unreasonable amount of time and effort to research your options to death. I expect the majority of hikers have a healthy survival instinct and eventually choose option one.

Not me. Of course my perfectionist character had to know it all and be one hundred percent sure. This is a big trip, right? I had read too many negative reviews of what can go wrong with bad operators to *take it easy*.

So I embarked on a herculean task that would keep me busy over many weeks, obsessed to find my single best option. I truly hope that my findings will make your life easier and give you a reasonable shortcut to option two.

Porter treatment

Hundreds of companies, almost an equal number of contradictory opinions, and price ranges from about US$1,500 to more than US$4,000 for the very same route and number of days – how would I even start to decipher all this information? Of course, pricing was an important consideration. Why these huge differences?

Fortunately, the online community broadly shared at least one common understanding: Budget operators can only afford to offer cheap prices at the cost of their staff. The worst off typically are the porters who do all the heavy lifting – rushing up the mountain carrying your personal stuff, your tent, your food and communal equipment on top of their own sparse necessities. Instead of resting when they finally arrive at camp, they will set up your tent, fetch water and prepare food so that everything is ready by the time you arrive. To make matters worse, they often don't even receive three meals a day, sleep in substandard conditions, wear worn out sneakers that are entirely unsuitable to their strenuous, load-bearing treks and need to make do with clothes that are inappropriate to protect them against the cold and rain. While hikers may believe they got a good deal from their operator, it actually means that their porters – despite all their misery – won't even receive their due minimum wage of less than ten dollars per day!

In order to improve the working conditions of the porters on Kilimanjaro, the International Mountain Explorers Connection (IMEC) established the Kilimanjaro Porters Assistance Project (KPAP), a non-profit organization registered in Tanzania, in 2003. They are an independent organization examining treatment practices towards porters, amongst others. All climbing companies can participate in their Partner for Responsible Travel Program without any fees. To qualify as a KPAP Partner for Responsible Travel, companies will be scrutinized and need to obtain an 85% performance level in their porter treatment against a set of minimum standards established by the Kilimanjaro stakeholders.[22]

KPAP found that in 2013, 47% of porters of non-KPAP partner companies didn't even receive two meals a day![23] Can you imagine – every second porter carrying heavy bags up Kilimanjaro exerting tremendous physical efforts only gets food once a day! For all their hard labor, they received an average wage of 35% less than porters of KPAP partner companies, barely US$5 per day. Fortunately, the trend is positive and practices keep improving. As of publication, 2015 survey results will show that porters of non-KPAP partner companies currently receive an average of two meals a day (versus three meals for those of KPAP partners). Their average pay is increasing to about US$7 per day (still about 30% less than KPAP partners). However, these are only averages, so some will be better and others worse off. To be certain one's porters are treated properly, at least most of the time, the least one can do is to make sure one's operator is a partner of KPAP!

For the purpose of writing this, I've just looked up the IMEC and KPAP websites to double-check their information. Yikes! Where is my operator with whom I have just booked? Their name doesn't appear among the KPAP partner companies. To make matters worse, KPAP warns that operators are using their name even though they have not been accepted as partner. Oh no! Up to now, I've been convinced that I'd already researched everything to the last detail. Slap-bang! Not so smart after all. I made the very same mistake that I'm trying to advise you against, blindly believing what is said on the operator's website and other supposedly independent reviews. Never trust the Internet!

"All our guides do work exclusively for us," my operator assured me when I asked them about their local subcontractor, but omitted to mention the name. I didn't insist because all their reviews were so good that they seemed trustworthy to me. Call me idiot, but this just highlights how difficult it is to find objective information. However, there still is hope for me. As of writing, only local outfitters are listed on the KPAP website, while my operator is an international company. Perhaps that explains?

And what about the big local operators, like Zara Tours, the African Walking Company (AWC) or Shah Tours? I can't find them on KPAP's website either. Several reviews on TripAdvisor suggest that there's no point paying more with an international outfitter because they would most likely just use one of those three local companies as sub-contractors. AWC is even said to be a founding member of KPAP.[24] Huh, but if they are that good, why are they not listed amongst the KPAP Partners for Responsible Travel? Yet another example of how difficult it is to find objective information of Kilimanjaro operators. My curiosity is sparked. I immediately write an email to KPAP to find out more.

KPAP reply within 24 hours, confirming that international operators working with local KPAP partner outfitters are not listed yet (though as of publication the full partner list will be published on www.mountainexplorers.org/club/partners.htm). To my great relief, my operator was a good choice, and I will find their name listed in future. Furthermore, it will be safe to assume that any companies not listed on their website are indeed no KPAP partners. KPAP are very appreciative about my concern and even offer to meet in person. How exciting!

Wait a moment – why would you care about all of that? Perhaps like me, you care simply for altruistic reasons because you wouldn't want to support mistreatment of the very people without whom you'd never make it to the summit. Perhaps, however, you believe that such considerations are better left to someone else, the *free market*. After all, if you don't go on your trip, three porters won't have a job in the first place. So isn't it better for them to at least receive a sub-minimum wage rather than being unemployed? Not an easy question and certainly I don't know the answer. However, here is why I care also for selfish reasons: I will rely on my porters to set up my tent properly, to boil my water properly, to prepare my food properly, to clean our communal toilet properly, and in the worst case to evacuate me down the mountain! Will they be able to do a good job if they are half starving, freezing and earning half compared to their peers from the group camping next to them?

I will have more thoughts about this later from my actual meeting with KPAP to learn about porter treatment from their firsthand experience. Stay tuned!

Experienced guides

Similar to the porters, a cheap operator will also more than likely save on the cost of their guides. More experienced guides will seek higher-paid opportunities and are less likely to work with them. Notable exception: Greedy guides who can get the maximum for themselves with operators who don't follow good tipping procedures by skimming the cream off the pot that you will leave for your porters in good faith. How is that possible? Because greedy guides are the best of actors: They will fool you into believing everything they say, and you will never even find out otherwise.[25]

Tipping aside, your own safety should come first, and that means first and foremost having experienced and well-trained guides. They should be able to manage the porters properly, set the pace and choose a path to maximize your chances of acclimatization; and they should be trained to look out for your health and safety. They need to understand under what condition you are safe to continue your hike, or when you are in danger of severe AMS and need to descend.

I believe if your guides have the right training and experience, you should never get into a precarious condition in the first place; but if you do, your fate relies on them taking the right decisions. In a worst case if you are unable to walk, they may even need to carry you down. For all these reasons, I would think twice before booking with a very low budget operator.

Furthermore, I've noticed guides in Western countries promoting themselves as very experienced because they have been to Kilimanjaro a few dozen times. This is NOT impressive. The most experienced guides are locals and have usually been to the summit well over 100 times, in some cases even more than 200 times. No one knows Kilimanjaro as intimately as the locals. Language barriers aside, local guides should be your number one choice.

Reading MG Edward's *Kilimanjaro: One Man's Quest to Go Over the Hill* provides shocking examples of what can happen when guides are not up to their task: The assistant guide wasn't able to speak English – so no chance of communicating with the hikers who he was supposed to take care of; tents were set up exactly where the rainwater would collect for two nights in a row so that the affected hikers ended up with wet gear; and worst of all, the writer was partly dragged up to the summit by his guide when he was already on his knees and thought he couldn't move anymore. MG Edwards may have been thrilled about what he believed to be great support in his summit attempt; to me it reads like irresponsible behavior by his guide to drag a client up despite alarming AMS symptoms. The number one objective of a guide should always be for their hikers to make it back down safely, not to get them to the top by any means.

In MG Edwards' case, however, it didn't appear that they had even gone for a very low budget option ("no frills" but above the lowest budget category). The operator had even been recommended to them. So what went wrong?

The problem might be that they went with a "small, independent operator". In principle, that sounds like a good choice, supporting small entrepreneurs rather than big companies. However, when operators are small, they may not have a lot of experience and you might serve as their guinea pig.

But it's also difficult to generalize. Other small operators may have accumulated a lot of experience as guides with a bigger operator before going independent. So what can future hikers do?

Insist on knowing exactly who your lead guide will be, how many years' experience he has guiding clients and how often he has summited Kilimanjaro as a guide. Many companies would advertise the total hiking experience of the entire company – beware! Who cares if an operator has hundreds of years of experience, if the guides supposed to take care of us have hardly any?

If in doubt, I believe that selecting a more sizeable mid-range operator may be the safer choice.

Equipment – sleeping comfort

Equipment is another way to save money for operators. The three most important components are tents, sleeping bags and any AMS-related equipment. There is a huge range in terms of quality and spread of additional *nice to have* equipment by which operators are trying to distinguish themselves from each other. Written confirmation beats future frustration. If something is not clearly stated to be included on an operator's website or in their booking documentation, it will most likely not be. If in doubt, ask. If left in doubt, beware.

Tents

Let's start with the easiest component. Tents are usually provided by operators and included in package prices. The main purpose of tents is to keep us dry and to protect against the wind.

Traveler reviews on TripAdvisor and other forums complain about leaking tents during rain, for example, "this is why I would not recommend Zara (at least until they sort out the problem): our tents were complete rubbish, just not waterproof. We got soaked every night (and I mean water running through the tent)."

Furthermore, I found that especially lower budget operators do not show the brand of tents on their websites. *If in doubt, ask* – true to my own philosophy and intrigued by the above review, I send Zara a customer inquiry.

"The models of our tents are Kilimanjaro outfitter," they reply and attach photos showing tents with big ZARA labels.

Kilimanjaro outfitter? Is this a brand?

"I can't find that model anywhere. Could you send me a link?" I follow up.

"The tents are known as Kilimanjaro outfitter and they appear as above pictures," they reply again, and I give up after two failed attempts.

I am not criticizing Zara Tours. They are the biggest local operator and hence by law of averages should also attract a greater absolute number of negative reviews. This is Africa. It would be surprising if all the climbs and disclosures were perfect all the time.

Sleeping bags

Assuming most tents actually meet their basic waterproof and windproof requirements, sleeping bags may well be our most important equipment. They need to keep us warm at freezing temperatures. Except for outdoors enthusiasts with cold climate experience, most Kilimanjaro hikers do not own and will never again need such a high performance sleeping bag. Thus, renting one seems like a good choice.

Again, hiker reviews are confusing. Some were fine with sleeping bags rated only up to ca. 15F/-10C, while others became extremely cold even though operators had promoted excellent models rated for much lower temperatures.

Our body's ability to keep warm is very individual. I know my body temperature control lets me down all the time, thus it was obvious for me that I wanted the warmest option. The reviews by hikers that told of freezing overnight, despite extremely low rated sleeping bags, kept bothering me. Would I end up the same?

Fortunately, I found a more technical explanation that gave me comfort: When sleeping bags are used over and over again, they gradually lose their protective functionalities. Probably that was the case with the unfortunate hikers. Hence, it is important to know not only the make of rental sleeping bags, but also how often they are re-used.

My operator confirmed that their sleeping bags are only re-used ten times and get cleaned after every trip. Phew, I should be safe. However, becoming obsessive in my research when finalizing this book, I will want to ensure I don't spread any ill-researched claims, and will send an email to the manufacturer to verify.

"With rental sleeping bags, 60-70 nights with 10+ washes is about right before they should be removed from rotation," a product specialist of the Mountain Hardwear Lamina™ Z Bonfire -30°

Sleeping Bag will confirm. "However, if this was your personal bag, with proper care it should last several years and many, many nights."

Great, so far so good as regards my operator. How about others? Again, I will be tempted to check the practices of Zara as market leader.

They confirm that I can rent "Black Stone Sleeping Bag–25-5C . . . always used for 2 years conservatively before removing from the rental stock. They are all washed after every usage."

That sounds promising; let's clarify.

"I cannot find the product website. What means -25-5C? Are they good for -25C? Sorry, I'm really worried about getting cold. Could you send me a link to the product so I can check? Great to know you replace them every 2 years. So that means they would go on 50-100 climbs before replacement (assuming 1 climb per week)?"

"Kindly note that we always providing/renting to our clients the same Black Stone Sleeping bags which are very good and conducive during the trek," they reply. FULL STOP. No more info provided.

If in doubt, ask. If left in doubt . . . ?

Foam pads

Finally, other than staying dry and warm, we also want some cushioning against the hard floor. Foam pads provide a rare opportunity for respite. They are typically provided by operators and seem to be fairly standard, no need to conduct yet another comparative exercise.

Luxury equipment

While with bad operators the quality of equipment may range from poor to worse, there seems to be almost no upper limit to the extent of luxuries provided by some very high-end operators. A few even provide personal stand-up walk-in size tents and mountaineering beds, prices naturally reflecting the exclusive nature of their arrangements. Good for hikers with serious back problems and/or without budget constraints, inconceivable for everyone else.

▲ ▲ ▲

Sleeping comfort was the easy part. Fortunately, the online community seems to agree that lower rated sleeping bags tend to be warmer, and that waterproof tents tend to keep drier. What a blessing for a change! Now comes the difficult part – AMS-related equipment.

Equipment – oxygen and safety

Welcome to the world of marketing nonsense and the abuse of human fears! Welcome to the world of confusions and bewilderment! Welcome to the realities of Kilimanjaro! Oxygen-related philosophies advertised by operators vary widely – from Gamow bags via personal supplemental oxygen systems to emergency supplemental oxygen and pulse oximeters to no equipment at all. For all these types of precaution or lack thereof, proponents and opponents seem to be living on different planets. Reading each operator's opinion in isolation sounded logical; comparing, by default, various contradictory opinions turned into a little research project on its own. Separating the wheat from the chaff – what a herculean task! As a novice to high altitude trekking, safety was my number one concern. After reasonably educating myself and considering different options, here are my personal conclusions – step by step.

Gamow bag

From the website of a luxury operator, I learnt about this wonder bag. According to Wikipedia, "a Gamow bag (pronounced Gam-Off) is an inflatable pressure bag large enough to accommodate a person inside. By inflating the bag with a foot pump, the effective altitude can be decreased by 1000 to as much as 3000 meters (3281 to 9743 feet). It is primarily used for treating severe cases of altitude sickness."

Sounds like a must have! Just to make sure, I double-checked other operators that appeared similarly trustworthy, including my preferred one:

"Our staff does not carry Gamow bags . . . because descent is the most immediate, accessible treatment" was clearly written on their website.

But what if problems happen overnight, as other websites claimed was common, and descent isn't possible? Are they all really that reckless?

Again – if in doubt, ask. So I did.

"It's very rare for climbers to need to be evacuated in the middle of the night," my operator replied immediately. "If they do, descending in the dark is much more effective. . . . We also have oxygen on hand that can give temporary assistance."

That made sense. Why would I want to stay up there if my body can't handle it? The debate was settled for me – no Gamow bag needed.

The only instance in which I would prefer to have one is when sudden severe AMS is more likely and immediate descent is difficult. To my understanding, that might only apply to the Crater Camp, where evacuation especially overnight is a burdensome task.

Personal Oxygen System

Moving on in search for state-of-the-art equipment, I learnt about the **ALTOX** Personal Oxygen System from the website of **Africa Travel Resource (ATR)**. ATR was included in my checklist following posts suggesting it might be most advisable to book with one of the two big local tour operators, Zara Tours or the African Walking Company (AWC). However, AWC does not take direct bookings, only via their two agents ATR (UK) and Peak Planet (US). Hence no surprise that **Peak Planet** was also offering the ALTOX Personal Oxygen System for rent to their climbers. So how does it work?

According to ATR, "an ALTOX Personal Oxygen System works by supplying oxygen directly into the nostrils by means of a small plastic tube, or nasal canula, connected to a small oxygen cylinder carried in a backpack. The really clever part of the system is the controller, or pulse dose meter, which detects when the user is commencing an inward breath and delivers a small and precise dose of oxygen during the first part of the intake, ensuring that the valuable oxygen reaches the deepest parts of the lungs. This method of dosing makes it possible for each oxygen cylinder to last for 7 to 10 hours, rather than the usual 40 to 50 minutes."

It goes on to explain how these systems have been proven by extreme high altitude ascents or sports as well as military use, and that testing on Kilimanjaro has led to overwhelming results. According to ATR, there are only a few operators who have access to that equipment and thus other operators may negatively comment about it simply because they do not have access to it.

Again, sounds convincing upon first read, doesn't it?

Skeptical as I am, of course I felt compelled to independently verify their claims. My own personal conclusions: Pure marketing gimmick, and outright dangerous in certain circumstances.

The problem is that the usage of oxygen does not allow your body to acclimatize naturally, masking any effects until it may be too late.

continually use supplemental oxygen up to a high altitude, your body and masking any symptoms, and if your equipment then was to fail or run out of oxygen for whatever reason, you may be in real trouble.[26]

Furthermore, as many experienced hikers point out and many amateur hikers have proven in the past by safely reaching the summit, Kilimanjaro is really not that high that it would necessitate such equipment, which was designed for usage at extreme altitudes (8,000m/26,000ft plus) or under extreme conditions (such as pilots of military aircraft or extreme sky divers).

Should you seriously doubt your ability to ascend Kilimanjaro without the use of supplemental oxygen but wish to do so nevertheless, I strongly recommend that you get proper medical advice prior to opting for a personal oxygen system. Furthermore, I suggest you ask yourself why you want to go there in the first place. We already know it's not such a beautiful mountain in comparison, and now we take any edge out of the adventure by *cheating* our way up there and simulating a lower altitude environment for our body? What's the point – just to tick a box?

Ask yourself whether that will still make you feel happy and proud of your achievement. I don't mean to criticize if that's what you want to do, just trying to encourage some reflection.

As for myself, I prefer to plan my hike to leave sufficient acclimatization time. Reading books written by serious mountaineers about 8,000-meter (26,000ft) mountains certainly has had an impact on my respect (or lack thereof) for Kilimanjaro, regarding altitude that is. I should add they had an opposite impact on my fear of cold, making me realize it's not only highly painful and uncomfortable. Scarily many climbers ended up losing their fingers and toes due to frostbite.

Should you wish to learn from a real mountaineer and away from the touristic Kili hype, I would highly recommend *No Shortcuts to the Top* by Ed Viesturs. It helps to put our amateur adventures back into perspective and maintain a healthy level of humility.

Emergency oxygen

In contrast to personal oxygen, however, most operators would carry bottled oxygen for emergency cases. This is not used to help people ascend, but only in case of severe AMS as a temporary treatment in combination with immediate descent. It seems pretty standard and I haven't seen any operators arguing against it. While I don't know whether it is absolutely required or just another measure to make us feel safe (there are no statistics on how often it is actually used), I feel better knowing that my operator will bring it.

Pulse oximeters

Similar to emergency oxygen, several operators use pulse oximeters to test the oxygen saturation in our blood. I have no conclusive view whether this is recommendable or not. While it sounds like a positive feature, I have also read reviews that the readings may give a false sense of safety and should only be used by someone who is well trained in interpreting the readings.[27]

My operator uses pulse oximeters to take measures of every hiker twice daily. I wouldn't know whether this is a *must-have* or just a *nice-to-have* piece of equipment.

medically trained guides

▲ ▲ ▲

In summary, rather than any AMS-related equipment, it seems more important to me that my guides are properly trained and experienced. With the wrong guides, the best of equipment may do more harm than good. Bottled oxygen for emergency cases seems to be a generally adopted standard, but I would be careful about paying extra for anything else.

Equipment – dining and post-dining comforts

Other items of equipment are more *nice-to-have* rather than *must-have* from the point of view of health, safety and summit success. Nevertheless, they may hugely impact our feeling of wellbeing on the mountain.

Dining facilities

It seems to me that all operators at least from mid-range onwards bring a mess tent including tables, chairs and complete tableware for meal times. While I do not attribute a lot of importance to it now, having a chair to sit on and a tent to congregate with my fellow hikers over dinner on those cold mountain nights will make a day and night difference from an emotional point of view.

Toilet facilities

What is, however, obsessively important to me now is how I will deposit my food after I have eaten it. Every single review I read repeated the same message: Don't even think of getting anywhere close to the public toilets. Smelly, overused, congested, decorated with leftovers . . . Yuck! One review was enough to convince me to stay clear.

To make matters worse, reviews suggested finding a private spot in the wild might not always be possible due to lack of trees and bushes to hide behind. Are they kidding me? I belong to the rare breed of Europeans who refuse to go naked into a sauna – now I'm supposed to moonlight in front of everyone else?

To top it all off, drinking as much as possible is imperative to stay clear of AMS. My operator recommends at least three liters a day. What to do? Should I drink most of it in the evening, so I can pee in the dark?

Not a good idea either. Other than ruining a good night's sleep, reviews concurred it may be neither safe to wander off far from one's own tent in the dark, nor appealing to venture outside into the freezing cold.

"Don't worry," reviewers want to assure me. Just use a pee bottle overnight.

Are they freaking kidding me?!

Nope – they are dead serious, even female versions seem to have become popular. Ugh – thanks, but no thanks. I can't possibly pee in my own tent. Here comes Ms. City Chic, and I'm stuffed. I can't pee, hence no Kilimanjaro for me.

Fortunately Kilimanjaro operators are a smart tribe. Of course they have discovered this newish market of city-chic first-time campers. Solution: Toilet tent complete with a portable plastic toilet!

Don't frown, that already seems to have become the default equipment of several operators. What a luxury, you might think. What an absolute necessity, I may have to disagree.

Hikers on Kilimanjaro have exploded from about 35,000 few years ago to 60,000 by latest estimates. I may just have found the reason why! Should the number of tourists ever go out of control and they need to cut back down again, let me provide some free advice to the Kilimanjaro National Park: Just ban portable toilets, and I'm sure you'll easily sift the wannabes from the well-deserved.

Here's the good news for my fellow wannabes: We don't need to influence our choice of operator by whether they bring a portable toilet by default or not. If it's not included in the price, it seems that all of them can add it upon request for a charge of around US$100. Note this includes the salary of one porter carrying and cleaning the toilet for the entire week. Sounds very reasonable and worthwhile to me, especially if you can share and split the cost amongst your hiking group.

For sake of completeness, I shall add that we will unexpectedly find decent clean toilet facilities replete with flush toilets and sinks with running water at two (out of eight) camps[28]. However, should I hike a second time, I would still want to have a private toilet as well – for my group that is, though you might even rent one individually for yourself. How snobby, I am thinking now. How good for the porter to have work, I will challenge my own thoughts.

Food and water

So far we have covered porter treatment, quality of guides and equipment. Hold on, we are almost there. Have you wondered what kind of food hikers get to eat?

Variety

Expect diets to be rich in simple carbohydrates, which are supposed to be easier to digest at higher altitudes: rice, pasta, bread, porridge. Devastating news for me – a religious carbophobe; good news for all the operators – carbs are cheap. Hence no surprise that lower budget operators seem to give you the same stuff dominated by carbs every single day. The mid to higher range ones try to offer variety and include a fair ration of fresh fruit and vegetables as well as protein for most meals.

Special dietary requirements

Many operators advertise they can accommodate any special requirements. That's most likely correct for vegetarians – welcome to the land of carbs! For more sophisticated requirements, they may not be able to source special food items in the country (at a reasonable price), nor may they be familiar with specific needs. If dietary requirements are very strict, caution with budget operator seems warranted. From my experience, they always tell us everything is possible, but many operators avoid providing specific answers to our questions. If in doubt, request a specific meal plan to avoid bad surprises when it's too late.

Warm or cold

Cooked food and hot beverages seems standard for breakfast and dinner with all operators. Dreaming of English breakfast? Sorry to disappoint – porridge will become the morning ordeal in lower budget versions.

How about lunch? We can live on a sandwich, right? At least that's what I am thinking right now, so let me jump ahead: Hot soup for lunch really makes all the difference on a cold day. And even if there is no warm food, at least hot drinks for lunch is a *must-have*, in my future humble opinion.

Diarrhea

Finally, the hygiene standards adopted by operators to safely treat our water and cook our food will greatly influence our odds of staying clear of traveler's diarrhea. While this continues to be a risk even with the best operators, beware and watch out for negative reviews. Remember – no flush toilets!

Group size

Group size may be another criterion explaining price differences. No matter whether on private hikes or group hikes, there will usually be at least one guide and one assistant guide. In order for them to be able to give proper attention to each hiker, the general recommendation seems to be around 10 up to a maximum of 15 hikers per group.

However, other than the number of hikers, there will also be differences in the number of guides and assistant guides per group. To my very positive surprise, I will end up in a group with a ratio of one guide for every two hikers (one chief guide, one lead guide and four assistant guides for twelve hikers). I doubt that would have been the case with any budget operator and would recommend future hikers inquire about the exact number of guides in your group for a better comparison across operators.

It may not be crucial for most of the time, but at least for summit night and day it will make a huge difference. When it's all dark and you only have two guides for your group of ten or more, you may not get to see them very often. Under those extreme circumstances of darkness, freezing wind, thin air and physical exhaustion, we cannot rely on our fellow hikers for support. Having a guide nearby and knowing they have the capacity to help if needed may make all the difference, determining whether we love or hate our summit experience, whether we return back home with fond memories or the wish to forget our nightmares.

Group tour offering

Kilimanjaro can be scaled either in a private tour or as a group tour. Private tours are only somewhat more expensive and allow the flexibility to go at our own pace and follow our preferred route any time of the year. Most operators will be flexible to accommodate our preferences upon request, assuming we give them time to plan and reserve a guide.

In private tours, however, we will miss out on the bonding experience with other hikers – often described as being one of the best parts of hiking Kilimanjaro by those joining a group tour. The drawback of group tours is that they are limited to fixed times and routes on offer, but that may be a blessing in disguise when otherwise overwhelmed by seemingly limitless choices.

In my case, I'm still not 100% sure whether I will be hiking alone or with friends, thus a private tour was off the table. Based on what I had determined to be the single best route and single best time of the entire year, I was looking for group tours for the Northern Circuit route late September. Only one credible operator passed my screen. Lucky me – I could save my decision-making energy this time round.

My operator choice

I eventually booked with Ultimate Kilimanjaro. They were one of the first websites I came across when starting my research about Kilimanjaro, providing a lot of helpful general information. They also seemed to tick all the boxes in terms of porter treatment, experienced guides, equipment, good food offering, and so on. I also found them very responsive and helpful in my decision-making process.

Finally, they did a great job being the first operator to market the Northern Circuit route to the *mass* market, as a group tour. By the time of your booking, I expect there may be a greater choice of operators for Northern Circuit route group tours as others will certainly jump on this *off-the-beaten-track* marketing opportunity.

As part of my research, I was also looking out specifically for negative reviews about Ultimate Kilimanjaro. Some outdated reviews on TripAdvisor complained about their previous local operator – Zara Tours! Meanwhile, however, they have made a conscientious decision to upgrade their services and moved away from Zara Tours to another local outfitter whose dedicated staff work exclusively for them, thereby being in a better position to quality-control their offering, and qualifying as a KPAP partner.

Perhaps Zara Tours had meanwhile also improved their offering and I could get a better deal directly with them? However, their website didn't mention the Northern Circuit. So I sent them an inquiry to double-check. Sure enough, Zara Tours jumped on their target. Yes, they would organize the Northern Circuit route as a group hike, and the price offered was about US$1,000 less than the price of Ultimate Kilimanjaro! Sounds like a good deal, no? Well, I wasn't convinced. After a closer look into the details of their proposed hike, I challenged them about the specifics of their proposed route.

"This is just the frame work of the itinerary can change depending on the stability of the climber, and how the guide will propose to go about, you can agree with the guide how you can and reach the summit easily."

Interesting, I wondered how these adjustments would work out on a group hike, or were they just trying to sell this as a group hike to me? So I asked them whether other travelers had already booked this tour.

"We do expect more people to join the tour though meantime there is now group already booked; the maximum is 12pax the minimum is 1pax."

I feared that my definition of group hike was very different to theirs, and I wasn't keen to end up in a 1pax version. Perhaps I just got unlucky dealing with a poor salesperson, or perhaps he just got unlucky dealing with a biased client. Having read several complaints on TripAdvisor by prior hikers didn't inspire much confidence in me.

Operator selection shortcut for future hikers

After everything I've learnt, I would recommend the following process to select an operator:

First, decide which route you want to follow and whether you prefer to hike in a private or group tour.

If you opt for a common route or would like to organize your private tour, I suggest you start with the current partners of the

Kilimanjaro Porters Assistance Project (**KPAP**) as listed by the International Mountain Explorers Connection (**IMEC**) on www.mountainexplorers.org/club/partners.htm to solicit their offers and/or check for matching group tour offers.

Only locally registered companies are permitted to guide in the Kilimanjaro National Park, meaning all international tour operators by default subcontract with a local outfitter. Contracting directly with a local operator will cut out the additional international agency margin.

If you wish to join a group tour on a less common route, like me, your choice may be limited to larger international agencies that contract with local outfitters. Again, make sure that your preferred company is listed by **IMEC** amongst their current agent partner companies, meaning that their local outfitters are approved by **KPAP**.

Compare offers not only by price but make sure you clearly understand what your preferred operator offers in terms of:

- Experience and composition of their mountain crew, especially your specific guide(s);
- Quality of equipment, including the make of their tents and rental sleeping bags as well as usage practices;
- Nutrition and variety of food;
- Group sizes, notably the ratio of hikers versus guides;
- Specific itinerary;
- Fair porter treatment (if in doubt, email **KPAP** at info@kiliporters.org).

Only when taking all these factors into consideration, you will be in a position to make an educated assessment and select the operator most suitable to your preferences and needs.

Unfortunately, as of publication, there is no neutral booking or comparison platform to further shortcut and facilitate the operator selection process. I hope to create such a platform to provide more transparency and ease the booking process for future hikers. Check www.kilimanjaro-uncovered.com for the current status. As of your reading, perhaps I will already be able to provide you with more helpful tools.

So many more things to prepare

After more than three months of researching my options, booking my Kilimanjaro climb feels like a huge accomplishment. My operator's booking confirmation email nicely summarizes what I have to do next: Book my flight, get travel insurance, arrange for any additional hotel nights, organize all my gear and equipment, start my physical training, get a medical check-up and recommended vaccinations and medications, and so on. On top of that, add my post-hiking arrangements for a safari and/or Zanzibar.

Clearly, my preparations are only just about to start, but with five more months to go I have plenty of time.

Fortunately, I have been quick to come up with a *to-do* list. Unfortunately – as a novice to the outdoors, hiking and Africa – I am starting from zero and that list keeps getting longer and longer. But first things first.

Hiking boots

END APRIL 2015

Hiking boots may well be the most important item of every Kilimanjaro hiker, and also the most difficult to get right. I already dreaded the multiple trips to stores that such a purchase would surely require, and didn't even want to get started. It was 6pm on Saturday by the time I browsed for the biggest store in my area. Instinctively I hoped for early closing hours, but it was open late. "Why can't

Switzerland be more European," I wished at the prospect of a terrible evening ahead. All right, no excuses. I would just go there and familiarize myself with the selection – step one of many more steps to come, so I thought. That strategy was confirmed as soon as I arrived at the store. Aisle after aisle filled with one and the same item: hiking books – all *same same but different*.

Of course I had done my research and knew what to look out for: mid-weight – not too heavy as I'm not going to carry much load other than my daypack and too much weight would just make every step unnecessarily more energy-consuming, but also not too light because otherwise I would lose stability and need to put much more effort into my legs rather than relying on my boots; mid-height to protect the ankles; Gore-Tex to keep dry; and leather to keep warm(er) – my number one priority.

A two-fold dilemma manifested itself as I skimmed the store's selection: First, most boots seemed to meet most criteria. Second, all the leather boots looked terrible. So I spent my time staring at the least unsightly pairs and wondering what to do next. Should I try on every single pair – an endless task; or start with the boots that looked best – a recipe for disaster; or simply give up – a shortcut to frustration?

Hopeless bewilderment must have been written all over my face. And then the miracle happened.

"Can I help you?" My guardian angel came to save me.

"Um, yes . . . Kilimanjaro . . . clueless . . . help!"

Christian turned out to be the most knowledgeable sales person I've ever encountered. Within few minutes he had narrowed down what had seemed like an overwhelming choice to just four pairs. To do that, he needed only two ingredients – the Kilimanjaro buzzword and the shape of my feet.

As I learnt from him, it is important that boots fit well at the sides. If too loose, sliding from side to side can cause blisters, loss of heat and less stability. The narrow shape of my feet ruled out a lot of brands, as typically a brand would always follow a similar cut – standard feet width in most cases.

Another revelation was my shoe size. It needed to be one size bigger than usual. The boot should be big enough to still tightly fit an index finger at the back while wearing thick thermal socks; otherwise I'd be pretty certain to end up with bloody toenails from constant pressure during the descent – not a nice souvenir.

"Let's start with this pair. Do you know how to bind your boots?"

What a question, of course I did . . . not know.

Christian turned out to be not only an expert sales person, but also a patient teacher. When walking uphill, tie your boots tight at the bottom but looser at the top, for stability and comfort. When walking downhill, loose at the bottom but tight at the top, to make sure your toes won't squeeze against the front. In order to prevent the laces from re-adjusting to an even level of tightness throughout, special crossing techniques in the middle do the trick. In addition, when feeling pressure points, e.g. from a hallux or crooked small toes, adjusting the binding at the front by simply not crossing over the shoelaces at that point provides more comfort. Who would have thought that there are so many different binding techniques and that they can make such a difference!

The store had an inclined walking ramp to test the boots, and so I spent my evening walking uphill and downhill with two different boots at each foot for comparison. If a boot didn't fit well, it was important to take it off quickly because otherwise my body would get confused whether any pressure was due to the previous or current boot.

As it turned out, the one pair that Christian gave me to try the very first also was the most comfortable, as well as the least unsightly in the selection. Having been patiently assisted for over an hour by who, by then, seemed to me like Switzerland's premier outdoors expert, I saw no point delaying my purchase decision.

"I anyway have plenty of time to trial them. If for whatever reason they turn out to be uncomfortable, I will just have to buy another pair," I mumbled to myself.

"No, no. In that case please come back and we'll find a solution. You should be happy with your purchase and in no case have to buy another pair."

Even though I had made my purchase decision, Christian still took the time to have me try on the boots with thinner hiking socks. My conclusion about the boots didn't change, but I also bought the merino wool socks he recommended, at my own request, that is. According to him, merino wool was the one and only material to go for. Finally, he took time to educate me about proper maintenance for optimum and long-lasting functionality.

"Make sure to proof your boots. It's best to wet them first; then the material absorbs the proofing spray better."

I follow his each and every word. Surely, you know that annoying question that every shoe salesperson seems to unfailingly ask at check-out: "Would you like to take a bottle of proofing spray as well?"

"No need, I have," I would automatically reply without considering whether I might need it or not, disgusted by their undisguised attempt to maximize revenues. Today was different.

"Which proofing spray do you recommend? Could I please also take a bottle?"

Only when everything seemed to be in place, I realized that the boots were not full leather, and my fear of cold took over again. Would I end up freezing?

"Oh no, leather anyway isn't necessarily the best choice," Christian assured me, "because it also reduces breathability. It's much better to work with different soles and socks to adjust for the climate. After all, you also want your boots to perform in tropical climate, not only when it's cold, right?" He had a point.

"Yes, I guess I'll just put on two pairs of thermal socks for summit night," I tried to comfort myself.

"I wouldn't do that. Wearing two pairs of socks causes sliding and rubbing which can cause blisters. I would rather recommend you to get some good functional insoles instead."

"Oh, OK", by now I fully relied on his expertise, "do you have them in store?"

Christian went on to explain that there are different versions. The better and more expensive ones use a special material that reflects the cold back away at the bottom. However, they need to be adjusted to one's feet after warming up with a special heating device. "We don't have that device in store over summer. It will only be back in September."

"OK", that sounded like the way to go, "then I'll just come back in September."

"There might be an even better option in the market, but we don't carry them in the store. They are called chili-feet. It's a Swiss invention. In essence, they produce heat from your movement. You may want to check them."

Wow, that sounded awesome! How often have you had a salesperson recommend you something they don't sell in the store?

To top it all off, "We have a promotion starting next week, but I'll give you the 20% discount already now so you don't need to come back. Let me give you my card so you can call if any issues."

Head of the Outdoors Department, I read on his card. My lucky day! What I feared to become a frustrating and tiring *shopping-without-buying* experience turned out to be an enjoyable 1.5 hours learning all about boots, socks and insoles, and returning home to tick my most important item off my shopping list. I'm so exci-ited, I just can't hi-ide it . . .

Back home, I can't wait to find out more about those miraculous chili-feet warming insoles. If they really work as Christian told me, they would solve all my frozen-toe worries – almost too good to be true!

Sure enough, the chili-feet website confirms what I want to read. Their innovative material creates heat purely from the pressure of walking, and customer reviews confirm that the chili-feet insoles work better than any other product on the market. Evelyne Binsack, a Swiss mountaineer, tested them on her way to Mount Everest and endorses that they kept her warm.[29]

If they work for Everest, surely they would also work for Kilimanjaro. Yippee! No more worries about frozen toes during summit night! Thanks to Switzerland for such cool inventions and beautiful mountains to trial them – what better country could I hope to live in when preparing for Kilimanjaro?!

Due to an overdose of Al Bundy when growing up, I had remained biased against salespeople of any nature, dominated by those focused on footwear. Surely they all are just focused on maximizing sales, so I thought and had since diligently turned down any offer of *advice*, proud of not falling victim to their sales scams. Instead, I prefer ordering my purchases online where I can find all the information I need.

More than technical knowledge, Christian has taught me two important lessons today. First, not all salespeople are crooks. Second, reliable expert advice is invaluable when buying technical gear. Don't even think of ordering your hiking boots online!

Keeping up the momentum

MAY 2015

For a few more weeks after booking my Kilimanjaro hike, I managed to maintain my level of excitement and cross out from my to-do list everything that needed immediate attention – no less, no more.

Booking my flight was probably the easiest of all preparations. However, it meant deciding upon my return date. Should I go for two or three weeks? Should I go on safari or to Zanzibar, or both? How many days would I need for each? Eventually, I settled on two weeks including a safari. Once the flight was booked with one-day acclimatization ahead of the hike, I reserved an additional hotel night at the same hotel that my operator uses – way cheaper to book this directly with the hotel than via your operator.

The hotel replied instantly to all my inquiries: "Regarding payment no problem you can pay cash," no credit card or down payment required. I started to fall in love with the friendliness and customer service orientation of the country and its people!

With my trip fully booked, it was time to take out travel cancellation/medical insurance – a mandatory requirement of my operator. They recommended World Nomads, a dedicated travel/medical insurance package solutions provider for international travelers.

Of course I could not just go with my operator's recommendation, but had to independently assess my options. What a tedious task, because as usual with insurance, the devil is buried in your terms and conditions. After confirming that my current medical insurance covers emergency evacuation abroad including higher altitude hiking, I hoped to simply add travel cancellation insurance on top, which logically should be cheaper than the full package. Mission impossible – travel cancellation insurance never comes cheap!

Lesson learnt: The combined travel/medical package solution of World Nomads turned out to be indeed the best offer in the market, even cheaper than travel cancellation standalone.

▲ ▲ ▲

Making safari arrangements has become a project by itself. The market yet has to learn to cater for single travelers. Prices are ridiculous, and both the concepts of single rooms and group tours seem to be non-existent. After sending out multiple requests for group tours, I received multiple offers for private tours. Me stuck alone with a driver in the middle of nowhere? No thank you, not my idea of fun.

Only one safari operator showed flexibility to accommodate my request and group me up with other travelers. However, I have not been able to find any independent reviews about that company, nor are they listed as a licensed operator on the Tanzania Tourist Board's website. Not a big deal, wouldn't they ask for a 30 percent down payment!

In principle, I am in favor of supporting local entrepreneurs, and I understand they would need a down payment in order to secure the hotels. In practice, frequent tourist scams destroy the credibility of small local entrepreneurs. How could I verify they were legitimate?

So the operator put me in touch with a prior client. To cut a long story short, I eventually met that client in person, which would give me sufficient comfort to proceed with the booking.

However, I still hoped to verify the operator's track record with the Tanzania Tourist Board. What did it mean if a company was not listed as licensed tour operator on their website? Unfortunately, they would never reply to my email inquiry. Only during my safari I will find out more: Applying for a tour operator license with the Tanzania Tourism Board is said to be a lengthy process and prohibitively expensive for small independent firms. Implicitly, this would suggest that they favor the larger incumbents over smaller entrepreneurs.

"They are all corrupt", I would hear time and again in the context of Tanzanian government organizations and large tour operators. "But don't quote me on that."

"Why not?"

"I don't want to get into trouble."

Are their claims true? By the law of averages, it sounds plausible. Unfortunately, I have no means of verifying any of this information independently.

▲ ▲ ▲

The best news of my entire month came from Jana.

"I've got my vacation request approved! So now I will also book," she delivered the news over drinks with the girls.

I couldn't believe my luck. Strike! I won't have to do it alone! One week later, it got even better.

"So have you booked?" I was keen to get her final confirmation.

"Yes, both me and Diego booked it."

"Oh wow, that's great! I didn't expect Diego to decide so quickly as well."

"Yes, there were only two spaces left in the group. So we went ahead to secure those."

Here you go – still five months to go but fully booked already. Starting preparations early had proven its worth.

▲ ▲ ▲

People keep asking me how I am planning to prepare physically for Kilimanjaro.

"I don't think I need to."

Questioning faces, jaws dropping.

Call me over-confident, but here's the thing: According to everything I've read, Kilimanjaro is more an endurance and altitude challenge than an athletic masterpiece. People of all shapes, ages and handicaps have scaled it. Yes, many don't make it or struggle severely, but that's usually due to the altitude and lack of acclimatization. When people struggle physically, it seems to be mostly people who are out of shape, overweight, at an advanced age or otherwise not enjoying good health.

What can I say about myself? I'm early 30s, in my best of health and reasonably fit. Kilimanjaro literature generally recommends frequent and long-distance walking as best preparation. In my case, going for a long Sunday afternoon walk falls into my mental category of *family activity*. I've never considered it a *workout* or difficult in any way. As part of my current normal exercise program, I train with weights two or three times a week and practice cardio activities like running, inline skating or cycling for fun on weekends. What more should I do?

For Kilimanjaro – nothing. For myself – I should probably paint the full picture. I live at a lake that has roughly the perimeter of a half marathon. One beautiful Sunday, I look out of my window. It's a warm sunny day; the grass is green and lush; the lake is blue and crisp. An untraceable chemical reaction in my brain makes me decide within the blink of a moment that I want to run around *my* lake, for the first time, never mind that I've only been a very slow casual runner so far. Do I have any doubts that I might not be able to run around the entire lake? Not the slightest. Of course I can do it! Full of energy and over-flowing self-confidence, running down one length of the lake matches my idea of pleasure. Wow, it's easy! On my way back up, my energy drains and pain sets in. I'm no longer enjoying my run, so I walk back and enjoy my walk instead, still excited that I've made it for the first time on my own feet. Outcome? My adventure leaves me with a massive blister on my foot, and on antibiotics few days later after my blister got infected and my foot has swollen to double its size. What have I learnt? I need to get proper running shoes! Can't wait to go back to my new favorite outdoor store.

Two weeks later, I'm back for another loop not only in proper runners, but with my new date – let's call him Marc – as well as Jana and Diego. We planned to do a proper hike, but my date had broken a collarbone, so our first time exercising together would have to be just an easy walk. I was concerned that Jana and Diego might have preferred more of a workout, but within minutes my fears have proven unjustified. While Marc and I are getting lost in conversation, Jana and Diego are falling behind.

"We have to slow down," I keep reminding Marc.

"I thought you guys wanted to exercise?" he teases me.

"Well yes, that's what I thought as well," I look at him helplessly.

We wait for Jana and Diego to catch up, just to repeat the same game over and over again. I'm stuck in between pleasing my new date and my new hiking buddies. Time and again I implore Marc to walk slower.

"I can't walk any slower than that," he would look at me impatiently.

I understand, walking slower than my natural pace feels equally hard to me, but Jana seems to be struggling already.

"Why don't we walk ahead, and then wait further down?" We all seem to agree that this would be the most sensible thing to do.

"Are you sure you want to hike Kilimanjaro with her?" Marc asks me incredulously as we walk off our pace.

"Why not? I'm sure she will train."

"Yes, but she's only got four months."

"She told me she has strong willpower. Anyway, there's no time pressure. It doesn't matter how fast she walks. And it seems the only really difficult part is summit night. I think she will just push through no matter how hard it gets."

"Yes, but what about you? It would be a nightmare to walk that pace for over a week."

"Oh, I'm not concerned about that. I think during the day everyone anyway just walks their own pace." At least that was the case in all the books I've read, including Tim Ward's *Zombies on Kilimanjaro* which was also based on a group hike with Ultimate Kilimanjaro. "And then we meet up again at the camp. It doesn't matter at what time people get to the camp."

Half way through, we pause and wait for Jana and Diego to catch up. It's a hot sunny day and the heat has drained our energy. Walking back together at a slow pace seems far easier now. I'm glad

y makes an effort to chat with Diego, giving me a chance
h Jana.

v is it going with Marc?" Jana teases me, and we keep
entertained chatting about our respective love affairs.

Who cares that we might not be walking the same pace? Having
someone to talk to and share some fun with seems way more
important to me. For that matter, we seem to be off to an excellent
start.

Sorting out my medical preparations

END JULY 2015

The months of June and July have left a big void in my
Kilimanjaro diary. Other than finalizing my safari booking, which
would fill an entire book on its own, I've hardly progressed towards
preparing for Kilimanjaro. Luckily, arrangements made earlier this
year are bringing me back on track and remind me that it's time to
get real.

"Tropical doctor," my calendar warned me few days ago that it
wasn't easy to get an appointment and I'd better make sure to have
all my questions ready.

That clinic was recommended to me by a friend specifically for
Africa and generally seemed to be the single best center for travel
medicine in Zurich. But of course I wouldn't just rely on their expert
advice. That's what normal people do, not me. Instead I conducted
my own research and brought along a long list of vaccinations and
medications that I was convinced I would need.

Usually, I only take medication if I really have to, but this was
freaking Africa. Without ever having stepped a foot onto that
continent, I wanted to take every single precaution, no matter how
small the odds and how big the costs involved.

According to Lonely Planet, the following vaccinations were (also)
recommended for Tanzania, aside from other vaccinations
recommended by the World Health Organization regardless of
destination: hepatitis A; hepatitis B; rabies; typhoid; boosters for
tetanus, diphtheria and measles; as well as potentially yellow fever for
entry requirements depending on the transit country.

To my bewilderment, my doctor declined to give me each and
every one of those. On the one hand, a quick look into my

vaccination records brought her to the conclusion that whatever had been injected into me throughout my past would protect me against hepatitis A/B, tetanus, diphtheria and measles for life, or at least another 20 years or so. On the other hand, she didn't consider yellow fever, typhus or rabies to be required given my travel plans. Yellow fever is only required for legal reasons when flying in via an epidemic country such as Kenya, but not in my case. And the likelihood of getting infected with typhus or rabies would be close to zero for me.

"But what if? I read that rabies can kill you," I protested.

"Yes, but it's really highly unlikely that you get attacked by a mammal when hiking Kilimanjaro or during a safari."

"I read there are monkeys on Kilimanjaro," I insisted warily, but that didn't help make my over-exaggerated vaccination demand any more plausible in her eyes.

"In the rare case of any incident with mammals, do you know what to do?" She went down the education route instead, and I shook my head. "Whenever you get bitten or even just scratched by a mammal, first immediately wash the wound thoroughly with soap and water for at least ten minutes. And then immediately go to a good hospital for further treatment. Even if you had vaccination, you would need to do that."

OK, I didn't get what I wanted, but at least I learnt something new.

Malaria

As if to make the point that there was something she could do for me after all and that I didn't make the appointment for nothing, my doctor seemed relieved to move on to malaria.

"Many travellers are under the impression that malaria is a mild illness, that treatment is always easy and successful and that taking antimalarial drugs causes more illness through side effects than actually getting malaria. Unfortunately, this is not true," Lonely Planet educated me when I started my research about Tanzania. Before that, I was one of those travelers, my erroneous beliefs dating back to when I lived in Asia and frequently traveled to endemic countries without worrying about medication. I don't know whether I was outright stupid, or whether the odds of getting infected or the types of malaria at that time were any different in Asia. "There are several types, falciparum malaria being the most dangerous and the predominant form in Tanzania.... The pattern of drug-resistant malaria is changing rapidly, so what was advised several years ago might no longer be the case.... Treatment in hospital is essential, and the death rate might still be as high as 10% even in the best intensive-care facilities."

I don't know what you make of that, but I have always regarded Lonely Planet as a trustworthy source of travel advice and the message was pretty clear to me: Don't even think of going there without antimalarial drugs!

A crosscheck on various other websites (such as those provided by the UK National Travel Health Network & Centre or the UK NHS) confirmed that there was a high risk of malaria in all areas of Tanzania below 1,800m (5,900ft). Taking malaria prevention tablets was recommended. The transit areas around the Kilimanjaro International Airport and Moshi are below 900m (3,000ft); therefore even travelers who only visit the country to hike Kilimanjaro cannot avoid potential exposure.

Since Malarone[30] has become available on the market, the prior debate in the scientific community about the best antimalarial medication seems to have become null and void (though there might be exceptions for people with specific physical conditions, budget constraints or other special circumstances). Take one tablet of Malarone one day before entering the endemic area, then continue daily throughout the stay and for another seven days after leaving the endemic area. Pretty simple, huh?

"Should I test it before the trip?" I asked my doctor with a long list of possible side effects in mind.

"That's not necessary. Testing is only recommended for the older drugs like Lariam[31]. You may get a headache, diarrhea or stomach pain, which are common side effects, but you have no choice anyway. It would be even worse with Lariam."

What an outlook! Time to rewire my mindset – expect the worst.[32]

"I'm also considering getting one of these small malaria blood testers," I mentioned in passing, keen to assess my doctor's reaction. Yes, you get the idea by now – I have driven my health considerations to the extreme and diligently noted down everything I read online. My doctor looked at me quizzically and I continued, "Because when I get fever on Kilimanjaro, then I can check immediately."

"I don't think you need that. It's highly unlikely that you would contract malaria despite taking Malarone. And even if, symptoms only develop after more than a week. By that time you would already be off the mountain again."

She had a fair point.

Sleeping sickness / insect repellents

Then my doctor mentioned the African sleeping sickness transmitted by the Tsetse fly.

"But I can't do anything about it anyway," because there is no effective preventive medication or vaccination against it.

"That's why it's important to avoid getting bitten in the first place."

Ah bah, tell that to someone who has suffered from mosquito and insect bites all my life! No matter what precautions I take and what amount of chemicals I dump onto my skin, these little bastards have always found my blood irresistible.

"Yes, I will get DEET," I knew it all. DEET is toxic, but I've found it to be the only insect repellent that prevents me from being eaten alive.

"Yes, get that for your skin. And get permethrin-containing spray for your clothes and other materials. Also avoid dark clothes and jeans."

"Jeans?"

"Yes, Tsetse flies are particularly attracted to blue."

Who would have thought that flies have a favorite color?!

Altitude sickness / Diamox

"We should also talk about altitude sickness and Diamox," my doctor progressed through her own checklist.

Diamox is a commonly used drug to prevent and reduce symptoms of altitude sickness or AMS (acute mountain sickness) in case of rapid ascent to high altitudes. However, it cannot completely prevent serious altitude sickness. [33] I have researched quite a bit about Diamox already and come to the conclusion that I prefer to summit Kilimanjaro naturally without taking any drugs. After all, I planned in sufficient acclimatization time, so I don't think I will need it. To the contrary, Diamox makes people pee a lot, which means most likely I would have to get up several times during the night. I prefer to have a good night's sleep instead.

"OK," my doctor nodded as I stated my logic.

Anti-diarrhea

"But I wanted to ask you about anti-diarrhea drugs like Loperamide," I moved on to what seemed way more important to me.

My doctor agreed it would be good to bring some just in case. In essence, Loperamide (or rather the Imodium contained therein) attacks the symptoms of diarrhea – obviously a big hassle on Kilimanjaro. However, Loperamide doesn't attack the cause, i.e. the bugs. Usually our bodies will be able to fight them without further antibiotics, but again I wanted to be extra-sure.

"Shouldn't I also bring antibiotics for more severe cases of stomach infection?"

"I think it's highly unlikely you would need that. Your operator would face serious reputational issues if they don't cook the food and boil the water properly."

"But what if?" I insisted again.

"Then I think most likely you will be able to get emergency antibiotics from your operator or someone else."

I usually don't like to rely on others, but given the low odds I relented and followed her advice.

Antihistamines

The clock was ticking, but I wasn't done yet. Antihistamines were next on my list. I tend to over-react to insect bites, which sometimes swell and itch to the extent of becoming truly unbearable. After suffering through a nightmarish experience with sand flies in Eastern Malaysia, I would always try to bring antihistamines when traveling to an insect-prone or underdeveloped country.

"You can just get them in any pharmacy without prescription, but let me give you a free emergency kit with a cortisone tablet," she kindly offered. "That's for serious emergencies only," such as if I should ever get bitten near my respiratory system.

Luckily, I'd been spared such a shock so far, but I gladly took on her advice and the emergency set.

Antibacterial ointment

"I'm almost done. Only one more question: Should I bring an antibacterial ointment in case of cuts or other open wounds?"

"Most travelers simply use commercially available hand sanitizers even on open wounds, but yes I can give you a prescription for that."

I previously never worried much about open wounds as they tend to heal by themselves, but after needing to take antibiotics for an infected blister and a recent hospitalization for intravenous antibiotics infusion from an even smaller wound, I've learned to respect the potential risks of open wounds. When traveling into the wilderness for over a week, better safe than sorry.

▲ ▲ ▲

My doctor must have been quite relieved when I finally left her after a long hour of non-stop questions. While I didn't get any of the vaccinations that I initially went for, hopefully I became a little bit smarter in the process.

Armed with my two prescriptions, I went straight to the pharmacy to progress my *shopping*: Malarone, Loperamide, antibacterial ointment, antihistamines, insect spray . . . and US$200 less in my bank account. Kilimanjaro doesn't come cheap!

A month of shopping

AUGUST 2015

When my operator sent me an email two months prior to departure to confirm final travel and booking arrangements, I woke up to reality: I no longer had half a year to prepare, but only a finite number of weekends that I could count on my fingers. As usual time flew, but meanwhile my *to-buy* list had expanded into some 40 items of gear and equipment as well as over 20 items of toiletries and accessories that I still needed to organize.

As I hoped to do more serious hiking in future, renting was not an option for most of my gear. Of course – as a perfectionist freak – almost each and every single one of these purchases had to be researched thoroughly. I wanted to know everything, I wanted to get it right, and I wanted to get the best price. That required time, time for which I easily found way more appealing alternatives to make use of over summer.

Belonging to the rare breed of females who dislike shopping and default online whenever possible didn't help to get me started. As I learnt from my hiking boots buying experience and soon became clear with other gear that had to be tried on or required reliable advice, I would have to actually visit stores physically. How dreadful! Getting there, squeezing past aimlessly meandering people, waiting for a sales person, waiting for my size from the storeroom, getting changed in hot and stuffy changing rooms, waiting to be told they don't have my size, waiting in front of the cashier, slogging back home, unpacking, cutting off the price tags . . . – why would anyone enjoy that?

Life-long experience warned me about my biggest challenge ahead: hiking trousers. What jeans makers had learned decades ago, sports brands had missed in their endless search for functionality: Not only mountains come in different heights, so do we! OK sure, I'm taller than average, but certainly not on the extreme. One thing I know for sure from a recent hiking experience getting caught in torrential rain and drenched in heavy jeans: They are out of the question for Kilimanjaro.

Dragging myself from store to store and trying on pair after pair of hiking trousers of all standard outdoor brands didn't help – standard brands only come in standard sizes. I was hopeless.

By coincidence, while visiting an Austrian outdoor outlet store looking for a good deal on skis, I found myself amidst aisles of hiking pants. Feeling like Alice in Wonderland, I went through their entire collection and marveled at all the qualities of high-tech fabrics: easy care, water repellent, soil repellent, oil repellent, stretchable, breathable, durable, odor control, cooling, windproof, thermal retaining . . . – How to even prioritize?

Eventually my height was a blessing in disguise; only three pairs were the right fit and thus turned an otherwise impossible task into an easy choice. Cooling for lower altitudes, thermal retaining for the summit, and odor control for in between. What more could I have hoped for? Only the neon pink color of number three made me hesitate until I got my priorities straight: Would I rather stink or look like a walking highlighter? I chose the lesser evil.

Thanks to ALLSPORT, an Austrian brand that I had never heard about before, but was seemingly made for people like me. After more than ten years happily abroad, I finally started to appreciate my country of birth!

Hiking trousers ticked off my list, I was still left with 60 more items to sort out. For a starter, I went back to my new favorite outdoor store. A junior sales person made me despair, until she excused herself and Christian took over. After advising me on my hiking boots and also proper running shoes, he surely recognized his loyal customer.

"Her AGAIN?!" He politely concealed his surprise, or perhaps he was simply used to customers returning time and again for his expertise second to none.

I came to trust his advice, and so within minutes rather than hours we cleared through my list with whatever their store held in stock.

▲ ▲ ▲

As I am a novice to serious outdoor activities, my Kilimanjaro research had taught me some essential clothing guidelines:

First, it's all about layers. Forget those thick skiing pants or that heavy winter jacket. They will only make you over-heat and sweat. Instead, go for layers that can be added on as required, each fulfilling certain functionalities. A base layer near your skin should be moisture-wicking and temperature-controlling, a mid-layer and insulation layer should keep you warm, and an outer layer should not only look good but protect you against wind and light precipitation or snow (softshell). In case of serious rain, a light layer of waterproof rain gear should always be in your daypack (hardshell). Simple enough and applicable to all outdoor activities, but in my case it required Kilimanjaro to learn these basic layering rules.

My second revelation was the existence of a wonder material for all base layers – merino wool, the one and only material to wear next to your skin. It keeps you warm when it's cold, it keeps you cool when it's hot, it draws moisture away from your skin, it is lightweight, and it has antibacterial properties. This means it can be worn for days before it stinks – an essential property for Kilimanjaro given strict weight limits restricting us to about three changes of clothing.

Ever heard of someone claiming they could wear the same underwear for over a week without stinking, and you thought what a load of nonsense? Well, perhaps it was a load of merino instead! Prior hikers tested and swore by it. Environmentalists and nature lovers will be pleased to know that merino wool is produced from merino sheep, hence fully renewable, recyclable and biodegradable. It was pioneered by Icebreaker from New Zealand, by learning from nature that it protects merino sheep against extremes – hot summers and freezing winters.

There was only one problem in my case: I have wool phobia. Even wearing the softest of all cashmere is torture to me. Would merino, described as exceptionally soft, be any different?

My last big revelation was the most obvious, but also the most essential in my initial research on whether I would dare to scale Kilimanjaro at all: There is no bad weather, only bad clothing. With the right clothing, we would be fine in any weather, no matter how cold, wet or windy. However, quality has its price, and that's not where you would want to save money.

▲ ▲ ▲

Armed with my newly gained knowledge and one of Switzerland's premier outdoor experts, I proceeded to buy my first merino gear. Trying on these long-sleeves in summery temperatures revealed an unknown masochistic disposition. How itchy! But that's just me.

"It will feel better on the mountain in minus temperatures," I comforted myself.

In stark contrast, my new mid-layer fleece pants felt like heaven on earth.

"They are also great for running in winter," Christian enlightened me.

Oh, so I could go for a run in winter without getting cold? Goodbye winter hibernation!

Having expert advice also came in really handy when facing an aisle of hiking poles. "So which ones are the best?"

"The best in the market are these LEKI Micro Vario Carbon poles. They are super light, you can fold them, adjust the height, quickly adjust your grip . . ." Christian demonstrated their easy usage but hesitated. "Those would also work, just a bit heavier, and you can't fold them."

"So why would you carry all those others if the first ones clearly are the best?"

"Well, because they are also the most expensive. Depends on how much you would want to spend—"

"Can they break?"

"Almost impossible, they are made of carbon. Unless you lose them, you would have them forever."

I was on a mission, no more explanations needed.

"Do you also have headlamps?"

"Over here," and not just a few, and entire shelf!

"So which one would you recommend?"

"Black Diamond are the best."

"OK, so which model?" I wanted to get to the point.

"I'd go for the Black Diamond Storm. It has all the functionality you'll need, and the price is good."

Christian demonstrated how by simply tapping I could adjust the light intensity, make it flash or even go into red light modus. What more would I need? Sold. Next.

Gaiters to protect against the mud were on every Kilimanjaro packing list as optional item. I didn't expect much rain, but of course

I needed to be on the safe side. A lightweight towel made of microfiber that would dry quickly was equally optional yet must-have for me. Finally, I was almost done for the day.

"Do you also carry CamelBaks?"

"Oh, you mean water bladders?"

The existence of such hands-free hydration systems was another revelation to me. They can be stored like a sturdy yet ultra-light and flexible plastic container in your daypack, and allow you to drink directly from a hose while hiking. Kilimanjaro operators would typically give you three liters of water for the day, for which they recommend to bring such water bladders. Plastic bottles are not allowed inside the Kilimanjaro National Park.

"We don't carry the CamelBak brand, but we have the SOURCE Widepac which I would highly recommend. It does the same, but is cheaper."

Same but cheaper? My alarm signal went on. "I read some of these CamelBaks make the water taste like plastic."

"Not this one, I've got the same and never noticed anything."

Sold.

The store was about to close and my stamina to continue my new personal-record shopping spree was about to collapse. I wonder who was most relieved when I finally left – Christian, my credit card or me?

▲ ▲ ▲

Before I could default to the convenience of online shopping, my shopping list had a few more important accessories that I preferred to buy in a specialist store with proper expert advice. Thus, the biggest outdoor store in Zurich (Transa) became my next target and made me feel like Alice in Wonderland again. Whatever I could have dreamed of, or whatever I could never have dreamed of because I didn't even know it existed, they had it all.

My eyes were my number one priority. "Snow blindness, or solar/ultraviolet keratitis is an excruciatingly painful state that comes from the sun burning the covering of your eye – the cornea. And it happens, very commonly if you don't wear sunglasses, or if you don't wear appropriate sunglasses in any bright light situation – especially easy to encounter at altitude," the Everest Base Camp Medical Clinic warned. I was convinced – for my eyes, more than any other body part, only the best of the best. Others seemed to agree, because sunglasses experts at Transa were in high demand.

No problem, I had enough distractions to get lost in while waiting, such as trying on different sunhats, or choosing amongst the dozens of thermos bottles. All the reviews I read seemed to concur that water would unfailingly freeze during summit night, so hikers would always be dehydrated by the time they reach the summit.

"Then why not bring a thermos?" I wondered and still don't understand why it doesn't feature in any of the Kilimanjaro packing lists. Perhaps the weight limit is the issue. Should I go for a smaller bottle to keep the weight low? No, the heavier full liter version seemed fully worth the extra pound to me.

"Sorry for the long wait," the sunglasses expert now gave me all his attention.

"Um . . . high altitude . . . wrap-around to protect against exposure from the side . . . highest level of UV absorption," I explained, and he immediately narrowed down an entire aisle of funky frames and colorful lenses into only two pairs that looked like straight out of Men in Black. I settled for the Adidas Elevation Climacool glasses, which seemed to be the absolutely best product in the market, or at least in Zurich's biggest outdoors store. Downside – quality doesn't come cheap; once more I managed to choose the most expensive item in their entire collection! Upside – durability and versatility justifies the price tag; once more I am looking forward to making good use of my new gear for all kinds of outdoor activities. Only the question of why I needed Kilimanjaro to finally invest in some decent gear remains a mystery to me. Shopping phobia might be the answer, so I had better keep up the momentum.

Waterproof rain pants were a tiresome affair to better be dealt and done with. Trying on multiple pairs that didn't fit wasn't helpful; realizing that each of them cost a fair bit of money made it almost mission impossible. Would you rather spend a lot of money for something that looks truly horrible, or would you rather spend even more money for something that looks barely acceptable? Going for a cheap poor quality solution was not an option. I had one of those in my cellar; and since getting sweat-drenched in freezing temperatures when hiking Mount Kinabalu I knew that breathability was more than just a marketing gimmick.

After trying and retrying different models in different sizes and lengths, having missing sizes ordered by the store, and returning the following weekend to try and retry an even more exhaustive set of different sizes, I couldn't spend any more time debating about the merits of expensive waterproof pants, because those were only the start of a long and tiresome 48-hour shopping marathon weekend to come. Every single item had to be ticked off my shopping list, at least that was the plan, and so I eventually settled for a pair of Haglöfs L.I.M III. They were independently recommended to me by both Christian and the Transa store as the most breathable, high-tech and lightweight product on the market; and they conveniently came with zips along the sides of the legs, useful when putting them on while wearing thick hiking boots and other layers underneath. More importantly in my case, they were the only pair of waterproof pants that came in size Small/Long, a surprisingly rare combination as we have established by now. Once more I managed to end up with arguably the most expensive product in the world of waterproof apparel! At this time I truly hoped to economize, yet was left without choice.

Next – more merino wonder products, and what a selection they have in the store! Merino wool comes in different levels of thickness. I hadn't given up hope yet that the ultra-light version for warm temperatures would feel tolerable on my skin. Touching the material with my fingers gave me hope, forcing it over my body made me despair. Imagine yourself wearing a coarse thick woolen turtleneck while exercising in hot, humid climate. Yuck – right? That's how that stuff felt to me in that changing room. But no worries, guarantee you would love it just like 99.99% of people. As for me, I'd rather stink!

Only the merino underwear shorts and sports bras felt tolerable. Having figured out the right size and cut for me, I was faced with my next frustration: They only come in bright green, yellow, pink and blue. How would that look underneath my ultra-thin hiking shirts? Not that I'd be overly conservative, but they were meant for backcountry Africa! Do the porters, guides and whosoever really need to see through what I'm wearing underneath? I would have to find better options online.

After freeing my skin again from all the wool, I stepped up my level of shopping efficiency, and within no time my little shopping basket was filled to the brim: a balaclava to protect against the freezing cold and wind during summit night; a multifunctional Buff headband/neckerchief to cover my hair once it starts getting greasy and unsightly; tiny compressed towels that miraculously expand into a proper wet towel when put into water; antiseptic gel which promises that one drop will *wash* both my hands; insect repellent; heaps of tiny toiletries; and water proofing spray that promises to turn my soft shell jacket into a brand new rain jacket.

That was one of the few pieces of required gear that I already owned, without even knowing about its high-tech functionalities. Would that outdoors jacket – that I received as a Christmas present long ago – be any good for Kilimanjaro? If in doubt, ask. So I asked Google about Northland Professional storm shell, and oh boy what a gem I had hidden in my wardrobe: windproof, waterproof, breathable, stretchable – all the qualities I would have been looking for. Best of all, it was made by a family business form my hometown in Austria. I had not the slightest clue about my country's hidden treasures in the world of outdoor apparel.

Once I'd satisfied myself that each and every potentially useful item at the outdoor store had made it into my shopping basket, I moved on to my weekly groceries that became equally dominated by Kilimanjaro: spare batteries for my headlamp, antiseptic blasters, blasters against blisters (just in case), and a series of wet wipes. The latter presented quite another challenge in itself. There was no such thing as *normal* wet wipes, but an overwhelming selection scattered across the supermarket: super-soft baby wipes for any mother's taste and preferences; multi-functional facial wipes that promised anything from antiseptic properties to radiant skin; and finally even a selection dedicated to adult intimate parts. Huh, I had already used up my decision-making capacity for the day and was in for some headache.

By Saturday evening when I unpacked all my shopping back home, I felt my most exhausted for a long time. A day in stores had worn me out and all further purchase decisions were happily postponed to Sunday, when I planned to simply order any pending items online, from the comfort of my living room. "Surely a quick and easy task," so I thought and indulged in a lazy evening. Ignorance is bliss.

▲ ▲ ▲

Feeling refreshed early Sunday morning, I set out after my most important pending piece of equipment: To identify the best possible (notably warmest) of all gloves. Again, that became a little research project by itself – first to identify them, and then to locate a retailer that would deliver them to a Swiss address. Following the majority of reviews and ratings online, I finally settled for a pair of Hestra Army Leather Heli mittens, trading off the loss of dexterity in mittens with the supposedly improved warmth that I would never find in finger gloves. Hestra conveniently provided a size chart drawing online which allowed me to identify my size (mind you even mittens require fitting!).

Ordering a pair of liner gloves for extra warmth and protection, especially when removing the mittens for dexterity, made me sigh with relief. The online community seemed to agree that fleece was the way to go, and optimizing for best price was my default for a change. By the time I was fully satisfied that I wouldn't need to worry about frostbite any longer, it was noon. I had dedicated my entire morning just to keep my fingers warm!

My afternoon bore another unexpected challenge. Newly convinced about the merino wonder material yet constrained by ultra-thin hiking shirts, I set out to order a skin-color merino sports bra. Given I had already identified the best cut and size in the store the day before, that should have been an easy task. Setback number one: Icebreaker Bras don't come in skin-color, not even a neutral white. Bet you all their designers are men – get real guys! All women would know that ordering bras without trying online is a tricky business, but faced without choice I was happy to give it a try. So I found Ibex, a wool clothing company, and got hooked on their products that had an enthusiastic following amongst the female online community. After consuming quite some decision-making capacity to identify my best cut and size, I was faced with setback number two: Ibex Bras don't ship to Europe. What a frustration, as if I had nothing better to do than idling my day away! Oh well, I accepted my fate stoically and set out to order my least ideal option by SmartWool, but guess what – they didn't ship to Europe either. So to cut a long story short, it took me an entire afternoon to figure out that obtaining a skin-color or even just white merino sports bra was mission impossible for the entire population of over 250 million women in Europe! How does that sound in terms of market development? Why no one had jumped on that obvious business opportunity remained a mystery to me, and I was back to square one. So I defaulted back to my all-time favorite – Victoria's Secret's Knockout. "It may not be merino, but at least it will look nice instead," I comforted myself.

What a day – nothing but gloves and bras, and it was already close to dinnertime! Everything else had to be dealt with quickly: merino panties, a second pair of long merino underwear pants, sleeping bag liner, spare laces for my hiking boots, dry shampoo, self-heating pads for fingers and toes, water purifier, and so on. Sounds simple enough, but guess what – even just identifying the best water purifier seemed like a science in its own right. Of course I could have trusted my operator who claims they treat water properly and there would be no need for additional water purifiers, but prior hikers warned me that might not be a good idea with any operator. So I educated myself and learnt that purification typically means overdosing on either iodine or chlorine, and accepting a chemical taste on top. I eventually settled for the Aquamira Water Treatment solution, which sounded like the least evil to me.

Finally, I dug out my trekking backpack from the cellar, confirmed with my operator that it would be OK to use (rather than buying a new duffel bag which all operators seemed to request by default for their porters to carry), and spent my evening testing whether all my gear would fit. More importantly, would I stay below the 15kg weight limit imposed by my operator? If not, I would have to make sacrifices and leave stuff behind – a scary prospect. What a relief when my scales only showed 8kg so far!

By the time I could finally relax and enjoy my weekend, it was Sunday 10pm. I had driven my habit of researching things to death onto a new level of extremes. At least no more shopping, so I thought.

▲ ▲ ▲

Solar charger – gizmo's

During the week, all my ordered gear arrived in perfect shape. Only one small hiccup set me off into another wild goose chase. Instead of dry shampoo, I received a bottle of shampoo for dry hair. Whoops – not much good for Kilimanjaro, was it? Infused with renewed research and shopping energy, I didn't just want to order any new dry shampoo. Now I needed to identify the single best option, and locate where I could actually obtain it in Switzerland – another useless evening!

At last I thought I was finally done with all my shopping, until the following weekend I ran a final crosscheck with another Kilimanjaro packing list, just to be certain. And sure enough, I found something amiss: portable solar charger (optional). Optional? I'm planning to write a book on my tablet, and we all know those batteries die within a day. How did I think I was going to do that? So a solar charger it had to be, and Alex had found a new little research project. Differences in size, weight, price, efficiency and performance all had to be weighed against each other. I finally optimized for the highest performance ratings of the RAVPower Solar Charger despite its *me!* ⍺

greater weight and size dimension. Something else would have to stay behind.

That was the easy part. There was something far scarier on that Kilimanjaro packing list: female urination device (FUD). I was aware of them, but so far had been too *cool* to even grant them the slightest consideration. Who needs those anyway? But now doubts were creeping in. Could there possibly be a valid reason for their existence? Why otherwise would people recommend them, including Eva Melusine Thieme, the author of my favorite Kilimanjaro book so far? Even Jana said she was going to get one, and she was an experienced mountaineer, not an amateur like me.

"Pee while standing, without getting undressed," online forums filled with positive reviews frightened the hell out of me: What if it didn't work? I didn't even want to think of the consequences – yuck! But there would be nothing to hide behind at higher altitudes. What if FUDs had indeed become mainstream? Then I would be the ONLY woman moonlighting in front of everyone else – shame! Fear took control of my senses, and Amazon took control of my Sunday – again!

▲ ▲ ▲

You might think by now I was finally done with all my preparations, but far from that. Other than figuring out the best option for my mobile and data roaming for Tanzania, my coming week was dominated by money – what would be the cheapest way to obtain US dollars? Despite a life of traveling, for the first time I was in need of cash in a currency of payment that I could not just withdraw from an ATM upon arrival.

"You can pre-order FX online and then pick it up at one of the FX specialists, that might be cheapest," my colleague advised, and sure enough Travelex had the best rates.

"I pre-ordered US dollars, but I still need to get Swiss francs. Where is the nearest ATM?" I would ask the lady at the Travelex booth.

"Oh, no need, you can pay by card here, much quicker," she pointed to the VISA and MasterCard signs at her terminal.

"But I don't have a VISA debit card, only credit cards," my experience working in financial services came in handy. While normally debit cards wouldn't charge for cash transactions, surely paying by credit card would involve cash advance fees.

"No problem, you can pay with credit card."

"Yes, but I don't want to pay fees."

"Oh no, of course not. Travelex doesn't charge you any fees for that."

She completely missed the point that my credit card provider very well might. Eventually she pointed me towards the nearest ATM, a two-minute walk that just saved me US$100. Travelex then worked like a charm, providing me with an amazing supply of small notes just as I asked for, so small it barely fit into an envelope. Great service, great price, just don't ask them for cash advance advice!

Only when writing this down, I realize that I cannot be 100% certain about the cash advance fee and better double-check rather than asserting half-truths. Technically speaking, perhaps my credit card provider would treat this like a purchase transaction (i.e. buying US dollars) and not like a cash advance (i.e. getting US dollars in cash)? So I check the terms and conditions as well as the fee tables of my credit cards, but cannot find the answer. Intrigued to find out, I call up one of my credit card issuers.

"Yes, for transactions in foreign currencies we charge a 1.5% foreign exchange fee," their service representative tries to make me believe, but clearly doesn't understand my question. I must be the first person ever asking her something so complex. Who else would bother?

"Are you sure? Because the transaction takes place in Switzerland, using Swiss francs."

"Oh, sorry then I don't know. It depends in which currency Travelex books the transaction."

"Yes, but usually when paying by card it gives the option to choose the currency. So assume they book it in Swiss francs. Would you treat this as a cash advance?" I re-ask.

"Oh yes, cash advance fee," she now confirms, "you can find all the details in our terms and conditions."

She obviously doesn't have the slightest clue. What a waste of time! But without a clear answer, I cannot let go. A written answer may take longer, but at least it will make them think twice.

"The transaction would be considered a cash withdrawal, hence the fee of 3.75% would be debited," I will read upon my return from Tanzania.

Here we go – don't use your credit card when paying for foreign exchange!

No time to take it easy

FIRST WEEKS OF SEPTEMBER 2015

Two more weeks to go, everything sorted and finally time to relax and enjoy the thrill of anticipation – was that even possible? No, of course not. My shopping spree would continue, because I made a fatal mistake: I went into a drugstore on the occasion of a trip to Germany. Having struggled to find any dry shampoo in Switzerland at all, and only at ridiculous prices, I stared bewildered at their very affordable collection in Germany: seven different brands and even more different fragrances, all promising to be the one and only. How to choose? Faced with an overwhelming task, cheap prices and sheer excitement, I dropped one each into my shopping basket. Over the coming weeks, I would test them all just to conclude that they are really all the same, differences in price and fragrances aside.

Mineral supplements that spoilt me for choice filled another aisle. I thought it would be a good idea to bring some magnesium/calcium fizzy tablets, both to avoid muscle cramps as well as to hide any bad taste of the water. Unable to choose between lemon, orange, grapefruit and more exotic flavors, again one of each brand found its way into my shopping basket. The one with the best taste would make it into my Kilimanjaro bag.

I should have left the drugstore by then, but as a health addict who rarely walks into stores, I couldn't help getting lost in their selection of nutritional supplements and medical wonders based purely on natural ingredients. Ginger-extract lozenges against nausea as well as charcoal tablets against diarrhea jumped out at me. Should I get sick on Kilimanjaro, surely that would be good to have! By the time I made it to check-out with a basket full of dry shampoo, fizzy tablets and supposedly healthy medication, the sales clerk probably thought that I was either a lunatic or working as a human guinea pig for a lifestyle magazine. As for me, I was as excited as a little girl at Christmas.

▲ ▲ ▲

There was another item on my Kilimanjaro preparation list that normal hikers won't need to worry about – baking my own snacks. I guess it's high time to fess up to another freakish trait of my perfectionist character. Over the past year, I've been following a rather strict no-carb no-sugar Paleo-like diet. That means that I religiously avoid bread, pasta, rice, potatoes and any forms of pastries or cakes, amongst others. Sounds like a masochistic cult? Maybe, I'm doing it obsessively voluntarily because I am in love with the results and the positive changes I have evidenced ever since. Never before in my entire life have I felt as fit and energetic. Why would I want to go back to my old *me* that struggled with body fat, lethargy and other supposedly normal side effects of civilized life? I could write an entire book about just this aspect of my past year, but that's better left to experts like Dr. David Perlmutter and Dr. William Davis whose books *Grain Brain* and *Wheat Belly* truly deserve to have made it onto bestseller lists.

So what does that have to do with Kilimanjaro? Everything! Less because I'm feeling stronger than ever before, more because the staple diet on Kilimanjaro is – guess what – freaking carbs! Help! My diet is my religion – I can't have any of those. In Dr. Davis' cookbook, I find my culinary rites: Trail Mix Bars and Chocolate Bomb Bars. Lacking the kitchen experience that you might normally expect from a 30-something woman, of course I had to run a trial version. Armed with a shopping basket full of organic nuts, seeds, cocoa, almond butter and the like, I set off to create my own version. Recipe for dummies – what a delight when the result turned out all right! I could just have refrigerated them and be done with, but no, they had to be eaten up and the procedure repeated in even larger quantity fresh before departure.

"Snacks, light-weight, high calorie, high energy (optional)," it says on my operator's gear list.

Light-weight AND high energy – how is that supposed to work? I had better check. Together with all the nuts I bought, my snacks weigh three kilograms. What a nightmare when faced with a 15kg total weight allowance! Have I gone too far? Not in my current state of mind; if need be, I rather carry them myself than let go of my religion.

▲ ▲ ▲

Another extraordinary item on my preparation list was finding a present for Jana. She will have her birthday on Kilimanjaro. What kind of present would be nice, but not add much extra weight?

Searching for ideas online brought me to Lala Salama, a massage and pedicure place in Moshi. Wonderful, surely that's something every woman would enjoy after nine days in wilderness. The only problem was timing. It had to be on the day of our return from Kilimanjaro, which happened to be Monday, their day off, and it had to be in the evening after their usual working hours, to leave enough time for a shower first. I tried my luck with Lala Salama and offered to pay them more for the inconvenience. They replied instantly, offered to arrange therapists for us even outside of their regular office hours and quoted me their standard price – what an amazingly tourist-friendly country!

Present settled; however, no birthday is complete without candles and something to unwrap. So I printed a little voucher that I could wrap up – easy; and stared at the packaged cake section at the supermarket – difficult. It had to be small, durable and survive my backpack. By now, I must have fully used up my Kilimanjaro decision-making capacity, because I had to pick up each and every sweet object potentially suitable to stick a candle on top multiple times and read whatever it said on their packaging before I was able to draw the obvious conclusion: A small brownie would have to do as cake replacement, and no there are no healthy versions. Dropping them into my shopping basket felt like transgressing my religion.

▲ ▲ ▲

So far, so good – I was still enjoying the process of preparing and learning a lot of new things along the way. However, the most cumbersome aspect of my last two weeks that I would rather have skipped was packing; or rather repacking as I already had almost everything packed up two weekends before my trip to make sure everything would fit. Repacking had started to become a never-ending process:

First, I repacked when adding my previously unaccounted for 3kg of snacks, just to realize that I was on mission impossible and would simply have to carry them myself in my daypack.

Next, I repacked after buying plastic zipper bags for extra rain protection. At least sorting all my gear into small zip containers had the side benefit of converting the mess in my bag into a neat arrangement – highly recommended!

Once everything was nice and orderly, a flash of insight told me I had better spray my gear with insect repellent in advance, so I wouldn't need to carry the spray onto Kilimanjaro. So once more I ended up unpacking half my gear, hanging up clothes all over the place to dry, and repacking again.

Finally, everything was neatly packed and I was satisfied that my bag weighed exactly 15kg. But I knew this was not the end of it. Now I had to repack everything again to make sure I would carry all my essentials in my carry-on luggage. This required figuring out what would be essential to hike Kilimanjaro if my check-in bag got lost. In my mind, all of it was.

After reloading most of the gear into my daypack, I realized that I was left with unused weight in my check-in luggage. So I repacked once more to add a separate bag and more fresh changes of clothing for my safari to leave at the hotel. By now it gives me the creeps when I just write the word *repack* – what a non-word!

▲ ▲ ▲

Finally it seems there is nothing left to do, other than celebrate. One last time, I'm hijacking our girls' night out to bombard them with the latest developments in my Kilimanjaro preparations. Rachael, who has heaps of hiking experience and also lent me some of her gear, is again sharing her encouragement and expert insights with me. How wonderful to have her as a friend! It almost feels like a fraud that I am going on this trip, having zero wilderness or trekking experience, while she has done it all. Together with Jana, we run through some essentials on our packing lists.

"Guess what, I also bought a female urination device," I amuse myself.

"Oh really? Which one?" Jana asks.

"I can't remember, it's pink . . ." and six girls crack themselves laughing.

"I wonder what the Tanzanian porters are thinking when all the European ladies turn up with their pink pee devices," Rachael tires to bring me back to reality.

"But I've got no choice," I try to defend my naivety.

"Just squat like everyone else."

"Jana also got one," I try to find an accomplice.

"Yes, but only for overnight in the tent. Not for during the day."

What? Peeing in your own tent? Next to Diego? OK Alex, some things you don't have to understand.

"But I read further up there's nowhere to hide behind," I'm holding on to my illusion that a device I cannot even get myself motivated to trial in my own shower might solve all my problems on the mountain.

"I also got solar panels," I excitedly move on to my other latest addition, just to cause yet another burst of laughter.

"What for?"

"To charge my tablet," isn't it obvious?

No, it's not. I'm further digging my hole, and attracting the entire bar's attention to our roaring laughter.

"And what do you need a tablet for?"

"To write my book," isn't it obvious?

No, it's not. Faces are moving from amusement into sheer disbelief.

"How about pen and paper?"

But I wouldn't have any of that. After years of neglect, my handwriting has become illegible even to myself, and retyping everything afterwards seems like a colossal waste of time to me. However, the girls have made me think. Back home, I test my typing on my tablet compared to my smartphone and realize that there's really not much difference. So while I abide by the power of technology, they just helped me drop an unnecessary pound and a half from my luggage.

My workout program

When I booked my hike, I considered myself in no need of a particular workout program for Kilimanjaro. Meanwhile, a couple of shorter hikes – a common pastime in Switzerland – have confirmed my belief and served more to trial my new gear rather than train my physique. I experienced first-hand the difference when it rains between wearing jeans (soaking wet – ugh!) and proper hiking trousers (dry in no time – yay!); the difference on a steep downhill path when hiking with poles (so much safer – wow!); the importance of expert advice when buying hiking boots (no blisters – wahoo!); and the impact of chili-feet warming insoles when it's not that cold (sweaty feet – oops!).

However, I think I owe you the complete picture of my current fitness level, so I don't set anyone up for wrong expectations. About a year ago, I completely changed my lifestyle, including diet and workout routines. What started more like an experiment instantly made me feel so good that it has become an addiction in itself and fuelled my yearning to stretch and challenge my body more and more. Hence, I've also continued to step up the intensity and frequency of my workout program over the past months. Was it due to Kilimanjaro? No, it was initially driven by luck – reading the right book that opened my eyes (*Grain Brain*), and perhaps a way more fundamental change in my life – being free and single again. Has Kilimanjaro given me an additional incentive? Yes, it undeniably has.

All my adult life, I've struggled to get out of bed in the morning and believed that I wouldn't function prior to having coffee and breakfast. At last, I have accomplished mission impossible – adopting a morning exercise routine. Now I have no more evening excuses, but instead I manage to exercise almost every day. During my initial weeks of motivational setbacks and body resistance, thinking of Kilimanjaro certainly helped me stay on track when I would rather have stayed in bed. By now, only two months since rewiring my sleeping patterns, my morning workout has turned into a real habit. I'm even looking forward to my morning runs, when the air is fresh and I have the trail almost to myself.

Would you also like to change your habits and exercise more? I can certainly attest the most common recommendation: Follow through for a couple of weeks of making an effort. After a while, your brain rewires and your desired change simply turns into routine. Reminding yourself why you want to change as well as visualizing yourself with your new habits can all help to break resistance.

Each morning, I alternate between running and training with weights. My whole life I used to believe weights are only for guys and bodybuilders – until eventually it was my turn for an epiphany moment. Immediately feeling and seeing the impact that working out with weights had on my body, I've followed through and gradually stepped up the intensity of my exercises. Best of all, a set of weights and an exercise mat are all one needs for an effective workout.

For legs in particular, I only do squats and lunges – simple yet highly effective. When I initially started eight months ago, I didn't even use any weights, but just tried to get the posture right. My muscles were still burning like hell. Once I got used to the movement, I've gradually increased my weights to currently 15kg on each side. If you want to strengthen your legs for some serious hiking, I would highly recommend these simple exercises. Run through three sets of 15 repetitions for each the squats and lunges every two or three days, and I promise you will immediately feel the results.

CHAPTER II

TRAVEL EPISODES

▲ ▲ ▲

"Wherever you go, go with all your heart."

—Confucius

.

On my way to Tanzania

18 SEPTEMBER 2015

"Bee-dee-dee-deep!"

I'm bright awake. Yoo-hoo! Today I'll fly to Tanzania, for my biggest travel adventure ever – hiking the world's highest freestanding mountain. Getting up has never felt any easier. My big day has arrived at last.

After almost a year of research, months of organizing all the right gear and weeks of packing and repacking, I can't wait to finally get going. Having gone over-board in all my preparations throughout the year, I feel as if I'd become an expert in all that's required, and with knowledge comes confidence: I will rock this mountain. I'm convinced that I've figured it all out and I don't have the slightest doubt that I will reach the summit. This is my only big vacation this year and I've pretty much dedicated my entire year to Kilimanjaro. Now I just want to get there and finally experience it myself; earn the trophy for reaching the top; and proof that everyone can get up and down safely without suffering altitude sickness or any other nonsense. According to everything I read, when you do it right, there's nothing daunting about it, other than the colossal hole in your budget of course. Preparation, preparation, preparation – and I've driven this to the extreme.

My flight doesn't depart until noon, so I have plenty of time to get ready. Obsessed about my health and fitness, I run through my muscle exercise routine one last time and reward myself with a bowl of mixed veggie, organic eggs, nutritious seeds and healthy oil – all part of my new lifestyle that I have adopted over the past year. Like a junkie, I am addicted to my regular dose of *feel good* boosters: right diet, regular cardio and simple strength workouts. I'm in love with the results, living proof of our huge capacity to transform our health and fitness levels by making these simple yet effective lifestyle changes.

Never before have I felt this strong and energetic. Oh yes, you got the message: I'm so full of myself!

Organizing all the stuff I would need has been the most time-consuming part of my preparation. By now I've packed, unpacked, repacked as well as checked and rechecked my packing list multiple times. But sure enough, when quickly skimming through it one last time before leaving the house, one item is still missing. When I finally close the locks of my bags, a heavy weight drops from my shoulders. No more thinking required, now it's time to reap the fruits of all that effort. And soon enough I know what that means – swapping my mental weight for the actual weight of these bags. Nothing can possibly require more physical effort than dragging them to the airport. Kilimanjaro, I'm so ready for you!

▲ ▲ ▲

These days I like breaking up my routines and habits, doing something new and different every other day. For today, I planned to strike up a conversation with my seat neighbor on the plane. I'm curiously looking forward to whatever conversation or acquaintance may arise from that, but am sorely disappointed. Not because my seat neighbor doesn't want to talk to me, and not out of lack of initiative. As I watch out for my victim, I only spot one other passenger seated so far away from me on the diagonally opposing window that I can barely make out his existence. Other than the two of us, the entire Business Class cabin is empty! Who would have thought so? This Turkish Airlines flight from Zurich via Istanbul supposedly is a busy route, especially Fridays. Um, have I missed a terrorist warning or something similar within all my mental fog? Too late, the plane is already in the air.

Well, what to do – I try to have a conversation with the staff instead. With three stewardesses and one chef (!) to share with only one more person, that should be an easy mission. The head stewardess hands me the menu with the typical airline forced smile.

"Thank you. What's going on today?" I try my luck.

Confused eyes look at me.

"Is the Business Class always that empty?" I clarify my question.

"Oh no, normally it's quite full," she assures me with an awkward smile.

"Because it's Friday, I thought it would be full today."

"Yes, just today".

Before I can follow up she quickly disappears behind the front curtain, barely to be seen again throughout the flight. Is it my outfit that makes her treat me like that? As advised by pretty much every Kilimanjaro operator, I'm wearing a full hiking outfit including my hiking boots. Instead of a handbag, my backpack lies next to me stuffed to the brim with all hiking essentials. If my check-in bags get misplaced, I'm prepared.

"Miss . . . ah . . ." The steward with the big chef hat struggles to pronounce my surname.

"Don't worry, it's a difficult name," I smile at him.

He insists and offers me his mispronounced version with a question mark.

"Yes," I agree so he would get over it.

"So Miss . . . ah . . . May I take your order? First, what would you like to drink?"

"What red wines do you have?"

"Ah . . . French and Turkish."

"What types are they?"

"Ah . . . sorry, I don't know. I'll check." He looks embarrassed.

"It's OK. Don't worry. Which one is better?"

"The Turkish wine."

"OK, then I'll have that." He disappears.

Huh, was that really such a difficult question for a chef?

After quite a while, he reappears.

"Miss . . . ah . . . May I take your food order now?"

"Sure. One question – what's in the stuffed eggplant?"

"Beef," he announces with a straight face.

"Are you sure? It says vegetarian on your menu." I point to the big VEGETARIAN label.

He just looks at me blankly, no words, no action.

"Could you maybe check?" I help him out.

"Sure," he disappears again.

After a few minutes he reappears, holding the actual dish.

"Miss, this is how it looks," he proudly shows me a small bowl still covered with aluminum foil that's partly peeled aside so I can peer inside.

"Thanks, but you don't know what's in the stuffing?"

"Sorry," he shakes his head.

What a chef! OK, let's try something else.

"What meat is in the kebab?"

"Beef," he assures me like before, happy that he can answer my question without thinking.

OK, this time it's more plausible and I settle with the beef kebab. What a surprise when I put the first bite into my mouth. It tastes like lamb!

I can't make sense of what's going on. Isn't Turkish Airlines top-ranked for its supposedly top-notch service quality? Why would they even bother employing such a useless fake chef? I must be in the wrong movie. Bring out the hidden camera!

▲ ▲ ▲

On my onward flight from Istanbul to Kilimanjaro, Turkish Airlines is driving surrealism to the extreme. After serving dinner, all flight attendants disappear. I can't get my seat to recline and try the call button. No reaction. After an hour, I'm getting thirsty and try the call button again. No reaction again. It doesn't even light up. Is it broken or has it been turned off on purpose?

Only once several hours after dinner they come through to take drink orders, on a seven-hour long-haul flight in business class! It takes them another 30 minutes to serve the drinks, even though the cabin is half empty. Next time they briefly re-emerge to hand out immigration cards.

"Sorry, could I please borrow a pen?" I dare ask.

"Sure, just a moment."

An hour later, they come through for duty free shopping.

"Ah, sorry," I struggle to get their attention, "could I please borrow a pen?" I try again.

"Just a moment," I'm told again.

Surely their definition of moment doesn't match mine. After two hours, I spot a pen in the front cabin on my way back from the bathroom. The flight attendants are animatedly chatting in what I assume to be Turkish.

"May I?" I pick up the pen. They don't even pay attention. "Sorry," I dare interrupt, "could you please bring me some water?"

"Yes, just a moment."

Obviously, the water never comes.

What an absurdly entertaining flight! This might set me off complaining under other circumstances. Not today. Today I'm too excited about my adventure and almost pleased about all these surprises. I can't wait to find out how my story continues.

On local grounds

19 SEPTEMBER 2015

Upon arrival at the airport, my *local* experience starts. It's my first time to Africa and I have no idea what to expect. I am lucky to be the third in line for visa upon arrival and immigration. The woman behind the visa counter is moving in ultra-slow motion, as if on sleeping pills. Has she only woken up from her nap? Must have, because making a cup of tea or coffee is her priority number one. She shall be excused. It's almost 1:30am. We are the only flight arriving that late. Meanwhile, the entire hall has filled up with our plane's travelers, tired and waiting. Phew, that puts my seemingly endless ten minutes waiting time into perspective. Finally it's my turn for the immigration officer who takes his time to enter information from my immigration card into his computer.

"Look at the camera". Silence. Waiting. "Put your right thumb on the scan . . . harder . . . wait . . . Put your right four fingers on the scan . . . wait . . . Left thumb, . . . all four fingers . . ."

What a procedure! After 15 long minutes, the immigration officer hands me back my stamped passport. How long will the unfortunate people at the end of the line have to wait?

Right behind the immigration counters, the conveyor belt is filling up with our luggage. My bags roll out within few minutes. Yay, they didn't get lost! At least one positive surprise this whole day! What's next? I warily make my way to the exit door.

As soon as I step into the arrival hall, men eager to earn money jump at their target.

"Taxi?"

"You need a car?"

"Where are you going?"

Undeterred, I skim the signs.

"Alexandra. Bristol Cottages."

Ah phew, what a relief! I move my eyes up and indicate to an elderly man that I'm the one he's waiting for. Instantly, everyone else got the message and leaves me alone.

"Welcome," he shakes my hand like a good old friend.

I only made the hotel reservation two months ago when I learnt that my operator had booked us into another hotel than anticipated. Rearranging my first hotel night to that same hotel was easy, and both hotels were extremely quick and friendly in their communications. As it didn't involve any prepayments and confirmation was only by email, I made extra-sure to reconfirm my airport pick-up with Bristol Cottages.

"Our driver will be there," the hotel director confirmed.

Now the person shaking my hand is so friendly, could it be the same person I was communicating with? "Are you Mehul?"

"Yes," he smiles.

Outside the airport, there is a smallish, mostly empty parking lot. The temperature feels pleasant. Soon I am safely seated in the back seat of a small van.

"How long is it to the hotel? 20 to 30 minutes, right?"

"No madam, MUCH longer".

"Oh really, so how long?"

"At least 30 to 40 minutes. Depends on the traffic."

"Traffic at this time? Early Saturday morning?"

"Yes."

OK, if he says so. I close my eyes in exhaustion from the trip, hoping to get a little sleep. The road sounds quiet and I'm just about to doze off.

"I sleep only three hours a night," Mehul feels the need to share with me.

"How come?" I politely respond to his conversation attempt, but by now I have no more desire to chat. The long flights have worn me out.

"My director Mehul asks me to pick up guests from the last flight at night, and then again drive guests to the airport for the first flights early morning."

His director Mehul? OK, I must have misunderstood earlier.

"So then you get to sleep during the day, right?"

No answer. I'm too tired to repeat my question. He would be silent for the remainder of the drive. Is he trying to make me feel sorry so I give him a tip? "No, sorry man," I'm thinking to myself. I already paid US$60 for the pick-up, which I consider totally overpriced for a country like Tanzania, like all the other costs of this trip. He doesn't appear exhausted or exploited, speaks English quite well and works with a decent hotel. His salary can't be too bad.

I open my eyes again when the car slows down.

"We are in Moshi now," the driver informs me.

There is no traffic whatsoever. We turn into a small side road and drive through a gate. The driver turns off the engine and I check the time. It's not even 30 minutes since we left the airport.

"The reception is closed now. The night guard will show you to your room."

It's pitch-black. I follow a man with a torch up a flight of stairs onto a balcony corridor. He unlocks a room and turns on all lights, leaving the door wide open. Ah, mosquitoes? Never mind. I'm still thirsty after my long flight with barely anything to drink and immediately realize that there is only one small bottle of water on the bedside table.

"Could you bring me another bottle?" I point and lift two fingers.

He nods and goes off, never to be seen again. Should I go look for him? I step outside and see nothing but darkness. I wouldn't even know where to go. After about ten minutes, I give up and get undressed for the night. It's already 2:30am and I can't wait to close my eyes.

And then I wait to fall asleep, and wait, and wait. A hungry mosquito circling over my head keeps me awake. I try to ignore this nasty bug. Go on, tonight you can have my blood and then shut up. But this stupid thing doesn't want my blood; it just wants to keep me awake.

"Zzzzzzzz," silence, "zzzzz," silence, "zzzzz," it keeps repeating the most annoying of all sounds until I finally have had enough. I fumble around for the light switch, drag myself out of bed and spray insect repellent all around my bed sheets. My lungs may suffer, but my ears are relieved, temporarily.

Then the silence in my room is taken over by the outside world. A crying rooster (yes, in the middle of the night) taking turns with intermittent surges of stereo music. People talking, cars, horns . . . Where do they come from all of a sudden? Wasn't the city deeply asleep when I arrived?

Finally, I drag myself out of the bed again to look for my earplugs. That must have done the trick. Next time I open my eyes, it's already daylight.

▲ ▲ ▲

I dress faster than I'd ever manage in Zurich, having on purpose left my make-up at home. The room is too basic to linger around, and without any coffee-making facilities I have a clear incentive to hurry. When stepping outside of my room, I find myself surrounded by green trees and gardens everywhere. Downstairs in the courtyard, there is an inviting lounge area with comfortable chairs and wooden paintings to one side, and an open breakfast area directly overlooking the gardens to the other side. What an oasis! It's a sunny day and the temperature feels pleasant both in the sun and under the shade of the trees.

"Good morning Mam," a friendly waiter invites me to take a seat in the breakfast area.

I look forward to a good cup of freshly brewed coffee. Surely in Tanzania they know how to do that.

"Would you like some eggs? Maybe an omelet? With veggie? And sausages?"

"Oh yes, with lots of veggie please. And water please. Ah, and coffee."

"Coffee is at the buffet, Mam."

My jaw drops. There are only sachets of instant coffee and I immediately think of Nescafe. Yuck, but some caffeine is better than none.

Sip–FLASH! That stuff is potent. *Africafe,* it says on the packaging. Best instant coffee ever.

What a lovely first morning – cold water, instant caffeine, oversize veggie omelet, pleasant sunshine and peaceful gardens. Is this what the life of travel authors is like? Sitting in places like this and typing on their laptops? My fantasies are going wild.

Two shapes in the garden wake me up from my daydreaming. Yay, that's Jana and Diego, my two friends from Zurich. We booked the hike together, but they arrived earlier last evening on a different flight.

"Hey, we made it," to Tanzania at least. That was the easy part. It's still good to see their familiar faces, just that they've never seen my face like that before.

"Don't get shocked, no make-up."

"Me neither," we giggle.

"How was your flight? The immigration was quite ridiculous, huh? I wonder how long the people at the end of the line had to wait."

"Yes, we were last in the line! We had to wait for an hour! And then, there was no car. The hotel forgot to pick us up."

"Oh no!" I'm picturing myself standing there alone in the middle of the night.

"We waited for 20 minutes. Then we asked someone to call the hotel. They said our pick-up was for today, not yesterday. Obviously they got it all wrong, and they didn't have any driver available."

"So then what?"

"We just got a taxi, and it was even ten dollars cheaper than the hotel pick-up."

"Phew, I'm glad this didn't happen to me. I don't think there were any official taxis when I arrived. It would have been scary alone as a woman with a random driver . . . Hey, you wouldn't believe what happened to me on the flight, like the worst service ever . . ."

"Ours was quite good, and they came through regularly for drinks."

They went economy on KLM and clearly made the smarter choice. While exchanging our stories, I realize how good it feels to be able to share my experience with them. Thanks Jana and Diego for coming along!

Meeting KPAP to learn about porters treatment

19 SEPTEMBER 2015

It's 10am and I keep looking out for the Program Manager of the Kilimanjaro Porters Assistance Project (KPAP). I contacted KPAP for reassurance about my operator choice, and their manager Karen kindly offered a meeting. We agreed to meet now in the hotel lobby. All I know is that Karen has short grey hair, so I'm looking out for an elderly local gentleman.

"Are you Alexandra?" A friendly-looking Caucasian woman tries to draw my attention.

"Yes?" Why does she know my name? And anyway, I don't have time, until it dawns on me. "Are you Karen?"

"Yes, good morning, how are you?"

I am so embarrassed. It never even crossed my mind that Karen is a common female name; neither did I bother to read more articles about KPAP online[34]. Picturing Kilimanjaro porters, I just took it for granted that Karen would also be a Tanzanian name for men. So much for trying to keep an open mind!

We walk to the KPAP office together. I'm glad Karen offered to meet me at the hotel so I don't need to venture out into the streets alone. Soon I realize that there's nothing scary about it and I'm embarrassed again that I ever felt differently. There is a surprisingly well-maintained church just opposite Bristol Cottages. Its car park is filled with modern SUVs and hatchbacks. People are selling hiking accessories underneath shady umbrellas on the sandy side of the road. We walk past Moshi's main bus terminal filled with big colorful buses, camel and coffee colored vans, white taxis with blue stripes and drink stalls underneath big red Coca Cola umbrellas. The street is bustling with traffic, mostly cars and just a few motorbikes.

"You'd better go on the sidewalk," Karen is considerately watching out for my safety while my attention is glued to her story.

I want to know everything. How did she end up doing what she's doing? I barely notice the street vendors selling anything from fruits and vegetables to shoes and clothes laid out on blankets along the wide dusty pavement; the women in long colorful wraparound skirts and the men dressed like back home.

"Will you find your way back?" Karen notices how I'm following her blindly.

"Ah . . ." Good question. I turn around to look back.

"You see that tall white building? That's Bristol Cottages."

"Oh yes, no worries, I'll find my way. So you said you didn't move here for KPAP?"

"I volunteered in Moshi with another organization and then KPAP was looking for a manager and advertised through the volunteer organization, so I joined them. This was back in 2004."

Over ten years of living in Moshi and fighting for proper treatment of the porters on Kilimanjaro! My mind cannot yet comprehend the level of self-less dedication required to lead such a purpose-driven life.

"That's The Coffee Shop. Our office is just behind." Karen points to a bungalow of concrete bricks with a big veranda. It looks as old and run-down to me as most of the buildings along the way. On the pathway in front, oversized cotton bras are hanging for sale on a wooden rack. Next door, there is a red brick building which I assume to be a local bar or restaurant. Locals are sitting outside on random red plastic chairs. Someone made an effort to have it look more inviting by putting up pots of green plants. Coca Cola signs everywhere. We turn into the dusty pathway between The Coffee Shop and that restaurant. "Here we are."

I hide my astonishment as we stop in front of a simple concrete structure with a flat corrugated iron roof and big metal doors that serve as windows when left open. Of course, what did I expect? KPAP is a nonprofit organization that relies on donations and Karen makes sure the money goes where it's most needed, not into fancy office space.

Karen introduces me to KPAP's three employees. I meet the office manager, fondly called Mama D by the porters; the assistant manager Adam who is in charge of the clothing lending program; as well as Zebe who oversees the KPAP investigative porters. Karen translates between us. I don't need to understand Swahili to feel their heartfelt welcome.

"I need to have a short meeting with Mama D and Zebe. Adam will meanwhile show you our office, OK?"

"Sure."

Adam speaks a little English. He seems excited about my visit and proudly shows me all their clothes. There are two big wooden wardrobes half-filled with soft-shell jackets and thermal shirts. On another wall, piles of green soft-shell pants are stacked on top of simple wooden shelves. It all seems to be good quality material. On the floor, there are baskets of warm hats, gloves and hiking boots. Adam also shows me a box of cell phones with names attached and their files with sign-up forms of all the porters. In essence, any porter with any climbing company can come to borrow clothes. He just needs to register his details once, and then every time he comes to borrow something, he leaves a valuable behind as deposit, such as his cell phone. That way, KPAP ensures that porters will always return their borrowed items.

"May I take photos?"

"Yes, yes," he happily models for me and beams into the camera. Surely he's not used to all that attention.

▲ ▲ ▲

"Sorry for the wait. Come, let's go next door to my office." Karen unbars the adjacent metal door secured by two padlocks. Inside, other than a simple desk, there are big bags stuffed with clothes.

"Is this for washing?"

"We prefer that the porters wash the clothes, but these are clean. These are a part of our clothing stock and are often reserved and pre-booked by partner companies for their upcoming climbs. All mountain crew – porters, cooks and guides – can either borrow directly, or often our partner companies pre-book what they need on behalf of all their porters."

Karen takes the remainder of her morning to patiently explain to me all about KPAP's history and work, the organization's achievements to date and the current and future issues that remain to be solved.

KPAP is an initiative of the International Mountain Explorers Connection (IMEC), a US non-profit organization, which focuses on improving the working conditions of porters on Kilimanjaro and in Nepal. KPAP receives its funding through donations and small grants.

KPAP Partner Companies don't pay a membership fee. That means other than treating their porters properly and proving this by attaining a minimum of 85% on their performance level every season, it doesn't cost them anything to become a KPAP partner.

In the early days, KPAP dealt mostly with tourists who came to them for advice about which operator to book with. Nowadays, in the age of Internet and online booking, tourists would usually book directly from home, and thus the focus of KPAP has long shifted to dealing directly with the porters.

The head office of KPAP is the one I am visiting in Moshi. They have four more offices – in Arusha as well as just outside of the Machame, Marangu and Rongai gates. The regional offices help especially with their Clothing Lending Program. KPAP have been able to collect a sufficient stock of good quality clothing as donations mostly from US ski resorts who have changed their uniforms. This was collected and shipped to KPAP by Rainier Mountaineering in 2011. Thereby, they are able to provide decent clothing to any mountain crew.

I remember reading on various websites that if you have spare equipment after your hike, you are encouraged to give it to your operators so they can distribute it to their porters. Other comments suggested that such gear never makes it to the porters, because either the guides keep it for themselves, or the companies use the better gear to rent out to other tourists against a charge.

"I'm not aware of such rental practices," Karen puts me back in place with my know-it-all attitude. "I think what's most likely to happen when porters receive gear is that they will sell it during the low season when they are in need of money. This is why KPAP has a Clothing Lending Program to make sure that the gear is used on the mountain."

"So if hikers have spare clothes and equipment, it's best they don't give it to their operators but bring it directly to a KPAP office for the benefit of all porters, right?"

"Yes and no. Climbers often want to donate their gear to the crew that helped them climb Kilimanjaro. We've also encountered climbers donating gear that would not be of value on the mountain. But if anyone wants to part with good quality kit that they would themselves wear while on the mountain, we'd be more than happy to accept."

With the Clothing Lending Program established and running smoothly, the key focus of KPAP has been to increase public awareness regarding the welfare of porters. "Raising public awareness is the most sustainable way to improve porters' conditions," Karen explains. "The more that tourists are aware of the proper working conditions and book with partner companies employing fair treatment practices towards their crew, the more porters will be treated properly by their operating companies and receive an appropriate compensation from their salary and tip. Then the porters would be able to provide for themselves and there would be no need for donations and charity."

In order to actually understand and monitor the situation, KPAP has specially trained porters who report on their climbs. Most KPAP partner companies have a KPAP investigative porter on most of their climbs. At the end of each climb, these investigative porters report back to KPAP about the porters' treatment by answering specific questions about each of the treatment standards. That way, KPAP get a first-hand account and can directly evaluate the performance of their current and prospective partner companies.

"So that gives you the stats for your partner companies, but where do you get the data from for your non-partner companies?"

"We're able to meet with porters who use our Clothing Lending Program, or outside the gate of Kilimanjaro and when meeting with porters in their villages."

When they do manage to interview porters of non-partner companies, the reports may at times reveal serious mistreatments – porters only getting one meal a day; porters not receiving an appropriate minimum wage; porters carrying more than the park's weight regulations; and so forth.

Karen gives me some shocking examples of how they found porters to be treated on various occasions. Why is this not made more public? If tourists only knew, it would fill a book by itself.

"This is off the records," she looks at me firmly and I put down my notebook.

Operating in an environment complicated by politics, vested interests and different cultural ways, she chooses her words wisely. There is a fine line between raising public awareness for a good purpose and revealing too many facts that may end up obstructing KPAP's ability to continue their work in the future.

"You know what's the most frustrating?" Karen continues. "It's when budget travelers don't have the money to book with a decent operator, so they book with a budget operator without realizing that their porters may be mistreated."

"Yes, I also thought about that question. It's a bit like the child labor debate. I mean, is it better for porters to be completely out of work and for the local economy to miss out on all the tourist revenues, or is it better to book with a budget company despite the way they treat their porters?"

I certainly don't know the right answer and I believe it is very difficult to judge on such questions. With the complex interplay of many broader socio-economic and environmental factors, I have chosen not to form an opinion. However, Karen looks at me as if I had just said the dumbest thing ever.

"If you ask me, those budget travelers should not climb Kilimanjaro."

That's a bit harsh? "But then the local economy misses out on the tourist revenues completely."

"Well, you see, the point is that it's hardly ever a question of having the money or not. They all have the money to travel to Tanzania and possibly go on safari or to Zanzibar. They have money to do these various things. KPAP is of the opinion that they should climb responsibly and make sure that their crew are being treated properly. So obviously they could afford the proper climb price, but they are simply not willing to sacrifice on their own vacation."

"Oh yes, I never thought about it like that before."

Karen just gave me an entirely new perspective. It's so true. In reality, budget and costs are hardly ever so tight that hikers couldn't afford to pay a bit more. The vast majority of travelers would go on a safari or to Zanzibar after their hike. This means they actually have quite a bit more money to spend. However, they choose to exploit the very people who help them summit and then spend money on the pleasure of traveling after the hike. They do this rather than pay a bit more to ensure proper treatment and perhaps sacrifice a bit on their remaining travels.

Of course most hikers may not consciously make that decision because they are not even aware of the porter treatment situation at the time of booking, nor may any issues become visible to them during the hike because they would hardly spend any time together with their porters. That's why raising public awareness is so important. Thus, please bear with me and contemplate that thought:

Whether we are aware of our porters' treatment or not, when we book with non-KPAP partner companies, we are actively contributing to porters' exploitation. As long as hikers keep booking with them, these operating companies, of course, have no incentive to change. If we spend money afterwards to continue our travels to Zanzibar or for a safari, we choose to exploit porters in favor of our own pleasure. Should you plan to hike Kilimanjaro yourself, please consider your booking arrangements from that point of view.

Many companies claim to be KPAP partners, but if they are not listed on the official IMEC website (www.mountainexplorers.org/ club/partners.htm), they are definitely not KPAP partners and lie to you. Chances are high that they probably don't treat their porters well, even if they claim to be part of some other porter welfare association. There may be one exception to this:

"I noticed in your statistics that even the treatment of non-partner companies has improved significantly in 2014. Why is that?"

"One big driver is companies trying to become partners and thus taking all our guidelines seriously, but we still classify them as non-partners in the survey until they are officially accepted."

But let's be honest – what are the odds you'll end up booking with one of those good but not yet certified ones? If in doubt about a certain operator, please send an email to KPAP (info@kiliporters.org) and I'm sure they will gladly provide you with more information.

"Karen, one last question: Assuming you get more donations, what would you spend it on?"

"Training, training, training of the KPAP staff. Our goal is to make KPAP sustainable with the work of the KPAP porter staff. They are dedicated to porter rights but only have primary school education, and they don't speak English."

"Yes, makes sense, but that shouldn't be too difficult. Can't you teach them?"

"No time, we are already working non-stop."

"Well, I guess all they need is a laptop, then they can just do an online course."

"Too expensive, Internet is very expensive here and they also do not have computer skills."

"How about volunteers, like foreign students, who'd like to do something meaningful during their vacation?"

"KPAP has challenges obtaining volunteer permits," Karen explains patiently.

I notice that I'm exactly what I don't want to be – a well-meaning *know-it-all* tourist who makes useless suggestions to the local expert. If it were so easy, surely KPAP would have done so already.

We walk back next door for me to say goodbye to Adam, Mama D and Zebe. There is another man.

"He is one of KPAP's investigative porters," Karen explains, "He just came back from the mountain and is giving his report about the climb."

She translates why I'm here and the investigative porter greets me warmly.

By the time I say goodbye to Karen and her team, my brain is racing wild. I feel humbled, like a fraud. Who am I stealing KPAP's time, trying to do any good while having my convenient and comparatively luxurious life back home in Switzerland?

It takes me the remainder of the afternoon to process and write down all my new impressions, no time left to explore Moshi, but I'm enjoying the comfortable hotel lounge instead. What a contrast between where I'm writing this book and where KPAP is doing all their work! What would have happened to the porters with the Partner Companies without KPAP? Would my porters only get one meal a day and carry excessive luggage for less than a breadline wage, without me even knowing?

I hope that by publishing this book I can make my tiny little contribution to KPAP's mission by focusing on where I might be able to help the most – raising public awareness. So in summary, should you consider hiking Kilimanjaro yourself, please check the KPAP website (www.kiliporters.org) to make sure your preferred operating company is listed among their partners. If they are not listed, please reconsider your travel arrangements or contact KPAP directly to learn more (info@kiliporters.org). Thank you for reading this and taking it seriously.

CHAPTER III

THE HIKE

▲ ▲ ▲

*"Strength does not come from physical capacity.
It comes from an indomitable will."*

—Mahatma Gandhi

DAY 0

Killing my Diamox rebel

19 SEPTEMBER 2015

It's 5pm and I'm so excited. This is the time of our pre-hike briefing. Who will be our hiking group members?

We are supposed to assemble in the lounge area of Bristol Cottages. Our operator's staff are easy to spot, all in blue shirts with the name Ultimate Kilimanjaro printed in white letters across the front. They ask us to take a seat while we're waiting for everyone to arrive.

Other than Jana, Diego and me, we meet Chris and Eva. I noticed them earlier today, a baldheaded guy and a girl with long brown hair. They were chatting to another group who just came back from their hike.

"Should I join their conversation?" I was wondering, but forced myself to write down my KPAP impressions instead.

Chris turns out to be an outspoken South African guy living in Dubai, and Eva is a young British girl.

"So where do you know each other from?" I ask them.

"Oh, we only just met earlier today. How about you guys?"

"We all live in Zurich, but I'm from Austria and . . ."

"I'm from the Czech Republic, and Diego is from Spain," Jana adds.

Two more people join our group: Ravindra and Farrah. Ravindra is American with Indian roots, wearing his hair up in a turban and a beard like in Sikh tradition, while Farrah is Iranian American. She looks like a Middle Eastern beauty with thick and curly long dark hair. They are traveling together, but Farrah lives in San Francisco and Ravi in Washington.

"So where do you know each other from?"

"From university, we did a medical degree together," Farrah explains.

"Ah, good to have two doctors with us!"

"Oh no, I'm just a nurse," Farrah is quick to clarify. "Ravi is the smarter one, he's a pharmacist."

"That's even better!"

They all seem to be more or less around my age, in their thirties. So far so good, but, "Where is everyone else?"

"We are waiting for some more hikers from the Stella Maris hotel," one of the guys in a blue shirt explains. His name is Baraka and he will be one of our guides. "They are stuck in traffic jam."

And what a traffic jam! There's already a lot of exchange about our hiking (in)experience going on by the time a van drives in with headlights on. It got dark meanwhile. Three hikers and a few more staff with blue Ultimate Kilimanjaro shirts join us.

We meet Giovanni, a quiet Italian guy with a thick beard. He is the only one in our group who looks like a real mountaineer.

Then there is Juli, a good-looking blond American woman. "I'm traveling with my husband. He stayed back at the hotel."

And there is Jeannette, a tall South African woman.

We are a very diverse group, representing nine different nationalities or ethnic backgrounds. I am particularly pleased to note that most of us are traveling single, only one more couple aside from Jana and Diego. This makes me feel more on a par with everyone else, rather than the fifth wheel.

"Welcome everybody! Everyone is here now, so let's start our briefing," one of the staff members takes charge. "There is one more hiker, but she is still on her flight. You will meet her in the morning."

He introduces himself and his colleagues, but I'm lost about who is who and their specific roles. There are too many of them.

The briefing just repeats the same information they have on their website, including a reminder about altitude mountain sickness and its symptoms in different stages, the need to stay hydrated and so forth. Eh, shouldn't everyone know that by now? Having over-prepared for this trip, I find the briefing rather boring. Perhaps they need to repeat all the information for safety reasons, just to make sure there are no idiots amongst us who may have arrived entirely unprepared?

"Hey Jana, did you catch his name?" I whisper.

"Robert, no?"

"Is he our lead guide?"

"I think so."

Robert also runs item by item through the entire gear list to make sure everyone has what we need. Phew, wouldn't everyone have made sure to pack appropriately back home for such a big hike?

However, Eva was unfortunate to have her luggage misplaced (on KLM via Amsterdam; so it indeed happens more often than you'd think) and she still doesn't know whether it would arrive in time, neither did she bring all essentials in her hand luggage. I would freak out under these circumstances, but she doesn't seem the tiniest bit distraught about her bad luck.

"Don't worry," Chris reassures her, "if it doesn't come on time, we'll share. I'll give you a shirt, socks and trousers. Anyway we just need one set each."

Oh wow, what an offer! I packed scarcely and wouldn't be sharing so willingly. My itchy perfectionist character cannot comprehend his generosity and their calm.

"Sleeping bag?" Robert continues through the list.

"Yes!" Almost all of us raise our hands.

After triple-checking that they wash them after every usage and only rent them out for ten trips, I decided it would be a waste to buy such a high-performance sleeping bag rated for -30F/-34C only for Kilimanjaro. Everyone seems to have come to the same conclusion.

"It says here a lot of you want a single tent. Is that true?"

"Yes!" Again almost everyone except for our two couples raises their hands.

"And me too, I didn't book it, but I'd also like my own please," someone adds.

Robert's eyes open wide and his jaw drops. I'm as surprised as he is, but in a different way. Normally operators team you up in pairs, but I decided to upgrade to a single tent for at least a little bit of privacy. That cost an additional US$300. "Would they all think I'm a solitary snob?" I was wondering, but to my relief it seems they all think like me. Yahoo!

"Why don't you share tents?" Robert tries to convince us otherwise. "The tents are big enough for three people."

He looks around but no eyes would meet his.

"Who wants to share with our twelfth hiker? She would be happy to share with you."

No volunteers.

"How about you?"

Eva shakes her head.

"Or you?"

I shake my head.

"And how about you?" He looks at Farrah and Ravi. "You don't want to stay together?"

"No, no, I want my own tent please," Farrah is quick to insist.

Robert's jaw drops even further and we are all amused. He thinks they are a couple.

"Um, that will be a lot of tents," Robert relents with a puzzled smile, while our group is starting to have fun.

"So what's your recommendation regarding Diamox?" someone asks.

Diamox is a commonly used drug to prevent and reduce symptoms of altitude sickness or AMS (acute mountain sickness) in case of rapid ascent to high altitudes. However, it cannot completely prevent serious altitude sickness.[35] The best way to prevent altitude sickness is to climb slowly and allow sufficient acclimatization time. That's exactly what we will be doing on our nine-day hike. I've researched the Diamox debate to death like everything else in preparation for this trip and confidently concluded that I wouldn't need it.

"We don't give a recommendation," Robert replies. "Some hikers take it and it helps them, others don't. If you've brought it, take it. If you haven't, no problem."

"I brought Diamox."

"Me too."

"I'm going to take it."

EVERYONE nods.

Huh, really guys? There's a little rebel in me that believes the pharma industry is brainwashing people's minds into taking way too many drugs instead of just adopting healthy lifestyles as a natural precaution and remedy. Right now, that little rebel is jumping up and down like crazy in protest, making my heart bounce against my chest. It wants to convert people to its passionate beliefs, to *save* them from their foolish beliefs (no offense please) and to feel less lonely on its own.

"So I'm the only one who didn't bring any?" I ask incredulously. "I thought the whole point of our long hike was to acclimatize naturally."

"I brought Diamox, but I won't take it if I don't need it," Chris is the only one who sees both sides.

"Listen, people, you need to take Diamox before you get symptoms," Ravi the pharmacist advises everyone on the proper usage and his recommended dosage. "I have looked into this in preparation and I highly recommend taking Diamox. It just makes you feel better and doesn't have any serious side effects."

Really? I remember reading an endless list of those, but I can't argue with a pharmacist about their frequency and probability. Only one side effect is indisputable:

"But it makes you pee a lot!" I protest. "I don't want to have to get up at night and go out into the freezing cold."

"Ah, you'll have to get up anyway."

"I brought a pee bottle."

"Yeah, me too."

People giggle, girls included.

Yuck, OK, that point goes to them. Serious mountaineers use pee bottles in their tents overnight. I'm not that serious yet, or perhaps I just feel that I won't need it.

"But don't you think that having a good night's sleep is more important than waking up all the time?" I try to bring them back to reason, my reason.

"Listen, people," our pharmaceutical authority speaks up again, "AMS is too dangerous to play with, people die from it. Given there is something that works and there are no serious side effects to Diamox, I would say it's almost irresponsible not to take it."

Yeow, what a slap onto my rebel's face! I look around the group for other opinions.

"Ravi is one of the smartest people I know, I'll go with his advice," Farrah comments.

No one disagrees.

"Really?! What a load of nonsense!" my little rebel is shouting inside me and making me cringe inwardly.

According to everything I read, Diamox may just give you a wrong sense of security, but it's still possible to ascend so rapidly that when illness strikes, it may be sudden, severe, and possibly fatal.[36] The Everest Base Camp Medical Clinic even discourages its prophylactic use, unless rapid ascent cannot be avoided or for persons who have repeatedly had AMS in the past. That's not the case on Kilimanjaro, and I would assume the experts at Everest know what they are talking about. In any case, one develops symptoms before it gets dangerous and always has the option to descend. In my mind, there's nothing irresponsible about not taking Diamox on Kilimanjaro. What's irresponsible is to continue ascending despite obvious symptoms.

So what's next? If I allow my rebel to speak up, this may set us off on the wrong footing. I put it to sleep instead. With our opinions set at opposite ends of the Diamox continuum, there's no point arguing any further. I'm here to make friends, not to start a war of beliefs.

"Do you have any statistics on hikers who used versus those who didn't use Diamox?" I get our guide back into the discussion.

Instead of satisfying my curiosity, I'm only triggering a baffled expression on Robert's face and roaring infectious laughter amongst everyone else.

OK, got it. How could I possibly expect our guide to know about statistics?

I rephrase: "I mean out of say ten hikers taking Diamox, how many make it to the summit? And out of ten hikers not taking Diamox, how many make it to the summit?"

"Sorry, we don't have that data."

Our group continues being entertained about my persistence. How could I possibly ask such ridiculous questions? On the opposite extreme, I'm stunned that our guide can't tell from his experience. High time for operators to run some proper surveys on this topic and bring some more transparency into this debate!

"But I can tell you it may not be a good idea to take Diamox and Malarone at the same time," Robert adds. "In our experience, hikers with the worst symptoms like headache and feeling dizzy take both. Once they stop one, they are better again."

"Really???" We all stare at him.

Malarone is the common anti-malaria medication. That it shouldn't be taken together with Diamox is news to all of us.

"So which one should we drop?" someone asks.

"Usually, we recommend dropping Malarone. There are no mosquitoes on the mountain. It's too high. Then, after the summit, you can start taking Malarone."

"Even at the first camp?" my rebel is waking up again.

"Even there."

"OK, then I'll just start taking Malarone after the summit," everyone in the group seems to agree, while I'm just baffled.

Am I really the only one considering the risk of malaria, which may end up lethally, to be higher than the risk of AMS, which can be prevented by descending before it gets too bad?

"I wouldn't do that." I dare suggest while fighting my rebel that wants to command the tone again. "Aren't you supposed to continue taking Malarone for seven days after your exposure? So if you get bitten tonight or tomorrow—"

"But there are no mosquitoes on the mountain he just said," someone interjects.

"But I'm already getting bitten right now."

"People, Malarone can also be taken as a triple dosage after the disease has been diagnosed, it's not such a big deal.[37] I consider AMS the bigger risk," Ravi our pharmacist sets the tone authoritatively and no one protests.

Am I in the wrong movie? I'm not a medical expert, but I've done my research. While I also started out thinking that malaria was not such a big deal, everything I've read specifically for Tanzania suggested otherwise. Malaria might be lethal even if treated properly post infection. Furthermore, it may not even be diagnosed properly because sometimes the incubation period can be very long and then one might confuse it with a cold or flu until it's too late.[38]

"Come on, tell them what you think," my rebel shouts at me.

"No, shut up," I swallow hard to suffocate it for good.

This trip is not for me to save the world but to have a great time with everyone else. "Let them decide their own fate and see for themselves that Diamox won't make a difference. I'll prove you wrong," I'm silently thinking to myself.

Suddenly all lights go off and it drops pitch-black. Our guides don't react at all. Just a power outage, must be normal around here.

"Are there any further questions? Otherwise we are done with the briefing."

"What about our insurance certificates?" Jeannette asks.

"Yes, good question!" we are all ears, eyes glued to Robert.

"Just bring them with you as part of your documents."

"You won't check them?"

"No need."

"Really?!"

I'm not the only one who is surprised.

"Travel insurance is required to participate on this trip" was written in bold red letters in the booking confirmation email. Hikers who couldn't provide proof of insurance wouldn't be allowed to participate. That made sense, but now they don't even check? No one is taking records of our insurance data and contact numbers?

"So who is going to call my insurance when I'm in trouble?"

"Haha, you'll die by the time they find your details," we joke as a better alternative to worrying too much.

Our guides remain completely untouched by our concern while we are all intimidated by the imminent unknown.[39]

"OK, so the briefing is finished. See you all tomorrow morning at 8:30." Robert and the other staff depart, together with our hikers from the Stella Maris hotel.

▲ ▲ ▲

"Dinner?"

"Yes!!!"

Everyone staying at Bristol Cottages reassembles at the dining area, and we continue to excitedly hypothesize about what to expect in the coming days.

"My hair!" All the girls have the same worry.

"We'll all stink anyway," everyone agrees.

"I just hope we won't freeze to death!" Some of us are only concerned about summit night.

"At least we'll have our own little toilet tent."

"Oh really?"

"Yeah, they're going to bring a plastic toilet up for us."

"Haha, how decadent!"

"Yes, but that was a key decision criterion for me. You wouldn't wanna go to the public long drops, yuck!"

"Haha, neither, same here."

All the worries of Kilimanjaro first timers . . .

"So does anyone have any extreme hiking experience amongst our group?"

"I've never even slept in a tent before," but that seems to be only me.

"I've been to the Everest Base Camp and I could feel the altitude, so for me I'm really most concerned about altitude sickness." Jana seems to be our most experienced hiker.

Other than sharing our fears and excitement, we also start getting to know each other. It strikes me that most are involved in some kind of development or socially responsible work.

Farrah is a nurse. "I was recently stationed in Liberia during Ebola . . ."

Wow! Not long ago I reviewed a potential investment project there (remotely, from my desktop in Zurich). When Ebola broke out, I remember thinking that I would never ever travel to Liberia and risk my life. Now I'm meeting someone who did exactly that, and I am in awe.

Ravi also focuses on developing countries in his work, currently in a program against HIV. Then there's a Canadian solo hiker who joined us for dinner. She is a medical professional working with MSF (Médecins Sans Frontières).

Chris is an orthotist. He tells me he has developed a special product for people with pronation issues.

"What's that?" I ask.

"It's when your feet are rolling inwards. Like you also have that."

"Yes, you're right, I've even got special running shoes for that." I'm surprised about his skilled eye.

"Yes many people have that, and it affects almost everyone once we get older."

"Oh wow, sounds with your product that's a massive business opportunity." My professional *me* awakes, trained to judge new ideas from their financial potential point of view.

"Maybe, but I don't care about money. I just want to help. I hope I can make my product accessible and affordable to as many people as possible."

I'm in awe again as he passionately explains his venture to me.

"So how about you?"

"I'm in M&A, mergers and acquisitions," I barely dare say what I'm doing for a living in this group of people dedicated to making our world a better place.

Other than Jana, who also works in banking, only Eva has a job that I can somewhat relate to. She is an accountant.

What a diverse bunch of people!

"OK guys, enjoy your last night in a proper bed," we all disperse back to our rooms soon after dinner for a good rest.

I'm falling asleep happily filled with a sense of excitement not only about our big day tomorrow but also about our fun and easy-going group. It could have been a lot worse, but now I already know we'll have a great time together.

DAY 1

Shifting my bathroom paradigm

20 SEPTEMBER 2015

From Moshi (850m/2,800ft)
via Lemosho Gate (2,100m/6,900ft)[40] by car
Distance — elevation — time:
80km/50mi⇨ — 1,250m/4,100ft⇧ — 5-6 hours⊕

to Mti Mkubwa camp (2,800m / 9,200ft) by foot
Distance — elevation — time:
6km/4mi⇨ — 700m/2,300ft⇧ — 2-3 hours⊕

There were not many times when I felt as excited as this morning. One was on the eve of my 20th birthday when I boarded a flight to Singapore for a six-month internship, yet had never been to Asia before. Now I'm about to go off into the wild for nine days, yet had never been a single day without running water nor slept in a tent before. It's this thrilling over-confident sense of anticipation about well-planned adventure, yet not without respect for the unknown.

Restless like a jumping jack, of course I had to get up early to enjoy my last shower and hair wash, just to realize that it doesn't work like that. Knowing I won't have access to running water for over a week doesn't make a shower with plastic curtains and an industrial soap dispenser glued to 70s style jaundiced bathroom tiles any more enjoyable, nor can I clean myself ahead of time, can I? So within seconds rather than minutes I move on to my priority number two. It's still dark and quiet as I sneak downstairs, but I find what I'm looking for: a thermos with hot water and sachets of instant Africafe.

Happy about my find, I carry off my extra strong concoction to keep me company while obsessively checking my packing list again one last time. Have I correctly put my nail scissors into my mountain bag, and my lip balm into my daypack, and my hairdryer into my safari bag to be left at the hotel? Sounds easy enough, but believe me it's BIG. I mean, who would want to end up with bloody toe nails and cracked lips because you got it all wrong? They say for any project it takes as much time as you've got. How true! I shouldn't have started packing weeks ago.

Only once every item has been ticked off my list again, by now barely readable from all the ticks and crosses and strikethroughs, I can allow myself to relax. It has become light meanwhile and another pleasant sunny day awaits me as I head back downstairs. This time, instead of empty tables, familiar smiling faces welcome me: "Hey, you're up early, come join us."

"And I thought I'd be the only one up already!"

"Good morning ma'am, omelet and sausages for you?"

"Yes!"

"So that was it, last shower, hey?"

"My hair is still wet, I washed it extra thoroughly this morning," Farrah points to her flowing mane.

"Me too, but I blow-dried it."

"What for?"

Good question.

"Yeah, I'm also really concerned about my hair," baldheaded and freshly shaven Chris chips in.

Obviously I'm not the only one high on endorphins, and so I end up enjoying nonchalant banter and chitchat with a bunch of blithe spirits while getting used to my new morning fare.

"All good?" Chris asks as Eva returns to the table.

"Yes, it's all here," Eva sighs.

Her luggage has meanwhile arrived, just in time. With that, we are all set to go.

Across the courtyard, we see men in blue shirts in the open lobby.

"Time to get real," we head over to join our guides.

There also is a girl with brown curly hair tied back. "Hello, I'm Lynn, just came in this morning." Lynn is our 12th hiker, a South African living in Canada.

Our guides ask each of us to fill in our details on a sheet of paper that has an empty table with questions for our daily health checks. One by one, they also clip a small device called a pulse oximeter onto our index fingers and ask us to remain still. Kilimanjaro operators frequently use such pulse oximeters to monitor their clients' blood oxygen saturation and heart rate. It's convenient and noninvasive, but my research also told me that pulse oximetry is not a fully reliable indicator of AMS and may give a false sense of safety. It's only one indicator amongst many. Most important is how one actually feels – headache, nausea, dizziness, fatigue, and so on – and they will also record that on the list.

Nevertheless, I am curiously watching the little digital screen as if the device were about to tell me groundbreaking news. My blood oxygen saturation settles at 98%, just about like everyone else. Anything above 95% is considered normal for a healthy person. According to my operator's website, it will fall into the 80s for most of us on the mountain. That's normal. Below 80%, they will monitor us carefully which I interpret as potentially sending us back down. Being the only one without Diamox, I have one clear goal to prove my point – keep that reading up.

While we are passing around our new toy device from hiker to hiker, our bags are being weighed. They are not supposed to be heavier than 15kg including the sleeping bag. Even though I weighed my bag multiple times at home, I curiously watch our guide Baraka lift it onto the hook. It's breaking the 15kg limit by a small margin.

"Too bad," I comment more to myself than to him, "I've got some more stuff in my daypack that I was hoping to squeeze in, but I'll just carry it myself then."

"Oh no, don't carry it yourself. Just put it in."

"Are you sure? I'm already above the limit. It's OK, I can carry it."

"No, don't worry, just put it in."

Wahoo, I feel as if I'd just won the lottery and excitedly repack my three kilos of snacks and a heavy thermos. Thanks to all my fellow hikers who packed lightly and left me their excess capacity!

▲ ▲ ▲

Bags loaded onto the roof of our bus and countless last toilet runs completed, it's almost 9:30am by the time we finally depart from Bristol Cottages. Half an hour later, we pick up the remainder of our hiking group as well as some more crew members from the Stella Maris hotel on the way.

A tall guy follows Juli onto the bus. "Good morning everyone," the two of them disappear into the few empty seats at the back of the bus, same as Jeannette and Giovanni.

Our small bus is just big enough to fit our enlarged group. It has six rows of two and one seats to each side of a narrow corridor. Half of our crew members end up standing because there are not enough seats. I notice a collapsible chair that folds onto the corridor next to my seat.

"Excuse me," I draw the attention of the person standing uptight next to me as the bus starts to move again, "would you like to sit down?"

He looks confused and doesn't react even though he has seen me pointing to the chair. Robert says something to him in Swahili. Only then he takes the seat. I am not sure whether he is a porter or what other role he has. All I know is that he would have been too polite to sit down next to me without someone inviting him, at the risk of our shoulders touching and making me feel insignificantly less comfortable, a liberty that he is not taking for granted.

"Hey Robert, can I ask you something?" I'm being sneaky.

"Yes sure, what is it?"

"What's the name of the local company that you work for?"

"Ultimate Kilimanjaro," he replies politely, probably wondering what an idiot he has amongst his clients.

Ultimate Kilimanjaro is written all over their shirts and caps. They are doing well with their branding, but I don't believe it is the same company. That was the only fishy item I didn't like about my US-based operator. Their booking form required me to explicitly acknowledge that independent contractors will perform the delivery of services locally and to discharge them of any responsibility for the actions of any contractor, yet I don't even know who these local contractors are. You don't need to be a lawyer to figure out that there's something fundamentally wrong with that from a client point of view. Given that I've got travel insurance and they had excellent reviews, I accepted the red flag; but whenever I don't get clear answers, I'm just the more intrigued to get to the bottom of things.

"So you only work for Ultimate Kilimanjaro, or also for other companies?" I rephrase my question and try again.

For a moment, he looks at me partly confused, partly suspicious, before his face changes back to cheerful.

"They keep me so busy, I wouldn't even have time to work with anyone else. I summit about three times every month. Just two days ago, I came back from my last hike."

"Oh wow, that's a lot!" I give up.

Fair enough if my operator wants to protect the identity of their local subcontractor for competitive reasons. They did well with marketing and putting together a very informative website. And not that knowing the name of their local outfitter would make any difference – good luck going after a Tanzanian company if need be!

After about an hour, we stop at a supermarket. This is our last chance to do any last minute shopping before heading off into the jungle. Most of us take this opportunity to pick up some more snacks or toiletries. The store is well stocked with all the international brands and items that someone going off into the wilderness might be craving for – from Pringles and Mars bars to Nivea cream and Kleenex wet wipes. Seeing travel-size Colgate toothpaste, I get tempted to participate in our shopping spree.

"Will it be enough?" I wondered in the morning after squeezing what seemed to be half of my small tube onto my toothbrush.

How is it possible that despite all my preparations I still find an excuse to make a purchase? Usually I hate these shopping stops on bus trips and wonder why everyone goes off buying unnecessary things. Today it makes me feel better to join the shoppers rather than just wait for everyone else to finish. Surely I used my time efficiently, right?

As we head on, the clouds have cleared and we get our first glance of the top of Kilimanjaro, emerging above a thick layer of clouds in the backdrop of an otherwise flat terrain. That's it? It doesn't appear as big and daunting to me as it was made out to be in other reviews. Perhaps it's because we are still too far away, perhaps because people tend to exaggerate to add more weight to their stories and achievements, or perhaps it's just me. Having read too many overly sensational reviews, I have set myself up to be hardly impressed by reality.

Only a few minutes later, the mountain is almost entirely hidden again behind the clouds. Instead, 4,600m (15,000ft) tall Mount Meru comes into view to our left, though blurred in the fog and struggling to attract attention next to its big brother.

The car stops in the middle of the road. A checkered herd of white, brown and black hides on edgy bones is crossing the road, goaded by two teenage boys with wooden sticks. What a striking difference between these cows walking on dry earth compared to the well-nourished ones lazily grazing all over Switzerland's lush meadows!

The countryside overall looks very dry and forlorn. Only a few houses, cows and goats are scattered here and there along the way.

"Robert, what do the people out here do?"

"Most of the people living in this area are farmers."

"Really? But it's so dry."

"That's because we are at the end of the dry season. In a month, it will all be green."

We pass some Maasai people in their traditional red blankets.

"Robert, there are a lot of different tribes in Tanzania, right?" Jana asks.

"Yes, we've got more than 120 different ethnic groups."

"And Sukuma is the biggest, right?"

"Yes."

"How do you tell the difference?"

"It's not possible, you cannot distinguish by the way someone looks. And it's not important to us. We are all the same. For example, me and also Baraka, we are Sukuma. In this area, most people are Chagga, like . . ." He indicates another guide, but I'm still lost about who is who. "Skoba is Maasai," I manage to catch. "In total, we six guides represent five different tribes. You cannot tell the difference, right?"

Indeed, no one for example would have guessed that Skoba with his average stature and roundish face is part of the Maasai tribe that our Western minds associate with very tall, lean bodies and long, markedly-shaped faces.

Every now and then, women in colorful clothing, kids walking with buckets on their heads, motorbikes and the odd car fly past my window. A handful of houses along the street, including a bank office and a small local shop, appear to be the biggest village in this area. Few lonely farmhouses sit here and there out in the dry fields, all with satellite dishes on their roofs. A sign in the middle of nowhere points towards an invisible high school some 2.5km off on a small side road.

Changing my gaze to the opposite window, I realize that the clouds have completely cleared and Kilimanjaro is now fully visible from top to bottom, surrounded by a vast plain of arid dusty land.

"Doesn't look that tall," I share my surprise.

"You must be kidding!"

"It's huge!"

"I can't believe we're actually going all the way to the top!"

"Wait until we get there!"

Obviously everyone thinks that I'm completely nuts. How can I possibly not be in awe of trying to make my way up there?

"Hey guys, I was also thinking of doing the Tour of Mont Blanc trek. Anyone heard of that one?" Chris already moves on to his next adventure.

"Did you just say the Tour du Mont Blanc?" Lynn, who has been quietly jetlagged so far, wakes up. "I am planning to do it this time next year."

"Oh really?"

"What's that?" Even though I live the closest to where they plan to go, I have never even heard about it.

"It's a ten-day hike that goes all around Mont Blanc via France, Italy and Switzerland. It's supposed to be one of the most picturesque hikes worldwide," Lynn explains.

So here we go, now I know who are the hiking pros in our group.

"We should do it all together!" Chris's eyes light up. He has found his accomplice.

"Yes!"

"I've been there and it's really beautiful," Jana confirms.

"I'd consider joining," because if the pros say it's that good, I'm not going to miss out on that fun.

"Great!" We're getting ahead of ourselves.

"You know what – perhaps we should wait first whether we can still stand each other at the end of the trip."

"Yes, we'll probably hate each other."

"Haha, we'll never want to see each other again."

▲ ▲ ▲

Two hours after we have left the hotel, tarmac gives way to dirt. We are going at city center speed, wobbling left and right as we navigate around vicious potholes, swaying back and forth as we take the less dangerous bumps head-on. Aha, so that's why it will take us until mid-afternoon to reach the gate.

All the reviews I have read already warned me that today would be a test of patience. We've come here to hike, not to sit in a car, but that's exactly what we're doing for most of the day. How easily I might have become frustrated with that. Not on this trip. I'm well prepared and my mind is set to enjoy every single minute of it. And it works! What a wonderfully relieving sensation to be moving away from civilization and leaving all its demands behind. Only this morning, I still cleared through my emails, read the morning headlines and checked my hair in the mirror. Now, for the first time in my entire adult life, I'm leaving it all behind, disconnecting from the world as I know it. No more worries about work, the latest news or whether my make-up looks all right. Is it possible to soak it all in and bring back some of this peace of mind to our civilized lives back home?

"Do you know any Swahili?" Robert breaks our silence. "Let me teach you the most important words: *pole pole*. Do you know what that means?"

"Yes, of course!"

"Slowly!"

It is mentioned in just about every single write-up or review of Kilimanjaro. *Pole pole* is how you make it to the top. And who hasn't heard about *hakuna matata* for no problem, made famous by the Lion King theme song. Other useful words are: *hatari* meaning danger, *maji* for water, and *jambo* to say hello.

"What's the word for toilet?" I ask.

"Toilet is *choo*."

"And how do you say I need, like I need a bathroom?"

"*Nataka*, you can say *nataka choo*."

"Or *nataka maji?*"

"Yes, but it sounds demanding," because literally it means I want rather than I need. "You can use *naomba* instead – *naomba maji*," meaning I need water. "But don't say *naomba* with *choo*, because it has another meaning."

All the guides laugh.

"What's the meaning?"

"It also means number two."

"Haha, we'll try it with our porters to entertain them."

"Later we'll have a training session for the toilet tent. The toilet porter will teach you how to use the toilet."

Can it really be that difficult?

"Sorry for the guy, he has the worst role!" Chris blurts out what everyone seems to think.

"Oh no," Robert corrects. "All the porters would like to be the toilet porter. He is considered superior to the others."

"Why?" we all want to know.

"Because he earns more."

"Fair enough for this tough job," we agree.

"And he is also allowed to come with us on this bus, the other normal porters not. It's him," Robert points to a guy with a red cap in the back row and says something to him in Swahili.

The toilet porter smiles proudly.

▲ ▲ ▲

It's noontime as we begin to approach the jungle. The acres are now looking moist. We cross a little river, the first sign of water we've seen all morning. There are men with a small truck pumping water out of the river.

Bushes are replacing the acres to the side of the road, before giving way themselves to trees. They are not the kind of lush rainforest trees one would expect near the equator, but of the coniferous type, just like back home in Europe, if not for the burnt grass to the side of the red earthen road.

We break for a short pit stop at a hut in the middle of nowhere and everyone disappears. Only Baraka stays back and hangs around with me outside of the bus. There is a rope suspended across the reddish earthen road behind the bus. Colorful pieces of clothes are tied all along the rope for better visibility. People at the hut must have lowered it for us and lifted it again after we crossed.

"What's this for?"

"To make people stop and pay."

"You mean private people trying to make money? So everyone has to pay?"

"They'd better do," he smiles sarcastically, "but we don't have to."

Juli's husband returns to the car, stretching his back.

"Hi, I haven't properly introduced myself yet. I'm Alex."

"Stewart, nice to meet you."

"Quite a bus ride, huh?"

"Yes, I can feel my back when sitting . . . but it's OK, used to be a lot worse, had spine surgery two years ago and couldn't walk for a year."

"Oh wow! So just a year after you're back on your feet you're already taking on this big mountain?"

"Well, I've turned 60 this year, so that was my timeline. But I can tell you my doctor wasn't too happy about it," he jokes.

What an extraordinary level of confidence and willpower! And I thought I'd need to hurry up before I get too old for such adventures!

When Robert climbs back into the van, he explains that they have just completed the paperwork for the national park. So maybe this was the official gate and not just some kind of local extortion as it seemed to me?

▲ ▲ ▲

Around 12:20pm, we arrive at Londorossi Gate, the official park entrance. According to the official gate sign, we are at an elevation of 2,250 meters (7,382ft). It's 47 kilometers (29mi) or 26 hours to Uhuru Peak (on the Lemosho route, presumably). That doesn't sound too bad, considering we have seven days to get there.

Some 30 hikers are already gathered under a roof with wooden tables and chairs next to the gatehouse. Everyone is having lunch here. Our guides give us two water bottles of 1.5 liters each to fill up our water bladders, a cardboard lunch box and a fruit juice. We all find ourselves some spare seats amongst the other hikers. Jana, Diego and I end up sitting next to a cheerful friendly girl from the Philippines who instantly strikes up a conversation with us. Like Farrah, she is a nurse and working in Liberia on the Ebola combat program, yet another example of all these good souls dedicated to a worthwhile purpose. I feel humbled. Is this trip trying to tell me something?

The lunch box contains a big piece of chicken that tastes surprisingly yummy, crisply grilled and perfectly seasoned, a burger with beef and a fried egg that's less exciting, two small sweet bananas and a muffin – more than enough for me. I feel spoilt with my triple protein shot of chicken, beef and egg out in the wild at the start of our adventure – so much more enjoyable than the predictable surf and turf at a fancy steak place.

While we are having lunch, our guides are organizing the porters. They are all queuing up to have their bags weighed, making sure none of them carries more than 20kg as required by park regulations. So while we each have a 15kg limit on our personal belongings, I believe Ultimate Kilimanjaro gives them additional things to carry in order to make full use of the 20kg allowance, as almost every operator would. The porters' own spare clothes and accessories come on top of that. This also means that because my bag weighs more than 15kg, it doesn't imply that my porter actually needs to carry more than others. He just gets less additional weight on top. At least that's my explanation and I hope my logic holds. Otherwise I would have made sure to carry any extra weight myself.

"Please go register," our guides beckon us over to the little gatehouse once we've finished lunch.

We add our name, passport number, name of tour operator and signature to a logbook used by all hikers passing beyond this point.

The weather is very pleasant, sunny but not too hot nor humid, with a nice cooling breeze. We hang around for another half hour waiting for the weighing to be completed and all gear and supplies to be put in place. *Hakuna matata*, any spare time flies by as we're only just starting to get to know each other. One thing for sure, we all love to talk nonsense and have a bit of fun.

"We should take a video of each of us every day," Chris suggests.

"Yeah, that would be funny to see the change," we agree, "from totally excited to leave me alone."

"I'm not sure I'd want see myself on a video after today," Farrah cautions.

"Me neither," we girls all concur.

"Let's start by taking a group photo in front of the gate sign," someone proposes.

"Yay, with the full crew!" we all agree.

"OK everyone," Robert calls our attention, "we are done, please get back into the bus."

"Robert, we'd like to take a group photo."

"OK, I take it for you."

"No, you need to come onto the photo. Could you help us call everyone together?"

Robert is calling out to all our guides to come join us.

"No, everyone please, also all the porters."

"Really? Um, OK."

He's calling out in Swahili and we see men getting off a big bus, their faces reflecting the opposite of our excitement.

Oh no, what have we done! "Robert, sorry, it's OK, no need."

But by now most of them have already gathered around the sign. Robert looks confused.

"So what would you like to do now?"

"Sorry, we didn't realize they were all on the bus already. It's OK. We will just take the photo with everyone who is here now."

We're trying hard to be considerate, but can't help being a nuisance instead.

"One, two, three . . . one, two, three . . ." Our new lunch buddy from the Philippines patiently clicks her way through our endless selection of cameras that we've hung all over her arms.

"We need to find a smarter way to do this," I wonder.

"Yes, let's just exchange our photos afterwards," others agree.

"We should create a shared drive and just upload all our photos there," Chris adds the practical solution.

"Agreed!"

Without realizing, we all have just tied the first knot of our bond that would keep us in touch way beyond our adventure.

▲ ▲ ▲

By the time we leave Londorossi Gate, it's already past 2:30pm. It will be another 30 minutes' drive to the point where we finally start our hike. To one side of the road, there is a thick forest of tall pine trees. To the other side, the trees are barely a meter tall and neatly arranged at equal distances from each other.

"They are all planted for business," Robert explains.

"You mean the short ones?"

"Both."

"Really? That forest looks quite old."

"Few years ago, there was nothing here. Soon, all the trees will be cut down again and replanted."

Past and ongoing destruction of the indigenous forest in the Kilimanjaro area has a major impact on the local climate and ecosystem, contributing to anything from inadequate water supply and erosion of soil fertility for local agriculture at the basin to melting ice caps on the top.[41] The issue has received significant media attention in past years and several reforestation initiatives as well as initiatives to stop further loss of indigenous trees are underway, but the current situation seems to leave significant room for further improvement.[42] Especially at the north-western slopes, most of the indigenous trees have been destroyed and converted into forest plantation, using fast growing exotic tree species, such as pine and cypress, and not replanted as required by normal rotation management. The width of the indigenous forest belt is at times reduced to less than a kilometer.[43]

Half way through our drive, so far on mostly even terrain, the road slopes uphill and, almost without transition, the vegetation finally resembles the kind of lush green indigenous rainforest that I expected for today's hike.

A few minutes later, our bus comes to a halt at the beginning of our hiking path. A big wooden signboard mounted on two tree trunks in a tower-like structure, just like the Londorossi Gate sign, announces that we are at Lemosho Gate.

"Are there any toilets?" I hear a female voice.

Robert points further up the road. I follow the girls, unaware of my imminent test of courage.

Yuck! So these are the infamous long-drop toilets – old dark wooden huts with a tin roof and no windows, but supposedly a fetid hole in the middle. They are barely big enough to accommodate one person. The wooden boards of the walls are so infested with whatever parasites have found a new home on them that the light reflects only shades of green from light mold to dark moss.

Without the slightest expression of visible intimidation, unless they are faking their cool as much as I am, one girl after the other disappears briefly and returns unharmed.

OK Alex, you can do this. Harden up! I hope any cobwebs would have been eliminated by now and take a deep breath. At least they are built in a way that you don't need to touch anything . . . Phew! Re-emerging back into sunshine and fresh air has rarely felt so good.

Our guides are still coordinating the porters and we keep busy adjusting our gear and taking pictures. It's 3:30pm by the time we finally start our hike.

Our group at Lemosho Gate

▲ ▲ ▲

Our *second-in-charge* guide Evance leads the way at a steady slow pace. We all follow behind him, on a narrow earthen path through the thick green jungle growth on both sides. Chris, Giovanni and I have taken up the position just right behind Evance, all eager to finally get going.

Constantly at first, someone is shouting "porter" from behind and we move to the side to let them pass. Carrying 20kg on their heads in addition to their own stuff, one porter after the other outpaces us swiftly, almost at a running pace. Within ten minutes, all our porters have overtaken us and moved far ahead out of sight. Once they have all passed, we've got the jungle almost to ourselves. Only every now and then, I hear someone shouting "porter" again and step aside. Men with bags, baskets and other heavy loads on their heads quickly walk past and disappear again behind the next bend.

"Evance, have you always worked as a guide?" I try to start a conversation.

"Not always, I started as a rescue porter."

"Oh wow, that must have been a tough job." Whenever someone gets injured or so sick they can't walk anymore, rescue porters would carry the hiker down on a stretcher. Here's my chance to find out the truth about Kilimanjaro's danger and death rate – all overrated in my opinion. "How many people really die each year on Kilimanjaro?"

"Many."

Um, I was hoping for a more specific number. "Do you know how many exactly?"

"Sorry, I don't know."

Why don't the park authorities track that? Or do they not publish the data on purpose? Perhaps they don't want the world to know how many porters find their ill fate on the mountain, such as when it rains and they get wet? I've heard horrible stories. After everything I've read, it seems unlikely to me that a tourist would succumb to altitude sickness. Surely they'd be sufficiently aware of the risks by now to descend before it gets too late.

"Is it mostly porters or also tourists?"

"Tourists also," Evance gives me another short answer.

"Really? So what is the main cause of death?" I'm not giving up yet. "Is it really due to altitude sickness?"

"Yes, altitude sickness, and also rockfall."

Rockfall? I thought there haven't been any lethal accidents over the past years since the fatal accident at Western Breach in 2006. "But that was long time ago, right?"

"No, just last week again."

What?! "You mean a tourist died from rockfall just last week? Was it at the Western Breach?"

"Yes, at the Western Breach. Two American tourists died."[44]

My jaw drops. I was close to booking that same route. That unfortunate tourist could have been me!

"Do you know what exactly went wrong?"

"No, I don't know more than that. We only just got the news."

Who would have thought so, that after ten years without any lethal accidents at the Western Breach, it just happened again! Lucky me that I've spent more time looking into it and decided for a safer route instead!

▲ ▲ ▲

While today is supposed to be a rather easy start, our hike is nevertheless loaded with steep uphill steps. It's good to have Evance slow us down rather than have us overexerting ourselves already on the first day. Had I done the same hike back home at my natural pace, I'd probably be breathing heavily and drenched from top to toe within less than half an hour. At Evance's pace, however, it feels more like a Sunday stroll to me. The weather is still very pleasant, neither too hot nor humid. It couldn't start any better. Everyone is able to keep up the pace and our group sticks together all the time, closely following each other's footsteps. Actually, not our entire group as Ravi and Giovanni soon went ahead at their own pace. Evance must have missed them, because whenever Chris and I get too immersed in our conversation and don't realize we are overtaking Evance, he asks us to slow down. "Alex, *pole pole*! Stay behind me." And we behave.

Stewart and Juli walk right behind us. "Have you done any other hikes before that?" I ask Stewart without realizing that I've just hit the jackpot. For most of the remaining hike, he would keep me entertained with bits and pieces of the exciting hiking and traveling destinations that he and Juli explored. The two of them are planning to move to Bali in a few years in order to write books and explore Asia. Stewart has an interesting family background tracing back a few generations and is thinking of writing his memoirs as a partly fact-based, partly fictitious story. I'm just about to ask Juli about the contents of her book when Evance stops, pointing towards the trees.

"You see?"

Um, not sure.

"Blue monkeys."

"Oh yes!"

Amongst the thick growth, they are barely noticeable to our untrained eyes.

Just a few minutes later, Evance stops again.

"Look there," he points high into the trees and again I struggle to detect his find. "Black-and-white monkeys," also known as colobus monkeys.

"Oh wow!" I've never seen monkeys like that before, with long plush hair and an immensely long bushy white tail. From the top of their heads all the way down to the end of their tails, they probably measure one and a half meters in total length. One of them is carrying its baby in front like a kangaroo. We all admire these beasts with the same kind of unconscious smile one can't avoid when looking at a cute baby, observing their movements as they jump from branch to branch, challenging us to clearly capture them on our cameras.

As we head on, Evance points out several more blue monkeys on the way, hidden in the grass and trees. I don't think any of us would have spotted them without our guides drawing our attention.

Every now and then, Evance stops. "Catch your breath," and we take a short break. "Drink," he continuously reminds us to remain hydrated.

Other than walking slowly, drinking lots of water is the second key success factor to stay clear of altitude sickness and to make it to the summit.

Without Evance's constant reminder, it would be all too easy to forget the golden rules. Knowing and doing are not the same.

▲ ▲ ▲

"Evance, you always say *mambo vipi*," to the porters walking past. "What does it mean?" I ask.

"Oh, *mambo vipi*, that's just an informal greeting, like *how are you*," or literally it would translate as *how are things*. The common response is *poa*, which also means *cool*.

Soon we start greeting passing porters the same way and they casually respond "*poa*" to us. It's fun to put our learning to practice. Another porter walks past and I cheerfully welcome him:

"*Mambo vipi!*"

"*Poa,*" the porter replies.

"*Kaka,*" Evance nods.

"And what does *kaka* mean?"

Evance explains that Tanzanians fondly call each other *kaka / dada* which literally translates as *brother / sister*. However, this can only be used for persons of roughly equal age. To illustrate, he would call me *dada* and I could call him *kaka*. When addressing someone in a senior generation, however, *babu / bibi* (literally *grandpa / grandma*) would be more appropriate. For example, Evance illustrates by fondly calling Stewart *babu* and Juli *bibi*.

Um, isn't that rude? Juli doesn't look like a *bibi* to me.

"*Dada* Juli," I say.

"No, *bibi* Juli," Evance corrects me. "*Dada* would be impolite."

OK, he's the expert.

▲ ▲ ▲

Just before sunset around 6pm, we reach our first campsite, the Mti Mkubwa camp. Some twenty tents belonging to other groups have already been set up, but I can't see ours.

Evance leads us to a tiny hut not much bigger than the long drop toilets. "Please register here," in the park's logbook, but I get distracted.

There are more blue monkeys all over the place. Seeing them close up, they look like your average small cheeky monkeys that like stealing from unsuspecting tourists. One of them is holding a slice of toast in each front paw and greedily snacking away on its plunder, suspiciously observing anyone who might try to take it away.

Huh, where is everyone? Our group has disappeared. Only Evance is still waiting for the last three of us to put down our names.

"Follow me," he leads us past the other groups into a small clearing.

There is a big black mess tent at the top of the clearing, followed by a dozen orange/off-white Mountain Hardware tents in three rows on a slight downhill slope, and finally a small black toilet tent at the lower end of the clearing. The tents all look just as I imagined, exactly like on our operator's website. Our bags are laid out on a plastic sheet. How nice for it all to be ready and waiting for us, and to have our own little spot surrounded only by trees!

A porter motions me to indicate my bag to him and picks it up for me. I follow him as he shows me to my tent.

Most of the girls have already disappeared into their privacy, while half the guys are happily rubbing soapy water onto their naked upper bodies. Stewart is even shampooing his hair. Not sure I ever wished I was a guy, but right now I'm definitely jealous of how easy it all is for them. I want too!

"So how does it work with the water?"

"Hot water is here Alex, just take." Evance points to a bucket next to the mess tent. It has a drainage valve at the bottom and sits on top of another bucket for easier access. On top of its lid, there is a bottle of soap. A wet plastic bowl lies aside on the floor amidst dry fallen leafs and branches. "Only one left, just take it."

"It's clean?"

"Yes."

I open the valve to pour a little water.

"Just take as much as you like. Also the soap, just take."

What a luxury! So this will be our shower over the coming week. With my little treasure bowl, I disappear into my tent, too shy to take off my shirt outside. Inside the tent, a foam sleeping pad inside a red/blue checkered cover like a Maasai blanket has already been laid out for me. It feels comfortable to sit on.

So how should I do my washing without spilling water everywhere? I lean half over the bowl in all kinds of awkward positions as I try to clean all body parts while keeping my tent dry. Um, that doesn't work so well. There must be a smarter way. Should I just go outside and strip like all the guys? My self-confidence is letting me down, and I end up using wet wipes instead.

My shirt that's meant to last for two more days doesn't pass the smell test. Fully aware that I won't be able to avoid getting smelly at some stage, I can't have that already on day one. I carefully give it a bit of a wash, hoping that it will dry overnight.

By the time I'm done with my little bit of washing, it's already dark. Time to put on my headlight. I'm shivering and have goose bumps all over. With the sun disappearing, the temperature has dropped instantly, perhaps to 15 degrees Celsius (60° F) at most. The cold has also woken up my bladder. Time to trial our fancy portable toilet! I put on a long-sleeve shirt and stumble towards the small black tent, armed with a roll of toilet paper. No one else is outside. It's pitch-black. Only some headlights faintly shining from inside other tents tell me I'm not alone in the wild.

The toilet tent is hardly distinguishable in the darkness against the trees right behind. It looks daunting, only faintly illuminated by my headlight. I unzip the tent curtain and barely make out in the dim light a tiny plastic toilet box that looks as if it had been in use ever since they invented plastic. Um, this is not the kind of modern spotless white device I remember seeing on our operator's website. Repulsed to even touch the lid, I feel helpless. This is probably the first time in my past thirty years that I don't know how to use a toilet. I must have missed our official training session, if there was one.

"Hello? Anyone around?" I cautiously call out for help.

The toilet porter runs to my rescue and illustrates proper usage: First, he opens the lid. Yuck, that doesn't look any better. Some brownish liquid spilled on the seat makes me cringe.

"OK, Alex, focus and harden up! It's too late to play the prima donna," I'm telling myself.

Next, the toilet porter pulls out a plug under the seat. This opens a hole between the toilet bowl and the bottom container that supposedly stores our waste. Then he turns around and slightly lowers his butt.

"Haha, OK," I nod. That part obviously doesn't require further illustration.

He indicates a roll of toilet paper inside a pocket of the tent curtain.

"OK, great," that's a positive surprise for a change. I thought we had to bring our own.

He moves on to indicate a pushing movement with his hand above a big off-white squeeze button to the back of the seat. Supposedly, that's the flush.

I nod again as he keeps looking at me to make sure I follow.

To conclude the procedure, he pushes the plug under the seat back in to close the hole and shuts the lid.

Looks easy enough.

"OK, thank you," I wait for him to leave.

He motions with his hands whether I would like to test the procedure while he is still here, but by now I can barely stand straight controlling my inner pressure.

"I'll be fine," I smile at him so he will leave me alone.

He understands and I quickly zip down the tent curtain.

First things first – I pull at the plug to open the hole, first gently, then a bit harder, but not as hard as I could in fear of touching or spilling anything. Nothing happens, this bloody thing seems stuck. I fail at this simple task. So I unlock the curtain and call for help once more.

The toilet porter runs to my rescue again. This time, even he struggles to get the plug freed, but when he pulls harder, that seems to do the trick. At least this time he leaves it open for me, quickly retreats and kindly closes the tent curtain from outside. Despair must be written all over my face.

After my obvious relief, I push the squeeze button, carefully, using a sheet of toilet paper to keep my fingers clean, as if that made any difference. Nothing happens. I try pushing harder and some water emerges, but not enough to pull the toilet paper down. I try again, but the result is the same. What to do? I'll just have to leave it for the next user. Sorry guys.

My mood has fallen off the cliff. This is not the kind of clean and convenient private toilet that I had expected. What am I going to do once my bowels start to move? No, let's not even think about it – better worry about that another time. For now, I content myself with obsessively disinfecting my fingers with my little powerful hand sanitizer that from now on I vow to keep in my pocket at all times.

With this basic imminent need satisfied, I realize that my body is still shivering from the cold. Who would have thought that it gets that cold in a rainforest!

So I crawl back inside my dark tent to put on another top layer. And what a relief that is: Even though I belong to this rare breed of people with wool aversion, I now find myself entirely comfortable within two layers of merino wool. When I tried them on back home at room temperature, I couldn't stand the scratchy feeling on my skin. However, merino has this unique property that nevertheless made me take the risk – it doesn't stink! Restricted by our weight limit to about three changes of clothing, I eventually got my priorities right and went with this one and only wonder material for all thermals. And what a wonder material that is – what felt like sandpaper now feels like cashmere!

Feeling nice and warm again, there's not much else to do in my dark tent. So I stumble my way to the big black mess tent, almost falling over twice.

"Be careful," I hear a voice but can't see who it is in the dark, "always look to the ground when walking at night. There are a lot of roots everywhere."

That makes sense; I'd better be a good girl. Why didn't I think of that myself?

A few others have already taken their seats in the mess tent, snacking from a massive plate of popcorn the size of a coffee table.

"Hello, welcome to our dining room!" They cheerfully invite me to join their jocular conversation, and my mood swings back from *toilet-encounter-disappointment* to *let's-have-some-fun*.

But first, let me describe our luxurious dining hall. There is a long table covered by a red tablecloth with black stripes (like the traditional Maasai blanket). The tent and table are exactly big enough to fit twelve decent-sized collapsible camping chairs with arm- and backrests, one for each of us. This will become our breakfast, lunch and dining venue for the coming week.

On the table, apart from the massive plate of popcorn, there are green thermos bottles of hot water; English Tea bags; instant coffee; milk powder and two types of chocolate drink powder; sugar and honey; some spreads including margarine, peanut butter, Nutella and jam; as well as tomato and chili sauce. The tableware consists of big yellow camping cups, white soup plates and bowls. We even have silver cutlery, wrapped in white paper napkins and nicely laid out on each plate. This will become our familiar table decoration setting throughout our mountain adventure.

As a coffeeholic, I pour myself a big cup of hot water and reach for the big tin of coffee. It's the same brand that they had at Bristol Cottages, Africafe. What a relief! I worried I would have to force down some horrible brown liquid over the coming days just to meet my caffeine cravings. Excitement takes over. Being used to drinking strong espressos, I need two big teaspoons of coffee powder to mix the big cup of coffee to my liking. After few sips, I feel my heart rate going up, as if I had just run up ten flights of stairs. What's going on? I'm usually immune to caffeine due to life-long overdoses, no matter how much and at what time of the day I drink it. "Perhaps it's just the altitude, not a big deal," I comfort myself.

Chatting away with everyone else, I keep sipping on my favorite of all drinks. It warms me up. Only when I finish my cup do I realize that my heart is racing at an alarming pace, ready to jump out of my chest at any moment. "Ba bump, ba bump," it is shouting at me so loud I'm surprised no one else can hear it. How curious! I've never felt like that before. And how scary! Am I starting to develop altitude sickness earlier than I ever would have anticipated? The pure thought of it freaks me out so much that I instantly promise myself to abdicate my addiction – no more late coffee for me. "Please stop, calm down," I plead with my heart to no avail.

The tent is slowly filling up with all our hikers, and our guides join us for our twice-daily health checks. As the measures using the finger blood oximeters are being taken on others, I feel my heart bouncing faster and faster. I feel stupid and vulnerable when it's my turn to clip that little pass-or-fail device onto my finger, keeping my eyes glued to the little screen as my blood oxygen saturation reading starts at 0 and moves up at an excruciatingly slow pace . . . 78, 79, 80, 81, 80, 79, 80 . . . That's exactly where I don't want it to be! At 80 percent, our guides might not allow me to continue. That would be my worst nightmare, completely beyond my range of imaginable possibilities until few minutes ago.

After a pause of perhaps no more than a few seconds, that seem like eternity to me, the number escapes the dangerous threshold and slowly, digit by digit, moves in the right direction until it eventually settles in between 97 and 98 percent. What a relief!

My resting heart rate, that feels like a 150+ marathon pulse, hovers just above 70 – abnormally high for me but of no concern to our guides. Lucky me! I've just learnt my lesson the easy way.

Other than noting down our oxygen saturation and pulse readings, our guides also ask each of us routine questions.

"Do you have any headache?"

"No."

"Are you dizzy?"

"No."

"Are you tired?"

"No."

"How have you slept last night?"

"Good."

"How do you feel overall?"

"Good."

Our answers are 99% identical, as would be expected for our first day. Instead of fatigue, we seem to be *high* from the excitement of starting our adventure.

Only Lynn is tired, but not because of the mountain. "Just got in this morning and couldn't sleep on the plane. Still jet-legged." Considering the circumstances, she looks surprisingly fresh.

"You'll get your dinner now," Robert concludes our health check, "and then we'll come back for tomorrow's briefing."

Our first mountain-cooked meal, how exciting! One of our waiters – yes, we even have two waiters! – puts a big pot onto the table, announces it as "cucumber soup", and disappears again.

"Did he just say cucumber soup?"

"Never had that before."

"Sounds odd."

"Any volunteers?" Someone grabs the ladle and hands out bowls to each of us. We try suspiciously.

"Tastes good!"

"What a surprise!"

"Can I have some more?"

"Me too!"

Our waiter comes back, this time with a massive plate of potatoes. There's no way our group could possibly eat all of that. The second waiter brings a plate of fresh vegetables – tomatoes, cucumber, lettuce, capsicum and avocado. Fresh veggies are my favorite and usually my staple diet. The plate is the size that I could finish by myself if I wasn't eating anything else. Will that be enough for all of us? I only dare to take a few pieces. When all of us have taken their helpings, there's still quite a bit left. "Anyone wants that?"

"I'm good."

"Not me."

"You sure?"

"Go for it."

Hooray, I feel as if I'd just won the lottery again.

Fried fish comes up next and we stuff ourselves crazy. Finally, they bring one more pot and announce it as veggie sauce. No one takes any interest in it. Who wants to eat sauce anyway? After a while, just out of curiosity, I peer inside. Yummy! It's not a sauce but a creamy veggie stew. This hidden treasure quickly draws everyone's attention and disappears in no time.

"What a great dinner!" everyone agrees.

"I'm totally satisfied," Chris adds.

"I knew it wouldn't be too bad", I admit, "but this was far better than I ever expected."

"How was your dinner?" Robert and the other guides have come back.

"Delicious!" we all shout excitedly, hands on our full bellies.

"Good, so let's start our briefing."

We all keep talking in parallel.

"First of all, I would like to teach you a little rule. Whenever I've got something to say to you, I want you all," Robert looks around the table at each of us for emphasis, "to listen, because it's important. But how do I know whether you are all paying attention? So from now on, whenever I've got something to announce, I will say *hip hip*. And then, so that I know that you all heard me and that you are paying attention, I want you to say *hop hop*, all together. And then, while I'm talking, please be quiet and listen. OK?"

"Haha."

"Yes sir!"

"It's like back at school."

He's got a point, we spend more time shouting to each other across the table rather than giving him our full attention.

"So let's try. I will say *hip hip* and then you all say *hop hop*, OK?"

"OK!"

"Haha!"

"Let's do it!"

"Psst, pay attention!"

All our eyes are fixed at Robert in anticipation.

"Hip hip—"

"Hop hop!" Twelve grown-ups shout in unison as loud as our vocal chords can manage, and then immediately erupt in laughter about our all-too-eager response.

Who would have thought that feeling like naughty pupils answering to a teacher can have such a high entertainment factor! Yes, let someone else take care of us and tell us what to do for a change. It's high time to shut off our brains for once and have others worry about us. How often do you get to experience such mental luxury in your grown-up life?

"Robert, I've got a question," I interrupt him before he even gets a chance to start our briefing. "What exactly is the role of our toilet porter?"

He looks at me confused, and everyone breaks out in laughter again. All the reviews of prior hikers mentioned the toilet porter constantly cleaning the seat after every use, armed with rubber gloves and detergent. Obviously that wasn't the case for us.

"I mean, is he only supposed to carry it, or also to clean it? Because when I used it there was some brown stuff—"

"Um, you haven't seen? There is a brush inside." A broad smile spreads across Robert's face, infectiously, enough to set off our whole group roaring like a bunch of drunkards.

"Yeah Alex, just do it yourself!" Chris bursts out what Robert was too polite to say, and by now not even our quiet assistant guides are able to keep a straight face.

I would love to clarify my question, but I've lost all muscle control. Only once my violently shaking belly muscles stop moving and my contracted throat allows me to breathe again, I am able to make another attempt.

"I was actually asking about the seat . . ." I rephrase my question. Robert is serious again.

"Normally, the toilet porter wipes the seat after every use with toilet paper," he answers politely. Clearly that wasn't happening. But now I want to know exactly.

"So just to be clear, only with toilet paper or does he also disinfect it?" assuming the unfortunate guy will in future do his job properly, which I think Robert will remind him to do.

"Yes, yes, with detergent. We use powder detergent. First he puts detergent on the seat," Robert illustrates with his hand like powdering a cake with icing sugar, "and then he wipes it with toilet paper," his hand now twitches left and right like rubbing a heavily stained cooktop, leaving no more doubts. Finally I've got my answer, loud and clear! "Next time you have problems with the toilet," he looks around the group, "you can ask her to help you clean for you. Now she knows how it works," Robert grins broadly, and we are all laughing our heads off again. He's definitely not short of good humor and knows how to deal with his prima donna clients.

It's loud and lively. Everyone seems to be talking at the same time, competing to chip in our insights of stupid talk for the sake of overall entertainment.

"Hip hip!"

"Hop hop!"

Our guide's little trick works like a charm; he's got our attention again.

"Robert, what should we wear tomorrow?" someone asks.

"What time do we leave?" someone else wants to know.

"What's the weather going to be like?"

"Do we need to bring rain jackets?"

"Wait, wait, be patient," Robert intervenes. "Let me first give you my briefing. I will answer all these questions. And then, if you still have questions, you ask them afterwards, OK?"

"OK," we all shut up.

Now he has us under control and our full attention.

"First of all, I would like to remind you to always be punctual when we ask you to be somewhere at a certain time. We are a big group, so we need to work together, OK?"

"OK!"

That seems like a reasonable request. It's true that many were showing up late for our initial pre-briefing yesterday as well as for our health check this morning.

"We should have a little punishment for those coming late," Chris proposes with a grin, and all of us instantly agree what that should be. Guess what—

"Cleaning the toilet!" we all shout in unison. I think Robert is beginning to like our little big group.

We obediently listen quietly (almost) for the remainder of his briefing. Indeed he clarifies what we need to know, but because we are a creative bunch, or may not have paid full attention all the time, we still come up with all sorts of both valid and less thoughtful questions. Robert patiently answers them all.

"Anything else you want to know?"

Finally no more remarks. By the time our curiosity is satisfied and our belly muscles tired of non-stop laughter, we are all keen to head back to our tents.

"And remember to keep your tent zip closed all the time, because there are a lot of bugs out here," Robert reminds us before wishing us a good night.

▲ ▲ ▲

I'm anxiously excited as I crawl into my dark tent. Have I mentioned that I'm scared of spiders (even more than of brown toilet seats) and find slugs so disgusting that I normally refuse to walk on grass in the dark? I feel so proud of myself right now for pushing my limits like someone at jungle camp just about to stick their head into a case of crawling worms. Of course I remember to zip up my tent as soon as I've squeezed inside. So what's next? Like settling into a new apartment, it takes me ages to position myself inside my sleeping bag and sort out all my stuff.

My camera battery is already flashing red, even though I gave it a full recharge in the hotel. No problem, it's time to test my brand new solar panels, which I bought just for this trip so I could recharge my phone in order to write this book. Robert said we have a long hike ahead of us tomorrow, so it may be too late again to get enough sunlight at tomorrow's camp. No problem, these panels conveniently come with holes and hooks so even I can figure out how to attach them to my backpack. How long will it take for my camera to recharge? I'm curious to find out.

"Don't forget to put all your batteries into your sleeping bag so they don't drain in the cold," Chris has reminded us over dinner, and I follow his good advice. Kindle, smartphone, spare batteries, camera, and the headlamp later on – all come into the sleeping bag with me.

Once I am finally all settled and starting to feel nice and warm with (or despite) all my edgy gadgets, an annoying thought crosses my mind:

"I forgot to brush my teeth. Shall I do it now?"

I see myself shivering in the cold.

"No way," I can't be bothered to get up again. "I'll just make up for it with an extra thorough morning brush." My lazy side has taken control.

I proceed to write down all my notes for this afternoon. Luckily, I've already got half the day typed up during our drive. But, annoyingly, I only realized today that the supposedly supercool Google keyboard doesn't work offline, or perhaps I was just too dumb to figure it out. So, instead of fancy word recognition, I end up with sore thumbs chasing every single letter. To cut a long story short, it takes me over an hour to type out the gist of what you've just read in five minutes.

"Should I have another look for that Google keyboard?" I wonder as I finish writing.

And sure enough – here it is, waiting to be selected under my language input settings. "Instead of typing like an idiot, I could have relaxed and read," I sigh while thinking of all the books about Africa that I made sure to download onto my Kindle and can't wait to start reading. Well, tomorrow is another day. Good night for now.

That's what I would have hoped for, but while my brain is getting tired, my bladder is waking up again. I don't want to leave my cozy warm sleeping bag, but this time I have no choice. There's no way I can win this fight until the morning, so I'd better get done with it. As I unzip my tent, my goose bumps are back, but not sure whether I can blame it on the cold again, or my silent coward that would rather stay in its safe confines. Who knows, there could be wild animals out there, right?

I listen intently – nothing but radio silence. I lift my butt and check my surroundings – nothing but pitch-black darkness. Not even the faintest light from any other tent to remind me that I'm not alone. Seems everyone is asleep by now. Slowly, step by step, I find my way towards the toilet tent, this time watching the ground, careful not to stumble again. Same as earlier but this time for a different reason, I can't wait to zip down the curtain. Phew, back within safe confines!

The seat is neatly covered in toilet paper. Um, what to make of that? Lazy return of courtesy by its prior user or authentic attempt to amend by the toilet porter?

"If in doubt, don't," Benjamin Franklin supposedly once said. He was a smart guy.

Cumbersome flush managed and trousers back up, it's no longer silent outside. "Grrr, grrr . . ." A deep buzzing sound brings my goose bumps back onto alert. Is this some kind of monkey or other beast, or just a snoring fellow? There's only one way to find out, and I instinctively hope for the latter. I slowly open the tent zip and shine my headlight off into the distance to check for any odd appearance. It falls straight onto the shape creating that sound – a female squatting in the dark!

Whoops, my head makes a nervous twist to divert the spotlight. "I'm so sorry, I didn't see anything," I utter with embarrassment. Who was that?

"I took a shortcut to the toilet tent," I hear Jana's cheerful voice pissing herself laughing, quite literally this time.

"Haha, good idea!" That would have been the smarter way to go about it, because I just realize that I've got another problem. Which one is my tent??? They all look the same. Wouldn't be good to crawl in to someone else's and scare them witless.

"I think your tent was the one on your left," Jana must have seen my confused face and points me into the right direction. She's the expert. So many things for me to learn on this trip!

Back cuddled into my sleeping bag and feeling warm again, it's finally time to relax and sleep. That should be easy enough, because I'm beyond tired by now and if there's one skill I've mastered to perfection, that's sleeping.

I keep twisting and changing my position left and right, back and front, straight like a soldier and bent like a fetus – nothing works. Even my customized tried and tested sleeping position lying flat on my stomach and squeezing my palms underneath my thighs in a way that makes others cringe at the thought of my contorted neck, but would normally send me to sleep in seconds, doesn't help. To the contrary, armed with my earplugs against snoring and peeing fellows, my own breathing makes me feel as if I were going to suffocate. And so I run through my sequence of twists all over again.

Mind you that's easier said than done. Every time I change the position, the sleeping bag liner twists around my body like a straightjacket and slides from above my head to under my shoulders, and my electronics squeeze against my body. So I end up spending more time re-adjusting my set-up rather than staying in any single position.

All night long I yearn for relief, but it's just not happening, and the night turns into a never-ending nightmare. Now I know what insomnia feels like, and I wouldn't wish it upon my worst enemy!

What's wrong with me tonight? I usually fall asleep quickly and sleep through without waking up a single time, no matter where I am. So far, however, my experience is limited to proper beds, and my skill is letting me down in this new environment.

Perhaps the late caffeine shot is to blame? Or perhaps it's due to the inclination of the ground on which our tents have been set up? My feet are lying lower than my head and I keep sliding downwards, uncomfortably twisting my feet against the bottom of my sleeping bag. In hindsight, perhaps I should have gotten up and turned my sleeping bag upside down, but I was lacking that tiny flash of wit throughout my sleep-deprived night.

DAY 2

Pole pole to the land of dust

21 SEPTEMBER 2015

From Mti Mkubwa (2,800m / 9,200ft)
to Shira 1 camp (3,500m/11,500ft)
Distance — elevation — time:
8km/5mi⇨ — 700m/2,300ft⇧ — 5-6 hours🕐

After an excruciatingly long night awake, I'm thrilled when I hear people talking outside. That's probably our porters who need to get up early to fetch our water. This means I will soon wake up from my nightmare of insomnia. Yippee!

Once the sunlight fills my tent, I start to get ready for the day. By the time one of our guides comes to wake us punctually at 6:30am, I'm already half way through packing my bag. As informed during our briefing yesterday, we are supposed to always finish packing first, then have a wash with warm water which will be ready for us from about 7:00am. Thereafter, we should proceed to the mess tent by 7:20am for breakfast, to be followed by our daily health check. By 8:00am, we should be ready to start our hike.

As I emerge from my tent just after 6:30am, a porter is already waiting for me outside.

"I take?" he points to my bag.

"Oh no," I shake my head, "please wait. I still need to wash and put my stuff back inside."

"Hot water," he points to the bucket.

"Already? Great!" I grab one of the bowls, pour myself just a little (lesson well learnt that too much is of no use) and head back to my tent.

It still feels too chilly to take off my shirt. Washing my face and brushing my teeth will have to do for my morning shower. Dry shampoo onto my hair and sunblock onto my face complete my beauty session in no time. Instead, just like yesterday, half the morning goes by obsessively checking again that I've got all my things in place exactly where I need them – hand sanitizer in my pocket, phone in another pocket, lip balm and tissues in yet another pocket, an Aspirin+C fizzy tablet for breakfast to guard against getting sick, water purifiers and remineralization tablets for my refilled water bladder, my camera attached to my solar panels . . .

So far so good, but now comes the real challenge. I'm still wearing my warm long-sleeve shirt and feel cold nevertheless. The trees are blocking the sun and the air hasn't warmed up yet. My short-sleeved shirt still feels moist from my evening rinse. Surely it will get hot again once we start hiking, so I just need to harden up until then, right? I swap my shirts in record time. Brrr, being bare-chested in the cold is the opposite of pleasant, and putting on a moist shirt just makes it worse. Quick, quick, a warm pullover needs to come on top. That will have to do for the morning.

Now I've got only one thing left to do – squeezing my sleeping bag back into its cover and lifting my bags out of the tent. The same porter is still waiting for me.

"I do it for you," he offers. "Just give me," he points to the sleeping bag.

"It's OK," I stubbornly resist.

I feel I'm a big girl and should be able to do it myself. Neither do I like the thought of my sleeping bag getting dragged and dirty outside.

"OK, now I'm done," I announce proudly as I crawl back out again.

The porter smiles and gives me his thumbs up. Just as he is relieved that I have finally got my act together and he can start packing up my tent, I am relieved that I can finally proceed to the mess tent for yet another shot of caffeine.

I shiver from the cold. Even Evance notices my discomfort and looks at me with a concerned expression.

"Are you OK?"

I feel stupid. Why do I risk catching a cold? I could just have put on a fresh dry shirt instead, but now it's too late.

"All good, just a bit cold in the morning. No need to worry."

"How did you sleep?"

"Not at all. But it's OK, I'm not tired," which is true, I'm bright awake. Either my body is still loaded with caffeine, or keeps producing adventure adrenaline.

"Why not?"

"Don't know. Maybe because I had coffee in the evening, or maybe because I have never slept in a tent before."

"Yes that might be. It's normal that our clients can't sleep the first night. Please don't drink coffee anymore in the evening, OK?"

"I promise."

"I think you will sleep better tonight. Oh, and please drop your water bladder," he points to a big wooden basket outside our mess tent. "We will refill them for you. After breakfast, you can pick it up again."

"OK," I run back to get it before joining the others for breakfast.

"Cold, isn't it?" they remark as I take my seat. Seems it's not just me who shivers.

Just as the past two days, my breakfast consists of eggs and sausage, plus extra strong coffee of course. There also is a big pot with hot oats porridge as well as white toast bread and the usual spreads. This will be our morning fare for the coming week.

"So today will be a long day."

"Yes, five to seven hours up the Shira plateau."

"Supposed to be really steep."

"I'm curious to see how tough it really gets."

"We'll only get lunch around 3pm when we arrive, so don't forget to pack snacks."

"Yeah, got my snickers packed already."

"Really? I thought we get lunch on the way." My recollections of yesterday's briefing are different from everyone else's.

"No, only when we get there, that's what they said."

I'm certain I heard something else. Surely I paid attention. I'm the one who has it all figured out, right? "Excuse me," I call over one of our guides. "When will we have lunch today?"

"Today will be a long difficult day. We'll only have lunch when we arrive at the Shira 2 camp maybe at three in the afternoon. Please all bring snacks. We'll give you some after breakfast and you can take what you like."

Um, OK, me wrong, lesson learnt again. So I haven't got everything figured out the way I'd like to believe.

They bring us a big plate filled with cookies, peanuts and fruit juices to choose our supplies. I prefer my own snacks and repack some into my daypack. When will I ever learn and become more efficient? To *repack*, ugh! I hate that word by now.

"Hip hip!"

"Hop hop!"

Giggles and laughter. Yes, we remember our little drill.

"Let's have our morning health check."

When it's my turn to clip the little oximeter onto my finger, the reading climbs up to 96/97% blood oxygen saturation before the screen goes dark. Seems the battery has gone flat. The assistant guide wasn't paying attention when the reading stabilized.

"Try this one," he clips a second device onto my finger. This time the reading stabilizes just above 80%, and the measuring guide informs the note-taking guide without the slightest surprise.

"No, no," I protest as if my life depended on it. "This cannot be correct. I want to try again."

This time it settles around 95% – so much about the accuracy of pulse oximeters! Surely our guides know that they are not reliable and only use them as a crosscheck, for the sake of proper procedure. I should know that too, theoretically, because that's what all my research told me. Practically, however, since I realized that I'm the only one without Diamox, these little devices have taken on disproportionate powers.

"Keep that reading up or you will fail," a superstitious voice is whispering at me. I think I'm not alone. Others are equally glued to their readings.

Oximeters aside, our guides know better about what really matters. "How are you?" "How did you sleep?" "How was breakfast?" "Are you looking forward to today?" they all constantly ask us informally.

"Clients sometimes don't tell us how they really feel, because they are afraid that we don't allow them to continue. Don't do that. You will all make it to the summit. We will get you there, no worries. But remember the number one priority always is to get back down safely. So it's important that you are always honest with us," Robert reminded us yesterday.

"I don't think our guides could easily be misled anyway," Chris remarks.

"Yes, true. Have you noticed how they constantly engage us in small talk?" Lynn adds.

"Yes, I think just by looking into our eyes and observing our body language they know how we really feel," just as Evance caught me out earlier. "I think they do a great job so far."

"Agree. I feel safe with them."

"Me too," we all seem to agree.

"Hip hip."

"Hop hop."

No more laughter. No more excessive shouting. Our little drill has become routine already. We are fully conditioned, like Pavlov's dogs.

"Please get ready, we are already behind schedule."

We pick up our water bladders from the big basket outside the mess tent. They have already been refilled for us.

"Do we need to add our own water purifiers?"

"No need, we've already sterilized it for you."

I rely on their guidance and just drop in my remineralization tablets. That's my prevention against both muscle cramps and bad taste. So far, however, the water tastes clear.

"Let's go," Evance asks us to get moving. We follow him back out from our private little clearing to the bigger campsite.

Beautiful singing of unfamiliar Swahili vocals attracts our attention. A group of porters is singing and dancing in a circle, with cheerful voices and soulful rhythm. Mesmerized by their performance, we pause to observe and listen. The air seems to vibrate with their energy. I have never experienced that before. They are so alive, so passionate, living the moment with infectious joy. How invigorating! No one wants to move.

"Please keep going," Evance needs to remind us again.

We continue past the bigger campsite back onto the trail, through the thick jungle. Within minutes the rainforest converts into a drier kind of coniferous forest with more needle-like trees. The terrain is almost flat to start with. Soon the morning sun's rays find their way down to us through the thick vegetation, making us feel nice and warm again. What a pleasant day, the weather couldn't be any better. There are no clouds in sight and the temperature feels like a comfortable 20 degrees Celsius, perfect for hiking.

Some of the trees have long whitish threads hanging down from their branches like angel hair on a Christmas tree. Looking up at them against the rays of the sun reminds me of fairyland, or probably of ghost land at night.

"Don't just look at the ground. Make sure to pay attention to your surroundings and soak it all in," I keep reminding myself.

Just like yesterday, Evance again does a great job keeping a slow steady pace. That way our group can stay together the entire time, in single file one after the other, and no one is running short of breath.

We continue our tradition to pass the time with random jokes and conversations, and each of us contributes the odd witty or perhaps less witty, but the more funny remark. As has already been crystallizing since we first met, Chris seems to be the biggest talker amongst us. He always has something to say. Stewart also likes sharing his hiking and traveling experiences. It sounds that he has already traveled the whole world and collected a massive stock of wonderful outdoor adventure memories. I am not overly talkative this morning. Like most of us, I simply enjoy the hike.

"What's wrong with you this morning? Not feeling so well?" Chris inquires.

"No, I'm feeling great. Why?"

"Because you're not saying much."

"Well, that's just how I am, I don't like talking all the time."

"Yeah right, I don't believe that. You're such an extrovert, been talking non-stop since we first met."

"No way, I'm a total introvert," or maybe something in between. Chris's comment makes me wonder. How quickly our external identities are formed, and how different these perceptions may be from who we really are!

We keep walking quietly, but not for long.

"Hey Alex, you know your solar panels aren't getting any sun?" Chris's voice resounds from behind me again.

"Oh thanks," these are the panels that I proudly hooked onto my backpack last night.

"Shall I readjust them for you?"

"No worries, I'll just do it myself during our next break."

"Why don't you want me to do it?"

"I don't want to slow you down. It can wait for our next break."

"I know your type. So independent." He's spot on.

"You're right, that's how I am."

"Why don't you just accept help when offered instead of insisting on always doing everything yourself?"

"Good question. Don't know, but I've heard that before. My friends tell me the same."

"You should listen to them."

"OK, you're right," I finally give in. Yet another lesson learnt for me. "You sure you don't mind?"

"Of course not! Why would I have offered it otherwise? Just stand still for a moment."

He swiftly works behind me, strapping my solar panels to the top of my backpack so they should get direct sunlight. Meanwhile, our group is overtaking us one by one and moving out of sight. Only one guide stays back to make sure no one gets lost.

"Sorry to make you fall behind."

"Ah, it won't take us long to catch up with them . . . OK, done."

"Awesome, thank you!" How nice to have such a helpful travel companion! I like when people are that honest and direct, really got lucky with our group.

Indeed, it doesn't take us long to catch up with everyone else. After another half an hour, we emerge from the deep forest. Tall trees give way to bushes, and we get our first glimpse into the far distance – a green hilly landscape covered by coniferous plants. However, the summit is not yet in sight.

Our path continues in a constant alternation of uphill and downhill slopes, until after about two hours we reach the bottom of the Shira plateau. What follows is supposed to be one of the toughest and steepest inclines of our entire hike. The next days would be easy by comparison.

"We'll have a break before we start the ascent. There are no more trees, so don't forget to put on sunscreen," Robert reminds us. The sun is burning indeed.

Everyone briefly disappears into the bushes, and I also look for a hiding place. This is out of my comfort zone again. I'm not used to mother nature as a toilet. Sure, I know it shouldn't be a big deal, especially not for someone who grew up in the Austrian countryside; had I just not become such a hopeless city girl . . .

Surprise, surprise – it wasn't difficult at all! Now I feel like a real camper. Why did we even bother with the horrible long-drop hut yesterday? Just like when I crawled into my dark tent last night, I'm again secretly proud of coping with our adventure just as well as everyone else, at least so far.

▲ ▲ ▲

"*Twende!* Let's go," Evance leads us on again, *pole pole* up the supposedly tough ascent to the Shira plateau. The terrain gets steeper, but *pole pole* seems to do wonders.

"That's it? I can do that, no problem, what's so difficult about it?" I wonder. Of course it's a bit of a workout, we'll be gaining some 500 meters (1,600ft) of altitude within three hours, but very doable for all of us nevertheless.

I walk next to Chris and Lynn. They are at least as much in high spirits and as little challenged by our walk as I am. We chat about the

Tour de Mont Blanc hike; or rather the two of them are talking about it while I am asking ignorant questions.

"Is it like here, that you go in a group and they carry your stuff?"

"You might be able to do it like that, but it's too expensive there to get porters," Lynn explains. "Though they've got roads, so you can arrange for your stuff to get transported by car."

"The good thing is they have nice huts along the way as well, so you don't need to sleep in a tent," Chris adds.

"True, but I was thinking to still do it on my own and just carry my tent."

"You mean you're going to carry all your stuff all the time?" I can't believe what Lynn just said.

"Yes, that's what I was thinking."

"Even your food? And what about water?"

"Oh, you can just buy it along the way. You just carry what you need for half a day, so it's not that bad."

"Ah, I see. But carrying my own tent, sleeping bag and all the other stuff still sounds pretty difficult to me!"

"I just like being out in nature. Somehow that makes it feel more authentic to me."

Wow! Just when I thought I've gotten well in shape, I realize there's still a long way to go. I admire Lynn's strength and silently set myself the goal to keep practicing until perhaps someday I will also be able to go for the real thing like her.

The higher we ascend, the fewer trees scatter the landscape that has by now changed from lush to olive green in a melee of needle-like leaves, woody twigs and uncovered earth. Thick green bushes that look perfectly uninteresting to my non-botanical eyes dominate the vegetation. Only a few flowery plants with red petals and long white stamens inside their open flower heads, the so-called *Protea Kilimanjaro* (a sub-species of the *Protea caffra*), provide a colorful contrast against the olive green landscape and the bright blue sky.

I overhear Diego and Giovanni speaking Spanish. Giovanni hasn't been saying much so far, choosing his few words wisely. Now I realize why – he's simply not that confident in English. I chip in some words in Spanish to their conversation.

"Oh, hablas español?" As soon as Giovanni realizes that we speak a common language, he transforms from a silent observer into a keen talker. This time I'm the one who struggles to understand. I learn that he was born and lives in Sardinia, has a technical university degree and works in an oil refinery.

"I've never been to Sardinia, but I heard it's beautiful."

"Oh yes, it feels like vacation every day. We have beautiful beaches and nice countryside, good food and sunshine all year round."

"So you've lived there all your life?"

"Yes. You see, I have a good job, they pay me well and our living expenses in Sardinia are very low. I get a lot of vacation, so I can still travel a lot. Why would I want to move?"

"Yes, that makes sense. Which places have you traveled to?"

"Many, but mostly in Latin America. It's easier because of the language."

Until this morning, Giovanni has been a stranger to me. No more. It's fascinating how speaking a common language makes such a massive difference to our ability to get to know and connect with the people around us.

"Let's take a break." Evance pauses. "Catch your breath. And drink."

We are about half way up towards the Shira plateau and can now look back down to see the entire hilly landscape. "We've come a long way!"

Like most of us, I unpack my snacks.

"What's that?" Chris asks.

"Ah, just my homemade energy bars – high fat, high protein, but no carbs."

"Can I try?"

"Sure, but I don't think you'll like them. They're not sweet." I hold out my little treasure bag to him and he takes a tiny piece.

"Tastes lovely. What's in it?"

Is he serious? I've never met someone who shares my extreme dietary preferences, at least no guys for sure.

"Walnuts, hazelnut flour, pumpkin seeds, sunflower seeds, pistachios, cocoa nibs, almond butter, coconut oil, dates, cinnamon . . ." I proudly recite all the ingredients.

"It's perfect. I really like them. Can I have another one?"

"Really? Of course!" I am delighted that someone enjoys my unusual baking creation as much as I do.

I check my phone to see whether we might have any connection. Yippee, all the bars are full! That's what all the other travel reviews said, that there would be mobile network connection out in the middle of nowhere, even far up the mountain. Hence, I casually mentioned to my dad that I would send him an SMS every now and then to let him know all is good. Same for my work. "No need to check my e-mails. I'll be able to do so and deal with anything urgent," I told them. How stupid, right?

So far, I have had neither mobile nor data connection. Relieved, I quickly type an SMS to my dad just to let him know that everything is great and he shouldn't worry, and to my work to let them know there's no data connection after all. Send and done – that's what I would have hoped for, but I'm not that lucky. My messages remain stuck. There's no connection after all. Ah, I could kick myself. Why have I not just set more realistic expectations? Then I wouldn't need to worry about that bloody phone now. Perhaps the reviews of other travelers were all based on the Marangu, Machame and Rongai routes, not this part of the mountain. "Never assume anything" is my mantra, and yet I did it again.

The next two hours to the top of the Shira plateau are quieter. We focus on our breathing rather than talking. Evance doesn't break anymore, just pauses briefly every now and then. "Catch your breath, drink . . . *twende!*" He keeps walking and we follow behind, some just like mountain goats, others breathing more heavily, but *pole pole* we all make it without major drama until a massive plain of heath land extends in front of our eyes as far as we can see.

Um, wasn't as difficult as they made it out to be. Or perhaps my muscle and cardio training throughout the year is finally paying off? Either way, I'm excited and relieved. No need to worry, I can do this. It's a piece of cake!

The remaining walk to tonight's camp is a very easy path, gently sloping downhill. Soon we glimpse our first closer view of the glacier on the top of Kilimanjaro at the far opposite end of the Shira plateau, piercing through in between constantly moving clouds that quickly hide this treasure again from our sight.

With supposedly one of the toughest stretches of the entire hike behind us, my excitement is pushing me back into my talkative mood.

"Hey Evance, are all clients like us, or do you also have more difficult ones?"

"I like all my clients," he answers politically, but he sounds as if he really means it.

"Who was the most difficult client you ever had? I mean in terms of age, or maybe any physical disabilities? I read all kinds of people come here."

"Yes, I've had all kinds of clients so far. Like last year, I guided two blind women, from Australia."

"Blind? That must have been difficult! So you had to stay next to them and tell them about every single step?"

"Yes, just like that," he's stretching out his elbow to demonstrate the support he was giving.

"You alone?"

"No, not just me. One guide can only guide one blind client at a time."

"But when they reach the top, they can't see anything." My mind is processing why someone would want to do that.

"Then I describe it to them, all the time I describe what I see."

"Wow, I couldn't do that."

"See that?" Evance nods straight ahead towards a hut and some colorful shapes, presumably tents. "That's our camp."

"Doesn't look far. We'll be there in ten minutes, no?"

"Maybe 45."

"Really?" It's difficult to tell distances up here where everything is flat and there are no visual benchmarks to guide our eyes. "Oh, what's that?" We are approaching an artificial assembly of stones, like a miniature replica of Easter Island without faces. "Does it have some kind of religious meaning?"

"No, it's just there, someone put it there," obviously. Knee to hip-high tower-like structures of random stones are scattered on a patch of earth the size of a tennis court. Someone must have had fun putting them there – perhaps a group of students or porters getting bored on a rest day? Not knowing the meaning doesn't keep us all from busily taking pictures of this curiosity. Whoever it was, they have created a welcome distraction on this otherwise uniform land of scrub.

▲ ▲ ▲

We reach Shira 1 camp around 2pm, earlier than expected. Seems our group indeed is above average and all of us are in quite good shape. The camp is set on a big plot of flat earthen land, perhaps the size of two soccer fields, on which the scrub has been removed to make way for tents. A handful of dingy long-drop huts mark the northern end of the field. Just like at Mti Mkubwa camp, we are not alone. A colorful selection of tents is spread out all over the campsite, some in groups, some individually. This time, there are no trees to create the illusion of being alone, but our tents are set up towards the far outer edge of the plot, a bit removed from everyone else. It still gives the feeling of our own little campsite. The wooden registration hut this time is a proper house with windows and a covered veranda. It reminds me of the stereotypical sheriff's house in a western movie.

Having walked right behind our lead guide Evance, I happen to be the first to register and walk over to our familiar tents. A porter immediately walks up to me and motions me to follow him. He leads me to one of the tents.

"Thank you. Um, and my bag?"

He opens the tent zip and points inside. My bag, sleeping bag and foam pad are already there. Oh wow! How does he know? Before I have time to think, he shakes my hand like a good old friend.

"I am Liber," he says and then retreats politely to leave me to my privacy.

Only then it dawns on me that he must be the porter assigned to carry my stuff, probably the same person who also showed me to my tent yesterday and came to pick up my bag in the morning, but I can't even remember what that person looked like! I feel ashamed. Did I really pay so little attention to him that now I can't even recognize his face? What a hypocrite, meeting KPAP and preaching about porter treatment, but then behaving like an ignorant client in real life! I reprimand myself to be more attentive and friendly to him going forward. It's all too easy on Kilimanjaro to get preoccupied with ourselves and feel a false sense of pride for our own achievements, forgetting the very people who make this possible for us and do all the heavy lifting.

"Alex, always keep the tent zips closed," Evance reminds me.

"Why?" I thought we left the bugs behind.

"Because of the dust."

Indeed! My shoes are no longer olive green but evenly covered by a red-brownish layer of dry earthy dust. For the first time, I pay attention to my hands. As if I'd just spent my morning gardening without gloves, I have dirt stuck everywhere in between my fingernails. How is that possible?

But first things first: My camera still hasn't charged properly despite Chris's clever rearrangement, and I also still want to charge my phone. So before I even wash my hands, I fix the solar charger to the side of my tent facing the sun.

"Be careful with your gadgets," Evance cautions, "don't leave them outside."

"Why? Do people steal?"

"Better be careful, we're not alone here."

"But I need to charge," I protest. "I'll have to take the risk."

"Put them inside. I'll show you how." Evance opens a tent zip. There's a second tent layer underneath. "Can you open from inside?"

I crawl inside and he passes me my gadgets, still connected to my solar panels outside. We zip the tent back up tightly around the cables.

"That's perfect, thank you!"

Now I have the mental capacity to focus on getting myself cleaned up. Our communal bucket with hot water is already waiting for us next to the mess tent. I wash my hands with soap and trickling hot water directly underneath the valve, just like a tap. What a luxury!

Our luxurious dining hall and shower facilities

Then I crawl back inside my tent to change my shirt and have a quick wash with a wet wipe while it's still nice and warm – yes, literally one wet wipe. With my bag already overweight, all supplies need to be handled economically. There's no capacity for excessive weight. And as I already learnt yesterday, water is not much use for washing inside my tent.

"Please go to the mess tent. Lunch is ready," voices from outside interrupt my little privacy time.

Already? OK, just let me check that I'm not sunburnt. I take a quick look into my small mirror. Shock! Dirt and dust is smeared all over my face. Have I been running around like that all day?

"Please go for lunch," the voice now comes from the shadow right next to my tent.

"Yes, yes," but I can't possibly leave my tent like that, can I? My brain goes into stress mode. Why don't they give us enough time to have a proper wash first? My hand reaches for a second wet wipe, the quick and dirty solution. It instantly goes from bright white to sooty brown, as if I'd just cleaned my shoes. Phew, at least it's no longer on my face!

On my way to the mess tent, a fierce wind that wasn't there just moments ago blows dust into my eyes and makes me shiver. It feels colder than it really is. The zip of the mess tent has been pulled down to keep the wind and dust outside. I quickly zip my way into its black safe confines. Only Lynn and Chris are there so far. "How nice and warm in here! And so light, I thought it would be totally dark."

"Snug, isn't it?" Lynn agrees.

"Snug? What does it mean?" I'm not a native English speaker and sometimes my vocabulary still lets me down.

"Like cozy, comfortable. Like when in winter you sit on your couch cuddled underneath a blanket with a cup of hot chocolate, that's snug."

How true! That's exactly how it feels in here, but my dust-smeared face is still lingering in my short-term memory. "I don't understand why they didn't give us more time to wash."

"True. It's almost 3pm. They probably want to space it out for dinner." Lynn is right. I still need to learn to let go of my city girl attitude and stop worrying about the way I look – being dirty is just normal up here.

"That's it. I also ran out of time and will need to continue afterwards," Chris adds politically, "only managed to wash my feet and boy they were as dirty as my fingers. The dust went straight through my shoes and socks."

"Me too!" Lynn agrees. "Dirt was stuck everywhere in my toenails. Felt so good to wash my feet!"

Really? That thought hadn't even crossed my mind. Now I can't wait to take off my socks.

Lunch consists of a creamy carrot soup, crispy grilled chicken, a massive plate of pasta and another veggie stew like last evening. There are also some fresh orange slices and small sweet bananas. It all tastes delicious. "We're really getting spoilt," everyone agrees. It's like camping for beginners – perfect for me.

"Hip hip!"

"Hop hop!"

"You've got your afternoon free today," Robert briefs us after lunch. "At 4:30pm, we'll have our introductory session. You will meet the entire crew. We meet back outside then."

For now, I cannot wait to run back to my tent, this time with a bowl of hot water for my feet. Butt inside, legs outside, I carefully peel off my socks, waiting for the disaster to unfold.

But I'm spared the shock. My feet look as clean as ever. Is that because my hiking trousers have that horrible elastic band at the bottom and hook onto the laces of my boots for a firm tight grip around their shaft? Real outdoors and hiking experts swear by functionality over looks. I'm not a hundred percent there yet, but one step closer.

I wash my feet, make an unsuccessful attempt of cleaning my fingernails, check my face in the mirror again to convince myself I didn't miss any obvious dirt earlier – and then what? Nothing, all stress for nothing. I've satisfied myself that I'm as clean as I could possibly get up here.

My phone is already fifty percent charged, and so I start typing today's notes. I love the new setup that Evance suggested. That way, I can write what you read while comfortably lying on my foam pad and at the same time leaving my phone connected to the solar panels outside. It's nice and warm in my tent, so warm that I've left my feet bare. I cannot hear anyone, just the wind flapping against the tent. How soothing! I would love to just close my eyes and take a nap. But what if sleeping now means another sleepless night tonight? That must be avoided by all means. I lose control of my eyelids, so I have to sit back upright in order not to fall asleep.

As I lift my chest, an unknown feeling spreads in my head, not a headache but a mild pressure towards the front. Reviews of prior hikers immediately emerge from my memory, about how altitude sickness first hit them after lying down and when getting up again. Is this the start of it all? Please go away.

▲ ▲ ▲

Just before 4:30pm, we all assemble back outside. Brrr, it feels chilly in the cold wind, but of course no one would want to miss that part. Robert introduces our entire crew to us. We have six guides, including Robert as our chief guide (the one responsible for everything), Evance as our lead guide (the one who leads the way), as well as four assistant guides: Baraka, Estomee, Samwel and Skoba. We cheer and applaud each of them.

"Next I introduce you to your chef," Robert continues. "He likes to be called Mr. Delicious, that's his nickname."

A very short guy with a very cute face proudly steps forward and we clap our hands like crazy.

"Hooray!"

"Yahoo!"

"And this is his kitchen helper, Mr. Armani."

A tall guy in a brown shirt with big Prada letters nods reservedly, just enough to indicate his existence.

The two of them couldn't be any more different from each other, nor could they be any easier distinguishable from everyone else. Mr. Delicious and Mr. Armani – that's easy to remember! Only after the hike I will find out that supposedly nicknamed Mr. Armani is actually called Amani (without the "r"), but his Prada shirt definitely helps to remember his name for now.

Our waiters are called Sostenence and Crispin. "Mr. Delicious, Amani and the waiters, they are porters as well," Robert explains. "Once they arrive, they immediately start cooking and preparing the table for you."

Big applause for each of them!

"They only work for you. For us, including all the porters and us guides," Robert waves his hand at the half-circle of about 40 crew members looking at us, "there is another cook. He also is a porter, and once he arrives, he starts cooking for all of us."

Wow, one person is cooking for all of them, after a full day of load-carrying labor! He deserves an even bigger applause, just that by now it's hard to go any louder.

"After you eat," Robert continues, "maybe you go somewhere else."

Laughter.

"This is your toilet porter, Dominick. As I already told to some of you, he is superior to all the normal porters."

A thunder of roars, cheers and hurrahs acknowledges his toughest of all roles.

"And finally, there are all the other porters to carry your bags, your tents, the communal equipment and all the supplies." The golden rule is about three porters per hiker.

One by one, the porters tell us their names and we applaud each of them individually.

"Now we would also like you to introduce yourselves to them," Robert requests.

One by one, we say something like, "Hi, I'm Alex. I live in Switzerland. This is my first time in Africa, and I love it!"

"Yahoo!" "Hooray!" The entire crew returns our applauses and cheers for each of us like for superstars, just that we haven't really deserved that. Surely, the hope for good tips at the end might be driving their behavior and fooling our emotions, but we all genuinely feel very welcome by them.

"And finally, our crew, the porters, we all have prepared a song for you," Robert announces.

That's the part I've been looking forward to, especially after the mesmerizing singing and dancing that we happened to witness this morning.

"*Jambo, jambo bwana . . .*" they start to sing for us in Swahili. We don't understand any of it, but it doesn't matter. It's the passion and joy in their voices, their rhythmic dancing and their smiling eyes that get us hooked. Our bodies start moving with the infectious vibe, and we all clap the rhythm.

Robert takes over the role as lead singer and all the porters sing the refrain – *hakuna matata*. No problem, indeed. We understand that! Keen to not only observe but to also become part of the fun, our voices join them for the refrain.

I could listen to them sing all afternoon, but unfortunately it ends too soon. Their warm welcome made me forget about the cold wind. Now I'm shivering again. After a series of group photos, everyone disperses into warmer confines.

▲ ▲ ▲

I crawl back into my snug tent to continue typing my notes. Snug, snug, snug – I like that new word. That's exactly how it feels in here. But back to work for me. Wow, my phone is already 100% recharged – the power of solar energy! But my camera is still flashing red – not working so well after all?

Cheerful voices from the mess tent fill the air. I can hear Chris, Lynn and our guides.

"You play cards?" one of our guides asks.

"Come, join us," Chris offers.

"We don't know that game."

"It's easy, I'll show you."

They are talking and laughing, obviously having fun.

"Should I go join them?" Ms. Fun is tempted.

"But then I need to type all my notes after dinner and it's going to get late again," Ms. Discipline protests.

"Ah, just scrap that stupid book idea and enjoy your vacation!"

"But I've already spent so much time on it."

"So what? That's because you idiot thought you would be done within an hour every day. Just because you've already wasted time doesn't justify wasting even more time. I'm the number one priority on this vacation, remember?" Ms. Fun is getting ready to make a move.

"But I've already met KPAP, wouldn't be nice to disappoint them now. And the Kili literature is still short of a review of the Northern Circuit," Ms. Purpose chips in.

"Yes, and someone to rectify that Diamox nonsense," Ms. Discipline has found an accomplice.

"We've come too far to give it all up so easily now!"

Two against one – that settles the debate, and Ms. Discipline forgets the world around.

▲ ▲ ▲

"Hey Alex, come outside and look at that." Chris's voice brings me back to reality. It's around 6:30pm.

"Look at what?" I shout back.

"The summit. The clouds are all gone now."

Shoes slipped into in record time, and my heart warms at the sunset view.

"Wow, it's amazing!"

"Beautiful, isn't it? How often do you get to see that?"

"Thanks for letting me know! Would have been such a shame to miss."

Indeed, all clouds have moved, and we have a crystal clear view of the top of Kilimanjaro and its glaciers. To be more specific, we are looking at Kibo cone, one of three volcanic cones on Kilimanjaro, and the one with the highest peak. That's where we're heading. The other two cones are Shira where we are right now, though it doesn't look like a cone, and Mawenzi to the eastern side, hidden behind Kibo. Shira and Mawenzi are extinct, while Kibo is dormant and could theoretically erupt again. It looks like a massive piece of rock, more wide than tall with a rather flat plateau on top, like Ayers Rock but with more moderate slopes. Right now, the setting sun envelops the rocky cone with an orange hue, making it look peaceful and benign.

We take a few pictures. Immediately, my camera flashes red again, even though it was plugged in all afternoon. The solar panels worked like a charm for my phone. Why has my camera not recharged? Tomorrow I will try again.

It's almost dinnertime. I quickly dissemble the panels and crawl back into my tent to fetch my headlight and to put on another jacket. When I reemerge just a few minutes later, I find myself in an entirely different place. Brrr, what just happened?! It's dark and freezing cold. The warm sunset has become a faint memory and the harsh mountain reality awaits us brutally, without warning.

In the mess tent, we all nestle into our seats with bent spines, raised shoulders and drawn-in necks, shivering while warming our fingers on a cup of tea or hot chocolate. Crispin brings in our familiar pot of soup – zucchini soup this time. I'm generally not a big fan of soups, but in this temperature hot soup tastes like the best thing ever. It immediately warms us up from inside. We also get spicy peppered beef, a bean stew and rice, followed by pancakes with Nutella filling – all as yummy as our chef's name. Thank you Mr. Delicious!

Despite the food warming us up for now, the prospect of a freezing night alone in our tents subdues our atmosphere. Reality has hit us earlier than we expected, and if it's already cold now, it will only get worse over the coming week. Our group is markedly quieter than last evening, processing what we've gotten ourselves into. We are no longer talking all over the place, no longer scrambling to chip in our comments and jokes. One person talks at a time, if at all.

"And I know a guy who proposed up here!" someone says.

"Not as romantic as he thought it would be, hey?"

"You wanna know how we celebrate bachelor's nights in Louisiana?" Stewart's train of thoughts has left the mountain.

"Oh he's got a great story there," Juli nods.

Sure, give us some distraction. We are all ears.

"You know how the waters in the swamps around New Orleans are all infested with crocodiles, right?"

"Yeah, alligators, they are huge!"

"You wouldn't want to go swim there."

"So that guy we know very well," Stewart continues, "he of course did what all boys do at bachelor's night, he got drunk with his buddies . . . and then we've got this local custom that the groom needs to prove his courage . . . so once they are all drunk, they take him out on a boat in the middle of the night."

Grrr, I see the dark swamp and a man in a tiny wooden boat come alive in my mind. "Is he alone?"

"No no, they all go together of course. They need to make sure he does what he's supposed to do."

Oh, taking the boat out there is not scary enough?

"So they all go out on the boat and then he needs to jump into the water."

"What?!"

"Why would he do that?"

"Sounds like suicide."

"Bear in mind alligators are not as aggressive as crocodiles," Juli clarifies.

"Yeah, they do it all the time and usually nothing happens," Stewart shrugs it off. "The groom jumps in and then the others drag him back into the boat, not a big deal."

My jaw drops. You could pay me millions I still wouldn't do that.

"But guess what happened to the guy we know. He jumps into the water, and as soon as he's in there, the other guys already see this massive thing charging at him . . . They immediately realize what's happening and so they're trying to get him back onto the boat . . . but these alligators are fast . . . so before they get hold of him, it bites into his arm . . . and of course the alligator doesn't let go . . . they manage to grab his other arm, and they are all pulling and fighting and struggling."

"Oh no!"

"Sounds like a nightmare!"

Our eyes and mouths are open wide, while Stewart is laughing like telling a joke.

"This is better than crocodile Dundee."

"So then did the alligator let go?" I ask impatiently.

"So then," Stewart carries on, "after pulling and fighting and struggling for ages . . . I mean you can imagine what a mess . . . these guys were all half-drunk . . . eventually they get him back onto the boat."

"And the guy was fine?"

"Well yeah, he was quite happy to be back on the boat. That sobered him up, you can imagine."

"And nothing?"

"No injury?"

"Well, his hand was like that," Stewart lifts his elbow horizontally with his hand dangling down vertically. "Not much left to keep it at his wrist."

"So then what?"

"They tied him up and brought him to the hospital. He was fine again for the wedding, just with a bandage."

Men – what a self-destructive species, I'm silently thinking to myself while enjoying my free evening program. Who needs TV or books when we've got Stewart to tell us his stories so vividly they come alive in front of our eyes?

▲ ▲ ▲

"Hip hip!"

"Hop hop!"

It's time for our health checks and briefing for tomorrow. The mild pressure in my head has disappeared again. Everyone is feeling good, other than the cold of course.

"Today was a tough day. We had a long steep hike, but you all did very well," Robert praises us. "Tomorrow will be easy compared to today, nothing to worry about . . . It's very dusty up here—"

"Yes indeed!"

"Haha, we figured that out by now!"

"Tomorrow it will get worse," Robert warns.

"Can it get any worse?"

"For those of you who brought gaiters, put on your gaiters tomorrow," he advises us.

"Why?" A critical voice asks. We all brought them in case of rain, against the mud.

"To keep the dust out of your shoes, and if you want to keep your trousers clean. Of course you don't have to, but we recommend."

Ah, that makes sense. I'm kind of excited that I can still make use of my gaiters in this entirely unexpected way and didn't buy them for nothing. It feels so much more *professional* with all that special gear.

"Tonight will be a lot colder than yesterday," Robert continues.

"Yes, it's freezing!"

"Haha, no need to tells us, we can feel it!"

"What's the temperature now?"

"Right now, maybe around seven degrees Celsius. Overnight, it may fall below zero."

"Already?"

"It's only our second night!"

We're not looking forward to the next ten hours.

"Be careful when walking at night," Robert continues. "There are a lot of stones everywhere. Always look down."

"I'm not planning to go outside in this freezing cold."

"Me neither."

"Yes, most of you have pee bottles. Just stay in your tent. For those of you who don't," just a few girls seem to fall into my category, "don't bother going all the way to the toilet tent. Just quickly pee next to your own tent and then go back to sleep."

Um, let's see about that. Robert doesn't want us to fall over in the darkness and hurt ourselves, but I have other priorities – avoid the flashlight on my butt!

"OK, so then I wish you a good night."

We can't wait to crawl into our warm sleeping bags.

Juli and Stewart have brought their toothbrushes with them into the mess tent and get busy with what they need to do while comfortably seated in the warmed-up tent. One teacup becomes their shared sink, the other one the tap. "Sorry for that, just so cold outside," Juli comments apologetically.

"What a great idea!"

"Yes, way too cold outside."

I almost forgot about my teeth again, but now I can no longer use that excuse. Should I also bring my toothbrush here? I ponder briefly, but no – the brutal truth is that I simply can't be bothered. I once read tooth brushing once a day is sufficient from a health point of view, assuming one does it meticulously.[45] It's time to test that theory. Others seem to have come to the same conclusion.

The temperature feels like minus already while I wait my turn in front of the toilet tent. Quick, quick, I can't wait to get back to my tent. Zip open, butt inside, shoes off, tent closed, and straight into my sleeping bag in full gear. Only my jacket comes off.

It doesn't take too long for the sleeping bag to warm up and for Ms. Discipline to forget the cold night outside while copying this afternoon down to electronic memory. Only after an hour, duty accomplished, do I realize that I'm in trouble again. Obsessed about avoiding AMS, I've drunk almost six liters of water today. That's double their daily recommendation. Now I have to pay for being overzealous.

I'm scared of the temperature shock as I open my tent again. Brrr, cold! Just like yesterday, it's quiet and all the tents are dark. Today, however, we are no longer in the deep sinister jungle but out in open star-lit terrain. In fact, the stars are so bright that Kibo cone is still clearly distinguishable against the night sky and I can make out our entire campsite. Squatters are in trouble! There are no hideaways. I peer towards the toilet tent. It couldn't be any further away from my own. The thought of a long march of suffering in the freezing cold is holding me back. But what if someone emerges from another tent exactly within my one minute of privacy? What the heck – keeping warm is more important. I follow Robert's good advice and huddle back into my tent in no time. Oh Kilimanjaro, you really make me change!

After 40 hours awake and without any coffee all afternoon, I should fall asleep in no time, right? Not quite so. Even though the sleeping bag is living up to its -30F rating, my own failure to get comfortable forebodes another restless night. I twist and change my position like a maniac, left, right, readjust the liner sheets, make sure not to lie on my phone, better lie straight, ouch that was my headlamp . . . solid ice . . . Yikes! That's my feet. Last thing I remember they felt nice and warm. What just happened? Ah, relief! I must have managed to doze off for a bit. Should I put one of my self-heating badges down to my feet? Too difficult to look for them, and better to save them for even colder nights to come . . . Brrr – not a promising outlook.

DAY 3

Learning Swahili and making friends

22 SEPTEMBER 2015

From Shira 1 (3,500m/11,500ft)
to Shira 2 camp (3,800m/12,500ft)
Distance — elevation — time:
7km/4mi⇨ — 300m/1,000ft⇧ — 3-4 hours☺

plus optional bonus hike
Elevation — time:
200m/700ft⇧⇩ — 2 hours☺

Faint voices make their way through my earplugs. Our porters are getting busy. It's 5am – still dark and too early to get up, but I'm happy like an insomniac. Five hours of solid sleep, what more could I ask for?

"Bee-dee-dee-deep!" My 6:30am alarm. Yay, I even got a bonus hour on top! First sunrays fill the tent. The air on my face no longer makes me feel as if I were stuck in an icebox, just a fridge with the door wide open. Yippee, let's get the day started – by sitting upright.

Crack, flap, and sag. Pressure on my right shoulder releasing. What was that? Oh yikes! The strap of my brand new Victoria's Secret sports bra just broke. I was too chicken last night to take it off in the freezing cold, too chicken to remove my shirt and get bare-chested even just for a few seconds. Now it's pay-back time. All my efforts to find a skin-color sports bra that wouldn't show through my ultra-thin hiking shirts just succumbed to vanity. And what an effort that was – bet you all the sports bra designers are men! Well, I guess some

171

things are simply out of our control, no matter how much we try to plan and prepare. The *white-sports-bra-look* it shall be for today.

Let's focus on something else. What's next? Hot water. I've kept some in my thermos overnight, hoping that drinking hot water first thing in the morning would help with bowel movements. After four days away from home storing all my food, I figured I should do something about it.

But hey – can't I also use my hot water for my compressed one-time towels? Then I could wash my eyes and put in my contact lenses straight away. Let's try. I pour just a little hot water into the thermos cup and drop in one of those white tokens. It's no bigger than the tip of my thumb and feels solid hard like a piece of plastic. Abracadabra, let the magic unfold. That little useless piece of nothing quickly soaks up all the water, expands in size, and voilà – it has transformed into a proper hand towel, like the ones they give you on planes. While it's still steaming hot, I spread it across my face. Wonderful, that feels so good! But it also turns cold quickly and I use the remaining humidity for other essential body parts. How exciting! Now I can wash and get 99% ready without even leaving the warmth of my sleeping bag. I've just redefined my morning routine. Why are thermos bottles not among the standard repertoire of any Kilimanjaro packing list?

I finish getting dressed and packing my bags while still seated within my sleeping bag. Only when all done, I slip outside to brush my teeth.

▲ ▲ ▲

Breakfast is the usual fare of eggs, porridge and white bread. With the sun up promising a warm new day, we are all in high spirits again, markedly different to our subdued dinner atmosphere. We survived last night – we can do this!

Jana joins the table last.

"Happy Birthday!"

"Oh yes, it's your birthday today!"

We briefly talked about it on the bus.

"Let's sing!" and off we go with eleven different tones but all as loud as we can.

"Yay!" Clap, clap, clap.

"Juli also had her 28th anniversary yesterday," Stewart reminds us.

Yes, Juli also mentioned that on the bus, she's celebrating 28 years of being clean and sober. It took me by surprise that she spoke about it so openly. People I know usually don't do that. Sober of what exactly? I didn't dare ask and I still don't, and no one else asks either. I guess it doesn't make a difference. Sober and happy, that's all that matters.

"Happy Anniversary Juli!"

"Happy birthday to you, happy . . ." and off we go again. Our singing pales next to the great voices of our guides and porters, but we all cheerfully participate nevertheless. It doesn't take much to make us feel happy and have fun as a group.

Our morning health check has become an unremarkable affair. My blood oxygen reading seems to have settled in at around 92 percent, the same as last night. The pressure I felt on my head last afternoon hasn't returned. No one else seems to have any complaints either.

As yesterday, it takes our group longer than 8am for everyone to finish their morning routines, collect water bladders and fix our daypacks.

"How did you sleep?" Evance asks me.

"Good, 50%!" I reply cheerfully.

"Why only 50%?"

"Still getting used to it, but hey, it's getting better. And I'm not tired at all."

"That's good." He watches me strap my solar panels to my backpack. "They won't get any sun like that, flip them around."

"Um, really? Why not?" I strapped them on top just like Chris taught me yesterday, one panel on top and the other two hanging down to the side.

"Because we're heading that way," he points east. "Those two won't get any sun. Put it the other way round."

"Oh, thanks," he's right and I readjust. Why didn't I think of that myself?

Meanwhile, others have formed a circle and are doing morning stretches. By now, it already feels nice and warm in the sun.

▲ ▲ ▲

We start our hike around 8:20am. It should take us about four hours to reach the Shira 2 camp. The terrain is almost flat to start with. We are crossing the vast Shira plateau towards Kibo cone, which remains clearly visible in the far distance. Knee-high bushes and football-size stones cover the earthen ground.

Our assistant guide nicknamed Skoba leads the way today. Giovanni and I follow right behind.

"Hey, Skoba, right?" I try to start a conversation.

"Yes?"

"Sorry, but I didn't catch your real name yesterday."

"Oh, it's Happy God. But you can call me by my nickname Skoba."

"Happy God? Like HAPPY—GOD? That's a nice name."

"Yes, but spelled differently."

"How do you spell it?"

"It's H–A–P–Y–G–O–D."

"Ah I see, Hapygod."

Silence.

"Have you been a guide for a long time?"

"Yes, more than ten years."

"Oh wow, that's a long time."

Silence again. Skoba is polite, but not very talkative, and I'm back to being a wound up chatterbox. What can we talk about?

"Skoba, could you teach us some Swahili? Like how do you say 'my name is'?"

"*Jina langu ni.*"

Dina gaga what? "Sorry, could you say that again? Slowly please."

Skoba repeats, slowly, again and again. Home run! He seems pleased with my effort to learn and turns out to be a very patient teacher, though without seeing anything in writing I barely progress beyond "*Jina lako nani?*" ("What's your name?"), "*Jina langu ni . . .*" ("My name is . . ."), "*Unatoka wapi?*" ("Where are you from?"), and "*Natoka . . .*" ("I'm from . . .").

Over the next hour, Skoba tirelessly repeats the same four simple phrases for me over and over again until I can finally hold on to them. Giovanni is doing far better – he already knows some basics from a YouTube course. Diego joins our language learning and together we all learn to sing the welcome song that the crew sang for us yesterday. It has a very sticky tune and goes like this:

> *Jambo, jambo bwana.* (Hello, hello Sir.)
> *Habari gani? Nzuri sana.* (How are you? Very well.)
> *Wageni, mwakaribishwa.* (Visitors, welcome.)
> *Kilimanjaro? Hakuna matata.* (Kilimanjaro? No problem.)

No doubt anyone coming to Kilimanjaro will hear this song. It's nice to understand the words and to be able to sing these lines together with our guides. While it may look simple enough when written down, it takes me at least half an hour to memorize without visual aid; and thus it keeps me entertained for a while.

We stop at a massive three-meter tall rock that protrudes like a landmark in an otherwise monotonously flat landscape, a welcome opportunity for distraction. Chris and Juli, both overflowing with energy, take turns to climb on top and have great photo shots taken, with the massive Shira plain and Kibo in the backdrop.

Crossing the vast Shira plateau

As we get going again, I continue my language learning with Skoba. I like to practice and constantly repeat simple phrases with him, and Skoba seems pleased and encourages my effort to learn. We refer to each other as *rafiki yangu* (my friend) or *dada/kaka yangu* (my sister/brother); Skoba in his quiet, polite tone, and me shouting out every single word in a shrill, highly exaggerated pitch.

Every now and then, Skoba asks: *"Jina lako nani?"*

"Jina langu ni Alex," I reply.

Or he asks: "*Unatoka wapi?*"

"*Natoka Austria,*" I reply.

Then I ask him back the same questions and he answers, over and over and over again, until it comes naturally without thinking too much. I also like to test my new vocabulary with our other guides. How pleasing when they can make out the meaning of my confused babble!

Juli overhears our simple exchange of words and also contributes some phrases that I don't understand.

"So you speak Swahili?" I ask her surprised.

"I picked it up when traveling through Africa," she shrugs it off modestly.

"How long were you traveling for?"

"Two and a half years, but it's already a long time ago."

"Two and a half years?! Wow! Just like that? How come? Where exactly did you go? Alone?" I know a lot of long-time travelers, but Africa still is a different league in my mind. You don't just go there for that long, and certainly not as a woman.

"I just set off on my own and went about everywhere. My plan was to traverse the whole continent from Dhaka to Johannesburg."

"On your own?! Like backpacking through Africa?!"

My concept of what you can and cannot do is shattered to pieces. All I can think of is Africa as a dark, dangerous place and all I can see is Juli as this gorgeous-looking woman with long blonde hair and perfect facial features. As a young woman traveling through Africa, her beauty must have been overwhelming and causing much attraction. Wouldn't she have been an obvious rape target? Uneasy feelings from blatant stares of lecherous men when traveling in India still linger in my memory. Surely most of Africa would be a lot worse than that. "Wasn't it dangerous? You never had any problems?"

"No, it was fine, I never felt unsafe."

So far I hardly spoke to Juli at all, perhaps due to lack of interest on my part. What do we have in common anyway? Or so it seemed to me, on first glance, even though I knew nothing about her. I overheard that she used to work as a waitress, and at breakfast Stewart mentioned that they live on the top floor of a five-star hotel that he had developed, so I immediately put Juli into my mental bucket as *good-looking woman married to a rich guy.* Not that there's anything wrong with being a waitress or good-looking or married to a rich guy, of course! The only thing that's wrong is my stereotyping. I struggle to maintain conversations with women whose interests are dominated by shopping, beauty salons and wasteful parties disguised as charity events, simply because that's not of much interest to me, and so far I haven't even bothered finding out whether there might have been a monumental flaw in my thinking. Now I realize I got it all wrong and can't wait to know more. "So how did it all start? Did you already know beforehand what you were going to do? And how many years ago was that?"

"It's a long story. Are you sure you want to hear it?"

"Oh yes, of course, we've got time – if you don't mind telling me."

"OK, so this was back in 1990," she begins to narrate. "I was working as a waitress at that time—"

"Wait a second. There wasn't even Internet back then, no mobile network, no Google Maps. How did you even get all the information you needed?" The problem is not that Juli doesn't want to tell me, but that I keep interrupting her with impatient questions before she even gets a chance to explain.

"Well, you wouldn't believe it, but I just used the good old Lonely Planet and a couple of Michelin maps. I also heard that they had a decent travel office in Miami, so I went there to get all the information I could."

Now how does that compare to my lazy trip planning while sipping coffee in front of my computer! "And how did you fund your trip? I mean two and a half years is a long time."

"I just saved what I earned as a waitress and financed it all from that. I went low budget, it wasn't that expensive."

"And how did you access your money? I mean, you probably didn't want to bring it all in one go because it would have been too risky."

"Yes, I used traveler's checks. Do you still know those?"

"Oh yes, I also used them on my first trip alone when I did a student exchange to Eastern Europe," I feel worldly-wise that I can at least relate this tiny bit of my experience to her adventure. "But you need a bank office to cash them in. Did all the capitals in all the countries have that?"

"There used to be American Express offices in the big cities, not in all countries, but it was OK. I even managed to get some mails delivered there."

"Oh, great. I was already going to ask you about that, how you managed to communicate with your family."

"Yes, long-distance calls were very expensive. I only called home briefly once every few months and that was quite an event."

"I can imagine. Your family probably got quite worried when they didn't hear from you for a while."

"Yes. One time I couldn't call them as I said I would. I was totally delirious, got malaria—"

"You had malaria?!"

"Yes, it happened when . . ."

I'm captivated as Juli keeps relating parts of her story to me. "So when Stewart said that you will be writing your memoirs, that's what you will be writing about, right? Your Africa travel story."

"Yes, not only, but it will become a chapter."

I'm deeply impressed. So far I've considered myself well-traveled and adventurous. Now I realize that I've barely started my journey, and for the first time in my life I wonder whether my ideas and preconceptions about Africa might be all wrong, just as those about Juli couldn't have been any further from the truth. I can't wait to read her story.

Skoba stops. "We'll take a break here. We have already crossed the Shira plateau. It's not far to Shira 2 camp, but the last bit will be steeper."

While talking to Juli, I barely realized how far we'd come. Hiking so far was as easy as a Sunday stroll. The landscape is still covered by scrub and bushes. Towards this end of the Shira plateau, however, where the path starts to incline more visibly, more and more loose rocks of dark volcanic lava peek through in between the scrubby vegetation. Patches of solid rock with soft eroded edges replace parts of the earthen ground.

There are some strange-looking trees reminiscent of giant candelabras, almost ten meters in height. They have long thin wooden stems that become thicker higher up before splitting into two thick branches that point straight up into the sky. Where they become thicker, the branches are entirely covered by tall wooden rosettes. Only at the very top end of their branches do some green leafy rosettes add a visible touch of life to their dry structure, almost like comic figures with long faces and unruly spiky hair. As I will learn from the respected mountaineering writer Audrey Salkeld in David Breashears' Kilimanjaro film of 2002 (the only serious Kilimanjaro film production I'm aware of to date), the strange-looking rosette structure is an ingenious survival mechanism to cope with this harsh climate. In essence, instead of the green leaves falling off when they die, they fold downwards around the stem like an insulation layer. These ingenious trees are called *Giant Groundsel* (members of the *Dendrosenecio* genus) and only exist in the alpine zones of mountains in equatorial East Africa – no wonder we have never seen them before.

Giant Groundsel tree

▲ ▲ ▲

It's getting cloudy, and our bodies are quickly cooling down during the break. Most of us start to feel chilly and put on a second layer.

"*Twende!*"

We get going again. There's a porter resting alone on a flat rock off the path, watching us pass.

"*Habari? Mechoka?*" ("How are you? Tired?") I shout over to him, keen to test what I learnt from Skoba earlier. Of course I've got the grammar wrong, but who cares.

"*Ndio, nimechoka! Habari?*" ("Yes, I'm tired. How are you?") He calls back with a broad smile. Probably he doesn't get a lot of crazy Austrian girls chatting him up.

"*Nzuri sana!*" ("Very well!") I am as excited as a nerdy schoolgirl about my simple conversations in this new language.

As we continue our hike, I follow behind Juli and her husband. At the age of 60, Stewart is the most experienced person in our group.

"So how's the property market these days?" I ask him, curious to learn a bit more from and about this successful man.

"Quite good," he answers politely, as if this young girl who can't shut up had just asked him about the weather for the sake of small talk.

"I also looked at some hotel and property projects at work, from an M&A point of view. So you do mostly hotels? What are the yields like in . . .?"

"Oh, so you are like an investment banker?"

"Sort of." Now we have found a common topic and I can talk confidently about what I do for a living with someone who speaks my language, different from our first evening when I felt like the odd one out surrounded by social aid workers. Stewart becomes his usual talkative self when he realizes that I actually understand what he's talking about. It all sounds very impressive and this time my first impression didn't let me down. He truly is a very successful man by the sounds of it all. "So you've always been a property developer, running your own company?"

"Always in development, but I started small as an employee in one of the leading companies in our area." In a nutshell, he worked his way up, took the company over with a partner and then went to multiply its business volume, taking it into a completely different league – so pretty much a storybook self-made entrepreneur. I'm very impressed.

Before we know it, there are some wooden huts, the – by now familiar – long-drop toilets that I'm not intending to get close to any more. Are we at Shira 2 camp already? It seems we are because our group have started registering their details on a small wooden table in front of a worn-out wooden wall that looks like an old school blackboard with a sunshade on top. "That roof won't be any good when it rains," I wonder.

"Yes, the registration hut is further up. We brought the park logbook down so you don't have to go there," Skoba clarifies my surprise.

I'm next in line after Juli. As part of our details, there also is a column for our age. I couldn't quite work it out earlier for Juli because she's got all this life experience yet projects so much energy and still looks very young. "So how old are you then?" No, I couldn't possibly ask that question, how rude. Now the number 57 jumps out at me. My brain is challenged to process. Can that be right? My mum is 57, but Juli . . . ? No, I can't quite believe it. Perhaps the number 5 is a 4? But no, it's clear and distinct. Perhaps that was meant for Stewart? But no, his 60 years are noted right on top. My concept of possibilities just got shattered again.

▲ ▲ ▲

It's about 12:15pm as we walk up the final steps on the path towards our tents. A thick layer of grey clouds is obstructing our view uphill. Supposedly, Kibo peak is hidden behind them. It's rocky and hilly up here. The tents of different groups are more dispersed again, some here some there, not all on one flat field. Our orange tents are all on one spot, almost giving the illusion of our own little private campsite again.

My porter Liber comes running towards me as soon as I arrive. Just like yesterday, he directs me to my tent; and my backpack, sleeping bag and foam pad are ready waiting for me inside. Perfect, how nice not to have to worry about any of that myself! Different to yesterday, however, I finally remember.

"Liber, *habari gani?*" ("How are you?") I greet him with an excited smile, pleased about my own progress.

"Welcome." He returns my smile with a hint of confusion about his weird client and politely retreats to leave me alone.

Today we've all followed Robert's good advice and put on our gaiters to protect against the dust. Looking at my hands confirms his prediction – today is worse, much worse! Not only my fingernails but also my entire hands are covered with a film of earthy-brown dust. It's so bad that I wait for hot water to wash my hands and face before crawling into my tent for a short break.

My phone is finding some networks again – Airtel, Tigo, Vodacom . . . All the big operators show up. I try to hook onto one of them in order to finally send off the SMS I typed yesterday. What a colossal waste of time. It just won't work. Could it be due to the cloudy weather? I don't know but one thing is for sure – I really regret having set the wrong expectations back home. While my parents are by now used to me traveling the world, their daughter going *alone* to Africa tore new fissures into their comfort zone, like a muscle that has not been activated before and hurts after first use. This is not how girls from the Austrian countryside spend their vacation. "Do you really need to go?" "Please be careful." "Who are you going with?" I heard these questions over and over again. Now I would like to help them feel at ease, but I can't.

▲ ▲ ▲

Today's lunchtime is at 1:30pm. We get crisply grilled toast with a thick layer of cheese inside – or is it pure margarine? It doesn't matter. Even though I usually avoid white bread like my worst enemy, this just looks too yummy to resist. Mmm, what a sensual delight! Next up comes our familiar pot of vegetable soup, followed by grilled chicken, hardboiled eggs and – best of all – a big plate of fresh vegetables. Tomatoes, carrots, cucumber, lettuce, avocado, capsicum – what a luxury! I desperately need some fiber. The hot water I'm drinking every morning has not been effective so far, neither has my package of dried prunes that I keep snacking from made any difference. I'm surprised our group is not scrambling for the fresh stuff. Am I the only one who has these kinds of problems? There is plenty left over.

"Um, no one wants that?"

"Go for it."

Finishing off the plate, I feel as if I'd just won the lottery again.

"Hip hip!"

"Hop hop!"

"How was your lunch?"

"Fantastic!"

"Delicious!"

"Perfect!"

"That's good," Robert seems pleased. "Today, you have your afternoon free. As I already briefed you yesterday, we will have an optional acclimatization hike later. Skoba will lead the hike. For those of you who join, we'll meet outside at 4pm. We'll hike up about

300 meters in altitude, stay there for a bit to acclimatize, and then come back down the same way."

The point of this hike is not to cover more distance, but to hike higher during the day than when sleeping at night. Climbing high and sleeping low – that's the third key success factor to making it to the top, just like drinking lots of water and going *pole pole* to gain altitude slowly.

Yesterday, our camp was lower than the ridge of the Shira plateau, so we had already hiked higher during the day than our night's camp as part of the normal route. This is ideal. Today's route from Shira 1 to Shira 2 camp, however, only went uphill. In other words, we will be sleeping at the highest point of our route today. That's why Robert highly recommended this acclimatization hike to us, and everyone decided to join.

For me, the only one without Diamox, this acclimatization hike is not only optional but a must. Within my overzealousness, keen to do whatever it takes to maximize my chances of acclimatizing naturally, I asked Robert yesterday whether it would be advisable for me to go higher than the 300 meters. I mean, "Shouldn't people without Diamox logically go higher than those with?"

"No, 300 meters is enough. We will all go together." He wouldn't even consider my proposal. I don't understand why, but he's the boss and I don't dare ask again.

"Any more questions?" Robert asks at the end of his briefing.

"Yes. How shall we do it with washing today?" Jeannette raises a good question. "Will you give us hot water after the bonus hike?"

"Oh, you haven't seen? Hot water is outside, you can wash now."

"And after the bonus hike as well?"

"Later, no need for wash." Robert is dead serious and quite surprised about the roaring laughter he has just caused.

"Haha! Who needs washing anyway?"

"Yeah, we'll just get dirty again tomorrow."

"Exactly, let's just all stay dirty!"

It's dusty as hell up here. For sure after the bonus hike we'll look just as we did when we arrived, covered from top to toe in earthy dust. Who would want to crawl into the sleeping bag like that?

"Robert, can't we also get hot water afterwards?" someone suggests once our laughter has calmed down.

"Please!!!" Twelve grown-ups look at Robert with puppy eyes.

"But it will be too cold to wash then."

"Just a little, to wash our hands?"

"Yes, please!!!"

"OK," he relents.

"Yay!"

"Thank you!"

"Hurrah!"

It's easy to make us all happy.

"OK, so please be ready at 4pm."

As soon as Robert finishes our little briefing, I immediately sneak out of the lunch tent in the hope of some privacy in the toilet tent.

Tent zipped down. Pants stripped down. "Anyone in there?"

You must be kidding me! "Yes, sorry, only just got here," I shout back.

"Haha, there's already a queue forming out here," says yet another voice.

"OK, got it." I hurry up. The flush is playing funny again. "Sorry for the wait, can't get that toilet paper down."

"It's OK, just leave it."

OK, I give up. "Sorry for that, your turn."

Oh how simple things like using a toilet are converted into pure luxury on this mountain! My privacy time will have to wait. I could, of course, use the public toilet facilities, but this thought doesn't even cross my mind. Only later I will learn from Juli that the ones here at Shira 2 camp were modern and clean. For now, I have already allowed all the horrible reviews I had read to bias my expectations.

On a positive note, however, our little plastic toilet has been kept more or less clean (as much as this is possible up here) ever since I've mentioned my initial disappointment to Robert and stirred quite some laughter along the way. It doesn't look as daunting to me anymore as it did on our first night, and I've even got the hang of the flush – most of the time that is, when I'm not exactly rushed to make a move. Left without a choice, I've got used to our new circumstances and learnt to make do with little faster than I ever believed possible.

It's still cloudy outside and a chilly wind blows up the dust, so I crawl inside my tent for shelter. I try to use my free afternoon to record my memory of this morning's hike, but my thoughts move back to my bowels. It's already the fifth day away from home and I've been stuffing myself like crazy with food over the past week. How is it possible that I'm still feeling so good? Whenever I had these issues before, my belly would feel like a stuffed soccer ball and I would hunch up in pain. No discomforts whatsoever this time round. To the contrary, my body feels good. Where has all the food gone? Could it be that all this exercising out in the fresh air makes such a difference, that calories get converted straight into energy when we burn them? I have no clue whether this is biologically possible, but my little pseudo-scientific explanation keeps me happy for now.

Only one thing leaves me worrying about my stupidity – why did I get one of these completely useless female urination devices? No woman is using them up here, at least not for daytime purposes, and I'm certainly not planning to do so either. While hiking, there have always been some rocks or other natural formations to hide behind. All my worries about moonlighting in front of everyone else have proven completely unjustified. Did I fall victim to one of those marketing scams that target our deepest fears? Being seen naked in public would certainly top my list!

Thinking of pee and poop, the afternoon has been flying past. Before I realize, it's almost 4pm. My tent hasn't warmed up all afternoon because the sun is still hidden behind the clouds, but at least it has kept me out of the wind. I'm not looking forward to facing the wind head-on again, but I only have one choice – harden up! OK, so let's get this done with.

▲ ▲ ▲

"Um, where is everyone?" Only Chris and Lynn are outside so far.
"Don't know."
"People are still getting ready."
Brrr, it's even colder than I expected and the cold wind makes my fingers freeze. I'm hopping around like an idiot in an effort to keep warm, but without much effect. "Should I go back to my tent to grab my gloves?" I wonder, but I know they're buried deep inside my bag. It's already way past 4pm and I don't want to make people wait for me. As soon as we start walking, surely my fingers will warm up again. We wait and wait, but people are still taking their time. Every minute standing still makes my body colder and colder. It feels like torture to me until I can't stand it anymore.

"Sorry, but I have to go now." I start walking.
"Yes, let's just go," Chris and Lynn join me.
"OK, you can go," Evance agrees. "Estomee will come with you."
What a surprise! This is the first time he doesn't call us back.
Sure enough, our fast steps and a little bit of sun peeking through every now and then make me feel warmer again.
"Now how good does that feel?"

"Yes, finally walking at our own pace."

"That slow motion gets really tiring after a while."

For the first time allowed to walk as fast as we please, the three of us are in our element. Finally, we can let our energies flow freely and it seems to have a striking impact not only on our mood and spirits, but also on the level of connection between us. So far, I don't know much yet about Lynn. She's an outdoor and hiking enthusiast, born in South Africa yet living in Canada. For a living, she is helping a company in the oil industry to navigate legal and regulatory matters. When she mentioned her job over dinner the other night, I was quite relieved to hear that I'm not to only one on the opposing end of the social benefit scale, compared to all the humanitarian and development-oriented professions that I'd met so far.

"So is your dad also a hiking enthusiast?" Lynn asks me. "He's probably quite proud of you for doing Kilimanjaro, hey?"

Interesting question. I've never even thought about it like that. Probably my desperate SMS attempt gave her that idea. "Not really. I think he's probably more worried than anything else right now. I'm the odd one out in my family when it comes to traveling and more extreme adventures. How about you?" I pass the question back to her. "Are your parents proud of you?"

"My parents already passed away a few years ago."

"Oh, I'm sorry to hear that. That must have been difficult." I can barely imagine the pain she must have been through. I always take it for granted that I still have my parents and assume everyone around my age would be the same, but of course that's not true and it takes such reminders to appreciate what we have.

"Yes. Hiking has helped me a lot to overcome the pain. My dad left me a small inheritance and I kept it to afford myself this hike for my 40th birthday this year. I think he would be really happy for me to see how I'm making good use of that money."

"Oh good. Do you have any siblings?"

"Yes, I've got a brother back in South Africa. I will visit him together with my husband right after Kilimanjaro. I am quite excited."

"Fantastic." I'm glad to hear that. It lifts the gloomy weight of our conversation. "Having a strong partner helps through difficult times, doesn't it?"

"Yes, certainly, he helped me a lot. How about you?"

"Still got a long way to go I guess. I was engaged already, but we broke it off a year ago, just wasn't right."

"Being able to talk with your partner openly about everything is really important," Chris joins the conversation. This then sets the three of us talking about relationships and what is important to make them work. It almost seems as if the free flow of our energies not only runs through our own bodies but also between us, as if it connects us at a deeper more personal and emotional level.

The clouds have dispersed sufficiently for us to enjoy direct sunshine again. No more need to walk just to keep us warm. The surrounding vegetation has become sparse. Only a few bushes have made it up here, leaving no more than boot-high pale scrub to cover the earthen and stony ground.

"Let's wait for the others," Estomee suggests. Our assistant guide has been following us quietly while we've kept talking non-stop.

To the side of the path, there's one of those odd rocks that pop up every few hundred meters out of nowhere, as if to prove the volcano's once mighty force, like the massive rock we saw yesterday in the middle of the Shira plateau. This one is just about big enough for the four of us to sit on.

"OK." We behave and follow Estomee's suggestion.

"Hey, let's take a photo." Chris unpacks his camera.

"I'll take one for you."

"No, stay. We'll do a group photo." He unpacks an extension arm and mounts his camera onto it.

"Oh, so you're going to set it on timer?"

"It's all here." He shows me the screen of his smartphone where I see myself from the camera's lens.

"Oh, that's pretty cool. So does it connect like via Bluetooth?"

"Sort of. It's a GoPro. It creates its own Wi-Fi network."

Not being very gadget-minded, I'm easily impressed about this simple yet smart connection feature. Why don't all cameras have that?

At the same time, I'm glad that he and others are taking a lot of pictures because I still can't get my camera to recharge. Even though I over-prepared for this trip, it didn't even cross my mind that I might need spare batteries despite my solar panels. Sharing equipment definitely is one of the benefits of hiking in a group.

▲ ▲ ▲

The sky is turning grey again and my body has cooled down from just sitting around. The remainder of our group is catching up with us. We can hear them already.

"I'm cold. Can we keep going?"

"Yes, let's go," Chris agrees.

Within sight of the others, Estomee doesn't object for us to hike ahead.

"I don't understand why they always make us walk in a group. Obviously some of us are faster than others," I speak my mind. "You know I was a bit extreme in my preparations and read all these books of other hikers who came here. They all just walked at their own pace, even the ones who hiked with Ultimate Kilimanjaro. I thought it would be like that for us as well."

"Yes, it became quite clear yesterday when we came up that steeper bit to Shira plateau that we're not all at the same level," Chris agrees. "Some were really struggling. I mean good on them, but still . . . they should just allow us to go ahead. That slow motion wears me out."

"Yes, I think they all did comparatively well, but I always feel like I need to break unnaturally. I can't do that for summit night. I will freeze to death if they make me walk like that," I vent my fears. "I always get that when skiing at higher altitudes – my fingers and toes just go dead and then it freaking hurts when they come back to life."

"Yes, for summit night we really need to split up into at least two groups. I can't do that either," Chris shares my concerns. "It would be a freaking nightmare if they make us walk like that all night."

"I just hope Robert will agree with that," I sigh.

"He'll have to," Chris reassures me. "Doesn't make sense otherwise."

"*Wewe ni nguvu kama simba,*" Estomee smiles at me.

Nunukaka what? "Sorry, I don't understand."

"I say you're strong like a lion."

"Haha, I like that. How do I say it?"

"*N-gu-vu ka-ma sim-ba* – strong like a lion."

"*Nguvu kama simba, nguvu kama simba, nguvu kama simba . . .*" I keep mumbling to myself in the hope of memorizing. "Oh, that's like *Simba* in Lion King," my mind connects the dots. "So it actually means lion?"

Estomee nods.

Ha, that's easy to remember!

Robert comes walking up behind us.

"Hey Robert, listen to that – *Gumu kaka simba!*" I shout out like a schoolgirl proud to show off her new learning with a broad grin.

He just stares at me perplexed as if to say: "What is she on about again?"

Estomee helps me correct what he has just taught me. I'm disappointed that I didn't get it right, but don't realize what I have just said instead. Only when back home, Google Translate will make me understand why Robert looked so disconcerted. Instead of exaggeratedly calling myself *strong like a lion*, I may just have accused him to be a *tricky brother*. Whoops!

▲ ▲ ▲

We stop our acclimatization hike just above 4,000 meters (13,100ft) altitude. This is the highest most of us have ever been, myself included. The so-called alpine desert zone starts around here, and indeed the landscape is bleak and barren. It's too high for any vegetation. We've left the scrub and odd bushes behind; only random rocks break the monotony of scree and earth.

In order for our acclimatization to become effective, we need to stay here for at least 15 minutes prior to descending back to our camp. I make yet another desperate attempt to hook onto one of the mobile networks popping up on my screen, to no avail. OK, what's next? My body has cooled down instantly without moving. A chilly wind makes the wait quite uncomfortable. The clouds are no longer breaking to give way to the sun, but have become thick and dark instead. Brrr, these 15 minutes feel like eternity.

"OK, we can go back down now," Robert finally brings my agony to an end.

On the way down, Stew happens to walk in front of me, and so we continue yesterday's conversation, or rather I bombard him with questions. On the one hand, I need a distraction from my painfully cold fingers; on the other hand, I'm curiously interested to hear more of his experience. "I was quite impressed to hear Juli's travel story. Have you two known each other for a long time?"

"Yes. We obviously both had our histories before that, but we've been married for over ten years now."

"That's a long time. How did you initially meet?"

"At one of my parties actually," Stewart tells me about the fabulous parties he used to host at his penthouse apartment. "Oh I tell you they were a lot of fun, bit wild." His voice turns cheerful in memory. "So for one of these parties, a mutual friend asked Juli to come along. She didn't want to go at first, really just got dragged along by her friend . . . and then we ended up talking the entire evening," and flash-bang-wow – sounds almost like love at first sight. I like to hear that, confirms my theory that there's no rush for me.

"Haha, so then no more wild parties for you."

"Oh, when we got married we continued to host parties together, different ones, more formal, like cocktail receptions, with hundreds of people."

Hundreds of people?! Not what I associate with a house party, admittedly. "You mean like charity parties?"

"Yes, we did quite a few of those. And at that time I was also involved in state politics, so we also did fundraising parties, quite a lot of parties actually."

"Sounds like you've been quite busy."

"Yes, we're doing less now, but over the past ten years, we would have more than 50 parties with around 200 guests a year."

"Really? That's like one every week!"

"Yes, on average we had at least one of those a week, sometimes two or three even."

"Fantastic! I couldn't do that, must be quite exhausting."

"Well, we both like hosting and entertaining people."

"You previously mentioned you also spent quite some time in Africa before, right? How come?"

"Oh yes, that's right. See, at the time when I was politically engaged and did all these fundraising events, I happened to become good friends with" the then president of the US! "At the time, he was looking for someone to lead the HIV combat initiative in Africa and asked me. I talked it over with Juli and we both agreed that would be a good thing to do, so we both moved to Africa for some time."

Wow! Now how often do you meet people with that level of energy and achievements? I'm impressed big time. Stewart and Juli are living very fulfilling and purpose-driven lives by the sounds of it all. Most of all, however, I'm impressed about how they have remained so very modest and down-to-earth along the way, roughing it up with us just like everyone else. What an inspiration! Who would have thought that one gets to meet people like Stewart and Juli while hiking off the beaten track to the top of Africa?

▲ ▲ ▲

While listening to Stew, I've almost managed to forget how cold I am and how frozen my fingers have become. Now I can't ignore it anymore. The stinging sensation in my fingers is taking over my capacity to focus and stay calm. It has converted into a burning feeling too painful to ignore. A few of us are already further down the slope, so I pick up my pace to follow them, rushing downhill as fast as my feet can carry me without losing stability. We arrive back at the camp around 6pm.

Hot water, that's all I can think of. Fortunately, the bucket is already waiting for us. Ouch, it feels like washing my hands in boiling water at first, but gradually my fingers are coming back to life. Phew, just in time before sunset! Within minutes, it's no longer my fingers but everything around me that feels freezing cold.

Dinner is expected for 6:30pm. This leaves just a bit of time for a *quick wash* as we call it up here in our newly-formed mountain lingo (but really *wet wiping* might have been a more appropriate term in my case at least), and to get everything ready for the night – grab the headlight, unpack the sleeping bag, put on a warmer jacket. I also find the small candle and brownie cake replacement for Jana's birthday, and the little voucher for a surprise manicure and pedicure treatment in Moshi that I had pre-booked for late afternoon on the day of our return. The brownie got squashed and might be no more than a mash underneath the packaging. What to do? Still better than nothing.

On my way to the dining tent, I'm so preoccupied with my little surprise plan that I barely notice the freezing cold wind. "Hey Crispin, could you do me a favor?" I pass my miserable birthday surprises to him. "Could you put this on a plate with the candle on top and then bring it in as a surprise after dinner?" He looks confused and reluctant. "Because it's Jana's birthday today."

"The wind . . . won't work."

"Like that?" I naively indicate a windshield with my cupped hand, as if this stood any chance against the raging air. "Just try, OK?"

"OK," he nods and walks off.

Brrr, only now I notice the stinging sensation from dust being smashed against my face by the brutal wind. Zip up, squeeze in, zip down. What a relief! It feels so s-n-u-g inside our mess tent, out of the cold wind and warmed up by everyone's body heat.

There is a plate of banana fritters on the table – hot and sweet, crunchy outside and soft inside. What a treat! I couldn't care less about my self-imposed diet right now.

Our veggie soup, this time pumpkin, is as delicious as ever and makes us all feel nice and warm again. Next up comes a big plate of pasta, veggie stew and minced beef in a red tomato vegetable sauce. It all tastes so yummy that I go for multiple helpings.

"There's still some left. Who wants that?" someone asks.

"I'm full."

"Me too."

"No, thanks," no one seems keen.

"Sure, I'll have that!" Tonight I'm definitely the biggest eater in our group, starting to develop a bit of a reputation: "Any leftovers? Give them to Alex!" My body has gone out of control, burning like crazy and shouting for more, but my pants feel looser than ever before. How is that even possible, and where is all that food disappearing to? Being used to a life of food constraints, I'm in awe about my own transformation. Whatever is wrong with me, I won't complain.

Robert and Evance join us in the mess tent. "How was dinner?" "How are you all?" They ask casually without moving away from the entrance, skillfully hiding our waiters behind them who I assume are lighting the candle. No one seems to realize. I hope the brownie doesn't look too embarrassing.

Our guides step aside, start to sing, and my jaw drops. The candle doesn't sit on top of a tiny squashed brownie, but atop a proper cake, happily presented by our chef Mr. Delicious. We haven't even seen him enter.

The cake is covered in chocolate coating and decorated with beautiful handwriting that reads *Congratulations* as well as both Juli's and Jana's names. It looks stunning, entirely unexpected. How is that even possible? How can they create such a piece of art at almost 4,000 meters (13,000ft) altitude, without an oven? That's beyond my imagination, blowing my mind.

While our guides, chef and waiters sing, with their wonderfully warm and passionate voices, Swahili words that sound like a local happy birthday song, we all clap the rhythm. The atmosphere is magical. Am I dreaming? In each and every one of our faces, I see a big grin and sparkling eyes, like kids in front of the Christmas tree. My eyes feel moist. I'm almost moved to tears. These people are terrific, giving not only Jana and Juli but all of us a very special moment, out of this world.

"Jana, Juli – when our chef Mr. Delicious heard it's your birthday today, he made this cake for you," Robert beams all over his face.

"So on behalf of the entire Ultimate Kilimanjaro team: Happy Birthday!"

"Hooray!"

Clap, clap.

"Wahoo!"

Whistle, whistle.

"Thank you!"

"Asante sana!"

"You guys are awesome!"

In the middle of nowhere surrounded by nothing but cold darkness, with only the barest necessities using their own skills, untiring energy and overwhelming kindness, they have created a very special birthday celebration that surely none of us will ever forget. And the cake not only looks beautiful, but also fully lives up to what our chef's name promises – simply delicious!

▲ ▲ ▲

Our health checks have become pure routine. Other than cold, which is no longer such a shock as it was yesterday, and fatigue, which seems normal after a day walking in fresh air, we are all still as good as we could be. Following Robert's briefing for tomorrow, most people are quick to head back to their tents. Having learnt my lesson yesterday, I stay back in the warmed up mess tent a bit longer in order to avoid the toilet queue in the cold wind.

"Is there still some hot water?" Robert looks for a spare cup.

"Yes sure, here you go," I help him pour some tea.

Robert sits down next to me. For the first time, I consciously take note of him as my peer, not just our guide. He's about my age, fairly tall and very good-looking, like a young Denzel Washington.

"So you said you've been to the summit over 100 times, right?"

"Yes, more than 160 times."

"Have you ever had altitude sickness yourself?"

"Me? No, never from the altitude. But I almost died before," he mentions.

Almost died!? "What happened?"

"Oh, it's a long time ago. I was only 20 years old, just started to work as a porter. It was only my second hike. We camped not far from here, at the Shira cave camp." He takes a sip of tea before he continues. "That night, it was raining heavily. I went to sleep as usual in my tent, but then I woke up in the middle of the night. I was freezing and my body was half numb. I realized that I was completely soaked and my tent was full of water." He pauses again.

"Oh no. That's horrible. What did you do then?"

"I dragged myself to the kitchen tent and spent the entire night next to the fireplace, but of course my clothes didn't dry and I was shivering all night." Robert hunches and crosses his arms to demonstrate.

"And I assume no one had any spare clothes, because carrying loads for the clients were too much already, right?"

"Yes, and it would have gotten wet in the tent anyway, like everything else . . . and all the porters needed whatever clothes they had brought for themselves."

Based on everything I had researched and heard so far, I'm not too surprised. I knew these things were and are still happening, but hearing this firsthand account from my own guide gives it an entirely new twist. It's becoming real and personal, no longer just rumors and statistics.

"So then what did you do? The guides didn't help you either?"

Robert sneers briefly, of course not. "By the next morning, I could barely stand. And when we set off for the hike, it started to snow."

"So then what?" I ask impatiently.

"They told me to get going and keep on moving in order not to freeze to death." And so Robert kept moving, with his wet clothes on the snowy mountain (!), as long as he still remembers.

They didn't send him back down? Now that's getting worse than I would ever have imagined. In shock, I stare at Robert with wide-open eyes, unable to comprehend the cruelty of our human race. No guide came to his help. "Keep going" were the only words of comfort seeping through to his half-conscious mind from his well-meaning porter colleagues. And that's what he did. Robert kept moving until at some point he lost consciousness and fell to the ground.

"Next thing I remember I woke up in dry clothes. Tourists had found me. They put their own clothes on me and had removed all my wet ones. They saved my life."

I swallow hard.

Robert completed the whole hike working as a porter (!) and miraculously hasn't suffered any long-term injuries.

"You mean you were fine again just like that?" That sounds too good to be true.

"I was quite sick and stayed home for a long time after we came back. It took me six months until I could move my fingers again."

"Oh no, sounds terrible! And then you came back to work as a porter?"

"Well, my mama didn't want me to. She asked me to stay and do something else."

"I can imagine!"

"But I wanted to become a guide, so I came back. I was fine afterwards, no more problem since then."

"So that was with that big operator, when you almost died?"

Robert nods.

It's the same big local tourism company that I almost ended up booking with myself! Thankfully, I went the extra mile to research the situation more thoroughly and found that they are amongst the worst in terms of porter treatment. It's so easy to get misled by all the manipulatively incorrect information online. Please, to all the sane and humane people on this planet – consult with KPAP and be well informed before booking your climb!

It's terrifying to hear such a firsthand account of porter mistreatment, and I'm feeling sorry for what happened to Robert. At the same time, it's like a bad story with happy ending, and I'm happy for Robert that he's made it so far, that he's now working as chief guide with a good operator. He seems to be truly enjoying his current role, showing a lot of good humor, endless patience and kind care for us tourists.

▲ ▲ ▲

Tonight it's already 9:30pm by the time I crawl back into my dark, cold tent. Last night's memory of feet like ice make me prepare better this time round. Two pairs of thick socks plus my merino leggings – that should do the trick. Should I remove my bra tonight? Trading temporary misery for more sleeping comfort and peace of mind, I clench my teeth and force my upper body into the freezing cold. Brrr, we girls really have to work a lot harder for that summit!

Once ready for the night, I type down my notes of the day as quickly as possible. If my thumbs just move quickly enough, I can stay in my warm sleeping bag and fall straight asleep . . . but no, my theory doesn't work. Journal completed within less than an hour and eyes ready to close, but my bladder is wide awake.

Oh well, after two nights of survival training nothing scares me anymore. To the contrary, I'm even optimizing my nightly pee run to the extreme. Just in my underwear leggings, I slip directly into my boots without bothering with the laces. Even though the toilet tent is really not that far away, I don't even consider going there any longer at that time. I've already figured out that I'm the only one up that late, and the whole procedure just seems too complicated. Instead, I just walk a few steps away from our tents and shamelessly moonlight under the ever-brighter moon, on daringly open terrain without rocks or bushes to hide behind. If anyone came outside against all odds, they would see me clearly and distinctly at my most private of all times. The risk is low, but even if – would I still care? Shame loses its shackles when there are more pressing needs to be met, such as minimizing my time in the freezing wind and cuddling back into my warm sleeping bag. Had someone told me two days ago that I would end up like that, I would have doubted their sanity. Civilized people don't do that, right? Hehe, proud to be wild!

DAY 4

Feeling so alive, yet alone

23 SEPTEMBER 2015

From Shira 2 (3,800m/12,500ft)
via Lava Tower (4,600m /15,200ft)
Distance — elevation — time:
7km/4mi⇨ — 800m/2,700ft⇧ — 3-4 hours☉

to Moir Hut (4,200m/13,800ft)
Distance — elevation — time:
7km/4mi⇨ — 400m/1,400ft⇩ — 2-3 hours☉

I wake up. It's still dark, must be in the middle of the night. Mother nature is calling me again. No, please not. I can't be bothered to get up and try to fall back asleep.

Tough luck, that's not working. I check the time. It's 5:30am. Oh, that's not bad! I finally managed to get a fair amount of sleep this night. Simple things in life can make one quite happy up here!

Soon it will start getting busy outside. I'd better answer my call before everyone else wakes up. Summoning up my energy, I crawl out of my sleeping bag and get mentally ready for the freezing cold outside.

Um, it actually doesn't feel too bad, almost pleasant. That's surprising, shouldn't it logically get colder overnight? Perhaps it's due to the calm air, perhaps because my body has stored sufficient warmth from inside. Whatever it is, the difference to last night is striking.

Back within my sleeping bag, I turn off my headlight, but my tent doesn't go dark. I can still clearly make out everything. How is that possible? No, the sun isn't up yet. That can only be the moon. Obviously I've noticed by now that the moon is quite bright up here

– it's stealing my privacy – but even within my tent? I'm in awe about nature again. So many new experiences these past few days – was I even alive before?

I close my eyes. From one moment to the next, my tent is filled with bright, warm daylight. I must have dozed off again. It's 6:15am, and I lazily snooze until our official wake-up time at 6:30am. What a welcome change to my first night when I couldn't wait for the day to start, or rather for the night to end.

As I'm starting my morning routine, it feels much colder again than just a few minutes ago. A fierce wind is howling outside, beating against the outer layer of my tent. The sun is no longer warming my tent; clouds must have come in between us. What a moody mountain, constantly changing between calm and windy, between sunny and cloudy, between warm (or rather cold but OK) and freezing beyond bearable!

I finish everything within the shelter of my tent, including wrapping up my sleeping bag and lifting my gear outside, before finally venturing outside myself. My fingers turn icy cold within seconds while tying my bootlaces, and move beyond cold to painfully burning while brushing my teeth in the freezing wind. Only the anticipation of soon zipping myself into our cozy mess tent and warming my fingers around a hot cup of coffee keeps me sufficiently motivated not to sacrifice my dental hygiene.

As usual, we are supposed to meet for breakfast by 7:20am. Today I manage to be done just after 7:10am. Practice makes perfect. I'm slowly getting the hang of the most efficient camping routine, and the wind makes sure I don't waste any time outside.

We are being spoilt for breakfast today – delicious egg frittatas with vegetables and even more delicious crunchy bacon, as well as a big plate of fresh pineapple slices.

There also is a large pot of chocolate millet porridge. "Does anyone want that?"

"No, thanks," shaking heads. Who would want such a bland taste and texture?

"Oh, I'll have some," Jeannette goes for it.

"Me too," Lynn joins the party, "reminds me of when I was a kid."

"Yes, me too, haha. We also used to have that," Chris shares their childhood breakfast memories. Our three South African hikers who have all moved to different corners of this world have found a common denominator.

Our guides join us as usual with our health check forms and the by now very familiar two little finger pulse oximeters. These tiny gadgets, that until only a few days ago I knew are totally unreliable, have found a way to manipulate my brain. I've granted them superstitious powers, and every time I clip them onto my finger I act casual but really I can't wait to see the result. Last night, my reading barely reached 90%, far lower than all the Diamox takers. That, of course, didn't go unnoticed by my little Diamox rebel. This morning it's back at 92%. Hooray, it seems to have stabilized.

"How did you sleep tonight?" Usually they only go through all these questions at night, but Evance remembers our conversations and asks me more like a good friend.

"Great, 100%!" I reply cheerfully.

"That's good." He genuinely seems to care.

Meanwhile, Chris has clipped the oximeter onto his finger. He sits next to me, and I keep a curious eye onto his reading. "Oh wow," it's already above 92% and still going up. "Are you on Diamox now?"

"No, I will only take it if I need it, but so far I'm still good."

"You guys are having a little competition or what?" Farrah jokes.

"No, I'm just really curious, scientifically speaking—"

"Yeah right," no one believes a word I just said. "I'm starting to get that tingling in my fingers. Does anyone else have that?"

"Yes, me too," others nod.

"I've got it in my toes," someone adds.

"That's normal. It's one of the most common side effects of Diamox," Ravi clarifies.

"Isn't that really annoying?" I dare ask. "It freaks me out whenever my hands or feet *fall asleep*."

"Yeah, like *pins and needles*," Lynn helps me again find the right English words.

"No, it's not a big deal," Ravi refutes my dare.

The screen on Chris's finger settles at 96. "That's impressive. How are you doing that?"

"Don't know," Chris grins.

I'm relieved that he doubles my statistical insignificance in refuting the Diamox nonsense (as I refer to it in my own mind, no offences please) to two against the rest of the world. Secretly, I still hope to prove my theory that there is no need to take Diamox for this hike, that we are even better off without it, without that tingling in our fingers and the constant urge to pee even in the middle of the night, robbing us off deep sleep for a whole week prior to summit night. So far, I haven't found any accomplices in my theory. To make matters worse, Giovanni's oximeter reading comes in at only 80%.

"No, I'm not taking Diamox yet," I overhear him say. Perhaps the device was just playing funny again, but it doesn't really help my theory, does it? While I'm silently shocked, he doesn't seem the slightest bit concerned. To the contrary, he seems to be doing just as fine as everyone else. That's way more important anyway, if these tiny gadgets just wouldn't mess with my brain. I can't ignore the fact that all the Diamox takers managed to keep their blood oxygen readings at 95% or higher.

▲ ▲ ▲

By the time we finish breakfast, the clouds have cleared and the air has calmed. That makes such a tremendous difference, like night and day. It feels nice and warm again, and the direct sunrays are refilling my energy levels close to the brim. What a lovely day!

While as usual some people need more time to get ready, the remainder of us have formed a circle and keep busy with morning stretches. Juli is the ever-smiling yoga girl (I really want to learn her secret!), and Giovanni also shares a couple of good stretches.

Instead of 8am as planned, we only start our hike at 8:40am. Seems these morning timelines simply don't work for our group, nor is there any reason to rush. With the sun keeping me warm and the time well spent in between, even my impatient rebel would agree with that.

Today we have a rather long and demanding seven-hour hike ahead of us. Our goal is to hike all the way up to Lava Tower at an elevation of over 4,600 meters (15,200ft), prior to descending to Moir Hut camp at about 4,200 meters (13,600ft) for the night. Moir Hut is not too far away from our current Shira 2 Camp, and a big part of our hike up to and down from Lava Tower will be on exactly the same path. The point of going up to Lava Tower is not to cover distance, but for acclimatization. However, there's the option to stop earlier and take the direct shortcut to Moir Hut, if we find it too exhausting. For people taking Diamox, it may not be that essential to reach Lava Tower; but I'm fixated and won't miss a chance to acclimatize naturally. "No matter what – you'll go up there," I've set my mind as soon as Robert briefed us about our options.

Together with Chris and Giovanni, we start walking our pace and gaining distance to the remainder of the group without even noticing.

"Alexy, Chris, Giovan!" I hear Robert's voice from behind. He likes calling me Alexy. His bemused smile when I initially introduced myself as Alex confirmed what he was too polite to say: "Alex is a guy's name."

"I call you Alexy, OK?" he offered politely, hoping to avoid any further embarrassments.

"OK," I liked the new twist to my identity.

Similarly, Lynn has become Lynny, and Giovanni has become Giovan. Perhaps the ending "-y" has a female connotation in Swahili? But then again Ravi was allowed to keep his name, like everyone else.

We pause, waiting for Evance in the lead and our group following him in single file. Robert and the other guides walk in parallel to the side of the path, keeping an eye out on everyone.

"Let's all walk together. Evance is our lead guide again today. Don't walk ahead of Evance," Robert reminds his unruly clients.

I feel like a rebellious student. In theory, I know that *pole pole* is the secret to stay clear of altitude sickness; but in practice, my body rebels against our artificially slow pace. It feels like the nightmares I used to have as a child, when I wanted to run away from an unknown persecutor but wouldn't move from the spot. My body wants to assure me that I am alive, that I can walk as fast as my mind pleases. I need Robert's constant reminder to slow me down, like a curious child that keeps reaching for the forbidden danger to test her limits. I follow suit, mostly, walking next to Evance, outside of the path. Walking on the path in a single line is boring. Balancing my way on uneven terrain over short scrub and rocks feels like a miniature obstacle course and keeps me entertained.

"I miss your story," this time Evance starts the conversation. He's gotten used to my constant chatter on the first two days when I was walking near him all the time.

I take this opportunity to ask Evance about Jana's birthday cake magic. "Tell me the secret, Evance. How could Mr. Delicious bake the cake yesterday without an oven? Did he make it already before we started hiking?"

"No, he did it yesterday. Just like that."

"Like how exactly?"

"Just put everything into a pan, on the stove, put aluminum foil on it and let it sit."

"That's it? So easy?"

"Yes," Evance nods.

"How does he know how to do all that?"

"We have special training courses for cooks, if they want to work on the mountain. There they learn how to do that," how to create fantastic meals with simple inputs and only the most basic cooking utensils. I'm sure Mr. Delicious was a great student, but what he presented to us yesterday surely went beyond that. Surly he must have used his own ingenuity to bring this art to perfection.

"Hey Evance, what are these bushes? Do they have a name?" I point with my boot at the greenish, white and yellow plants scattered here and there.

"Oh these? They are everlasting plants."

"That's easy to remember!" Everlasting plants – how fitting! I don't need scientific terms; his answer fully satisfies my botanic curiosity.

▲ ▲ ▲

Giovanni walks quietly. He never says much when our group converses in English all the time.

"Giovanni, cómo estás?" It's time for me to challenge my brain again with a little bit of Spanish practice.

He seems pleased with my attempt of conversation and politely ignores my rusty confusion of words and grammar. We exchange bits and pieces of our travel experience – a complementary match between my Asian and his Latin America stories. Giovanni loves Latin America and knows the entire continent inside out. He did a lot of cool things there like snowboarding (or rather sandboarding) in the world's highest dunes in Argentina and hiking up Machu Picchu. Machu Picchu has long been on my list, but I wasn't aware that I could also hike up there. I mentally rewrite my bucket list.

Next time I look up, I notice that Chris has re-hooked his solar panels to the front of his body, attached to the straps of his backpack. With his shorts, knee-high socks and these rigid black squares the size of a big opened book dangling down from his chest all the way to this belt, glistening silver in the sun, he looks like a geek in search of extraterrestrial being.

"That's smart," I'm thinking to myself. I'm impressed about his clever technique, and perhaps even more so about his self-confidence. He couldn't care less about the way he looks, only functionality counts. I've mounted my panels onto my backpack as usual, but we are walking towards the sun. My dead phone hasn't recharged – obviously, it's not getting any sun back there. Now I know how to fix that.

During our next break I copy Chris, never mind sporting an equally or perhaps even more ridiculous look myself. If he doesn't care, why should I? Our panels (we happen to have bought identical ones) conveniently come with hooks. Within seconds, I've fixed them to the front straps of my backpack. That was easy. Now they are also dangling down my chest. To describe my complete appearance: I changed my trousers to my pink ones this morning. They are the fluorescent kind of pink, like a highlighter pen. By coincidence I also put on my purple sweater. Without a mirror to remind me, I only became conscious about my color combination during breakfast, when people politely remarked about my *fashionable* outfit, and we all know what that means on the mountain: Get real, girl! So in my candy-colored outfit and with my solar panels all over my front, I could easily break the record for the weirdest-looking hiker ever. Together with Chris, we are geek central life on Kilimanjaro. Ah, brilliant, we've got a good laugh about ourselves – having fun can be that easy!

We keep hiking, but my body forces me to stop a few times with total loss of muscle control. I can't stop laughing imagining myself walking like this through downtown Zurich. Picture that: Pink pants, purple sweater, solar panels all over the front, ankle-high boots, space lens sunglasses made for the top of Everest, a safari sunhat like back in colonial times, the hose of my water bladder dangling in front of my mouth and armed with high-tech carbon trekking poles that would make airport security go wild. What a curiosity! Or would they just arrest me straight away?

I definitely wouldn't want anyone back home to see me like that, but out here in the middle of nowhere I couldn't care less; or perhaps I just feel as if I'm amongst kindred spirits and don't need to hide behind a respectable appearance.

▲ ▲ ▲

After about an hour or two, the sun hides behind clouds. It immediately feels colder and most of us put on a soft-shell jacket to feel comfortable again. We can also start to feel the increase in altitude with our breathing. I notice a slight pressure on my front, just like that afternoon at Shira 1 camp. It's not painful (yet), but enough to make me shut up in order to focus on my breathing, and to slow down in order not to make it worse. Chris is the only one who still rushes up the slope ahead of everyone else. He doesn't seem to feel anything and only makes stops every now and then to wait for us. By now, Robert has given up constantly calling him back to slow down.

We break at noon after reaching the top of a rather steep ascent. Everywhere we look, there's just sand and scree. Even the persistent scrub can no longer survive up here. In the far distance on top of yet another ridge where our path and the barren landscape seem to fall off into the grey nothingness of clouds, Lava Tower rises up like an oversized dark rock that only supernatural forces can possibly have created – the once mighty volcano. It reminds me of the typical dark fortress at the end of a long desolate path in evil fairytale lands like Mordor. Tiny black dots of crows are busily circling the sky, like vigilant birds of prey spying for the dark forces in the castle.

On a distant ridge almost parallel to our path, we can make out hikers on the Machame route, one of the most popular routes. It joins the Lemosho route near Lava Tower. We're following the Lemosho route for the first part of our hike, but while both Lemosho and Machame will continue eastwards along the southern slopes of Kilimanjaro, we'll head back westwards to make our way around Kibo cone on its rarely-visited northern slopes.

We all unpack our snacks that we brought to tide us over until late lunch when we reach our camp. As I am about to dig into my nuts, I notice our guides silently watching us eat without any food or water for themselves. This is not a sight I can bear. "Would you like some?" I offer one by one and each of them happily holds out their hands. No need to ask twice.

"Thank you, that's enough," they all quickly make sure I don't pour too much.

Farrah also makes the round with her pack of seeds, and our guides accept our little treats more than willingly. Of course they are as hungry as we clients are, but their only mission is to make us happy. Sharing with them feels like win-win. It makes us happy to give something back to them, and I'm starting to realize that I can't possibly eat my three kilos of snacks all on my own. I overdid it again, but this time I'm glad about my miscalculations because now I have plenty to share.

▲ ▲ ▲

"*Twende!*" That means let's go. We know that already. Evance uses it all the time. He knows we like to use simple phrases in Swahili. It makes us feel as if we spoke their language, even though ten words barely qualify for even the most basic.

We continue our hike. The higher we go, the more our fitness level and age lose their relevance. Juli, Jeannette and Stewart do not seem any more challenged than the younger ones in our group, including myself. We're all moving at the same speed, limited by the same amount of air we can breathe and the same need to acclimatize slowly.

I'm glad that Robert and Evance kept slowing us down. By now, I have no more urge to go any faster than that. *Pole pole* – that's all that seems to matter. Is it really? "Hey Stew," I want to find out, "how did you prepare for this trip? I mean, you're doing so well, did you do any special training?"

"Oh yes! Been training over the past nine months."

"Like other walks and hikes?"

"Yes, a fair bit of those, and also in the gym every day."

So here we go, *pole pole* matters now, but it's really the invisible discipline and groundwork that makes it all look so comparatively easy on the surface. Stewart seems to me like the perfect proof that everything is possible if you really want it.

▲ ▲ ▲

At our next break, Jana decides to stop the acclimatization hike to Lava Tower and head to our camp early.

"Are you OK?"

"Yes, I'm fine, just really tired. I think it's better for me to take a nap and save my energy."

"Yes. That's probably right. Have a good rest." I really hope she recovers for tomorrow and feels better soon.

Baraka stays with her, while the rest of us continue upwards, fighting the loss of energy and headaches that are starting to creep in with some of us. I got lucky and am feeling surprisingly good, relieved that the pressure I started to feel earlier has disappeared again. Walking slowly, taking deep breaths and drinking lots of water – all of that definitely helps a lot.

"I've got this crazy headache," Chris confides in me.

"Really?" He, who has been running ahead like a mountain goat and stunning me with his super-human oxygen readings? "I thought you were fine, because you kept walking ahead. I couldn't keep up your pace, ran out of breath long time earlier," I stutter in between gasping for air. "Why didn't you slow down?" I must sound like his mum.

"I was fine, but now it feels like my head is ready to explode."

"Well, just slow down and stay with us."

"Yes, I will now," but at the same time he's already a few steps ahead of me again, as if he does not yet want to accept any physical confines.

We cannot see the thin air, only feel it when we've gone too far too quickly. If not for Robert and Evance's constant reminder to slow down, I would have run straight into my own trouble.

There are a handful of other hikers ahead of us. So far, we have only had porters overtake us during the past three days, but never came across other tourists while hiking. Seeing them provides a welcome distraction in this desolate landscape. I see Chris, true to his open and friendly self, excitedly catching up with them and trying to strike up a conversation with two girls. The remainder of our group also follows suit, exchanging friendly hellos and *Jambos* in passing. Everyone in such a remote place is excited to see other human faces.

"I think they were Japanese," Chris tells me after we've overtaken them.

"Yes, I heard them speak Japanese. I saw you talk to them."

"Yes, haha, I tried but they didn't say much."

"Maybe they just didn't understand your mumbling." That's my non-native speaker excuse for sometimes struggling to understand Chris with his South African accent.

"Yeah, their English wasn't that good," or perhaps they simply had to prioritize the usage of their lung capacity.

"You know, gasp, I find myself running out of breath, gasp, walking and talking, gasp. How do you do that?"

He just shrugs. "But my head is killing me," and finally he accepts our speed limit.

During the last hour up to Lava Tower, we hardly talk to each other but focus on our breathing instead. Diego develops nausea and needs another break. Skoba stays back with him while the remaining ten of us keep pushing on; still following Evance's slow and steady pace, accompanied by Robert, Estomee and Samwel.

By 2pm, we find ourselves in front of the big dark rock – we've reached Lava Tower.

"So that's it? We're not going up there?" I ask Evance.

"You want to climb up there? Perhaps you'll need to come back another time."

"Oh, haha, I thought there was a path up there, maybe." Naivety knows no limits, especially not in thin air.

The rock rises some 100 meters straight up into the sky. Imagine standing on that square in front of Notre Dame in Paris and looking straight up to its Western façade on a foggy November morning. That's exactly what it reminds me of, like a medieval European village square dominated by its imposing church that speaks of super-human forces; just that we have a scientific explanation for its creation: volcanic plug.[46] This means hundreds of thousands of years ago lava shot out from a vent underneath the rock's base, but then cooled, hardened and eventually closed the plug. In layman terms, I'm picturing a water fountain that freezes to solid ice in mid-air.

On active volcanoes, such plugs might lead to explosive eruptions when the magma pressure underneath becomes too big.[47] Again, to help me internalize what that means, I'm picturing the cork on a champagne bottle exploding with delicate liquid after shaking just a little too much. Good that this thing is dormant!

At over 4,600 meters (15,200ft), this will be our highest elevation for the coming three days, until we reach base camp. We'll stay up here for about 30 minutes to acclimatize, and then head back down. That's it? Wasn't too difficult after all! I turn around to celebrate our mutual achievement, but most have already sat down. "Um, shall we do a group photo?"

No one reacts.

"Perhaps we'll do it at the end, when we need to get up again anyway," Juli suggests.

Only now I realize the blend of exhaustion and suffering from headaches or nausea written over most people's faces, eyes closed or staring into the void. OK, I get it. It was a very strenuous hike after all, and people are feeling the thin air as expected. I'd better leave them alone. Um, so why do I not feel it?

To the contrary, I feel more alive than ever before, so alive that I can't possibly get myself to sit down and rest. It feels as though my energy wants to keep flowing and celebrating. My little *high* takes me by surprise. Why is my inner engine not striking in protest against our long walk, against the lack of oxygen?

Most likely I just got lucky that my body is predisposed to thin air, but the rush of endorphins is currently blocking that thought from my complacent brain. Instead, I like to believe that I'm fully in control of my own fate, and so of course my brain uses this opportunity to pat myself on the shoulder. Well-done! I never used to be particularly athletic or crazy about sports in my past 30 years, just about average. What a tremendous change! Surely that's all because of my healthy lifestyle, because of my new diet and my exercise regime. Well deserved! I knew I did the right thing, but didn't expect the impact to be so profound. Triumph and euphoria! Please can I never wake up from this wonderful dream?

It almost seems too good to be true, and indeed my highly exaggerated opinion of myself shows that I'm suffering from AMS just as much as everyone else, only in a different way – altitude euphoria. That's my self-diagnosis in hindsight, because I experienced a similar euphoria when I reached the top of Mount Kinabalu on Borneo five years ago. What a tremendous amount of luck! Not only do I seem to be genetically predisposed to handle altitude abnormally well, I even get an entirely legal *high* out of it.

There's only one big problem: No one else in our group *suffers* my symptoms. I long to share the way I feel, to call it out loud, to hug and celebrate, but I can't. Would you rather be connected in exhaustion, or alone in euphoria?

▲ ▲ ▲

I crawl up behind some rocks to alleviate the consequences of my overzealous water consumption. Yuck, shriveled toilet paper everywhere. Nothing rots up here any longer; the thin air preserves it forever. So far we were lucky and spared such sights that other reviews had already warned me about, but at Lava Tower we've come to the crossroads with the busy Machame Route.

Really, people? Can't you be more considerate and not leave your shit behind? That's exactly why I'm using wet wipes that I store in my own little garbage plastic bag until I can dump them into our communal waste bag at our next camp. Can we all do that please, or have a more open dialogue to come up with the best solution?

While I'm navigating my way towards a safe spot, I notice crows all over the place, constantly picking something off the ground and observing every moving object. What are they doing up here, where there's nothing to eat? Are they feasting off our human leftovers?

If crows could speak, I'm sure they would say: "What are you doing here, pink lady? Have you brought us something to eat?"

I walk around to explore our surroundings, but there's not much to see. Diego and Skoba have meanwhile disappeared from our view. They must be on their way to our next camp already. Behind Lava

Tower, there's nothing but grey clouds. Other than us, there is another group up here having their tented lunch directly in front of Lava Tower, spoiling my pristine photo-shooting attempt.

Evance keeps walking around, just like me. "Remember the accident that I told you about, when the American hikers were killed by rockfall just a week ago? It was just there." He nods towards the northern side of Lava Tower.

"Oh, so the Western Breach is just there?"

"Yes, just there, behind that bend."

I follow his gaze down another stony slope that soon disappears behind a rocky outcrop. That section is known to be dangerous because the melting glaciers are releasing rocks unpredictably, which then fall right down onto unsuspecting hikers on that infamous Western Breach route. There had been no lethal accidents since 2006. Thus it would have been tempting to take the risk nevertheless, thinking that "it won't happen to me" because the odds are so low. Or perhaps some people like this extra thrill of real danger. Or perhaps they don't spend enough time looking into it and are simply not aware of the risks. Either way, after hearing this devastating news, I'm really glad I've decided against the Western Breach route to Crater Camp that I was so tempted by myself.

As I still feel itching to move, I keep busy stretching my legs with yoga moves. People probably think that I'm a bit crazy. Just as I can't relate to their exhaustion, they surely can't relate to my euphoria.

All of a sudden someone grabs my waist, lifts me up into the air and spins a few circles. It's Chris. The earth is spinning under my eyes. I shout and giggle as my baby niece does when I play airplane with her. When my feet touch the ground again, I can barely stand straight. "Ok, now I'm also dizzy, haha. Don't do that again, I'm too heavy for you," but Chris doesn't reply and just moves on to some other distraction. I guess like me he simply has too much energy left and needs yet another challenge. How good to know I'm not the only crazy one!

After thirty minutes of just hanging around, it's getting cold. Yes, me and my cold again. My body isn't good at keeping warm, despite all the food that I keep stuffing into myself.

"Ok everyone, get ready to go," Robert and Evance break the inertia.

Hurrah! I can't wait to get going, but not everyone seems pleased about getting back up again.

"Can we do a group photo now? Please!"

"Yes, come here everyone," Chris is getting as excited as I am, and slowly our group is coming back to life. Simply moving our bodies and standing together closely seems to be doing wonders, bringing back the energy. We don't just take one boring photo. No, it needs to be something different. "Everyone raise your left leg," Chris shouts and we all follow suit, giggling at our own foolishness. Oh I love this bunch. Who would have thought that simple life can be that much fun, especially when high on endorphins!

Our group at Lava Tower

▲ ▲ ▲

The walk down is of course far easier; and even though mostly cloudy, it feels a lot warmer as soon as we've left that top elevation where the wind blew in from all sides. Within few minutes, we pass again the same hikers that we overtook earlier and some new faces still making their way up to Lava Tower.

"Well done!"

"You're almost there!"

"It's not far!"

We encourage them, over-excited by our own achievement. Would they really want to hear that, to be reminded that we are already on our way back down while they still seem to be fighting for every single step? I don't know, but one thing for sure: Now it's no longer just me, but we are all in high spirits and got some good laughs along the way. Perhaps we are all a bit light-heated from the thin air, perhaps ecstatic about what we've just accomplished, perhaps simply enjoying the liberated feeling of no worries and being totally at ease and peace with our surroundings, or perhaps it's a combination of all of those.

I won't even remember what we laugh about – other than yet another fit of laughter about my ridiculous outfit, which shall be imprinted in my memory forever – but I will remember having the giggles almost non-stop. In fact, I've rarely laughed as much over multiple consecutive days as these last four days on our hike. It almost feels as though I've found my tribe here on this trip. Going through this adventure together as a group is starting to form a strong bond between us all. No wonder team building exercises based on adventure outdoor activities are so effective!

Nevertheless, it's been a long day and we are excited when we finally spot Muir Hut camp in the distance, at the bottom of our stony path. The camp sits like a tiny Lego village at the base of an endless grey wall of sand that stretches all along the camp's northern perimeter from the east to the west, as wide as our eyes can see. Supposedly we'll have to conquer that wall tomorrow, if we want to escape to the northern unchartered terrain of Kilimanjaro, off the beaten track.

▲ ▲ ▲

By the time we reach the camp after 3:30pm, lunch is already waiting for us. Robert joins us in our mess tent, grabs the ladle and helps us serve our meals. That's a first. Why is he doing that? I feel bad about him serving us. "Don't worry, Robert, we can take care of ourselves."

"You all had a tough hike," he replies cheerfully, "you deserve to have a good rest."

"But you had an even harder day with all of us! Have some food yourself. We've got more than enough."

"Yes, sit down with us," others encourage.

"I have already eaten in the kitchen."

"Really? We only just got back."

"Yes, I ate quickly."

"OK. But really, no need to serve us, take a rest."

"OK, then I'll leave you all to it," and he leaves. In hindsight, I wonder whether he simply enjoyed hanging out with us.

"What a great guy!" we all agree after he's gone.

"Always so helpful and cheerful," I admire his character.

"Yes, isn't he?" Lynn confirms.

"And good fun, great humor!" Juli adds.

"Yah!" Jeannette nods.

"And very handsome and charismatic – a true leader," Chris summarizes.

Presumably Ultimate Kilimanjaro sends some of its best people on this relatively more challenging Northern Circuit hike, and indeed I couldn't imagine any better guides than Robert and Evance.

Just like our connections with our guides, also our lunch seems to be getting even better by the day, or perhaps I'm just getting hungrier. Aside from the usual veggie soup, there is a pot of lovely steamed chicken in a red vegetable sauce. We also get a somewhat less exciting pasta/veggie mix, as well as fresh orange slices for desert. The meat eaters in our group are always spoilt for choice, while the vegetarians – half the girls, that is – have to make do with what comes on the table. The chicken is so soft it melts in my mouth and makes me wish for more, and more, and more. I am about to reach for my umpteenth helping.

"Ravi isn't here yet, perhaps we should also leave some for him," Eva and Farrah considerately watch out for him.

"Oh yes, sure," I feel guilty like a naughty girl. It has already become a running joke (or truth) in our group that I'm eating much more than the others: Any leftovers? Alex will finish it up, but now I've gone too far without realizing.

Ravi finally joins us in the tent and only takes one piece of chicken. "I'm not that hungry," he comments.

"Really, you're not going to have the remainder?"

"No, go for it."

Strike! My voracious belly and my guilty mind have been waiting for him to say that. It's my lucky afternoon.

"How can you eat so much?" Farrah asks.

"You must have a naturally high metabolic rate," Jeannette suggests.

"Yes, like a natural bundle of energy," Juli believes.

"No, not at all." I know people like that, and I've always envied them. It feels strange and revealing to be viewed like that myself all of a sudden. The high in my energy levels that I'm feeling on this hike is still new to me. It's so different from my own self-perception, from the way I felt and lived for most of my life, and from how most people I know would describe me. "I've actually struggled with my weight all my life. Only about a year ago I changed my diet. I think it's all because of that."

"Tell us your secret. What exactly do you do?"

"Well, it's quite simple actually. Avoid pure carbs and sugars, but eat as much protein and fat as you like. Protein is so important for our muscles, especially when doing sports. I think that really makes a big difference. Don't understand why people go for all the pasta instead of the chicken."

"Yes, like Paleo style," Chris knows what I'm talking about. He's the only one in our group who shares a very similar philosophy about what we consider to be healthy.

"But that would be hard for us vegetarians. Couldn't eat anything then," Farrah is right. Low-carb and vegetarianism don't go well with each other. Neither would our planet be able to cope with everyone eating as much meat as I do, but in awe of my own *transformation* I couldn't care less.

Had I done this hike one year earlier, I may have struggled hard with today's hike. On top of that, without months of preparation and rewiring my mindset, I would have been totally freaked out by now with the lack of amenities – no running water, no heating, no fresh daily change of clothes. Exchanging this for constant dirt in my fingernails, greasy hair and cold feet doesn't sound like a good deal. But instead, to my total surprise, I'm starting to enjoy this new freedom and liberating feeling associated with our simple lifestyle. Who would have thought that letting go of it all can be that much fun! Evidencing this tremendous change in myself today is blowing me away and refueling my perpetual endorphin production, leaving me in a constant feeling of *high*.

▲ ▲ ▲

After lunch, the clouds have parted and the sun is re-energizing our campsite with its blissful warmth. It makes such a difference, like summer or winter. I use this opportunity to mount my solar panels onto my tent for a full recharge of my phone. It reaches almost 100% within two hours. I still can't believe how well these panels work and get excited every time they prove their worth. Nature and basic lifestyle is great, but the power of technology to make our lives easier equally has its charms.

More importantly, however, we all use this sunny window for a thorough cleaning session. Yesterday was too cold to bother beyond basics. Today it's toasty warm in our tents. I strip off all my clothes and take my time, enjoying not being cold or in a rush for a change. My fingernails, however, are beyond repair; dirt is stuck everywhere. Some people have brought a nailbrush, which might have been a good idea; but it's also a never-ending fight, so perhaps not such a big omission after all.

Once I otherwise feel nice and clean again, the afternoon sun leaves me another cozy hour to recall the events of the day and make good use of my recharged phone to write it all down. It's quiet outside. Others are probably reading or taking a nap. How nice it would be to just close my eyes! The memory of my restless first two nights still lingers and helps me resist the temptation.

All of a sudden I shiver. My toasty warm and bright tent has become dark and freezing cold. When the sun goes down around 6:30pm, it does so without warning, brutally, from one minute to the next, and takes all its warmth with it. We are near the equator. The concept of dusk doesn't belong here. At our elevation of more than 4,000 meters (13,000ft), Arctic nighttime temperatures have converted my tent from sauna to icebox before I even realized that it had gotten dark. Even after putting on my warm layers, I can't bear to stay inert in my tent any longer and make my way to the mess tent ahead of dinnertime in the hope of a hot drink to warm me up.

A fierce wind hits me outside. I find Eva standing outside the mess tent in just a hoodie, no jacket. "Are you not cold? Why are you not going in?"

"It's a bit cold," she admits.

This sounds like a humongous understatement of our Arctic temperatures to me. I hear our guides talking inside. Between lunch and dinnertime, it's their chance for a bit of a break and fun, playing cards or drinking tea.

"Didn't want to interrupt them," Eva explains.

The cold wind has blown away my concept of politeness, and we quickly zip our way into the tent. Our guides look up in surprise at our early appearance and get ready to move.

"No, no, don't worry," we tell them and settle into seats at the other corner of the table, with raised shoulders and ducked heads.

Eva is sitting quietly with her hands in the front pocket of her hoodie, waiting patiently. Opposite her, I am squeezing my crossed arms against my belly and can't help shaking my crossed legs violently in a desperate attempt to conserve and produce body heat. I'm only able to think of hot water and soup. Time slows, converting the minutes until dinner to hours of pain.

One by one, we hear the zip go up and one hiker after the other appears in a thick jacket, hunched, shivering, turning their back to us while quickly pulling the zip down again, before uttering a few words that unfailingly contain one and the same commonality: "Cold!"

Our tent quickly fills up, but stays remarkably quieter than usual. Most people are exhausted and about half have a headache. The high altitude is finally showing its true face.

"Haha, look at Eva," Chris points out, "while we are all freezing in our jackets, she just sits there in her hoodie like in her living room." Chris is always coming up with something to say, to lighten our atmosphere, and to praise others. And how true, Eva seems entirely comfortable by now, quietly observing everyone else's misery, probably too polite to say: "What's wrong with you all? Isn't it nice and warm in here?"

"Yes!" we all agree with Chris. "How do you do that?"

Eva just shrugs.

"And have you noticed how she walks?" Chris carries on. "While we were all struggling on that last bit, she always looks so relaxed." He copies her serene expression. "No poles, but always with that Nalgene bottle dangling down from her hand."

"Yes, like on a Sunday stroll," people agree. I realize how little I've paid attention so far, too preoccupied with myself.

Jana and Diego join us in the tent. We haven't seen them all afternoon.

"How are you?" Everyone wants to know.

"I had a nap and now I feel good again, thanks." Jana has regained her strength. "But now Diego has caught a cold and got fever," so her mood hasn't lifted. She suffers along with him.

I feel bad that I'm feeling so well (cold aside) while others are suffering, especially my friends from Zurich who I had asked to come along with me on this trip. "Do you need medicine? I've got lozenges and vitamin C and—"

"No, thanks, we've got everything."

OK, what else could I do for them? I keep thinking.

"Jana," I draw her attention again because she sits at the opposite end of the table.

She looks up at me as if I'm a big nuisance.

"Would you like more of those heating badges? I've still got heaps," I try again.

"We've got everything we need," she replies shortly.

OK, got it, I'm not helping, but unintentionally making her feel even more stressed. Jana is well organized and has everything they need. It seems best to just leave her alone. Is she angry with me? I hope not, but the thought keeps nagging me.

▲ ▲ ▲

Our dinner consists of vegetarian toasted sandwiches and a green banana-potato-beef-veggie stew. Yes, such combination does exist! Green bananas are a starchy non-sweet staple in Tanzania. They fabulously blend into the stew, and taste just like floury potatoes. For the vegetarians, there is an identical pot without beef. Food is good as always, but within three hours after lunch no one feels much appetite.

"Hip hip!"

"Hop hop," we mutter in response, quieter than ever before.

It's time for our health check. I've been expecting our oxygen saturations to improve following our acclimatization hike, but they've actually come down on average. Most are now settling in the low to mid 90's% range. That's strange. I curiously watch my own reading until it stops at 92%, unchanged. I'm disappointed, still attributing superstitious powers to this device. Perhaps the acclimatization effect won't show until tomorrow?

One by one, Evance runs everyone through the standard questions, until it's my turn:

"Do you have a headache?"

"No."

"Are you dizzy?"

"No."

"How did you sleep last night?"

"Good, 100%."

"Are you tired?"

"No." My last answer is different from almost everyone else's. The cold has made me wide awake.

"How do you feel overall?"

"I hate to say it, but I feel great."

People stare at me. I can feel scorn in their eyes and thoughts. Yikes, have I just actually said that? Evance smiles, he's got one less hiker to worry about, while I cringe inwardly. Why did I have to say that? No one wants to hear that, a simple "good" would have been sufficient.

While trying so hard to be considerate, my mouth has just outfoxed my self-control and spoken the truth. I'm still wowed about how my body handled our big challenge today. The fact that everyone else seems so exhausted makes it even more astonishing, because it reminds me that it wasn't as easy as it felt to me. My heart still aches to celebrate and shout it out loud, but I have no one to share my feelings. While physically *high* amidst this downcast vibe, my emotions are suffering from not being able to freely speak my mind. I feel lonely and would blame myself for the remainder of the trip about the sentence I've just uttered. "I feel great" – that sentence shall be banned from now on. But isn't there something fundamentally wrong about feeling bad for feeling good?

On the other hand, people like Eva, Juli or Lynn have equally made it through the day energetically and without any suffering. They are silently and modestly keeping their strength to themselves in respect for everyone else. How can they do it? I will find no answers. Our group's sparse conversations and silent thoughts are dominated by negative sentiments of suffering and exhaustion.

Robert senses the drop in our group's morale. "Today wasn't easy. It's normal that some of you don't feel well. We expect that by now. It happens on every hike. Fatigue, headache, nausea, catching a cold – it's all normal. Don't worry. Your headache may be gone again by tomorrow. It may not even come back later. This is no reason to worry, and it's no reason to doubt that you will reach the summit. Stay positive. You will see, tomorrow will be different." He sympathizes both with our group's physical as well as emotional state of mind.

"There is one more thing I would like to ask you all," he looks at us as if he's about to bring bad news. "We are almost halfway through our hike. Do you have any suggestions for improvement for us? For me, or the other guides, or the chef, or the porters, or anything else – what can we do better?"

We stare at him in disbelief.

"If there's anything you don't like, please tell us now so we can change. If you tell us only after the hike, it's too late. Then we can't do anything to make it better for you. So please tell us now."

We feel almost embarrassed by his question. How could we possibly complain about anything?

"Robert, are you serious? You and the entire crew have been amazing."

"You couldn't have supported us any better."

"Without you, there's no way we could have come that far."

"Thank you for all your efforts."

"Please tell everyone thank you, you are the best."

"OK, thank you," he doesn't seem to fully believe us, "but if there's anything later, please just tell us. Don't wait. OK?"

"OK. But really, there's nothing," we try our best to assure him.

▲ ▲ ▲

Once done with our briefing for tomorrow, we all eagerly disperse back to our tents by 8:30pm, hoping to find some warmth under our sleeping bags. While I've been saying that every evening so far, tonight our longing for warmth and rest is more pronounced than ever before.

As soon as I've crawled back into my tent, I squeeze my legs into my sleeping bag. Next I pour a hot cup of water from my thermos and drop in a dose of Aspirin+C, just as I already do each morning. I'm used to eating lots of fresh produce and this is my preventive measure to avoid getting sick from a sudden vitamin withdrawal. Having seen Diego's suffering scared me out of my wits and reminded me how important it is to stay healthy up here. My nose is starting to block up and I already see myself with chills and fever, unable to breathe, suffering through a freezing long night alone in my dark icebox tent. What a nightmare! This must be avoided by all means. Now I hope that a second dose of vitamin C may do the trick.

After a few sips from my hot power water and within few minutes under my sleeping bag, I miraculously don't feel cold anymore. To the contrary, it's rather comfortable and my legs have become toasty warm. While typing my journal as usual, I am getting hungry again. My homemade energy bars make for an excellent desert. I keep reaching mindlessly into my bag of supplies like a bag of popcorn while watching a movie, and one by one my bars become victim to my nocturnal appetite. Next time I reach, only crumbs are left. Have I just stuffed half a kilo of energy bars into myself? Where has it all disappeared?

Usually I would feel guilty and ugly as sin after such an uncontrolled snack attack. Not tonight, not on this mountain. My trousers still feel looser than when I bought them. Whatever spell this mountain has cast on me, I like the change. It makes me laugh about myself as if I were an actor in my own comedy.

I'm picturing the reaction of my fellow hikers, if only they knew – disbelieving stares, disgusted faces or uncontrolled laughter? How can she still enjoy eating, after all the food she devoured this afternoon? And why is she not tired and sleeping like everyone else?

I don't know, because that person is as new to me as to all of them. Never would I have thought that typing notes for a book while snacking bland trail-mix bars and sitting cross-legged in my warm sleeping bag on a freezing dark mountain could feel as entertaining as watching a movie while eating popcorn on a cozy couch at home. So snug!

As usual, I finish my journaling around 10pm and still need to venture outside into the cold once more for the night. A symphony of loud and deep snoring provides the background music for my three minutes under the stars, while faint talking and laughter from the mess tent makes me smile. Our guides seem to be in a good mood, they have deserved this break. Once I put my earplugs in place, however, I quickly doze off and forget about everything around me.

DAY 5

Into the wild away from popular routes

24 SEPTEMBER 2015

From Moir Hut (4,200m/13,800ft)
to Buffalo Camp (4,000m/13,200ft)

Distance — elevation — time:
12km/7mi⇨ — 200m/600ft⇩ — 5-7 hours🕐

It is already daylight when I open my eyes. This was my most restful sleep so far. I only remember waking up twice during the night, but both times quickly fell back to sleep. Even though I feel like newborn this morning, I don't want to get up. My tent still feels as freezing cold as it was all night, and I can hear the outer layer of my tent flapping in the wind. Like yesterday, the sun is not directly hitting our camp yet, and that makes a colossal difference.

After getting ready as usual within the warmth of my sleeping bag, I dread stepping outside to brush my teeth. My fingers are getting cold before I've even slipped into my shoes, and hurt by the time I've tied my soft bootlaces that cut into my flesh like the edge of a knife. Ouch!

A biting wind tempers my mood. I desperately move my legs while brushing my teeth, but my blood circulation doesn't get going. Alternating between left and right hand to brush my teeth while hiding the other one in my pocket doesn't do the trick. It just leaves me with painful sensations on both.

My fingers change from burning red to deathly white. With my numb stubs, I struggle to get the zip of my gaiters up. It seems stuck. Bloody gaiters! Bloody zip! Bloody wind! Bloody everything! The more I try, the more frozen my fingers get, the less feeling I have left. I hate this feeling of numbing cold, desperate pain and utter helplessness. It's miserable, the dark side of hiking. It robs me of all positive emotions and makes me feel frustrated.

Just in time before losing my temper, the first sunrays from behind the mountain ridge tell me there's hope in sight. It's around 7am. Within moments, the sun returns sufficient warmth to our campsite and brings my fingers back to life. With the pain subsiding, my mood instantly changes to positive. How nice that the sun is back! What a blessing!

I couldn't possibly imagine being stuck up here in cloudy rainy weather. Don't even think of coming up here off-season when you may not get to see the sun – the misery would be beyond my imagination!

Nevertheless, I still can't get the zip of my gaiters to work. My tent is right next to the kitchen tent.

"*Samahani.*" ("Excuse me.") I draw Crispin's attention and helplessly hold out my gaiter. "I've got a problem with the zip. Could someone help me?"

He nods and speaks a few words to a nearby porter who immediately comes to my rescue. The porter goes out of his way not only fixing my zip but also helping me force the gaiter over my shoe.

"*Asante sana, asante sana . . .*" I keep saying, overwhelmed by his helpfulness.

He immediately dropped whatever he was about to do, gave me all his attention and wouldn't stop before being fully convinced that he had done everything possible to make me happy. Once convinced that I am fine again, he politely withdraws to let me carry on with my day. They all really take good care of us, no matter what problem we have and no matter whom we ask for help.

▲ ▲ ▲

Our breakfast consists of our familiar omelet, chocolate millet porridge and toasted white bread with spreads. I usually don't mention the bread because it's always there and doesn't attract my attention. However, for all normal people, I guess I should point out at least once that it's usually freshly toasted, crunchy and warm, not just soft and boring. Duty completed. Now I can move on to the little treat that I've got in store for myself – energy bar crumbs. Of course

I wouldn't want to let them go to waste, despite all the energy that I already stuffed into myself last night. Instead, I excitedly mix them with hot porridge for a welcome alternative to my daily omelet. Yummy! Who would have thought that porridge could be such an interesting delight – warming, tasty, smooth and crunchy. I'm pleased with my little bowl of brownish mash like a Michelin star chef with his sophisticated creation. Happiness needs no luxury.

Yesterday's acclimatization hike still hasn't improved our blood oxygen readings, just stabilized them. Mine comes out at 92% again. In hindsight it makes sense. Moir Hut is after all still 400m higher than our prior Shira 2 Camp. Without the acclimatization, we may have suffered badly. With the acclimatization, we are all more or less fine. Most headaches have disappeared overnight, just as Robert predicted. Diego also feels a lot better this morning. His cold is almost gone. What a quick recovery! Seeing him smile again also lifts a weight off my shoulders, and, of course, even more so for Jana. She has returned to her cheerful disposition. My late night vitamin C shot has also done its trick and cleared my nose. In a nutshell, our group overall is doing very well, ready and energetic for this new hiking day. Our regular dose of sunshine certainly has a big impact in getting us back on track, rewarming our bodies and boosting our morale.

▲ ▲ ▲

From today's hike onwards, we're heading north, breaking away from the Lemosho and Shira routes. This is the part for which I couldn't find any prior traveler reviews, which initially gave me the idea to start writing this book. How exciting! Finally we're heading into real wilderness, on a path less traveled, away from the more popular routes. I should add that even so far, we mostly had the hiking paths entirely to ourselves and even our campsites didn't feel crowded or *mass-market*. The only time we came across other tourists was yesterday near Lava Tower, though they provided more a welcome distraction than impacting our wilderness experience. So there are ways to avoid migrating with an entire village if you are prepared to stay away from the busy Machame and Marangu routes.

Moir Hut camp sits at the base of a giant caldron with only one flat opening facing downhill, not where we want to go. So for the first part of our hike, we can't avoid a steep ascent back on the outside of the caldron, to the top of the ridge. We need to hike up the steep wall of grey sand that we saw on our descent yesterday.

I position myself in line behind Eva, taking the chance to learn a bit more about her. First thing I notice is that Eva seems to have become friends with Jeannette; they like walking together.

"So Eva, you mentioned you are from Bristol. That's in the south, right?"

"Yes, south west, near Cardiff and Newport."

"Oh, not in the south near Eastbourne? I think I went there once on a school language trip."

"No, other side. At the same height as London, just on the west coast."

"Oh, I see," I had confused it with Brighton. Hearing west, I'm thinking of Manchester and Liverpool. "So what's the area like there? Is it very industrial?"

"Not much industry, it's mostly farmland. We've got a lot of agriculture."

"Oh, I see," I confused it again. "What a shame, I lived in London for two years and don't have the slightest clue!"

We keep walking silently, but I can't shut up for long. It seems like such a waste of time not to talk and learn from others. "How about you Jeannette? What made you do the hike?"

"Oh, I'm turning 60 this year. I always wanted to do it, so then I set myself the target to do it before my 60th birthday. And here we are."

"Oh wow, how ambitious, that's great!" I like being surrounded by people like Jeannette, Juli and Stewart who are proving me wrong and giving me new inspirations. One doesn't need to be young to do crazy things like hiking Kili and have fun along the way. "You're South African, right?"

"Yes, but I live in Sweden."

"Oh, how did that happen? Do you have family there?"

"Yes, my husband."

"Oh, that explains. Where did you meet him?"

"In Saudi Arabia. We both lived there for a few years."

Saudi Arabia?! Oh, now that's getting interesting! I've never met a woman who lived in Saudi Arabia before. Curious to hear more about her experience in that country, I bombard her with questions: How is it to live there as a woman, how did you find work, is there an expat community, are you allowed to import alcohol?

We're getting stuck with the last question – no alcohol? "That would be so difficult. Once I went to Brunei for a weekend and we went to a steak place for dinner. Steak without red wine is like breakfast without coffee for me, but they wouldn't sell any. However, importing was allowed. So to make it worse the table next to us had some, and watching them felt like torture. That's when I realized I'm addicted to red wine!"

"Haha, yes, you can neither import nor buy alcohol in Saudi, but a friend of mine just produced it at home."

"Oh really? How?"

"Just from sugar and yeast, I think. It even tasted quite good."

Wow, I learnt something new again! So it's not only possible to bake a cake without an oven at 4,000 meters (13,000ft) altitude, it's even possible to home-make your own alcohol — the wonders of chemistry.

Before I can satisfy my curiosity to hear more, and perhaps to Jeannette's relief, Robert is putting me back in place. "Alexy, stop talking." He knows who is the instigator of our shenanigans. "This is a steep ascent. I want everyone to focus on your breathing for now. Once we reach the top of this ridge, you can talk again as much as you like for the rest of the day."

We immediately obey. Robert is the boss and knows what's best for us. Hearing others panting, I realize that Jeannette has been walking, talking and breathing normally, never mind the steep ascent in thin air. What an incredible level of fitness, especially for someone about to turn 60!

In reward for our meditative silence, staring at the footsteps of the person in front of us and step by step increasing in altitude at our familiar *pole pole* pace, a direct view of the summit glaciers awaits us towards the top of the ridge. There is not a single cloud in sight. The landscape alternates between tones of brownish grey, from a dirty fawn of the earthy sand all the way to blackish dark brown shadows of rocks and ridges. We are too high up for any green sign of life. The glaciers stretch horizontally in a thin line on top of a grey rocky cone, faintly blurred, overexposed under the morning sun that has only just risen from behind.

View to the glaciers one hour after leaving Moir Hut

We take a break to catch our breaths. The remainder of our day is said to be relatively easy, with a gradual repetition of moderate upward and downward slopes.

I still haven't given up on my camera and check whether it may have gotten enough of a recharge in the morning sun. The solar panels have by now become a constant decoration of my backpack. The battery of my camera dies as soon as the focus lens has opened. This time, however, it doesn't even allow me to close the lens anymore. Evance notices my despair.

"Put it under your shirt."

"You mean the camera?"

"Yes, then it warms up."

I follow his advice. After few minutes I try again. Just as Evance predicted, warming it up has done the trick. The camera obeys and retracts its lens, but then it instantly goes dead again. Now I know that the battery is defunct and finally give up on it.

While our group still recovers from the steep ascent, our porters pass us with our heavy loads on their shoulders and heads. They don't ever break, but keep going all the way. Surely our next camp will be fully set up again by the time we arrive.

Aside from our group, there is an elder couple with their private guide breaking at the same spot, heading the same way north. So we don't have that side of the mountain entirely to ourselves as I thought we might have, but surely it will still be far less busy and more authentic than on any other route.

The onward path bends behind a rocky outcrop, leaving both Moir Hut camp and the view of the summit behind us. The clouds roll in almost predictably around 10am, just like yesterday. For about thirty minutes, we walk on an assembly of flat disc-like rocks rather than scree and earth, like a pile of debris after a massive explosion.

"Clients tell us they can get mobile network here," Evance points out to me. "Try." He knows I've been looking for it, and indeed all the local networks show up on my phone again. Some of us try to use this window of opportunity to send a short text back home, but we are still unable to register on any of the networks. It would work for Diego a bit later, but no luck for me.

Once we have left the rocky path behind us and reached the northern side of the mountain, our view extends all the way down into Kenya and all the way into the far away Serengeti plains on the horizon.

We keep walking in single file on a proper path, well-trodden, markedly cut into the earthy terrain from repeated passage. Wasn't this supposed to be a new route in wilderness? I didn't expect to find a beaten track. As usual whenever I don't know what to do or think, I ask Evance. "Isn't this a new route? How long has it been operating?"

"No, it has been around a long time, just like the other routes."

"Oh really? But who was using it?"

"Locals, and in private climbs."

"But no group tours?"

"No, not so many."

Turns out it simply hasn't been widely commercialized yet. My operator did a good job with their marketing.

We take another mid-morning break and refuel our bodies with our own snacks. I have brought along some more of my homemade energy bars (still have a second bag after my nocturnal feast last night), but as yesterday I can't bear eating while our guides have nothing, looking at us with glassy eyes. Again I offer each of them a piece.

"*Rafiki yangu, habari gani?*" ("My friend, how are you?") I smile at Skoba, pleased to make use of the few words I learnt from him.

"*Nzuri, na wewe?*" ("Good, and you?") He responds like many times before.

"*Nzuri sana*" ("Very good"), I repeat the two words which have by now become my standard response.

After I've completed my round and each guide has gladly accepted a piece, there's nothing left for myself. Whoops, but so be it. I've been eating way too much on this trip and don't feel hungry yet. They have just saved me from unnecessarily stuffing myself.

We keep walking, quietly, monotonously. No one is talking. That's no fun. I'm usually a rather quiet person, but this mountain has magically changed my character. Each and every minute in silence is a lost chance to communicate, to connect and to satisfy my greedy mind. I decide it's time to get to know our guides better. They take so good care of us all the time, but we really don't know anything about them. Baraka happens to walk behind me, and so I ask him whether he has children, just to start the conversation.

"Not yet," he replies, and all the guides laugh about my innocent question.

"Why is that so funny?"

"Baraka is only 23," Robert explains with a broad smile.

"Oh really? So who is younger – Baraka or Estomee?" My mouth moves as my brain is processing.

They all laugh again.

"I thought Estomee was the youngest," I keep digging my hole.

"How old you think he is?" Robert teases me.

OK, so I guess that means he is older. "24? 25?"

"No way," they keep laughing.

"He is 29," Robert enlightens me.

Whoops, hopefully they are not offended by my gross miscalculations. I already know that Robert is 32 (a year younger than me), Evance is 40 and Skoba is in his early forties.

Moving on, we learn that Robert, Evance, Skoba and Samwel all have kids, and a wife of course. We are often so focused on ourselves and forget that our guides and of course all the porters have a private life and families, just as we do. In order to come with us, their job requires them to be away from home for an extended period of time, over and over again. Surely they would miss their families.

"But I would like to have many wives," Robert announces with a prankish smile.

"Oh really, why?" Lynn joins our bantering.

"One wife is not enough." Robert smiles to himself.

"Why?" Lynn, Farrah and I all curiously want to know.

He's got all the girls' attention. Robert is Mr. Charming – tall, well-built, handsome, smart, humorous, easy-going yet always in control. I wonder whether any female hikers have ever tried their luck on him. His wife surely is a very lucky person.

He keeps us waiting, weighing his answer.

"Why, Robert?" we don't give in.

"Because I would like to have 20 kids," he pulls our leg.

"Yeah right!" It's so much more fun to hike with guides who like to joke and are not just serious all the time. But on a more serious note, "Do people when they get older rely on their kids to support them financially?"

"No. It used to be like that, but it's changed," Robert explains. "Many parents in Tanzania nowadays try to make their own provisions, it depends on their economic means and how well off the kids are. It's different from family to family."

▲ ▲ ▲

By noon, we have descended into a thick layer of fog, and the hike is starting to become dull and repetitive. The landscape doesn't change. There's a seemingly endless repetition of uphill and downhill slopes. We can never see beyond the next hilly ridge, if at all. Sometimes the fog is so thick our view is limited to no more than ten meters at most. With our decrease in altitude, the vegetation has noticeably increased again. We are back in the land of everlasting plants, as Evance likes to call these bushes. However, it all still looks rather grey, brown and desolate in this fog.

I give up any attempt of conversation and succumb to our monotony, meditatively following the person ahead of me, allowing my brain to shut down. I'm not thinking anything, silence everywhere, inside and outside. By now, I've finally also slowed down my inner pace to match our group. My body has learnt to behave. I no longer rebel against it. Or perhaps everyone is walking a bit faster today. Benign slopes make for quite a difference.

We spot a black tent on the top of yet another hilly ridge. In need of some break from the dullness, we are excited.

"That's our lunch tent!"

"Yay!"

"Finally!"

We already know from our briefing that we will receive hot lunch today on the way. The prospect of something warm to drink and some form of calories, no matter what, provides a welcome twist to our monotonous past two hours. We reach our lunch spot by around 2pm, over six hours since I had my tiny bowl of porridge and crumbs.

Hot water for coffee, tea or chocolate and a plate of muffins are already waiting for us, and we don't need to wait much longer for our freshly prepared lunch.

We get veggie soup (surprise, surprise – but I can't get enough of that hot stuff on this cold mountain; not as boring as it may sound), something that looks like a potato frittata (we are told it is spaghetti with eggs), as well as fabulous vegetarian and veggie/chicken wraps (made of a freshly fried dough similar to Indian Chapatis). Adding some spicy curry ketchup turns these wraps into a heavenly meal. Too bad there is only one for each of us; I could have devoured five of them!

I unlock my phone to take a picture of our lunch and can't believe what I find. Dozens of emails have made their way onto my phone. So after all, I've got data coverage but still cannot hook on to any mobile network. Keen to use this rare window of opportunity, I quickly type an email to my dad to say that I'm fine, as well as an email to my work to say that they shouldn't expect to hear from me again over the coming days. Both reply within a minute. My dad must be relieved to hear that I'm well after all. It's nice to hear back from him so quickly, and also a big relief for me. Now I don't need to worry about that bloody phone nor my network coverage anymore, everyone's expectations finally managed the way I should have from the start. However, seeing all these emails freaks me out, and so – loyal to my over-organizing character – I spend the remainder of our lunch break making sure that there are no burning fires and happily deleting as much as I can. "Sorry guys, not being very social during lunch today."

"Hip hip!"

"Hop hop!"

"Please get ready, we'll continue."

It's around 3pm. There is another tour group having lunch at the same location. We saw their luxurious tents at Moir Hut camp last night. Their tents are so big and tall that you can comfortably stand up in them. Some of the tent zips were open, and so we could see that they had proper beds and even bedside tables! We couldn't believe our eyes when we saw that. So that's what a luxury version of camping is like. As written in big letters on each of their tents, their tour operator is called Thomson Safaris. I can't remember coming across them when researching alternative tour group operators for the Northern Circuit route, so I'm intrigued to find out more.

As luck would have it, two of their hikers are standing outside and greet us collegially as we are about to move on. Here's my chance, I take the opportunity to find out more.

"Hey guys, are you also on the Northern Circuit route?"

They look at each other confused. "I think they call it Grand Traverse," the girl replies.

"Is it also a nine-day hike and goes around the mountain?"

"Yes, it also goes around, but ten days," the guy confirms.

"Ah, I see, probably similar, just with an extra day," I'm quick to draw conclusions.

"Yes, probably," they are very friendly.

"I actually looked quite intensively for alternatives and didn't know there was another operator following that route. Do you mind me asking how much you paid?"

"Was it about 7,000?" The guy looks at the girl.

"Yes, a bit over 7,000," they both agree casually, as though this were just about average. 7,000 dollars! I try hard not to show what I'm thinking. This is ridiculous! Why would someone pay so much?

"I see, thanks for the info. Enjoy the rest of your hike!"

"Thanks, you too! All the best!" Very friendly, I must have done well to hide my thoughts.

7,000 dollars! I can't believe what I've just heard. That is even more than the most expensive quote I received when doing my research, which was about US$5,000 for the Crater Camp via the Western Breach. Of course I can't resist immediately passing on this new piece of information to my fellow hikers.

"Guys, listen to that. Wanna know how much they paid?"

"How much?" Of course they all want to know.

"More than 7,000!"

"No way!"

"That's crazy!"

"Just to get a stand-up tent and bed?"

"And probably it's not even any softer than our foam mattress, just that it sits on a frame rather than lies on the floor."

"4,000 bucks more just for that?"

"I like sleeping in our tents, makes it so much more authentic."

"Yes, that's exactly the fun part of camping."

"There's no way this price can be justified," we all concur.

Evance smiles. He seems amused about our outrage and pleased about our conclusions.

"Is the food they get any different from ours?" I ask him.

"No, it's all the same."

"So the tents and beds are the only difference?"

"Yes, just that."

We are all stunned. Why would people pay so much more for that? Perhaps the added expense is worthwhile when you have serious back pain (as Stew also keeps saying that getting in and out of the tent is the biggest challenge for him on this trip, though he handles it well nevertheless), or if your company pays for it as some kind of team building offsite, or if you've got so much money that it really doesn't matter anymore and you prefer an even more *exclusive* experience?

While we can't believe why the Thomson Safaris hikers paid that much, they probably feel sorry for us given our comparatively rough camping conditions, and surely wouldn't want to swap with us either. We feel good about our choice, oblivious that we might not have all the facts to come to premature conclusions.[48]

Shortly after lunch, we need to scramble some ten meters straight up a wall of rock. It's the first section on the entire hike where the word *scramble* applies, in a limited sense, without drama, over some huge stones that require a bit of energy and holding on to the upper stones to lift our bodies up. On top, we take a short break to catch our breaths. Most people find a rock to sit down.

Farrah is pale as chalk. "I'm dizzy." Her stomach revolts from this almost vertical ascent and associated interruption of oxygen flow right after lunch.

"Would you like a ginger lozenge? They're supposed to be good against nausea." That's why I'm carrying them with me as part of my daypack medical essentials, but so far I didn't need them.

"Oh really? That would be great."

I'm excited to be able to share what I've got.

We keep walking.

"Are you feeling any better?" I ask Farrah.

"Oh yes, much better already."

"That's great!"

Perhaps the lozenge really worked, or perhaps it's simply a function of renewed oxygen flow. Whatever the reason, I'm delighted that I might have been able to help. Yes indeed, I'm not just glad but extremely content.

My feelings are taking me by surprise. Why would this get me so excited? I'm starting to realize how some of my happiest moments have been when doing something for others, no matter how small and insignificant. I felt extremely content when offering my snacks to our guides, I like it when our waiters place the big pots of food near me so I can grab the ladle and serve everyone else, I enjoy when I can contribute to our group's entertainment by making some stupid remarks every now and then, I smile alone in my tent when I can praise others in my journal (knowing they will get to read it), and now I'm happy about this tiny ginger lozenge for Farrah.

On the opposite spectrum of happiness, I felt most unhappy (or rather my only unhappy moment so far) when I saw Diego and Jana struggling last night, when I couldn't do anything to help and felt rejected. Hiking quietly in nature gives me time to observe and reflect upon my own behavior and emotions. We're doing that all too rarely, aren't we?

The remaining hike leads us back down to moorland. There are noticeably more and thicker bushes covering the earthen ground.

"See that? Elands," Evance points out some hoof prints.

"Ela—what?" I've never heard that name before.

"Antelopes, right?" Farrah clarifies.

I obviously haven't been on my safari yet. Everyone else seems to know that elands are types of antelopes. So why do they come all the way up here where there's nothing to eat?

"To lick alkaline," Evance explains. The rocks higher up on Kilimanjaro are very alkaline, and so elands go all the way up to above 4,000 meters (13,000ft) in order to refill their mineral supplies.

"Will we get to see them?"

"No. Humans rarely get to see them up here. They avoid us. Usually they only move at night." Only the tracks they leave tell us their story.

"Robert, how far to the camp?" Farrah wants to know. It's been a long hiking day.

"Not long, maybe another hour," Robert smiles understandingly.

OK, that's not too bad, we all set our minds and expectations. 20 minutes later, around 4:30pm, we find ourselves in front of our tents. Robert obviously knows how to keep us happy – promise little, keep expectations low and over-deliver.

Our tents are set up pretty much in the middle of nowhere, on a slope with only a few patches of flat ground. It's not an official campsite. There are no signboards and none of the ugly wooden long-drop huts that have become such a common sight at all the other camps. Wonderful, that's why we have all come on this route, for some real wilderness experience! It feels so much more authentic rather than hiking with a small village.

The mountain vista and associated feeling, however, are different than I had expected. The fog has cleared on the lower slopes, opening our view again all the way down into Kenya and the far distance. There are no rocks, no steep cliffs, and it doesn't feel aloof from the rest of the world. The slopes look green and move downhill gently, before gradually transitioning into an expansive hilly plain. It gives me the feeling that we are still connected to the world. I would just need to run for half an hour and be all the way down again, never mind that we're still at 4,000 meters (13,000ft) altitude.

The camp of the Thomson Safaris group has been set up at a bigger site some 30 minutes further along the path. We can see their tents. That's where we would have stayed otherwise, if we had this part of the mountain entirely to ourselves.

Within few minutes, everyone has disappeared into his or her tent. Have I just missed something? Perhaps people just need some rest and private time. There's no hot water yet to wash. I prefer to wait outside. Getting in and out of my tent is one of the biggest nuisances on this trip for me, not just for Stewart. I'm not keen on repeating that procedure any more than absolutely necessary. It seems to require so much more energy than hiking all day, even for people without back pain.

Speaking of nuisances, getting out of my warm sleeping bag at night to pee in the freezing cold tops the list. Though optimizing that procedure and getting used to my evening routine is making it less of a nuisance by the day. Instead, it is competing with my newfound nuisance number two − frozen fingers in the morning when clouds temporarily block the sun. On the positive side, my initial fears of not being able to wash my hair or not having a decent toilet have proven unjustified. I simply cover my hair with a sunhat or beanie all the time so I even forget it's there, and drinking hot water first thing in the morning combined with snacking on dried prunes has finally accomplished its purpose. So in a nutshell, my nuisance list is actually pretty short.

While I'm waiting alone outside, the Thomson Safaris group passes our camp. They all smile at me, and we exchange a series of hellos and *Jambos*. When the same couple that I've asked about their route and pricing comes along, we wave and greet each other like good old friends. Everyone seems excited about a little bit of fresh social interaction.

▲ ▲ ▲

Crispin carries a big plate of popcorn into the dining tent and I follow this temptation. Better to sit alone in the tent and stuff myself with popcorn than waiting in the wind. To my surprise, I find Juli sitting there, alone. "Oh, I didn't expect to find anyone in here."

"Yes, I'm giving Stew some space in our tent to settle in. He likes putting everything in place first."

"I see," and reach for the popcorn.

"I thought you don't eat carbs?" She catches me cheating.

"Yes, I try to avoid them, but this looks too good."

"I'm quite impressed how disciplined you usually are."

"Oh, I wouldn't say that. I just stuff myself with all the good things," like swallowing half a kilo of energy bars for desert, "so there's not much temptation left. I've been doing this for a year now and I'm feeling much better than ever before. Previously I didn't have that much energy. I'm just so fascinated to observe how much capacity for change we all have."

"Yes, I agree. We all have the full potential inside us, just need to access it."

While I have no clue about the spiritual meaning of stuffing ourselves with popcorn, somehow we start sharing our spiritual concepts. Before long, Chris also joins us in the tent. Not sure whether he's been following the smell of popcorn, or whether he's heard us talking, or is just escaping the wind while also waiting for hot water.

"I believe our minds directly influence the wellbeing of our bodies," Juli continues.

"Yes, exactly. And just by controlling our thoughts and beliefs we can influence and change our lives the way we want," the three of us agree.

It turns out that we've all read the same books and share a very similar life philosophy. I don't often meet people with whom I can debate these concepts. It feels again as though I've found my tribe.

Once the hot water is ready, however, and the plate of popcorn half empty, we disperse to clean ourselves. Only when taking off my hiking boots, I realize that my socks are damp from sweat. Yuck! That's because I've tested my thick chili-feet insoles today, in preparation of summit night. They produce heat purely from the pressure of walking, an awesome Swiss invention and – according to all my research – the warmest insoles currently on the market.

I was totally excited when I first learnt about them because frozen feet (next to frozen fingers) were my biggest fear about summit night. The only thing that left me wondering was whether putting these chili-feet on top of my normal insoles wouldn't squeeze my toes too much. They come in two different versions of thickness, and I only got to test the thinner ones back home because it was still too warm. Even the thinner ones had made me sweaty within minutes.

Would the thicker ones on top of my normal insoles still feel comfortable? Now I know. I simply tied my shoelaces a bit looser this morning, and these chili-feet worked so well I even forgot they were there. My feet felt cushy and warm during the entire hike. Yippee, no more need to worry about cold feet during summit night! A new worry has emerged instead: chili-feet = stinky feet? I happily take that risk.

Even though we don't get as much sun this afternoon as we had the prior days, it still feels warm enough in my tent for a comfortable wash. Even my solar panels get enough sun this late afternoon to recharge my phone battery above 50% by the evening, despite me incessantly draining it to take pictures, check my emails (bad habit, I wish the connection wouldn't work so well now!) and type my journal for the rest of the afternoon. Yes, sorry for mentioning my panels again, but I can't get over how well they work. They still excite me every day.

▲ ▲ ▲

I hear the mess tent getting lively. There are no walls up here. The confines of our tents give us the illusion of privacy, but really everyone can hear everything, all the time. It sounds they are having fun. I'd better head over to join the action.

Only now I realize that it's gotten dark already. It's 6:30pm. An icy wind hits me by surprise. My body instantly drops into a state of frozen shock. I've not felt that cold before – yesterday was a warm-up by comparison – and zip my way into the mess tent as fast as my fingers can move.

So far only half our group are assembled, all hunched and cuddled into their thick jackets. Robert, who stands tall and seems entirely unimpressed by the low temperature, is entertaining everyone, because they are all laughing. "So be a little careful when leaving your tents tonight."

"Why?" I've missed the story.

"Because there are animals in this area that move at night, like elands or buffaloes."

"Ha, no wonder this site is called Buffalo Camp!"

"I'll get them to bring you some ginger tea," Robert looks at Ravi before he leaves.

"Are you OK?"

"Yes, just getting a cold, I've got a really sore throat," Ravi's hoarse voice says it all.

"I still have heaps of ginger lozenges, would you like some for your throat?" I offer. "Or I've also got proper sore throat lozenges."

"Yes, the ginger ones would be good, thank you," Ravi accepts.

I'm pleased that I can help and share whatever I've got, but – what have I just gotten myself into? Now I need to make another trip back to my tent in the icy wind. I'm not looking forward to going outside again, brrr. It makes me feel as though I were really going the extra mile, on these ridiculous ten meters back and forth to my tent that seem like a walk through hell.

The cold wind feels even icier now than just few minutes ago, deathly, immediately taking all life from my nose and fingers. We're definitely having the coldest night so far. I'm shivering incessantly, but it's not only me. When I'm back, I notice that everyone is shivering. There is no hot water yet to make hot drinks, neither to warm us up from inside nor to warm our fingers holding the cup.

Our waiter Sostenence brings us a big pot of hot pumpkin soup. We all look around the table with quizzical and eager eyes. Should we be polite and wait for the rest of our group to arrive?

There is unanimous agreement: "Let's start!"

Table manners succumb to basic needs, and hot soup really does wonders. It instantly makes us feel warmer and comfortable again. Gradually, the tent has filled up and everyone has gotten their priorities right, ahead of any social interaction – putting something warm into their bellies. Other than the soup, we also get tasty meatballs that remind me of Spanish Albondigas, accompanied by mashed potatoes and veggie stew – a hearty dinner for a rough climate!

With the drop in temperature and yet another long hiking day behind us, the evening vibe in our mess tent is getting quieter by the day. Our adventurous excitement has faded into routine. We focus on eating and once again look forward to our warm sleeping bags.

Someone whispers into my ear: "When Robert says *hip hip*, we all say *Robert*."

Got it. I pass on the message to the persons next to me. For the past days, we've dutifully answered *hop hop* each time we heard Robert or Evance say *hip hip* to draw our attention, as we learnt on our first day. Let's give it a little twist, just for the fun of it. We smile at each other conspiratorially, looking forward to cracking our joke. Yes, when stuck in a dark and freezing cold tent, we crave for entertainment and even the most innocent jokes make us laugh.

We don't need to wait long. Soon Robert comes into our tent to start his briefing.

"Hip hip—"

"Robert!" everyone shouts out loud before bursting into laughter about our successfully completed shenanigans.

Our guides can't help but laugh as well. Robert seems particularly pleased with our new way of answering, and so we decide to permanently swap our drill response. He says *hip hip* another few times during our briefing, as usual. A big smile spreads across his face each time we respond with his name. That's the beauty of our rough and simple life up here. Small things make us extremely happy.

"Hip hip."

"Robert!"

Smiles.

"Be careful when leaving your tents tonight. There are animals here. They move at night."

"What animals?" people want to know.

"Elands. But not only, also buffaloes, monkeys, stray dogs."

"Buffaloes?"

Now he's got everyone's attention. I'm more concerned about stray dogs.

"When you leave your tent, first stick out your head. Look to each side." Robert demonstrates with big eyes, moving his head left and right. "When you see it's clear, then you lift your butt out."

We are glued to his instructions like kids to fairytales, unable to distinguish fiction from reality. Is he kidding us, or is this serious stuff?

"Are these animals dangerous?"

"What are we supposed to do if we actually encounter them?"

"Has a buffalo ever run over a tent?"

Robert keeps a straight face while we all blurt out our thoughts.

"What do I do if I pee and all of a sudden a buffalo stands in front of me?" Farrah changes our conversation back from serious to entertaining. My mind plays the scene: Farrah squatting, realizing some dark skinny legs in front of her that were not there a second ago, pulling her head into her shoulders and slowly looking up with big wide eyes, into the expressionless face of a buffalo with massive horns, starting a frozen staring competition as neither of them moves.

Robert just smiles. Suffice to say there hasn't been an actual encounter between hikers and those animals before. They tend to follow a different path and avoid campsites. But just in case, Farrah demonstrates to us her version of what to do when meeting a beast.

"You know what they tell you to do in the Yellowstone national park when you come across a mountain lion?" She stands up tall, raises her arms like the horns of a deer, fingers bent like the claws of a predator, opens her lips as wide as possible while clenching her teeth and goes "arrrrrrrh" – enough to set us all off again into roaring laughter.

▲ ▲ ▲

As usual, we head back to our tents around 8:30pm. This seems to have become our daily bedtime. I dread stepping back out into the icy wind, but to my surprise it feels a lot warmer now, almost pleasant. It's always like that after dinner. Hot food makes such a big difference. It doesn't even bother me too much anymore that I still need to expose my buttocks to the freezing wind. Most surprising of all, I'm not even worried anymore if anyone might see me in the dark, and mind you the dark I'm referring to is becoming ever more lucid under the growing moon. You could spot a buffalo from half a mile away.

I pick my private spot just a few steps away from our camp as I can't be bothered to walk any further, behind a bush barely tall enough to cover my knees, to appease the tiny bit of leftover civility that mandates that I look for the highest object within ten meters of my tent. I'm satisfied this bush is the best option at hand.

In fairness, I could have used our toilet tent of course, but that's far too cumbersome. Why waste energy opening and closing the tent zip; trying to pull the plug out; getting frustrated that the plug is stuck; pulling it out again with much force which sometimes makes water from nowhere spill on my fingers and I can only hope it came from the top container; making sure not to touch anything with bare thighs or carefully laying out paper on the seat; pushing the flush; getting frustrated that the flush isn't strong enough to pull down the toilet paper; pushing the flush again with much force; closing the plug; unzipping the tent again; and, finally, carefully sterilizing my fingers with hand sanitizer? And all that without the added assistance of moonlight, and at the risk of inhaling some leftover gases – thanks, but no thanks!

Just as I'm about to pull down my three layers of pants, Ravi walks up the same path to also find his own little private spot. We have a small laugh about it.

"Don't worry, I won't look," he obligingly keeps walking a few more meters further up behind my back and that's it, no big deal.

In the end, we're all humans with basic human needs. It took me a few days to learn what Jana already knew on our first evening. Does it require climbing Africa's tallest mountain for that realization? Perhaps for me finding back to nature and humanity is what this trip really is all about. Tonight I feel as if I've finally become a legit hiker and camper.

▲ ▲ ▲

I'm more tired than ever. My tent is set up on a slight slope, like the first evening when I struggled to fall asleep and partly blamed it on sliding downwards. Tonight I'm smarter. I have repositioned my foam pad diagonally across my tent, so I can lie with my head down, feet up. I also try for the first time my self-heating badges, stuffing a big one that's meant for my back all the way down my sleeping bag towards my toes. I close my eyes and lie waiting in anticipation of some warmth; waiting, still waiting, and waiting a bit more. Nothing. This stupid little thing doesn't work.

So I turn on my light again to also unwrap some of the self-heaters for my toes and hands. I stick the ones for my toes onto my socks and squeeze the hand warmers into my liner gloves (yes, I'm wearing gloves tonight). Then I must have fallen asleep, just to re-awake soon after with burning hot hands. These stupid badges are setting me up for a bad night, but l am relieved they actually work. I will need them for summit night. Not so sure about my toe warmers, however. They are neither hot nor cold. My feet have become comfortably warm, but that could simply be my own body heat. At least I should be good for tonight, well insulated against our nighttime frost. Can I please sleep now?

Nope, not that lucky tonight. As soon as I doze off, I wake up again, and again, and again . . . Unable to find relaxation despite my fatigue, constantly twisting and changing from side to side and from back to front, the night is becoming unbearably long. I'm already looking forward to the morning.

DAY 6

Getting bored of fog, soup and pole pole

25 SEPTEMBER 2015

**From Buffalo Camp (4,000m/13,200ft)
to Third Cave (3,800m/12,500ft)**

Distance — elevation — time:
8km/5mi⇨ — 200m/700ft⇩ — 4-5 hours☺

plus optional bonus hike

Elevation — time:
200m/700ft⇧⇩ — 1-2 hours☺

I wake up to faint chatters from outside. My tent is already filled with daylight. It's around 6am. After struggling to sleep through the night, I wish I could sleep longer now. I don't want to get up yet, just that my bladder won't let me anyway, so I'd better get the day started.

By the time I scramble out of my tent after my quick morning routine, it's already nice and sunny outside. The air is crisp and calm. Today my fingers don't freeze while brushing my teeth. The sunrays feel pleasant and instantly boost my energy, immediately erasing my memory of a dreadful sleepless night.

There is not a single cloud in sight, and so Kibo, which was hidden from our view yesterday, shows itself clearly and distinctly – a wide grey hump with some white lines on top, the remainders of the glacier. It seems closer than ever before, as if within an hour's walk we could reach its base. And it doesn't look that tall. "What's the big deal about it?" I wonder.

We can also see all the way down again into Kenya and the far horizon, where a greyish layer of morning dew blurs the edges and melts into the intense blue sky. Even more so than yesterday, I feel as if we were just on a hill and it wouldn't take long to run down. Comparing the plateau downhill that's probably at some 2,000 meters (7,000ft) of elevation with the glaciers uphill, I would never have guessed an altitude difference of 4,000 meters (13,000ft) in between. There are extreme athletes who run all the way up and down in less than a day. Call me crazy, but now my mind can comprehend how such a feat might very well be possible.

The zip to our mess tent is open this morning. It's such a pleasant morning, no need to hide from the wind. Half of our group is already inside. There is a big but almost empty plate of fresh watermelon. Multiple pieces of leftover rind are piled on everyone's plates. Ha, after being scolded the other day at Moir Hut for eating too much chicken before Ravi arrived, this sight makes me feel better. Seems I'm not to only one who forgets about sharing equally when faced with delicious treats – first come first served. But the reminder was appropriate and served me right. Now I dare only take one piece to leave enough for the people still coming. If there just were more of it!

As usual, I pour myself a cup of hot water and add a massive spoon of instant coffee, already anticipating my second cup after that. Given my sleeping issues, I've only been allowing myself coffee in the mornings. That's a big change for a coffeeholic like me, who is used to about ten espressos throughout the day. I take a sip. That's the moment I'm looking forward to every morning, to appease my addiction.

Ugh! My throat tightens from the bitter taste. That's not how I remember it.

I keep drinking as I'm used to, but every single sip becomes a torture until I give up, not even half way through my first cup. The thought of this sour liquid in my stomach makes me feel sick. Is that the same stuff I've been savoring for a week?

Yes, it is. For the first time in my entire life of hopeless addiction, I can't stand coffee. Could it be that all the exercise in fresh air and living detached from civilization without the need to constantly focus and think has changed my palate? Is my body letting me know what is good for me under my current circumstances? To all the smokers and heavy drinkers – perhaps you should consider a trip up here. It may work wonders!

Sostenence brings our familiar pot of porridge. "Beans," he comments as he puts it down.

"Beans?!" Excited faces look at each other and eagerly lean forward to peer inside.

Indeed, steaming hot white beans in a red sauce, just like English breakfast beans, make us scramble for the ladle. What a welcome surprise and change from our everyday fare! Canned beans have never tasted so good before.

Both Giovanni and Chris have started taking Diamox this morning, in preparation for our base camp hike tomorrow. Now I'm the only one left without. Like every morning and evening, I curiously watch my blood oxygen saturation reading. If I can't make it to the summit because of lack of acclimatization, it's because I'm the only idiot who refused to take Diamox, and I've only got myself to blame.

My blood oximeter reading climbs to 94%. I'm excited as if I'd reached the summit already. We spent this night about 200 meters lower than last night, so it makes sense that my reading has gone up. But it hasn't gone up for everyone, and my reading has changed from below average to above average.

I'd love to say that this refutes the whole Diamox debate and proves that you don't need it, but of course I'm not statistically relevant and might just be the odd freak of nature, the extreme spike on the bell curve for altitude acclimatization. Perhaps having spent some time as a kid in the Austrian Alps has prepped me to handle altitude well, or perhaps I'm simply genetically preconditioned. Who knows? This is something you'll only find out for yourself when you actually try and do it. I got lucky this time round. But I'd better not jump ahead; there are still some 2,000 meters (7,000ft) of altitude between the summit and us.

Way more important than our pulse oximeter readings is how we actually feel, and as far as I can tell, our group is in an excellent condition. No one has a headache or any other signs of altitude sickness. Our long hike to ensure sufficient acclimatization time has been paying off so far. Now only Ravi needs to 100% recover from his cold – he's already feeling a lot better than last night – and our group will be in perfect shape for the big challenge.

▲ ▲ ▲

Our hike today will be rather short. We expect to reach the Third Cave camp within 4.5 hours, in time for lunch. Nevertheless, these 4.5 hours feel like a long day. It's not because the hike is challenging, to the contrary it's easier than any other day before, and not because of the weather, which couldn't be any better. It feels long because the hike starts getting boring and repetitive.

We see the same landscape over and over again, our little jokes that made us laugh so much just a few days ago have lost their entertainment factor after hearing them over and over again, and conversations between us are getting less engaged. As for myself, I'm silent in my own thoughts for the biggest part of the hike. According to our guides, this is an entirely normal pattern they experience with each and every group: Total excitement at the beginning transitioning into a quieter interim period when people develop first signs of altitude sickness or simply get bored, followed by a renewed wave of excitement for the final summit push.

There are only a few very short stretches along the path that provide for some distraction and require a bit more concentration, such as a short yet steep scramble over a three-meter tall rock. Skoba has positioned himself at the bottom and Samwel at the top, to make sure no one could possibly fall over. Our safety is their priority, but it also means taking the edge out of any challenge. I stubbornly refuse Samwel's helping hand that's reaching out to lift me up. Doing it all by myself makes me feel better.

Without much entertainment otherwise, I pay attention to the vegetation. Most of the ground is covered with the by now very familiar so-called everlasting plants – short bushes that grow anywhere from only a few centimeters up to knee-high. There are boring green ones without any flowers, your average type that probably wouldn't even get any botanist excited. There's also a type of shrub that's covered with fingernail size yellow or white flowers on top of prickly stalks that are so pale they look grey, or brown when they dry out and give way to new ones. They are just as boring as the non-flowery green ones, because they are all over the place.

Every now and then, a different kind of plant distinguishes itself against the monotonous scenery. Amongst my little entertainments, we pass a plant that I've never seen before. It stands up over a meter tall, in a shape that could easily pass as the phallic symbol of Kilimanjaro, though I would later find out its real name – a so-called *Giant Lobelia*. It has a base of reddish rosettes from which a green longish outgrowth with an intricate honeycomb-like surface erects itself into the air. This variant only grows in the mountains of East Africa, just like the *Giant Groundsels* that we saw on the way to Shira 2.

Giant Lobelia on the northern slope of Kilimanjaro

We also come across a few more of those *Giant Groundsels,* just that this time they don't look that giant at all. They are the young version, barely taller than the surrounding bushes. Only their first few layers of green leaves have sprouted into the air, like the top of a stemless palm tree.

Amongst our other few excitements during today's hike, we catch up with the Thomson Safaris group while they are taking a break. We pause for a few minutes at the same spot. There's a reason we all choose the same rest points, usually related to an assembly of big rocks – the perfect hideaway for some private time while stripping down our pants.

As soon as everyone has re-emerged, we continue onwards.

"Hey look, we can't see those guys anymore!" Chris comments after a few minutes.

I look back and indeed, "Seems we're doing quite good!"

"Yes, I think our group is quite fit."

Our unchallenging takeover maneuver makes us feel good about ourselves. However, by now none of us has any ambitions left to walk faster than our familiar *pole pole* pace. Even Chris stays behind Baraka (our lead guide today) almost the entire time, and I've also lost any drive to overexert myself. To the contrary, I've wound down my inner clock and even learnt to enjoy the quiet serenity of our slow and steady pace.

It is becoming ever more evident that making it to the top truly is all about *pole pole*, just as they all say and as I've read so many times. Our fitness levels and age have close to zero importance up here. Jeannette and Stewart are doing just as fine as we younger ones, perhaps taking their time a bit more on downhill slopes, but walking uphill just as fast and steady as everyone else. And Juli still is such a bundle of energy and positivity that I struggle to believe she put down her real age on that registration board.

As usual, the clouds roll in mid-morning, soon blocking our view of Kibo to the right and Kenya to the left.

Jeannette happens to walk behind me, and I'm still curious to hear more about her time in Saudi Arabia. "We didn't get far with our conversation yesterday," I break our silence. "I was still gonna ask you how you ended up in Saudi Arabia."

"Oh yes. Well, I was fascinated about the Middle East culture and the country," Jeannette patiently starts to explain. She simply wanted to move there and purposely looked for a way to make it happen. However, back then (and probably still now), it wasn't possible to simply go and live in Saudi Arabia without a job. Thus, via an agency, she found herself a nursing job in a hospital.

How courageous! Moving to Saudi just like that, as a woman and on my own initiative, would have never crossed my mind.

"Where exactly did you stay?" Chris chips in, appearing from out of nowhere. He likes moving back and forth within our group in order to join or start different conversations. "I also lived a few years in Saudi," he explains.

Jeannette and Chris exchange bits and pieces of their experience; or rather Chris is keen to share, Jeannette listens politely, and I ask eager questions. It turns out Chris has traveled the entire Middle East region. Right now, he lives in Dubai.

"I've never even been to Dubai," let alone anywhere else in the region, because so far it seemed uninteresting to me.

"You should come visit. I think it's one of the most fascinating places," Chris's eyes sparkle as he talks about his host city and region.

"Yes, I really should," listening to him and Jeannette I'm for the first time intrigued to go and see for myself.

Learning from and getting inspired by the people around us — that's one of the most rewarding aspects of hiking Kilimanjaro in a group, at least for me.

▲ ▲ ▲

We pass the remainder of our morning again in meditative silence, until we spot the familiar orange color of our tents in the far distance.

"Yay!"

"Finally!"

Seeing the finish line stirs more excitement than ever before, even though it has been the least challenging day so far. Bored by monotony, we are looking forward to lunch, to escape our lethargy.

On our descent to the camp, I finally take the opportunity to have a conversation with Jana. Since we've started our hike, she hasn't said much to me, other than politely acknowledging my attempts at conversations with a few short words. Nor has she asked me to join her on any photo this entire week. Her distance has been bothering me, and I'm worried that I've done something wrong. I thought we would get to know each other a lot better and become closer friends on this trip, like partners in crime, but the opposite seems to be happening. Perhaps I've hurt her by being overly cheerful and energetic when she didn't feel too well two days ago? Do I need to contain my positive emotions more in order not to make others feel worse? I want to find out and apologize, to get rid of whatever has come between us.

"Hey Jana, how are you?" I catch up from further behind to walk next to her.

"Good, how are you?"

"Good, good. Um, listen, we haven't spoken much so far. I just wanted to see whether everything is OK. Did I do anything wrong?" I muster up my courage to speak my mind and ask her directly.

She looks a bit stunned. "No, why?"

"Well, because we haven't been talking to each other since we started the climb."

"Oh, yes, I just don't like to talk while hiking. I prefer to focus on the hike."

"OK, sure," but that's not what I mean. I don't want to give up easily and get to the bottom of it. "It's just that even when we have breakfast, or lunch, or dinner, you don't talk to me."

"I'm sorry if you got that impression," Jana apologizes. "I wasn't aware of that. I'm not doing it on purpose."

"OK, no problem, all good then," just that I'm not convinced yet. "But if there's anything, please just let me know, OK?"

"OK. But really, there's nothing," Jana reassures me with a benign voice.

"OK. I'm glad to hear that," I shut up again to leave her to her quiet hike and stop being a nuisance.

I'm relieved that we've had this conversation, but I'm still not satisfied, not having my friend mentally with me on this mountain. After all, what was the point of doing it together in the first place?

My mind wanders off, speculating about what's really going on. She has Diego to share her experience, so she doesn't *need* me . . . Um, that doesn't feel good. Or she finds me outright annoying, but doesn't want to hurt my feelings by telling me? . . . OK, that feels somewhat better. Or perhaps she thinks that given we have such a great hiking group and we all get along so well with everyone else, I don't *need* her either . . .

Whatever the reason, being ignored still feels like a bitter pill to swallow, even if she's not doing it on purpose. I'm so glad that we opted for the group hike and that it's not all couples or close friends sticking together. Thanks to everyone for being so open and friendly. Otherwise I would be feeling really awkward and lonely right now . . . Or perhaps that's exactly the beauty of this trip, not knowing what it will bring us? And perhaps if Jana and I were talking to each other all the time, I wouldn't have a chance to make new friends with everyone else? Yep, I like that explanation, a misjudged twist of serendipity. Thank you universe for giving me this awesome hiking group!

That works! I immediately feel better again. The magic of influencing our lives by controlling our thoughts, just as Juli, Chris and I concurred yesterday.

▲ ▲ ▲

We reach the Third Cave camp before 2pm. There is another small group camping here. They must have come up on a more direct shorter version of the Rongai route, which approaches the summit from the northern side. However, their tents are set up a short distance away behind some rocks. We can barely see them, and so it still feels as if we are out in the wild and have the entire campsite to ourselves. The Thomson Safaris group must have gone a different way. Their tall tents are nowhere to be seen.

"*Karibu!*" Liber welcomes me with his, by now, very familiar broad smile.

He is rather short, with a haggard angular face and gaunt body, but his firm handshake makes me feel his strength. It's probably all muscles; whatever little flesh covers his bones, that is. His hands and fingers are gigantic, the ones of a piano player in a different kind of world, but made strong from a life of labor. His palm feels cold, but his smile is warm and sincere.

"*Liber, habari?*" (How are you?) I respond to his welcome.

"*Nzuri. Habari?*" (Good, how are you?) He seems pleased about my little attempt at friendly conversation in his language.

"*Nzuri sana, asante.*" (Very good, thank you.)

Liber opens the tent zip for me. As usual, my stuff is ready waiting for me inside.

"*Asante sana,*" I thank him once more. Just a few simple words, yet they make such a difference.

Admittedly, the first time Liber shook my hand, I was a bit shocked, almost disgusted, as if it were dirty, untouchable. Surely he wouldn't be able to wash his hands after having to touch God knows what, right? I told myself not to be such a prick. Without him, I wouldn't even have a tent to sleep in. Who would be carrying my heavy stuff? And why would his hand be any dirtier than mine anyway? I'm constantly touching the same tent that he built up for me and don't feel anything wrong about it either. Nevertheless, I'm still secretly washing or disinfecting my hands each time right after he welcomes me. Does this make me a bad person? Call me a hypocrite.

We've got 30 minutes to settle in until lunch is ready. My hair exudes a rancid odor even though I've been spraying it every morning with dry shampoo and some other stuff that's supposed to overpower anything unpleasant with a nice floral scent. Today, I've been distressingly aware of that odor all morning, hoping no one else would notice, and can't wait to hide away and do something about it.

When I take off my beanie, the hint of rancidity converts into a pungent smell. I end up spending the best part of the 30 minutes rubbing baking soda into my hair and brushing it out again.

No, I haven't gone nuts. According to everything I've read in preparation (how to *wash* my hair having been a big part of my research!), baking soda is supposed to be one of the best natural cosmetics. There's even a whole *no poo* (no shampoo) movement out there with heaps of followers who've stopped using shampoo. Baking soda is one of their little shared secrets to make it work. It not only sucks up excessive sebum, but also neutralizes smells. I've tested it at home in order to get my hair used to less frequent washing and it worked well for one or two days, the longest I've ever managed without shampoo. But up here on my fifth day without, I realize I will never become religious about *no poo*.

When I check the outcome of my half hour treatment session in my small mirror, my hair looks as greasy as before. It's beyond help and only a good old shower will be able to fix it. Only the smell is gone. Has the baking soda sucked up most of it, or has my nose just become insensitive in a desperate attempt at denial and self-preservation? To err on the safe side, I dump another big dose of floral spray onto my head and put my beanie back on, before consciously joining my nose in its state of denial. I can't see my hair, thus it's not there. Ignorance is bliss.

As my tent is right next to the mess tent, I can hear people gathering for lunch. So I go join them. The first thing I notice is Lynn's hair – completely uncovered and perfectly intact, tied back in a jaunty way. She clearly is the hiking pro in our group.

"How do you do that?" I'm eager to learn her secret. "Your hair looks so good!"

"Oh no, it's nothing," she shrugs it off. "I just tie it back." Lynn is not the kind of person to get freaked out about looks. She looks good in her natural way and totally at ease with herself.

"But it's not greasy at all. How is that possible? I've tried everything and nothing works."

"Oh, I just rub baby powder in every morning."

Ah, here we go. She obviously knows what she's doing, without even thinking much about it. So baby powder is the secret worth sharing. Next time I'll try that too!

Lunch is pure delight – banana fritters (!), leek soup, a massive plate of raw vegetables (!), a big pot of chicken (!), and French fries. I love it all, especially the assortment of fresh veggies including slices of cucumber, capsicum, red cabbage, onions and even some mango. And the chicken is a clear favorite amongst all us non-vegetarians. It tastes soft and tender, coated in a savory sauce of capsicum and tomatoes, with just about the right amount of seasoning.

"Hip hip!"

"Robert!"

"Did you like your lunch?"

"Ye-es!"

"We got fresh food delivered all the way from Moshi this morning. So we've got a lot of fresh food, enough for the next four days."

That's what they usually do on the Northern Circuit route, getting a second delivery of fresh produce from the Rongai route in the north. That way, they don't need to carry all the food from the start and make sure it stays fresh.

"This afternoon, we've got another bonus hike for you, but it's optional," Robert continues. "For those of you who want to go, we start at 4 o'clock."

As usual, we ask a lot of questions.

"This will lead us up in altitude only 200 meters, no higher than we've already been today," Jana summarizes the crux of our debate. "So it won't help our acclimatization, right? And we'll just go up the same path that we'll follow tomorrow, so we won't even see anything new, right?"

"Yes, it will help your acclimatization only a little bit," Robert confirms politely.

"I think it's much better to save our energies for the next two days. I'm not going," Jana states what seems to be the general opinion.

"Yes, what's the point?! This is stupid," Diego agrees.

Wow, I haven't seen the two of them so outspoken on the entire trip.

"So what is the point of it?" Stewart demands a better explanation. He looks at Robert incredulously, and we all follow his gaze.

For the first time, our chief guide smiles awkwardly and looks a bit overwhelmed by our sudden shitstorm. We are all ears, waiting for Robert to respond.

"Because we know that some of you have come here to walk," Robert has regained control, "so we give you a chance to walk. Some people get bored if they've got a whole afternoon without anything to do," he explains patiently, "they complain about just lying around in their tents. So we give you an activity . . . only if you want . . ."

"So just to be clear," Stewart mocks, "you mean we go walking just for the sake of walking?"

As if we hadn't walked already way more than enough during the past days! Who would voluntarily opt to walk any more than necessary?

Diego, Jana and Stewart are in strong agreement – they won't go. Everyone else is watching quietly, partly entertained by the heated debate, partly weighing options.

Call me crazy, but I'm still keen to walk. It's got nothing to do with boredom. I could easily entertain myself typing my notes or finally starting to read one of the many books about Africa and Tanzania that I've made sure to save on my Kindle for this purpose. So far, I haven't even had the chance to open any of them. But in essence, just as Robert says, I've come to walk. What's more, I don't want to miss out on any fun or opportunity to spend time with my fellow hikers. I will have enough time to read afterwards. My priority right now is the mountain and the company of my fellow hikers. Surely only a few of us will think like me and opt to go on this bonus hike?

"Um, I think I'll still go," I cautiously confess my intentions, "anyone else coming at all?"

To my surprise, eight of us raise their hands. I've found my tribe!

"I twisted my ankle today," Ravi explains his no-show of hands.

Ouch, he really has a streak of bad luck.

And Diego, Jana and Stewart stay back for obvious reasons, to enjoy a quiet afternoon and save their energy. That makes total sense. Tomorrow we start our big day(s). We'll hike up almost 1,000 meters (3,300ft) in altitude to base camp; we'll try to sleep in the afternoon, which will be difficult for most of us; and we'll embark on our big summit night late evening the same day. As I would have expected for most of us, they don't believe in hiking non-stop just for the sake of hiking and find it completely ridiculous to waste energy right now.

What I didn't expect, however, is that the majority of us are hiking freaks like me who literally enjoy walking for the sake of walking, no matter how much we've walked already and how much more still lies ahead of us. We are not a random sample of the population, but extreme outliers on the distribution of hiking enthusiasm. That actually makes sense. Why else would we all have booked the longest possible route up to the summit?

▲ ▲ ▲

Everyone heads back to their tent for a short rest. I find it nicer to stay in the mess tent where I can keep drinking hot tea and sit upright while typing my journal. Our guides come in and play cards. I think they always do that when the tent is free after lunch and after dinner, when they get a break from their multitasking as babysitter, coach, boss, teacher, psychologist, entertainer and friend.

Evance doesn't join their game.

"You're still here?" he prefers to talk to me instead.

I look up from my phone.

"Yes, it's nicer here, drinking tea," I explain and keep writing, about how we passed the Thomson Safaris group earlier. "Evance, do you know are the Thomson Safaris porters paid more than others?" I'm still curious to find out more.

"No, it's all the same."

"I still can't believe why their hikers are paying so much more."

"Estomee worked with them before," Evance tells me to support what he's just said.

He asks Estomee something in Swahili and Estomee replies, but seems annoyed by the question.

"Yes, he says it's all the same," Evance translates for me.

"So it's just the beds and the standup size tents, that's the only difference?" I still can't believe it.

"That's it," Evance nods.

I'm flabbergasted.

Later on, the rumor starts amongst our group that they also have a shower. Does that explain part of the price difference? In hindsight, I will verify with Thomson Safaris directly – no, they don't provide showers for their group tours[49], but yes, their staff receive some of the highest wages and are treated extremely well. This is yet another example of how difficult it is to find out the truth about Kilimanjaro operators. I'm sure Evance gave me the best of his knowledge, and yet it may not have been the full story.

I keep typing my notes.

"Are you working or playing games?" Evance asks me curiously.

"Um, writing my diary, just for me, taking notes, just to reflect," I'm telling half-truths and feel bad about it.

Ravi and Chris also come back to the mess tent for some company. I feel like such a spoilsport, staring at my phone rather than talking to them, but I'm keen not to leave all the typing for after dinner. I wish I could tell them the truth, tell them that I'm planning to write a book and only have good things to say. However, I want to keep that for the end.

I don't want to bias my experience. I don't want you, dear reader, to think that our guides only did so well because they knew I would write about them. The truth is, they have been the best possible guides so far without the faintest idea of my publication intentions, and I prefer to keep it like that for now, natural and authentic.

▲ ▲ ▲

Our bonus hike truly is a walk just for the sake of walking. The sun peeks through to start with, but clouds would keep it out of sight for the remainder of the afternoon. We walk uphill on a very gentle slope for about 45 minutes and take a short break to make the acclimatization worthwhile, for whatever little benefit we can gain from it. As nobody needs to rest, we keep entertained taking different kinds of group photos. On one, we all stand in a circle and put our right boots together inside. Surprise, surprise – they all look the same! Covered in dust and sand, what may have been green or black or brown or blue to start with, now all looks grey and faded.

On the way down, I feel a renewed surge of energy, energy that wants to flow, to get converted, to come alive.

"Evance, is it OK if I go ahead and run back down?"

"OK, but be careful," he agrees.

Evance knows that there is no risk. There are not many stones I could stumble over, and no wrong turns that I could take.

And so I set off on a 20-minute jog down the hill. Yippee! It feels so invigorating to finally be moving again at my own speed. I instinctively stretch out both arms to my sides to feel the energy, just as I used to do as a child, as if I could fly. With everyone else behind me, and our camp still out of sight, it almost seems as though I had the entire mountain to myself. What a wonderful feeling – nature and free-flowing energy, it makes me feel so alive!

Further down, I notice two people walking uphill. As we approach each other, I realize they are the same elder couple that we met yesterday. They are visibly enjoying their hike and each other's company. "*Jambo!*" I call out, and they greet me back with their friendly smiles.

Once back at our camp, it doesn't take long for Chris and Giovanni to arrive as well, ahead of the rest of the group.

"Oh, you were quick!" Good to know I'm not the only freak who enjoys a faster pace and some time alone on this mountain.

"Hey Alex, did you see the elder couple?" Chris asks me.

"Yes, we already saw them yesterday."

"Yes, exactly. How old do you think they are?"

"Um, not sure, 65?"

"No way, they must be in their seventies!" Chris has a much better sense about these things than me. "What more could you wish for when you reach that age! Still being so fit and healthy, and to have a partner with whom to come up here and to share such an experience. Don't you think?"

I didn't even think about that, but now that he mentions it, "Oh yes, sure, absolutely, that would be great," I agree with him.

"Hey Alex, let's make a pact. If we're still single when we're 70, or single again, we meet back here and do this hike again, together."

"Haha," I like his thinking, "sure, let's do that!"

"Deal!"

We jokingly shake hands to seal the pact. Chris beams as if I'd just made his day. He has this rare talent to give people his full attention and make them feel special and good about themselves.

It's getting chilly, now that we've stopped moving. I'd love to continue our banter, but the sun will be setting soon.

"Um, sorry, but I wanna go wash before it gets too cold. See ya later."

"Yeah, sure—"

I've already turned my back on him and disappear into my tent with my little bowl of hot water, excited about what's coming up next: new clothes!

Following general recommendations, I only brought one fresh change of clothing for every third day. We now only have three days left, so finally I can change into a fresh layer of underwear, thermals and hiking pants. What a luxury, I feel like a newborn!

Changing my merino underwear definitely gives me some peace of mind, but they've kept their promise and persistently resisted the take-up of body odor, contrary to merino socks that stink just like any other! More than my underwear, however, I'm excited to dump my pink hiking trousers. Not because they are pink, but because their fluorescent bright color shows every little bit of dirt, and there's a lot of dirt on them by now! Seeing the stark contrast of brownish grey smear from top to toe made me feel filthy, even more so than my greasy hair that I can't see.

No haute couture could get me as excited as my last pair of hiking trousers. I've been looking forward to wearing them all week. Olive green with heaps of outside pockets and promising to have all the qualities that I could possibly wish to have on summit night – they make me feel like a pro. Never mind that I have already been educated by the real pros in our group how to spot an amateur by their trousers: If they sit tight, that hiker clearly is a first timer who still focuses on looks. Yep, spot on, that's me! Pros would go for saggy ones to account for all the layers they may want to fit underneath. Whoops, that might actually become a problem . . .

▲ ▲ ▲

Before leaving for dinner, I realize that I have barely finished my three liters of water that we get every morning and try to gulp down as much as possible. Usually I would have a refill in the afternoon as soon as we arrive at the camp. I try to drink most of it during the day while hiking in order to avoid getting up overnight. That's been working well for me, also because I'm used to drinking a lot. Some people, however, really struggle to finish their daily three liters. If you are the type who barely drinks a glass a day, you may want to incorporate drinking into your exercise program. Drinking water, that is.

Dinner is becoming a repetitive affair. People seem to be mostly exhausted, more mentally than physically.

"This hike is starting to feel a bit too long," we all agree.

"No matter how well they cook and take care of us," there's a limit to how long even the best veggie soup pleases our palates.

And without much change in scenery, the entertainment factor is decreasing by the day. We've seen enough sand and everlasting plants by now.

"Seven days would have been enough," Chris expresses what everyone seems to think.

"Yes, nine days is too long," others concur.

"I just want to finally go up there and get it done with," everyone seems to agree.

"And go home," someone adds.

"And have a shower," we all nod our heads.

I can see their point and of course I wouldn't mind a shower either, though it's bothering me less than I expected. And I am of course also looking forward to summiting. That's what we all came here for, right? But for me it's not about getting it done with and going home, it's more out of curiosity about summit night. I want to feel challenged again! But I keep that to myself. Some people seem terrified about the pure thought of summit night.

"Yeah, it's getting boring. But if you go for seven days, you'd have all the crowds on the other routes, and less time to acclimatize," I only dare express my opinion about our route. "I'd still book the same route with the same guys all over again."

"Me too," some people volunteer.

"I like having our own little camps," Lynn adds and we all agree.

"Yes, they should just shorten the route," Chris is becoming creative. "We should tell them to cut out some days."

"Yes," others nod.

Um, he's got a point, but not sure how they could possibly shorten the route.

"Hip hip!"

"Robert!"

"Hey Robert, we think you should shorten the route . . ." Chris offers our insights to him.

Robert just nods and smiles politely. What is he supposed to do with a bunch of grown-ups complaining that they're getting bored?

It's time for our regular health check. After my morning excitement, I look forward to some further improvement. We are at a lower altitude than the past two days. Our blood oxygen saturation can only go up, right?

My oximeter reading plateaus between 88 and 89, it won't reach the 90% mark. Shock! How is that possible? Has my run made it worse?

"What an idiot," I reprimand myself, "tomorrow you'll go very, very slowly," when we'll gain 1,000 meters (3,300ft) in altitude up to base camp. Risking altitude sickness is not part of my agenda and has to be avoided by all means.

"I also stopped taking Diamox again," Chris informs me. His measures read even worse than mine, barely reaching 80%, the magic threshold.

"Really? Why?"

"I will take it if I need it, but I feel good," he explains.

Ravi, our pharmacist, is skeptical. He and Chris like giving each other a hard time. Almost predictably at least once during dinner, they would disagree about something. It's quite entertaining to watch – Chris the declared atheist and Ravi the Sikh by appearance, yet equally atheist, banging together, both sporting a great sense of humor and ability to laugh about themselves for the enjoyment of everyone else.

"That's a load of rubbish!" Chris would speak his mind.

Ravi, quite the opposite, would lift his arms to both sides like a preacher man, and in a more politically correct tone seek the support of the masses:

"People of this nation. You may have heard . . . BUT . . ."

It's hilarious. We all love their little theatrical display. It's like your daily evening soap, gathers you in for the first few episodes, quickly becomes run-of-the-mill, yet you keep watching because it still makes you chuckle each time round and you've got nothing better to do.

Tonight, Ravi reminds Chris of what we all already know: "Diamox is only effective if you take it before you feel sick. If you get sick up there, it's too late."

I'm with Ravi. While I should feel relieved to have a partner-in-crime against what I still believe to be a load of nonsense, seeing Chris's poor reading makes me more concerned that I may not have a partner-in-crime at all. I don't want him to get sick. He needs to get up there to the summit with me. How dreadfully boring and lonely would that night feel without him!

"You sure you don't want to take it now?" I try to convince Chris otherwise.

"I'm good," Chris stays firm in his resolution. He won't be taking it.

Overall, however, from a physical point of view, our group is still doing great. Only Ravi is having an unlucky streak with his twisted ankle while still not having fully recovered from his cold. But nobody has any noteworthy altitude symptoms. Boredom and fatigue are our only complaints.

As I was lying awake for most of last night, I'm longing for a good night's sleep. Tonight will be my last chance before our big summit night. Thus, I leave the mess tent as soon as we're done with our briefing.

While I'm settling into my sleeping bag and getting comfortable for the night, I hear Chris talking to Robert in the mess tent. He's confirming numbers with him to prepare our tipping: How many crew members within each category do we actually have?

Tipping is customary and a big thing at the end of each hike, no matter which operator you book with. There are recommended ranges for how much each lead guide, assistant guide, cook, waiter, toilet porter and porter should get. Jeannette proposed at the start of our dinner that we had better sort this out now, before all the summit exhaustion. We agreed that we'd better tip in the group rather than individually, and – following Jeannette's suggestion – appointed Chris as our spokesperson. He happily accepted this role, which also means figuring out how much each crew member should get and what this means for each of us. I am glad he's taking care of it. I wouldn't have the energy to think about it right now, let alone run any calculations in my head.

I also hear Jana's voice, joking to Chris and Robert. She sounds cheerful and energetic, fully recovered following her afternoon break, while I can't wait to close my eyes.

DAY 7

Into thin air

26 SEPTEMBER 2015

**From Third Cave (3,800m/12,500ft)
to School Hut base camp (4,750m/15,600ft)**
Distance — elevation — time:
5km/3mi⇨ — 950m/3,100ft⇧ — 4-5 hours☉

I wake up and it's still dark.

"Please don't tell me it's still in the middle of the night," I implore my phone.

"5:30," it beams at me.

At last! After a week, I finally managed to get over seven hours of uninterrupted sleep. Just in time for tonight's big summit night!

This night, I followed Evance's advice to keep my feet warm: "Sleep without socks, then you won't have cold feet," he'd already told us a few days ago.

Without socks? That didn't sound right, when stuck in an icebox, and so I spent three nights experimenting with two pairs of socks and self-heating badges instead, to no avail.

"Hey guys, guess what: I followed Evance advice to sleep without socks," Farrah told us excitedly yesterday morning, "and it really works! I had warm feet all night."

Based on her endorsement and because nothing else worked, I finally decided to give it a go as well. It wasn't easy – I had to drum up all my courage to take off my socks in the freezing cold, but it really worked. My feet felt nice and warm all night long!

Without even putting my socks back on, I just slip into my boots bare feet for a quick toilet run. Everyone is still asleep. The moon has become so bright that I don't even need my headlamp to find my way. Kibo is brightly lit up by the moon and millions of stars. It looks much more like a real volcano from this angle in the east, not like the wide plateau we saw from Shira 2 on the western side, but its slopes appear more gentle than ever before. It just sits there like an oversize frozen sand dune, peaceful and benign, welcoming us to explore if we really hope to find anything interesting up there. The air is crisp and calm. There's not a single sound other than my own breath and footsteps – pure serenity.

Night view of Kibo from the Third Cave camp (© Giovanni)

I calmly walk back to my tent and snooze for another hour, oblivious to the ghost hovering and watching over our camp. – Yes, ghost! At least that's what I will see in Giovanni's glorious night shot.[50] You don't believe in ghosts? Me neither – please enlighten me of any scientific explanations!

▲ ▲ ▲

We've got yet another beautiful morning. Without any obstructing clouds, the rising sun immediately warms up our tents, gently welcoming us to open our eyes and get ready for the day.

After weeklong practice, I have optimized my morning routine to the extreme: Lean onto my left elbow and use my right hand to pour a bit of hot water that I've kept overnight into my thermos cup. Drop in a tiny compressed one-time towel to let it soak up the water and convert into a steaming hot towel. Sit up in my sleeping bag. Enjoy the hot towel over my face and clean my eyes. Put in my contact lenses. Pour some more hot water into my thermos cup and drop in a vitamin C fizzy tablet to dissolve. Put sunblock onto my face as well as a thick layer of sunblock lip balm on my lips and all around my nose (which has become red and dry from the constant exposure to sun and wind). Take a sip from my hot vitamin C water for an instant warm-up from inside. Take off my shirt. Use the wet towel (that's meanwhile unfortunately no longer warm) to wipe other essential body parts. Cover my armpits with a thick layer of deodorant. Put my clothes onto my upper body. Dump a big portion of floral spray onto my head and sweater for a fresh touch, and hide my hair under my beanie. Finish my hot vitamin C water and force myself to finish any other leftover water in my water bladder. Drop two new remineralization tablets into my empty water bladder. Pack up most of my stuff, except for my toothbrush, toothpaste and thermos. Drag my feet out of my sleeping bag to put on my socks and trousers (yes, everything so far happened within the wonderful warm and cozy comfort zone of my sleeping bag). Stuff my sleeping bag into its cover bag.

This was all easy so far, now comes the tough part – open my tent and put on my hiking boots and gaiters. I don't like this part. It requires getting my hands dirty touching the gaiters, and messing around with the zip that keeps getting stuck.

I don't like the next part either – lifting my butt outside of the tent to stand up, while juggling my toothbrush and thermos in one hand, and making sure I don't need to dirty my other hand on the floor mat. That requires more leg and core strength than the entire hike!

The remainder is easy today in the sunshine: I can brush my teeth at length, no longer needing to jump around like a teenage hip hop dancer in the vain attempt to bring any blood circulation back into frozen fingers. Finally, wipe any leftover toothpaste from my lips with the back of my hand that I went to extremes to protect from getting dirty, just to then wipe the same into my hiking trousers. Yes, I've got a high-tech fast-dry towel, but no, I stopped using it on day two – too complicated.

To continue, finish any leftover hot water in my thermos. Lower my butt back into my tent to store away my tooth brushing utensils and lock my bag. Finally, after one last bloody time lifting my butt outside of my tent, drop my water bladder into our communal basket for a refill, and bring my daypack to the big plastic tarp that has been laid out as interim floor mat for our bags. As it's sunny this morning, I also position my solar panels on top of my daypack to start recharging my phone battery.

Finished!

That wasn't too bad, right?

I'm glad I can leave my big backpack, sleeping bag and foam pad inside my tent for our porters to sort out. Just like fairies, they take care of all the tough bits and pieces, and make it all seem so easy.

▲ ▲ ▲

On my way to the mess tent, I run across Jana; and so I try to use this opportunity to reconnect.

"Good morning! How are you today?" I ask her cheerfully.

"Good" is the usual short answer I would receive, "and how are you?" she asks me back today, making an effort to be polite and smile.

"Great, thanks! Lovely weather!"

Silence.

She keeps smiling at me, patiently bearing with my attempt at small talk and waiting for whatever I might say next. Surely she'd rather just get on with whatever she was about to do. We have again reached this invisible daily limit of conversation that the mountain seems to have imposed on us.

"OK then, see you at breakfast." I'm trying not to be a nuisance and leave her to finish her own morning routine.

Having mechanically progressed through mine, now comes the fun part: Proceed to the mess tent, enjoy the friendly good morning smiles of my fellow hikers and pour myself a nice hot cup of hot coffee . . . um . . . tea!

I can't believe I voluntarily opt for tea instead of coffee, listening to the caprices of my body that no longer demand any caffeine shots. What's wrong with me?

Our breakfast is testimony to yesterday's fresh food delivery: There's a big plate of fresh orange slices and watermelon, this time more than we can finish; and our omelet is mixed with green vegetables, giving it a freshly appealing touch.

Our oxygen readings are all fine and there are still no signs of altitude sickness in our group. Everyone is in high spirits today, looking forward to our big night tonight – summit night! Or rather most of us are looking forward to finally getting it done with and heading back down the mountain.

"Listen, for the tipping," Chris runs us through his calculations of last night, "I've taken their guidance and increased it by 10%, because they're really doing so well. So for each of us, that would mean . . ."

"Yes, sounds good," we all agree.

On the one hand, it sounds very reasonable because we are all extremely satisfied with everyone's performance (though I read that we shouldn't pay more than recommended, but I don't want to be a nuisance to bring this up now). On the other hand, I think we are all relieved that Chris took care of the math for us.

We take our time to prepare for the hike, there's no need to rush. I check my phone battery. To my surprise, it's already charged more than 50% during our breakfast hour. Yes, sorry, here we go again. I just can't get over how well these panels work. And this time I really need a good recharge because my phone will also have to act as replacement camera on the summit. This is BIG and important for me right now. I mean, what's the point of going up there if I can't even take photos to remember the experience?

I'm not the only solar panel enthusiast in our group – four of us have brought them. That's one third of our group, too many to classify us all as freaks. But it gets freaky now – we all brought exactly the same model by RAVPower! Seems we all went to the same extent to research the best model and came to the same conclusion. And no, RAVPower isn't sponsoring me. I'm simply a very satisfied customer who loves their product.

As I pick up my refilled water bladder, the water looks different – clear, not murky white. I'm certain I left two remineralization tablets inside. The thought of putting my lips around a mouthpiece that someone else has been sucking on for a week makes me feel nauseous.

"Hey guys, does anyone happen to have the same water bladder?" I just want to double-check.

People shake their heads. I guess I should know that by now. If there were any duplication, surely we would have noticed before.

"Alexy, what's wrong?" Robert immediately realizes that something is amiss.

"Don't worry. I just want to make sure that this really is my water bladder. Perhaps they just emptied my remineralization tablets thinking that it was waste. No big deal."

But Robert worries. If a client isn't happy, he won't rest. He starts asking around again and verifies with every hiker that nobody has the same model. That makes me feel awkward: "Don't worry," I repeat.

But Robert wants to get to the bottom of it and asks amongst the crew. I hope he's not giving them a hard time.

"They thought it was dirt," he confirms, "sorry."

"Not a problem at all," I reassure him while impressed how much efforts he puts into making sure that I'm satisfied. But speaking of areas for improvement, "Hey Robert, by the way, you know the toilet frequently runs out of paper. I really don't want to complain, but could you perhaps ask the toilet porter to just always leave a stack in there?" I remark cautiously.

I feel bad for saying anything because the entire staff goes out of their way all the time to make sure we are happy. Any kind of criticism doesn't seem justified in light of their huge efforts and hard work, but he asked us to tell him if they can do anything to improve. That's what you get when you constantly outperform and over-deliver. A week ago, I was surprised that they provided toilet paper for us at all, now I complain that it's not always there.

Robert immediately tells the toilet porter to go fix it. He also shows me a black bag.

"The toilet paper is always in there, you can take," he educates me politely. "It's because the porters have already started packing up."

Only now I realize that indeed there always was a black bag in the toilet tent, but I never even bothered to look inside. I feel ashamed about my own stupidity and behaving like an annoying prima donna again. Sorry Robert and Dominick – I apologize!

▲ ▲ ▲

Our hike to base camp starts like a Sunday stroll. We follow the same moderate path of yesterday's bonus hike, though it feels and looks different today. Yesterday, the clouds and fog blocked our view into the distance and made everything look brown and grey. Today, we have a bright blue sky and clear view of Kibo to our right. It looks tiny in my eyes. "What are those Kilimanjaro horror stories all about?" I wonder. It can't be that bad by the looks of it.

As we slowly increase in elevation, fewer and fewer everlasting plants are defying the treacherous climate. They gradually give way to a desert of sand and stones, dry ground eroded from the wind and lack of humidity. By mid-morning, as in all the past days, the clouds roll in and hide Kibo from our view.

"I miss your story," Evance wakes me up from my daydreaming. He is so used to me talking non-stop.

OK, let's have a conversation.

"Evance, is there any mountain you would like to climb if you could, I mean worldwide?" I ask him.

"Machu Picchu," he replies immediately.

"Yes, I'd also like to go there," we've got something in common.

"Do it with us," Evance recommends.

"What do you mean? Does the same company that owns Ultimate Kilimanjaro also have an operator in Peru?"

"Yes, also there," Evance nods.

That's great! I make a mental note to look into that upon my return home, for planning my next trip. Having been super satisfied with them so far in Tanzania, sticking to the same company sounds like a safe bet.

"I may go there next year," Evance continues.

"Oh wow, that's great!" I'm surprised. "How come?"

"They do hiking meet-ups for all the guides globally. I may go next year."

"Wow, awesome! Maybe I will even see you there again." I'm so happy for Evance.

He smiles.

I think if he or I were born into a different kind of world, we'd become good friends. I'd really like to see him again and do another hike with him.

To our left, Mawenzi comes into view. With 5,149 meters (16,893ft) at its highest point, Mawenzi is the second highest peak on the Kilimanjaro massif. It also is the third highest peak in Africa, just 50 meters short of Mount Kenya. Towering from behind a rather plane expanse of sand, Mawenzi looks like a mountain in its own right, but strikingly different from Kibo that welcomes us with its benign-looking slopes. The top of Mawenzi looks sharp and spiky like a crown, its walls steep and stony.

"Can you hike up there?" I ask Evance.

"Not everyone. You need technical mountaineering. But now it's closed. There was an accident last year. Two hikers had to be evacuated by helicopter. The park authorities don't allow it anymore."

"Let's play a game," Robert tries to entertain our group.

"OK, what game?" we're up for that.

"It's a country game. The first person says a country, and then the next person says another country that begins with the same letter that the other one ends."

That reminds me of my childhood. I loved these kinds of games.

"Let's try," Robert suggests. "Giovan, you start," because Giovanni walks at the front.

One after the other, we move through our line to half way. Then there's silence. The people behind either haven't been paying attention or can't be bothered. It doesn't matter. Giovanni, Jana, Juli, Stewart, Eva and I keep playing, intermittently, without order, with drawn-out periods of silence in between. Whenever everyone seems to have lost interest, someone randomly names another country. The periods of silence get longer and longer, until they become permanent. Game over.

We keep walking silently. The clouds become thicker and cover the sky. Without the blue of the sky or the green of any plants, we find ourselves again shrouded in grey and brown.

Walking without talking, without connecting, without learning something new seems like such a waste of time to me. I'm not usually like that, but this week I just can't shut up. Blame it on the full moon. So who's my next victim?

Samwel leads our hike today. I jump the line to walk next to him.

"Hey Samwel!"

"Yes?" He looks at me warily.

"I haven't spoken yet much with you. So where are you originally from?" I start the conversation.

It must sound like a bad pick-up line to him. I don't know anything about him, other than that he's the one with red-lensed sunglasses – little clues one picks up on initially to make it easier to distinguish who is who. Otherwise, all our guides wear the same blue Ultimate Kilimanjaro shirts and jackets. Jeannette keeps praising Samwel. He helped her take photos with her camera along the way. We've all got our own special guardian angel guide who we tend to ask for help or when we've got questions. For Jeannette, that's Samwel; I would always ask Evance; and for most others, that's Robert.

"I'm from Moshi," Samwel replies.

"Ah, that's convenient. How many kids do you have?" I guess everyone likes talking about their kids, don't they?

"I've got two kids."

"How old are they?"

Ah, older than I would have thought.

"So they go to school?"

"Yes, they are both at primary school."

"How many years of schooling do you have in Tanzania?"

"We've got 13 years, and then university."

That's just like where I come from, I'm thinking to myself. But where would they go to university? Would kids from Moshi even have a chance to attend university? Surely not everyone can afford to move to a bigger city?

"So when the kids go to university, they have to move to Dar es Salaam?"

"No, no, we have a university in Moshi."

"Oh really? That's convenient."

In that little countryside village that barely has a few proper roads? Where instead of supermarkets traders spread their goods on the sandy pavement?

"Can they study everything in Moshi? Or are their certain courses like medicine or engineering for which they need to go elsewhere?"

"What a dumb question!"

No, just joking. Samwel is of course keeping that part to himself. Only the surprised look on his face hints at my ignorance.

"Yes sure, everything. Moshi has the second biggest university of Tanzania. You can study whatever you want there."

"Oh wow, I didn't know that. That's great."

Yes, indeed, there's a lot of things I don't know yet, that I may have read but not internalized, that I decided to ignore as not important, that I would only research later on because I'm writing this book. For example, the municipality of Moshi has almost 200,000 inhabitants, that's eight times the size of the town where I went to university. It's bigger than Geneva, the second biggest city in Switzerland. What arrogance and ignorance to assume they wouldn't have a proper university, just because they don't have tall buildings and fancy sports cars! I'm ashamed of my stereotypes, assuming all of Africa would be poor and lacking basic infrastructure.

This trip has been quite an eye-opener for me. People in Tanzania, in essence, live just like in my part of the world – they have families and kids, they have regular jobs, they hope to send their kids to university, they have decent hospitals. Of course, the average income per capita is lower and they have their own social problems. However, the stereotypes in our Western society that I've allowed to shape my image and story, associating all of Africa with poverty and illiteracy (let alone war and disease), couldn't be any further from the truth, especially if generalized for every single country, every single family, every single individual. I really need to see and learn more about this beautiful continent!

"How about military service?" I continue our conversation for the sake of it, this time without any preconceived ideas.

By now, Chris has also jumped the line to join our conversation, probably also looking for some distraction from the silence.

"Like for example in Europe, a lot of countries used to have compulsory military service that all the boys had to attend, but then they changed to a professional army," I explain my question. "How is it in Tanzania?"

"It used to be voluntary, but they just reintroduced it two years ago. Now everyone has to go."

"Only boys?"

"Both, boys and girls. But when they attend university, they can delay it."

It's now about two hours since we left Third Cave Camp. While talking to Samwel, the hiking path has become steeper and more demanding, and the air has become thinner. It's not so easy anymore to talk and walk at the same time. Remembering my poor blood oxygen saturation readings, I shut up. It's time to focus on our breathing. No one talks anymore. We walk slower than ever before, like our last hour up to Lava Tower, gaze focused on the sand and scree in front of our feet. Whenever I try to speed up or say something, my lungs immediately put me back in my place. This is not the time to fool around and miss out on precious air. I focus on taking deep breaths with every single step, determined to avoid a headache or nausea by all means.

We spot a buffalo carcass further up the sandy slope. Our guides had already mentioned that we would come across such a curiosity today. It demonstrates what Evance told us two days ago, that buffaloes come up that high, over 4,000 meters (13,000ft) in altitude, to lick the alkaline rocks.

The carcass sits tall on a prominent rock. Someone has repositioned it there, like a tourist attraction. To us, it's the only visual distraction on today's hike, other than the view of Mawenzi. I can't wait to actually reach it, less to see it close up, more to catch my breath while taking a photo. It looks so close, like a minute's hike away, but would take us another ten minutes to reach.

The carcass lies on the rock with limbs drawn in, head lifted up into the air, as if it were curiously looking into the distance, waiting for someone to come along. It looks peaceful and clean, dry and well preserved. Its beige hide fully covers its bones and is partly covered with brown patches of thinning fur. Only its eyes have been picked out by crows, and its horns removed. Everything else looks intact. What a strange curiosity indeed!

Buffalo carcass on the way to School Hut base camp

Simply walking around the rock on which the carcass sits takes a humongous effort to deliver sufficient oxygen into our lungs and brains. I take a quick photo and keep moving, almost afraid that if I pause too long, my body won't allow me to go any further, keen to have this morning hike done with.

A steep slope of sand and scree rises in front of us. It's that illusory type of slope where one can only see clouds above its edge, where one doesn't know how much further it slopes uphill once we reach that edge. For half an hour, we endure the toughest stretch of our hike so far, not only because it's steep. This is the highest we've ever been at, the air the thinnest we've ever breathed. Every step forward requires a deep breath in or out. When we stop paying attention to drawing air into our lungs for just a second, or when we try walking just two steps faster than we should, we immediately find ourselves breathless and light-headed.

As I finally reach the edge of that slope, it turns out to be of the good type, flattening from now on, letting me see what I wouldn't have dared to hope for.

Our tents!

They appear no bigger than dots in the scenery, but their warm orange color glows amidst the dusky backdrop.

Excitement. We're almost there! Just ten more minutes!

Our camp is settled at the base of a big brown wall of rock, roughly as tall and wide as the public façade of Buckingham Palace, but slanting at the sides. An insinuation of a steep slope rises to our right, but the low ceiling of fog protects its mystery.

The path looks so flat and easy that I want to speed up. My legs want to run, my lungs scream for a break, my brain intervenes: We'll get there eventually, slowly, no need to rush; the most important thing is that I'm getting enough air, otherwise I may spoil your fun. It's not about steep or flat, it's about air or no air. Right now, there simply is not enough. I've never felt such a pronounced difference between my energy and my lungs before. They are not in sync.

I see Stewart walking some fifteen meters ahead of me. He must have kept walking when we took a break. Under normal circumstances, I could just run up to him. Up here, it's impossible to catch up on such a distance.

It takes us another half hour to reach the camp that looks so close. At 1:30pm, we're finally there, at School Hut base camp.

We've got the entire camp to ourselves. The other group from the Third Cave camp hasn't come up the same way. Indeed, we haven't seen any other hikers the whole day. We are spoilt to seemingly have the entire mountain just for us to enjoy, though the association with joy and pleasure doesn't come easy when trying not to suffocate from moving our legs faster than our lungs can squeeze oxygen out of nothingness.

As usual, my porter Liber welcomes me with a congratulatory handshake and shows me to my tent, with my bag, foam pad and sleeping bag ready waiting for me inside.

We still have about 30 minutes to recover and settle in until lunch, but today we don't get any hot water for washing. There is no water source near the base camp and all the water for drinking and cooking needs to be carried up from our prior camp. Does this mean our porters have to make the same trip twice, once with our gear and once with our drinking water? Most likely yes, but I don't know and I don't ask. Right now I have no capacity to think about that. I'm happily ignorant, glad that others take care of us, no matter how. I cleanse myself with wet wipes and prepare my stuff for the summit hike.

▲ ▲ ▲

Freshly fried vegetable puffs are bringing some excitement back into our meal fatigue. They are wrapped like a small calzone pizza with a crispy layer of dough outside and a savory steaming hot filling inside.

"Hip hip!"

"Robert!"

"You like your lunch?"

"Ye-es!"

"Thank you!"

"Yummy!"

"We are at 16,000 feet [4,800m]. It's not easy for your bodies to digest meat at this altitude. That's why there's no chicken today. Our chef Mr. Delicious has prepared this food especially for you today, so it's easy to digest."

We're all glued to his voice; today is important, no instruction to be missed.

"We will have early dinner today, at five thirty. Please go to your tents and try to sleep."

"Will someone come wake us up?"

"Yes, at five thirty we will come wake you up. Just try to sleep. Then, after dinner, we will have our briefing about summit night."

It might seem like a very serious affair to leave for after dinner to discuss, but we've already had a week to barrage our guides with questions about our big night. There's only one unknown:

"What time will we leave?" someone asks.

"Maybe at midnight, maybe at eleven. We'll discuss after dinner. And then you go to bed early today."

"Yeah right, I won't be able to sleep anyway," someone comments.

"Me neither," others agree.

"OK, just try. Please go to your tents now and have a good rest. See you later," and off we all go.

So far, I have not allowed myself to nap during the day. Usually I feel the urge to use our afternoon break to type my journal before events disappear from my memory. Not today, today there are bigger issues at stake – to have a good rest for summit night and to preserve the battery of my phone for taking photos on the summit. I crawl into my sleeping bag and close my eyes.

"Hello . . . Hello-o?" A voice outside makes me open my eyes again.

"Yes?"

"Dinnertime."

Eyes wide open.

"Okay!"

Wow! Have I just slept three hours? I must have fallen asleep as soon as I closed my eyes.

"Well done!" I'm thinking complacently.

I didn't expect to sleep so well, after all those restless nights. Perhaps the altitude or skipping my coffee entirely this morning has made the difference?

I feel a hint of excitement. It's slowly starting to get serious, only a few more hours until we will start our summit ascent.

Our camp has gotten dark in the shade of the big rock behind us. The clouds have descended below us. They block the view down to about one hundred meters from where we came earlier today, but leave a clear blue sky above us. Mawenzi, which in the morning adorned our view to the left before disappearing behind the fog, now lies behind us. Its spikey crown breaks through the clouds and radiates a soft yellow hue in the setting evening sun which is directly illuminating its flanks.

"Hey guys," I rub my hands as I walk into the mess tent, not only to warm up my fingers as usual but also as a gesture of excitement. "It's getting real!" I'm sporting an abnormal smile of eager anticipation. "How did you sleep?"

"Ah, not at all, I'm too excited."

"I wasn't tired yet."

"I can't sleep in the afternoon."

So I'm the only one who got some sleep?

Juli comes in with a big bag.

"I've got something for you," she announces and starts handing out huge American energy bars.

"Thank you," "Thank you," everyone is pleased about her present, and Juli about giving.

"Alex, I know you wouldn't like it," she skips me considerately, knowing about my self-imposed strict no-sugar diet. I'm glad she doesn't make me say no.

"Thank you," "Thank you," everyone else happily accepts her treat and Juli's sparkling eyes wouldn't need any explanation:

"We've got heaps of snacks left. And we love to share."

Like lunch, our dinner consists of food that's supposed to be easily digestible – onion soup, spaghetti and a veggie/mushroom sauce. Most people only go for small portions. "I'm not hungry yet, we've only just had lunch," everyone agrees.

Farrah hardly eats anything at all. "I've got no appetite up here," she explains.

The spaghetti tastes starchy, but I like it anyway. Maybe because I normally wouldn't allow myself to eat any and now I've got an excuse. This is the last hot meal we'll have for the next 20 hours. Isn't this the time to load up on energy? I follow my voracious reputation and instinct to go for several helpings. Altitude is supposed to make us lose our appetite, but it clearly has the opposite effect on me.

"So how many layers is everyone going to put on?" someone asks.

No one wants to get sweaty hot, or miserably cold either. Prior hikers recommended different things at Bristol Cottages. Some got too hot walking in full winter gear, while others were cold despite putting on every single layer they had brought. It's very individual.

"I'll go with four," Chris announces.

"I'll put on everything I've got," most of the girls concur that we need five or six layers.

"Hey guys, remember what Evance said about the couple whose camera didn't work, how no one loaned them a camera so they couldn't even take a picture at the summit?" Chris recalls. "We're not going to be like that, right? We'll loan our cameras if someone needs it?"

"Absolutely," people nod their heads.

"Everyone can have our camera," Juli agrees.

"I wouldn't necessarily give my phone to them. I'd help them take a photo myself and then send it to them by email," I admit.

"Yes, that's it. We'll get their email addresses," everyone agrees, still unable to believe how people can possibly be so mean and not even help someone else take a photo at such a special occasion.

It has gotten dark outside. The air is loaded with anticipation. It's this special kind of atmosphere of anxious excitement, like when one needs to get up in the middle of the night to catch an early morning flight to an unknown destination, or when one prepares backstage for a big performance, or an interview for one's dream job, or your university graduation ceremony.

There's an unmistakable hint of forced optimism.

"We'll all get there, we'll all make it up," we keep saying, but I'm not so sure everyone truly believes that about him or herself.

Unspoken fear is written in some eyes. At least no one's got any signs of altitude symptoms, other than loss of appetite. Ravi still feels his ankle unfortunately, but is willing to quietly accept his added burden and go for it nevertheless. Overall, we've got no major complaints. Our long acclimatization time has definitely been paying off, so far.

"Hip hip!"

"Robert!"

All our six guides are present for tonight's briefing.

"We will all come with you. Evance will lead us. And we will have four assistant guides to help you: Skoba, Samwel, Estomee and Baraka," Robert points out one after the other, as if we met them for the first time. Have previous hikers ever not know their guides by now? "We will also have two summit porters. They are strong porters who come with us all the way to the summit. They can help carry you—"

Laughter.

"Please not!"

"I don't want to be carried up."

"If I can't go any further, I'll just stop."

"It would be such a cheat," several incredulously exhilarated voices intermix with mine.

Chris and I spoke about that previously.

"I read in some books that people got carried up by their guides because they couldn't walk anymore," I mentioned, "and they all loved their guides for that. I think that's really stupid. A good guide shouldn't do that. It's dangerous. They should send you back down immediately."

"Yes, what a cheat!" he agreed. "I wouldn't want to say I got carried up there. What's the point? I want to do it on my own, or I just stop."

Robert patiently bears with our nervous outbreak of laughter, but stays serious throughout. The responsibility for our safety rests on his shoulders.

"For some of you, your backpack may become too heavy," he clarifies. "They can help you carry. Or they may support you on the way down, if you've got bad knees."

We're not capable of thinking about the way down yet. Going up is all that matters.

"Some of you have asked us what to wear," Robert carries on. He usually briefs us for the following day, such as whether we need a warmer jacket or just a rain jacket. Today he goes item by item, hiking for dummies: "On top, you put on your first layer, your fleece, your down jacket, your wind jacket," and so forth; at least four layers on top, three layers at the bottom; one or two pairs of socks; gloves and optionally liner gloves; a balaclava or beanie or both.

We've all already made up our minds what to wear, but we listen attentively to double-check, for additional reassurance that we haven't missed anything.

"When the sun is up, it will be very strong. Don't forget your sunscreen and sunglasses.

"So what to expect?" Robert moves on. "Some of you will get sick from the altitude. Remember, that's normal. Maybe you'll get a headache. Maybe nausea. No problem. Maybe you'll need to vomit . . . maybe you'll vomit once . . . or maybe four times . . . that's normal . . . just vomit . . . and then keep going."

We all laugh hysterically, anxiously entertained like a class of students after being told that some will fail the exam but may get a chance to study harder and sit through it again, each of us hoping to be spared the extra trouble. I hate feeling nausea and can't possibly imagine being able to keep going nevertheless, and certainly not after throwing up. Yuck, that would feel horrible!

"The most important thing is to stay calm. Don't panic."

OK, that should be easier. Robert has already summited over 160 times. He has the best possible experience. We all fully trust and rely on him to take good care of us. As long as he's there, we'll be fine.

Liber and another porter come into the tent.

"I'll now introduce you to your summit porters. This is Mr. Liberaty . . ."

We welcome him with a round of applause.

". . . And this is Mr. Charles."

We all applaud again.

"If your backpack gets too heavy, you can give it to them."

Before coming on this trip, I thought we'd have perhaps one lead guide and two assistant guides, three in total, as it seemed to be the case for other hiking groups whose reviews I had read. Having eight (!) guides and porters accompanying us twelve hikers to the summit exceeds my expectations big time. It means we'll be less than two hikers per guide. Even in the worst possible scenario if one of us can't walk anymore, they'd be enough people to carry us down. What could possibly go wrong like that?

Evance takes over: "It will get very cold and your water bladder will freeze. After you drink, blow air back inside. Then it doesn't freeze so quickly, but it will freeze. Some of you asked me what to do.

No problem. You use your Nalgene bottle. What you do is you put your Nalgene bottle like this," he holds his bottle upside down to demonstrate. "Then the water starts to freeze from the top," he points to the upside-down bottom of the bottle. "When you drink, you just turn it back around." It should remain liquid near the opening.

Smart technique. I'm glad I wasn't aware of that back home, otherwise I wouldn't have brought my thermos which I wouldn't want to miss now that I've discovered all its other uses.

"Now you decide as a group two things," Robert picks up again. "First, what time do we leave? We can leave at midnight, or we leave earlier, at eleven. Then we may see the sunrise from the summit. We'll all go up together as a group," he's already preventing any discussions of splitting up, and I can feel my heartbeat accelerate. "On the way down, we will form smaller groups. Those of you who feel confident enough with your knees can slide down quickly and others will walk downhill."

"We should also all walk down together as a group," Stewart interjects.

"Let them walk faster," Juli intervenes.

"The slope downhill is very sandy. There will be a lot of dust after each of us. That's why we need to go in small groups and leave a gap behind each other. It's quick to come down, almost like skiing, you will see," Robert explains.

No one really cares much about our descent yet at this point in time. We'll worry about that part once we've actually accomplished the bigger challenge. Most worry about getting up to the summit in the first place.

I worry about freezing to death on the way while walking at a zombie pace, and I don't like the direction our conversation is going. Should I make another attempt to try and have us form two groups for the ascent as well? Will Chris raise the point? By now it has become crystal clear that some of us walk a lot slower than others. Why is Robert forcing us to walk all together? I'm sure I'm not the only one who would opt for the faster group. There would be at least four of us.

"If you want to go fast, go alone. If you want to go far, you go together," Jana concurs with Stewart from the opposite end of the table.

Yeow! That feels like a slap into my face. She hasn't been that outspoken for the entire week, apart from yesterday's bonus hike discussion.

"Yes!" everyone nods and agrees with Jana.

She has set the tone, so it seems to me.

OK, I totally get that, and so far it has been wonderful to hike as a group and share my experience with everyone else. But what about: "If you want to keep your body warm, go at your pace. If you want to get frostbite, go as a group." I bite my tongue. Am I selfish to think differently? Why are slower hikers allowed to be anxious about physical exhaustion, but faster hikers are not allowed to be anxious about freezing? Why is it OK to suffer from high blood pressure, but not OK to suffer from low blood circulation in my extremities? Does nobody here know the pain when your blood no longer reaches your nose, fingers and toes?

I was counting on Chris as my accomplice to push for two groups, but he just sits there quietly. Has he meanwhile changed his mind? Seemingly, I'm the only person who doesn't see the point of making all of us go the same pace, and that won't be enough to have Robert accommodate my wish. I don't want to be perceived as unsocial and keep my mouth shut. It's group pressure life in action. OK, in the big group it shall be. I'll just put on every single layer of clothing and hope for the best.

"Let's leave at eleven, we won't get any sleep before that anyway," Stewart proposes.

"Yeah, me neither. I'm too excited," others agree.

Why not? I think I will, but this is not the time to preach about meditation and inner relaxation. I read in a prior review that they made it up too early and it was too cold on the summit to wait for sunrise, so they started their descent in the dark. That must be avoided by all means. I want to be up there for sunrise.

"But then we'll be up too early," I interject.

"I don't think so, we'll need that time," Chris wakes up again.

"Really? What time is sunrise?" I look at Robert.

"Sunrise is at six fifteen."

That's over seven hours (!), much longer than others needed in what I read.

"Guys, if we leave at eleven, it will be dark when we get up there." I try to push for midnight. I'm the one who has over-prepared for this trip and figured it all out, so I think.

"Listen," Chris speaks up, "we'll see the sunrise anyway, so we may as well leave at twelve and then we either see it from the top or on the way."

"Yes exactly," I like his thinking.

"But we'll need the time," Jana pushes back.

"And we can't sleep anyway," Lynn agrees.

"Yes, let's leave at eleven," Stewart says authoritatively.

"Alex, we'll need the time," Chris tries to intervene.

"Really? No way!"

"Evance says so. Hey Evance, we'll need the time, right? If we leave at eleven, we'll just get up for sunrise, right?"

"Yes, your group will need the time," Evance confirms. "We know our clients. Your group will need seven hours minimum."

How dreadful! I can already feel my fingers freeze in the slow motion.

Chris gives me a conciliatory look.

OK, I had better shut up and deal with it. If Chris can do it, I can, I'm telling myself. But he is a guy and surely he doesn't suffer from cold fingers and toes . . . Oh well, I brought all these self-heating badges and hot water, I'll be fine, I'm trying to comfort myself. With this, the debate is settled and I resign to our majority vote, swallowing hard to drown my frustration.

"OK, so we leave at eleven. We will wake you up at ten. Then, before we leave, you can have a hot tea or coffee, and we'll have cookies for you. Pack up your bag and leave everything in your tent," Robert summarizes our action plan. "In the morning, your porters will pick up your stuff and carry it to our next camp. Just bring your small backpack.

"So now you have to decide on the second question, where we stay tomorrow night. There are two options – Millenium Camp or Mweka Camp. Millenium Camp is a bit closer. From Uhuru Peak, you can get there in maybe six hours. The other one is another one and a half hours further down."

I don't really care. My competitive me intuitively opts for the one further away, just because I can and it increases the challenge, and because I believe the guides may prefer Mweka Camp in order to save time on our last day. I'm sure they can't wait to get home to their families in two days. But I leave it to everyone else to make that decision. So do most of us. We can't think that far ahead and have no benchmark for comparison.

"I think the closer one," Jana volunteers an opinion. "After this night, I don't think we'll want to walk any further than necessary."

Some people nod.

Chris takes charge again: "Robert, it's difficult to decide that now. We don't know how we will feel tomorrow. Can we decide that tomorrow after the summit?"

"OK, you can also decide tomorrow."

That was easy.

"We are done with our briefing. Try to get some sleep now. We come wake you up at ten."

We all quickly disappear into our tents, picking up our refilled water bladders on the way. I ask Crispin if I could have a full liter of hot water for my thermos, so I won't need to bother with that later on.

"We need to boil more."

"OK, I'll just wait."

He reaches out for my bottle. "You can go. I'll bring to your tent," he kindly offers.

What a service!

On the way back to my tent, it's so bright that I don't even need to use my headlamp. The terrain is uneven and full of opportunities to stumble, but the moon sheds more than enough light. What a nice surprise! Crispin and the moon have restored my mood, I'm happy again.

"Your water," I hear Crispin's voice once I've barely taken off my shoes.

Great. Now I only have one remaining task – to get some rest. With all my clothes on, including my thick insulation jacket, I crawl into my sleeping bag and surrender to my duty.

SUMMIT NIGHT

Fighting alone and together

26-27 SEPTEMBER 2015

**School Hut (4,750m/15,600ft
to Gilman's Point (5,685m/18,652ft)**
Distance — elevation — time:
5km/3mi⇨ — 900m/3,000ft⇧ — 5-7 hours☺

"Wake up," a voice brings me back to reality.

Already? Wow! I must have fallen asleep again as soon as I closed my eyes, another full three hours. Lucky me!

"Wake up!"

"Yes, thanks, I'm up!"

Not only that – I'm bright awake. This is it! The moment of truth has come at last. I'm excited to finally get this big day started, but at the same time scared of the cold night awaiting me outside.

We've got an hour until we will start our hike, no need to rush. I take my time to put on pretty much all the top layers that I've brought along and that might be of use to keep me warm: a sleeveless merino top, two thick long-sleeved merino shirts, another long-sleeved polyester thermal undershirt, two thick long-sleeved merino sweaters, my insulation jacket, and my wind/water resistant soft shell jacket. With all these eight layers (or nine including my merino sports bra), I feel like a Michelin man, barley able to move.

I go a bit lighter on my legs, including merino thermals, mid-layer fleece pants, windproof and thermal retaining hiking trousers, as well as waterproof pants – four layers in total (or five including my merino shorts). That's only half as many layers as on top, but twice as difficult to put on in this tent that right now seems confining and small. How do you do that if you're sharing a tent?

Until tonight, I thought that I might have lost weight on this trip, but right now my hiking trousers tell me the opposite. I can barely close them on top of my thick fleece pants. Or perhaps that's because I bought the non-professional tight version that doesn't allow for much underneath?

If you still wonder what exercise to do in preparation for such a trip, try the bridge pose – upper back and feet down, butt up. You will definitely need that unless you prefer to get dressed outside in the cold!

At least my head is relatively easy to take care of, though pulling a balaclava over my face for the first time in my life also adds a touch of adventure to this body part. It should be warm enough theoretically, but I still put my beanie on top just to make sure, and in order not to look like a bank robber on the summit photo. I also keep my thin Buff neckerchief for whatever little bit of extra warmth it might be able to provide.

To keep my feet warm, I use my thick chili-feet insoles and stick one pair of self-heating toe warmers to the outside of my thick ski socks. Our guides advised us to put on two pairs of socks, but I trust the chili-feet insoles should be more effective than a second layer, and there's not enough space for both.

My hands will be covered in liner gloves and brand-new mittens. I'm curious about whether they will keep what they promise, after I spent almost half a day researching the warmest possible mittens on the whole planet. But just in case, I also stuff self-heating finger warmers into them. Expecting my nose to get leaky, I tie a handkerchief to my mittens. That should be an easier solution rather than messing around with tissues, allowing me to wipe my nose without even taking my mittens off. And just in case I still need to take my mittens off, they've got convenient handcuffs, so I can just leave them dangling down my wrists and not worry about losing them. I love this efficient construct – all devised with only one purpose in mind: To keep my fingers warm. What could possibly go wrong?

In my inside pockets, I put my phone and spare batteries for my headlamp. Keeping them inside should prevent the batteries from draining in the cold. Within easy reach in my outside pockets, I double-check that I carry my lip balm, ginger lozenges (against nausea) as well as some wet wipes (in case I need to pee).

In my daypack, I carry my three-liter water bladder and my thermos filled with one liter of hot water, my sunhat, sunglasses and sunscreen for the day, heaps of nuts and power snacks, another pair of hand and toe warmers, as well as my valuables and passport as usual. And of course I'll be holding on to my hiking poles as always.

My big bag that I leave behind for the porters to pick up in the morning has deflated from brimming full to half empty. No wonder – it's all on me now (!), layer after layer cramping my agility like a straightjacket.

With everything in place, it's time to get out of my tent and to face the harsh temperature outside. Part one is not an easy feat – bloody clothes and gear weighing me down just like full-on scuba diving gear that always makes it so hard to get back out of the water. Part two makes me forget that feat in no time. – It's not cold! It's not cold! It's not cold! It even feels warm, relatively speaking of course, within all my layers. The air is calm, and the starlit sky looks peaceful and clear of any clouds. I can't believe our luck. My worst fears are nullified. If it's not cold, then nothing can go wrong.

A flush of happiness hormones makes me feel exhilarated, my most confident ever. I'm looking forward to this night like an actor before Oscar night, anticipating the long walk over the red carpet, certain of the imminent award, and looking forward to days of celebrations and feeling good about myself thereafter.

By the time I reach the mess tent shortly after 10:30pm, everyone else is already seated around the table. There are half empty cups of hot tea or coffee and a plate with a few cookies. Seems people have been here for a while. It's quiet. They look at me as if I'm the latecomer. Chris busies himself to find me a spare cup.

"How did you all sleep?" I dare ask.

"Ah, not at all."

"Neither."

"I just want to get going."

"And be done with."

"Assuming I make it."

"Of course we all make it!" I try to encourage them.

"Yes, we'll all get there," Juli and Lynn agree with me.

Forced smiles and nods.

Within my exhilaration, I don't understand why the mood is so subdued.

Chris has found me a spare cup. It doesn't look clean, but as long as it's not in use it's good to go. I mechanically pour myself a cup of tea, just following my instinct. Never would I have thought that my body doesn't shout for caffeine at the start of this biggest of all nights.

There is not much conversation going on. Everyone is just waiting to get started.

"OK everyone, please get ready," Robert finally gives us the signal.

We move back outside and I'm strapping my backpack on, but some people are still messing around with their gear, doing whatever I would have thought they should have done by now. Seeing that we won't leave for a while, I make a last trip to the toilet tent. And what an effort that is! Peeling down and up five layers of tight trousers and pants that are not meant to sit on top of each other, while unable to bend my elbows properly under seven layers of long-sleeve shirts, within the confines of a dark narrow toilet tent that's blocking all moon light – nothing can be harder than this Herculean task! Going through that procedure again must be avoided. I plan to drink little on the way up.

"Let's go. Why is everyone so slow?" Chris tries to find an accomplice in me as I return.

"Don't know," but I don't dare say that I'm the last one back from the toilet tent. This makes me as guilty as everyone else.

"Please line up," our lead guide Evance gets us organized.

Slowly, people are moving into place. I feel so hot within all my layers, even just standing around, that I open the zips of all my jackets and store away my mittens on top of my backpack for now.

"Jana, come here," Evance asks her to walk right after him.

As soon as she and Diego have repositioned to the front of the line, Evance starts to walk. And off we go, finally! It's already 11:20pm.

My body is expecting Evance's familiar slow and steady steps, excited to march off into our big night, but our pace is not just slow. It's excruciatingly slow, as slow as a dead snail. I constantly need to pause after every single step in order not to run into Chris who's walking in front of me.

"We're not even moving," Chris vents what I don't dare to think anymore.

In a group it shall be. I want to enjoy tonight, and as long as it's not cold and we get up there by sunrise, I don't mind whatever pace Evance deems appropriate.

There is a short steep incline to start with, scrambling up a massive rock the height of a five-story building right behind our camp. Surely it will get better afterwards. My only concern is whether it might get cold and windy once we've left the rock's protective shield.

"Why didn't you say anything at the briefing?" I want to know why Chris left me hanging. "I thought we were gonna push for two groups?"

"Robert wouldn't let us anyway."

"You're probably right. If it gets too bad, maybe we'll still split up later on," I comfort myself.

The night stays calm and pleasant, and the path soon turns rather flat as it winds horizontally around the Eastern side of the mountain. Nevertheless, we continue walking very slowly. I feel I'm in a slow motion movie, in permanent break mode, unnaturally restraining my legs and interrupting their natural motion. We hardly seem to make any progress. My lungs feel sufficiently filled with fresh air to allow conversations and random jokes, though I hear others already breathing very heavily. As a group, that's the pace we need to follow, we couldn't possibly walk any faster. I've moved beyond frustration and accepted the reality. Now my mind is set to make the most of it.

Chris seems to have a different view; his fancy altimeter watch tells the truth. "We're not gaining any altitude," he confides in me with an unmistakable hint of frustration.

I'm happy, happy that after all I'm not the only one who would wish to walk faster, happy that I'm not the only freak in our group, happy that I can share this experience with someone who feels like me.

Our view now reaches all the way down into Kenya where randomly lit houses mirror the star-filled sky. It's so nice and peaceful up here. There's not a single sound other than our own steps, not a single wind whisper, just our own breath moving the air. My worst fear of getting miserably cold is proving unjustified, and with the slow pace of our group I don't think I could possibly run out of breath or develop any worse high altitude symptoms myself. If others can handle it, I'm sure that I'll also be fine. This is the night I've been working towards for the greater part of this year and I'm determined to enjoy every single bit of it. I should be grateful that we're walking so slowly, because this gives me enough time to soak it all in. If I had the choice, I wouldn't possibly want to be anywhere else right now. I couldn't be any happier.

Some people need to pee or catch their breath, so we take a break. Already? Haven't we only just left our camp? "OK, Alex, this is not the time to get frustrated," I keep reminding myself, "just relax and enjoy the view."

Evance smiles at me understandingly, almost apologetically. He knows this snail pace must feel like torture to some of us. "Don't forget to drink," he reminds us.

I take a tiny sip only to oblige, but remain determined to make it through the night without pulling all my five layers down and up again.

I gaze down into Kenya. Up here, the view doesn't gradually slope down as it did at Buffalo Camp. It no longer looks as though we could just run down. This time we just see a hundred meters of a gentle downhill slope, and then abruptly the lights underneath in the far distance, as if we were hovering on a detached far away slab of rock, like on the moon looking back down on earth. I have never seen anything like this before and wish I had a camera to capture this mesmerizing sight. My phone has worked well as a camera replacement so far, but it's useless at night. "Anyone got a camera and could take a picture?"

"Don't worry, I'm taking photos." Giovanni already has his professional camera out.

"Great, thank you," I sigh with relief, knowing that he is a very experienced photographer.

Summit night view into Kenya (© Giovanni)

Shortly after we continue walking, we scramble over some knee-high rocks that take a bit more effort.

"*O sole mio*," Giovanni's singing voice breaks the silence.

This reminds me about a situation in Spain when a native English-speaking friend asked me over dinner while ordering *solomillo* which means sirloin steak in Spanish:

"Why do the Italians sing about steak?"

I found the confusion between *"O sole mio"* and *"O solomillo"* hilarious back then and can't help laughing about it all over again.

"Hey Giovanni, you wanna hear something funny?" I tell him the joke, but he doesn't react much. Has he not understood me, or does he simply not find it funny? I decide to drop it, but keep silently laughing to myself. Perhaps the thin air is having more of an impact on me than I'm aware, giving me a bit of light-headedness again.

The path keeps bending around the eastern side of the mountain. Soon we see short lines of dotted lights, both downhill and uphill. Our path is now merging with the busier Marangu route as well as the Rongai route. Both had their base camp at Kibo Hut, not too far away from School Hut. We are no longer alone in the wild, but that doesn't change the serene atmosphere. Seeing these lights even adds a touch of romance and beauty to the entire scene, as if we're part of something bigger, a pilgrimage or a solidarity march.

As soon as our paths have merged, we are no longer walking alongside the mountain on a moderate inclination, but make a sharp right turn facing straight uphill. The onwards path winds like a snake up a steep slope, so steep it wouldn't be possible to just walk straight up. "OK, so this is where the tough part starts, it couldn't possibly remain that easy all the way up," I'm thinking to myself. Now we're increasing in altitude with every single step and the air is becoming noticeably thinner from one moment to the next. No one talks. We all just follow the monotonous footsteps of the person right in front of us, focusing on our breathing: Step, breathe in, step, breathe out, step, breathe in, step, breathe out. My mind is clear; I don't think of anything other than controlling my breath.

All our guides are taking great care of us, continuously asking everyone how we feel, reminding us to drink water. Naturally they are paying most attention to those struggling, but even I feel there's constantly someone by my side, asking me how I am. Whenever one of our guides asks me, *"Alexy, habari?"* I cheerfully shout back, *"Nzuri sana!"* I know this is a tough night not only for us, but also for our guides. So I want to assure them there's one less person to worry about, I'm fine.

After what must have been over an hour since our last break, I take a sip of water, more out of curiosity than thirst. The tube of my water bladder isn't frozen yet, still allowing me to drink normally. But the act of drinking is not an easy task up here, difficult to accomplish while walking. As I swap a breath for a sip of water, I immediately feel a lack of oxygen. Using my short breath to then push the water back down the tube to prevent it from freezing reminds me of the last time I had a shisha and inhaled a bit too eagerly, leaving me feeling light-headed for a while. Breathe in, breathe out, breathe in, breathe out; that's all I'm thinking. It's almost like meditating, and I'm losing any concept of time.

▲ ▲ ▲

We take a break at a bend that is big enough so we don't block other hikers, and that conveniently has many big stones to sit on, or to hide behind in order not to moonlight in front of everyone. It's around 2am. The temperature has dropped a little, but I still don't feel cold. Sitting on a rock facing downhill, I realize that the imposing Mawenzi peak is now in full view, rising straight up in front of us, surrounded by stars all around its crown. While others do whatever they need to do, I just sit there quietly and look at the view, mesmerized.

Our break drags out longer than I'd think necessary. What are they all doing? Looking uphill, it seems that we haven't even started our real challenge yet. There's no end in sight to the line of lights, no end to the massive black wall that seems to slope all the way up into the sky. At our slow pace, will we ever make it to the summit before the mid-morning clouds roll in? We've hardly made any progress so far, and several hiking groups have overtaken us already.

"Evance, tell me the truth, like that, we'll need another 12 hours to the summit, right?"

I want him to say, "Don't worry, we'll get there in time," because I still trust that it will be fine.

Evance just nods. Yes, we'll need another 12 hours.

I'm not surprised. He only confirmed what has already become evident.

It takes me a moment to process, then . . . Boom! Reality hits me, brutally, like an avalanche. So when I'm up there, I'll just be looking at clouds and fog? What's the point of it all? Everyone makes it up there by early morning so they have a good view before the clouds roll in! But I'm not allowed to, even though I could?! Getting Evance's confirmation pulls all excitement and positivity from under my feet and makes me fall into overwhelming frustration. My mood flips like a swing from mania to depression. I can't help feeling wronged. I have trained and prepared massively over the past nine months for this very night, and now my only chance of getting a good view from the top of Africa is jeopardized by being forced to walk in a big group, at a pace half my own natural speed! My dream has just evaporated, my masterpiece shattered into a thousand pieces. Sorry guys, but right now this doesn't seem fair to me. Yes, I'm selfish, I want to have a good view when I'm up there and not just look at clouds. The feeling of anger is rather alien to me, but in this very moment I'm swallowing hard about this entirely unnecessary bad ending to what should have been the highlight of my year, about my loss of control, about others dictating my fate without any clear benefit to them other than perhaps glee, wanting to hold me back so they don't feel left behind themselves? What does that have to do with me? Why do I need to suffer on their behalf?

We finally continue our hike. I'm still processing my emotions, trying to sort my act out and accept my fate. Within only a few minutes, while I'm still sullen and self-absorbed, it feels as if the wind has picked up significantly, and the temperature dropped to below freezing from one moment to the other. I don't know whether it actually dropped or my body simply got cold because of the long break.

My fingers and toes start to freeze. I need to put on my mittens, but they are still in my backpack. Taking off my backpack while walking is too difficult, would consume too much air. I feel stupid. Having just had such a long break, I can't stop again to take out my mittens. Stripping my backpack off and strapping it back on takes too much time. I should have done it during the break. When we don't break, we all constantly keep walking, slowly, but walking nevertheless. Pausing at this altitude means falling far behind, and for whatever illogical reason I can't get myself to do that. It would be a defeat that I don't want to allow myself, conflicting with my emotions about walking so slowly. In any case, getting cold so suddenly doesn't make sense. It can't possibly be so much colder now than just five minutes ago. Surely getting my body back into motion will warm my fingers again. I just need to hold on for a few minutes. Wiggling my fingers like crazy, I desperately try to get my blood flowing again. Jumping around as I did in the mornings, when my fingers froze while brushing my teeth, is not an option. There's not enough air.

After about ten minutes, I realize that my fingers won't come back to life like that. We are not moving fast enough for my body to reheat. Instead, my fingers are no longer just cold, but burning painfully like being in boiling water. I know that sort of pain. It freaks me out. I've felt it before and cried for half an hour when the blood started flowing again because it was so painful. Is my worst fear eventually coming true and I'll end up with frostbite? My mind goes crazy. "The most important thing is: Don't panic," I remember Robert's warning. Exactly. I'll just ask one of our guides to help me quickly grab my mittens, not a big deal. I keep looking out for a guide, but they all seem busy with other hikers. After what feels like an eternity, but perhaps was no more than a minute, I finally locate Skoba. He's not attending to anyone else.

"Skoba, sorry, can you help me?"

I immediately get all his attention.

"I've got my gloves at the top of my bag. Can you help me get them?"

I move to the side to let others pass and he starts looking. It should be quick.

One after the other group member walks ahead of me. I'm getting impatient. Why is it taking so long?

I hear a zip. That can only be my side compartment. Why is he looking there?

"At the top," I repeat.

He keeps looking.

"They are not there."

Of course they are, why is it so difficult? My impatience turns into annoyance. There are not many things that make me lose my temper, frozen fingers is one of them.

"Alexy, what's wrong?" Robert is the last in line coming up.

"Just getting my gloves."

"OK, but hurry up."

Robert keeps walking. He knows we'll catch up.

Finally I take my backpack from my shoulders and grab my mittens myself, as expected right from the top. Skoba is patiently watching me, with bare fingers. Perhaps he just didn't hear me clearly in the wind, but I'm not capable of thinking that far. I'm oblivious of my manner towards him. Am I rude or do I manage to contain my frustration? I won't be able to remember, but the thought, that I might have been as cold to him as my fingers were to me, will make me feel ashamed, will make me want to say: "I'm sorry. Thank you for trying anyway. I know you just wanted to help."

Right now, I can only think of my fingers, pain, frostbite, and being far behind everyone else. I quickly strap my backpack back on and we keep moving. Finally I can hide my fingers underneath my thick mittens, but they are already frozen solid and it doesn't seem to make any difference. The hand warmers that I have left inside don't help either. They were supposed to remain warm for six hours but haven't even made it for four. I wish I had taken a new pair from my backpack, but now it's too late. I can't take my backpack off again and fall behind even further. That will have to wait for our next break.

There's not much I can do for my frozen toes, other than putting up with it and hoping for the best. The toe warmers don't help either, rather the opposite. They feel ice-cold. I regret having used them at all. Even my supposedly foolproof chili-feet insoles are not working any longer. I silently blame me being cold on the slow pace of our group. Neither is my body getting enough exercise to keep warm, nor are my insoles getting enough walking pressure to produce heat. It's not fair – that's all I can think. I'm boiling inside with anger and frustration, while freezing from the outside and drowning in my own self-pity.

It's lonely up here in the biting wind, staring at the ashen sand that's so frozen cold that it scrunches with each step, marching my own funereal pace, without a companion to share how I feel. Can I go on like this for four more hours throughout the night? If my fingers don't come back to life, I'll need to call it quits very soon, but I'm not ready yet to give up.

The path becomes steeper and the air ever thinner. I focus my attention on my breathing to avoid developing a headache or nausea. Catching back up with our group takes a huge effort. No longer can I rush ahead the way my muscles would love to do. Whenever I try to walk faster, I begin to feel dizzy. I need to take deeper and deeper breaths with every single step. Eventually I catch up to the end of our line.

Another group quickly walks up behind us. Our guides ask us all to step aside and make space to let them pass. I don't have much interest in them, just frustration that they move faster than us. The rumor starts to spread later on that this was the Thomson Safaris group. Apparently, they all looked fresh and well groomed, indicating that they must have had access to shower facilities. I'm not so sure about that. In hindsight, I will find out that it can't have been the Thomson Safaris group because they summit during the day, not overnight. And certainly they wouldn't provide for a shower, especially so far up the mountain where there is no water at all.

We keep walking, still as a group, but the gaps between us are widening. It's not possible to see all the way to the front of our line, nor all the way to the back. We are probably spread across two or three bends of the serpentine path. Within my emotional fog of cold and frustration, and my physical struggle between catching up and the need to draw sufficient oxygen into my lungs, these painful five, fifteen or thirty minutes will soon become blurred in my memory, partly erased by my human need to forget everything unpleasant. On the one hand, I would still remember trying to regain my prior walking position towards the front of the line. On the other hand, I also remember walking behind Stewart and Juli for a while, wondering how they can keep up that pace, barely able to re-catch my own breath, contentedly following their footsteps without any urge whatsoever to move any further ahead.

"Oh Alex, you go ahead," Juli realizes I'm behind her.

"It's OK." It really is, I don't know how you guys are keeping this up so well. You're doing great, I mean to say, but I don't have any breath to spend on actually saying it.

"No really, I know you like going in front. Just go ahead," she smiles at me.

How is she doing that? How can she be in such good shape and still be so positive and considerate?

"Thanks," I try to quickly get out of their way, summoning up all my strength to speed, breathing heavily.

I see Chris further up and give myself another push. Eventually I manage to catch up and regain my prior position. Phew, finally I can *relax* again, no more need to walk any faster than everyone else.

"You're back! I thought you'd gone already," Chris immediately acknowledges my renewed presence.

Aw, so nice to finally have a companion again! I want to share my feelings of frustration, to let go of it and feel better. He's my only hope of understanding how I feel right now. Surely he must be equally frustrated, given his comments earlier on.

"I asked Evance, we'll not even make it up by noon," I stammer while panting for air. "The clouds will be in. We'll not see anything," my brain feels dizzy from talking. "My fingers and toes are already frozen," I gasp, "because we're so slow". I must share what I think, even if I'm almost fainting from lack of oxygen. Come on, give me some "f" and damn words; let's share our frustration.

Chris just looks straight ahead, keeps setting one foot after the other.

"I've already surrendered," he replies with a friendly yet resigned tone.

That's it? That's all he has to say? I'm not even sure what he means by *surrendered* – surrendered to our group's slow pace, or surrendered to the thin air leaving even him no choice but to walk slowly? It doesn't make a difference. Surrender is surrender. Yikes! So I'm still alone after all?

No, then I'll just surrender as well. If he can be so calm about it all, then I'll just try to do the same, to equally surrender to everything that's out of my control right now. There's no point fighting an emotional struggle that I can't win. Hearing his unperturbed voice helps me to also get my feelings under control and calm down.

The night turns long, rough and boring. Step by step, breath-by-breath, we slowly increase in altitude, silently making our way up an endless zigzag path of steep left and right bends connected by somewhat more manageable straight stretches. It's a tough hike that requires all my focus and attention to control my breath, but my mind now is at peace. All I need to do is to follow the person in front of me. Time is no longer important.

The ground is covered in earthy dust that's frozen solid. At least that's a positive surprise. Other hiker reviews all mentioned that for every step up, they kept sliding back down in the scree halfway, multiplying their efforts. Seems that doesn't apply to our route but only to the south-facing slope from Barafu Hut.

At times we take very short two-minute breaks, just to catch our breaths. Our guides remind us all to drink and I want to follow their guidance, but nothing comes out from my tube, it's already frozen.

"Hey, you saw Mawenzi?" I ask Chris, facing downhill and nodding towards the crown-shaped mountain surrounded by stars rising in front of us.

"Yes! Beautiful, isn't it?"

A simple exchange of words, yet it means so much. I'm not alone. Chris is still here with me.

We keep walking, following the same monotonous and slow step-breath-step-breath pattern. My fingers are slowly coming back to life underneath my warm mittens. With the pain subsiding, I regain my composure and my inner strength.

Other than Evance in the front and whoever walks at the end of the line, all other guides walk to the side of the path, parallel to us. They keep changing their positions, shortcutting our zigzag path straight up or down the steep slope if they need to, like shepherds keeping an eye out on each of their sheep. There always is a guide nearby, sometimes Estomee, earlier Samwel and Skoba, at times Robert though I get to see a bit less of him because he keeps an eye out on our weaker group members. No matter which of our guides, including our summit porters Liberaty and Charles, they would rarely pass without asking:

"*Alex, habari?*" Baraka walks up beside me.

"*Nzuri sana,*" I breathe heavily.

It takes me quite some effort to reply just two words. While I'm comparatively "*nzuri*," "*sana*" has become a lie. I'm definitely not very good anymore, just good, but there's nothing Baraka could do to restore the "*sana*". I want to assure him that he doesn't need to worry, and to delude myself.

The person in front of me pauses.

"Catch your breath," Evance's voice tells us that this is just a short one-minute break.

Baraka smiles at me, encouragingly.

"Any chance we make it up before eight?" That's when the clouds usually start rolling in. Why do I even ask this irrational question to which I already know the answer? I'm not sure. Perhaps I just want to hear a second opinion, perhaps I just ask for the sake of conversation, perhaps because his smile gives me new hope.

We start to move again.

"Yes, sure. Even earlier."

"Really?" is all I manage to utter before re-catching my breath. That can't be right.

"Yes, I think by seven thirty at the latest we'll be at the summit," Baraka reassures me expertly. He says it casually while walking up a steep incline, like on a Sunday stroll.

I can't believe what I'm hearing.

"Best news ever!" I use all my breath to reply and can't say more than that. No need for more words, we understand each other. Despite the darkness, he must have seen the instant flash in my eyes, and I see him beam back at me. He knows he's just made me very happy.

So perhaps Evance didn't understand me earlier on, my unnecessary frustration just the result of an innocent misunderstanding. There is no reason to worry after all. We'll get up there in time.

My pendulum swings back, no longer stuck in apathy. I instantly feel positive again, almost elated. Even my frozen toes become more bearable, walking on this new glimmer of hope. It may be the most strenuous night of my life, but I'm at peace with our harsh conditions.

▲ ▲ ▲

I hear Jana breathing heavily.

"Break," she begs Evance.

There are no stones nearby, just frozen earth. It's not convenient to break, nothing to sit on, no stones to hide behind for those who need to pee.

"Yes, we'll break. Not good here. Soon," Evance skillfully leads her on, her and all of us behind because, at least up to me, we can all follow their conversation.

"How long?" Jana wants to know.

"Just a little bit further," Evance replies, over and over again, repeating the same question and answer game.

It does the trick. We all keep walking, pushing through just a little bit longer, and the little bit turns into an eternity. Hissing breath like a bellows becomes our constant background music, like a percussion instrument that knows only two tones – wheeze, break, whoosh, break, wheeze, break, whoosh, break – high on the inhale, deep on the exhale.

By now, I have no more ambition or urge to walk any faster, feeling the limits of my own body. I need to take very deep breaths to make sure I don't feel sick. Whenever I don't focus or waste my breath on just a few words, I feel an immediate flash of nausea, reminding me where I am. So then I focus again – deep breath in, step, deep breath out, step, deep breath in, step, deep breath out, step. That does the trick for me, helping me to quickly regain a clear head. But yes, I'm challenged to get enough oxygen into my lungs and barely manage to keep pace, even though I could be considered comparatively young and fit. I don't want to even imagine the suffering others must be going through right now. I'm starting to feel grateful for walking in a big group, for others slowing me down, for Jana setting a pace that I can still manage reasonably well without getting sick. And I'm impressed about how well everyone keeps pushing on despite their struggles. If it weren't for others slowing us down, it would be me breathing that heavily now and begging for a break.

We finally take a slightly longer break, five minutes, long enough for everyone to strip off their backpacks and either drink or pee, but barely long enough for both. I'm glad I didn't drink too much and don't need to bother with my multiple layers of pants, don't need to expose my fingers and butt to this freezing cold, don't need to make the colossal effort of squatting in this thin air. Instead, I've got time to finally unpack my thermos. It's been a while since my last tiny sip from the long frozen water bladder. But it's not thirst that motivates me right now, rather the prospect of getting something hot into my body. I look around for a flat piece of rock or ground to position my thermos cup. The rocks are uneven and slanting as far as I can tell, and the ground is sloping downhill everywhere, too frozen solid to flatten even just a tiny spot to place my cup. I try to pour while holding the cup in my other hand, but the thermos is too heavy. I'm afraid of spilling water and getting wet along the way, not a risk I want to take. Evance happens to stand next to me.

"Could you help me for a moment?"

"Sure. What is it?"

"Could you hold my cup for a bit?"

"Give it to me," he readily holds out his hands.

While I pour carefully, I become aware that he is holding my cold stainless steel cup with his fingers only covered in thin liner gloves, as if he didn't even notice the cold air.

"I'm sorry," I feel so bad.

"Don't worry. I'm here to help you".

"Are you not cold at all?"

"No, I'm fine," he smiles warmly.

I don't know whether he is just very tough on himself and a very good actor, or actually has an amazing blood circulation that keeps him warm. All I know is that if it were me without thick mittens in this freezing cold and windy night for hours, I would be frostbitten by now and no longer able to hold anything. Our guides are amazing.

Robert lights a small torch into my face, my eyes. He probably does that with everyone, checking that we're OK. Apparently, our eyes tell a lot about our true state in this high altitude, whether we are OK to keep pushing. I assure him that I'm fine. That's not even a lie. I'm actually feeling quite good right now, in my element. I'm facing downhill, looking at the beautiful Mawenzi peak surrounded by stars. How often do you get such a sight! And I'm standing right next to my guardian angel, Evance, who I can always rely upon to take care of me. What a comfort! And I'm drinking hot water, warming from inside. What a luxury! That's all I need to be happy. I really don't understand why bringing a thermos is not among the essential items on all packing lists. How come no one thought of this before?

Our break is just about long enough for me to finish my water, to wipe my nose and to put on more lip balm.

"Get ready."

That's Evance's command to put our backpacks back on.

"Already? I still need to drink something," Jana complains.

"Hurry up!" Evance remains firm.

"It's not long enough. I can't pee and drink at the same time!"

She has a point, but I'm more concerned that my body may cool down again just standing around. I think that's also the reason why Evance now keeps our breaks so short. I'm keen to get going, while Jana feels stressed. That's what you get when you make warm-blooded and cold-blooded creatures walk together.

"Let's go," Evance keeps pushing.

And off we go again, slowly, step by step. My hands were warm when we started our break, so I didn't even bother with my second pair of self-heating hand warmers. But now, just as we continue walking, I realize that my fingers have gotten freezing cold once more during our break, during the five minutes not covered in my thick mittens and without moving. Why did I not realize that a minute ago? Too late, I haven't learnt my lesson. Now I need to wait again until our next break, whenever that happens. At least my body overall doesn't feel cold. My eight layers of clothing on top are keeping me warm, even when we're not moving. I'm glad I put them all on. It's just my nose, fingers and toes that get to feel how cold it really is, to let me toughen up and *earn* the summit.

Our ascent is slow and monotonous, a training in mental endurance, a draining of emotional sensitivity. Everyone is fighting for themselves. There's not enough air to cheer each other on; no breath is lost on words. The extent of my talking has reduced to a simple *"nzuri"* whenever a guide asks me how I am. I can't manage *"sana"* anymore for lack of air, and for a better reflection of my true state.

I hear the wind and my own breath, and Jana's constant heavy breathing. I know she is fighting hard, but she has an iron will. Evance is taking care of her. "Keep going!" "Don't stop!" "Jana, come!" He keeps mentally pushing her on step by step.

The night is long, very long. We hardly take any breaks; if at all, we just stop for two minutes to catch our breaths. When we break too long, some people might decide to just give up and stop pushing further. It's better to keep moving, slowly but constantly.

My backpack is getting heavy. The hip straps keep sliding upwards on my slick waterproof pants. I push them down over and over again whenever we stop for a little, but it's a pointless fight. Just one step, and they are loose again, leaving the entire weight on my shoulders and back. It probably weighs just over five kilos, but feels like fifty.

After what seems like an eternity, we take another five-minute break. I can't wait to take off my backpack for a while. This time, I manage to find an even spot on a rock to position my thermos cup, so I can pour the water myself and don't need to bother our guides. I also remember to get a new set of hand warmers. However, as I switch on my headlamp to open them, there's just a very faint, hardly noticeable light. My batteries must have drained quickly in the cold. I ask Baraka who stands next to me to help me shine his light on the packages for a moment. As soon as I'm done unwrapping my hand warmers and stuffing them into my mittens, Evance asks us to get ready again.

"Alex, take mine," Baraka kindly holds out his headlamp for me.

"Thanks, it's OK," I reject his offer. I don't want to be a burden, nor do I need a headlamp to walk. I can manage without.

"No please, take it."

I'm overwhelmed by his effort to help me.

"Don't worry. I'm good. I've got spare batteries. I'll put them in at the next break," I lie again.

Sure, I've got spare batteries, but messing around with these tiny batteries in the dark, which requires exposing my bare fingers to the freezing cold, does not seem like a worthwhile effort. Anyway, I feel sufficiently confident to continue and complete my hike without. The moon is saving me.

Everyone is lining up again behind Evance: Jana, Diego, me, Chris, Giovanni, Lynn, and so on.

"Stewart, you go in front." Robert wants him to walk right after Jana and Diego. "Baraka will stay with you."

I step aside for Juli to pass as well.

"No, it's OK. I'll just stay behind."

She knows the guides will take good care of Stewart. They are the experts and there's not much we can do to support each other.

We start walking. Baraka steps to the side and waits while I follow uphill on a steep bend.

"You sure?" He smiles at me cheekily, his hand readily positioned at his headlamp. He doesn't give up easily, but I'm equally stubborn.

"Yes," I beam back at him.

Going through this night together does wonders. It no longer feels like client and guide. We've become friends.

My fingers feel frozen cold again after our break, when I had my mittens off. I thought the hand warmers would help, but they don't feel warm at all. They just make the poles harder to grip. I should have saved myself the energy and loss of heat while unpacking them. In hindsight, a second pair of warmer mid-layer liner gloves might have been a smarter addition to my packing list, but obsessively researching the warmest possible mittens was certainly time well spent.

Just after our break, the terrain is getting steeper and stonier. At most of the bends of the zigzag path, we need to scramble over rocks, at times higher than our knees. For each of these ridiculously high stones, we need to summon up colossal efforts to drag ourselves up one more level, sometimes impossible without using our hands for added support. Our guides are always there, offering us their hand to help lift us up when needed. I'm still good, or rather stubborn, not willing to accept any hand that reaches out my way. I can do that, by my own force. I've got it stuck in my head that I need to get up there 100 percent by my own strength and I can't let myself accept any help.

But our guides and summit porters are amazing, cheerful and helpful throughout, as if the thin air doesn't bother them the slightest bit. Robert is walking behind, towards the second part of our group. At times, he's calling out to Evance at the very front and they exchange bits and pieces of information in Swahili. I assume Robert is checking in every now and then to make sure we're all still fine at the front of the line, or to coordinate when to make the next short two minute break to catch our breaths, or perhaps asking Evance to slow down to allow people at the end to catch up.

I don't know how they do that. Interrupting my breath while walking to utter few syllables already makes my head spin. How can they still shout entire sentences to each other?

By 4am, several amongst us are clearly suffering, panting loudly and needing to sit down from time to time. In the end, we are all fighting our own battle, silently inside, capable of focusing on no more than just the next step, just the next breath.

When our morale is lowest, the night the darkest, the wind the coldest, and the temptation to quit the most persuasive, Robert starts to sing. All our guides immediately join in, offering us their solace and encouragement. The vibe of their voices, authentic and benevolent, creates one of the most mystical moments I've ever felt, reuniting our entire group all the way from Evance at the very top down to the last guide at the end of our line, from Jana at the front all the way down to our last hiker.

We can make out our names and countries in their vocals, between repetitions of "*bomba*" ("cool") and "*nyoka*" ("snake") and other unfamiliar words, followed by the familiar refrain, "*hakuna matata*". But it's not about what they sing. It's much more about how they do it, full of heartfelt warmth and sympathy, and how they integrate our names and countries in their singing, encouraging each of us while at the same time reconnecting our entire group.

I don't know how they do that, how they can walk, breathe and sing at the same time. Their singing makes me smile and I join them, silently in my mind, saving my breath for my walking. It gives me a renewed push of energy and motivation, from lethargically dragging foot after foot and resigning to the cold to actively enjoying the process of hiking again. It's not so bad after all. We'll get up there eventually. The night can't be that much longer. And when do you get a free concert under the starts, above 5,500 meters (18,000ft), with beautiful Mawenzi in the backdrop?

Even though the terrain is getting steeper and steeper, our pace feels slower and slower, and ever more manageable to me.

▲ ▲ ▲

Evance, Jana and Diego at the top of our line are always within my sight, followed by Stewart and Baraka. Chris, Lynn and Giovanni are also nearby. The three of them all seem to be doing well, as expected, all very strong hikers, but we don't have enough air to exchange how we all really feel. I'm clueless as to what's happening further down our line. At times Evance keeps shouting back to the guides behind, probably making sure that the hikers they are looking after are alright, or asking whether we should make another very short break. But we don't break anymore; we just keep walking, *pole pole*. I assume everyone further behind is still more or less fine.

Little do I know that Farrah is suffering from serious nausea. Robert is taking care of her. He's repeatedly asking her to throw up so she would feel better, but that doesn't work for Farrah. At some time in these early morning hours, she would even report seeing him in a blurred, funny way. She must be feeling as if she's in the wrong movie. I don't know how she managed not to panic and call it quits under these circumstances, how she managed to summon up the strength and willpower to keep going despite her misery. Retinal hemorrhage with associated loss of visual acuity is common in high-altitude trekking. As far as I understand, it's not dangerous to start with, but could become more serious with continued ascent and therefore needs to be monitored. So that's why Robert is constantly checking our eyes with his little torch. And remember, nausea is normal up here, so Robert keeps pushing her on with his words, knowing it's safe to continue.

Neither do I know how much Ravi is fighting due to his twisted ankle and his cold that would in fact turn out to be a respiratory viral infection and take a month to resolve. He doesn't see the point to keep going any further and would turn around, if not for Eva. She is not leaving his side, keeping him company as well as motivated. Ravi asks Eva to leave him behind and keep going her own faster pace, but she won't leave him. She wants him to succeed, even though it means that she herself is falling behind. They move slowly but steadily, Ravi fighting his pain dragging foot after foot, making sure he doesn't keep Eva from reaching her own dream, and Eva persisting in her belief in him. So after all there are still heroes amongst our group who have the capacity to take care of others despite their own struggle. I couldn't do it right now.

As far as I understand, both Juli and Jeannette manage their ascent without any major altitude symptoms, other than shortness of breath like all of us. They stoically fight their own battle, silently inside, showing me that my theory of hiking Kilimanjaro now, while I'm still relatively young, is all nonsense. There's no limit. I admire their modest greatness – doing amazing things without the need to brag or even just talk about themselves.

At times I hear Jana say that she can't go any further. No longer just "break," now she is pleading "no more" to Evance in between breaths.

"Keep going!" Even though Evance normally is such a sweet gentle guy, he knows when to be tough and keeps pushing her on with his words, like an army officer drilling his solider.

Jana is panting very loudly, like when a tennis player hits the ball, hard and with all her strength, over and over again, for every single step. It sounds angry and violent, desperate yet determined. I know she is summoning up all her last bit of energy, and that she has an iron will. Yet it sounds to me as if she will stop and turn around any moment, because I would. But Evance's steady slow and patient pace – one foot at a time – miraculously encourages her to pull all her strength together and continue, fighting for every single step, all the way up. She is here to make it to the top and won't give up no matter what it takes. I couldn't do it like that and would have given up long time ago.

Diego is silently following her footsteps, keeping her company. He seems to be doing OK, but that's just what I can tell right now. In reality, he's bravely fighting inside, living through a nightmare, bearing his own suffering without drawing much attention, while at the same time supporting Jana as much as he possibly can.

I also see Stewart struggling, in a different inconspicuous kind of way, quietly, at times swaying faintly as if he's getting dizzy and losing control of his muscles. He is walking just ahead of me, closely followed by Baraka who is watching over him. I can see how alert Baraka is. He's keeping his arms lifted and his knees slightly bent, constantly ready to jump and support Stewart if needed. And indeed, some of these knee-high stones in this ridiculously thin air would temporarily tilt Steward's balance, daring him to stumble and give up. But Baraka would immediately reach out and catch him, helping him to immediately regain control. And Stewart keeps walking, stubbornly, by his own force, both exhaustion and determination written all over his face. He is not the kind of guy who gives up, and he wants to make it up there by his own strength just as much as everyone else. With very strong willpower, he keeps pushing on against all odds, step by step.

"I need to sit down," he says after a while and lowers himself onto a rock. His face is ashen. Robert is racing uphill. Knowing that Stewart is in good hands with Baraka and Robert, I continue onwards in my own struggle. I don't have the energy to even say a few words of encouragement. Will he be able to make it to the summit? It doesn't seem likely. The odds are heavily against him.

"Good luck man," I hear Chris's voice, but I don't hear any of what follows.

"OK, you can sit, but only five minutes," Robert instructs Stewart.

Robert is the expert and knows what's in our best interest. He is our boss and we would follow his instructions all the time, like well-behaved pupils following their teacher.

Not Stewart, not in this moment. Twice Robert's senior and unused to being bossed around by anybody, he stays true to his own character: "I'll tell you when I'm ready," Stewart replies authoritatively and takes control of his own fate.

▲ ▲ ▲

The rocks are getting higher and higher, the slope steeper and steeper. There is no more frozen earth, no more in-between bits of gradual include. Every second step seems like a step up a gigantic staircase, along a never-ending black wall, all the way up into the sky.

There are some parts where you wouldn't want to stumble, risking a fall more than a few meters down into nothing. Oh yes, you could certainly die up here, no more dangerous than the Swiss Alps where hikers fall to their death all the time, but yes, no more denial that Kilimanjaro also has its steep slopes.

Our guides provide support where required, position themselves at precarious spots like a safety fence and hold out a supporting hand when the rocks are more than just knee-high. But some of us don't easily accept help, myself included. Giovanni, Chris and Lynn all jump up the rocks like mountain goats, breaking out from our line and finding their own paths. It's obvious they all are very strong, experienced hikers. And they seem to be coming back into their own in this last, toughest hour of our long night, just like myself. The slower our pace becomes and the more others are struggling, the more it seems doable to us. We've got enough time to pause and catch our breaths.

Chris is even getting talkative again, relatively speaking of course. "It's minus four degrees," he informs me according to his fancy watch.

"Only? Feels much colder." I would have estimated at least minus ten degrees Celsius, to justify my temporary suffering and loss of control with my fingers and toes. So it's not that bad after all. Perhaps the icy wind made it feel worse.

We scramble over some high rocks again. One of them is so ridiculously high that I need to lift myself up with my arms. Our summit porter Charles is holding out his hand, kindly offering to pull me up, but I'm still stubbornly refusing any help. I want to do it all by myself. Just as I swing myself into the air, I feel someone pushing me up from behind. Chris quickly jumps up after me.

"Thanks, but no need, save your energy," I mumble sullenly.

"I know, haha, finally got an opportunity to touch your butt," he jokes, impishly excusing his urge to help.

"Yeah right."

And we laugh.

We laugh cheerfully, just as we did all week, despite the fact that we're now at over 5,500 meters (18,000ft) in thin air, climbing up a colossal mountain that should make us feel sick and desperate by all rational standards of comparison. After three hours of dark silence and lonely struggles, this simple exchange of words makes all the difference, waking me back up from my apathy that I had fallen into once more. I'm glad that he's here and cheers up the atmosphere, makes me feel connected again while everyone else is busy with their own thoughts, silently trudging along.

Just a few steps further, Giovanni's "*o sole mio*" breaks the silence. He is just one step ahead of me. I find it funny all over again. This time because it's ironic, singing about the sun while walking under the full moon. I want to share my thought with Giovanni and make him laugh. How would I say it, is it "*o luna mio*" or something else, I ponder to myself. I'm not sure. Explaining myself to him would be too difficult, deprive my lungs of too much oxygen. I focus on my breathing instead and keep my little quip to myself, laughing about it silently while admiring Giovanni's strength and energy. How can he walk and sing at the same time? Does he not feel the lack of oxygen at all?

"No more!" Jana demands.

She is way beyond her limits. Is it still safe for her to keep pushing? I don't know. Evance is the expert. We break for a minute. It's 5:30am.

"See the lights up there?" Evance points towards the top of the dark, steep wall of rocks and stones. "Those are hikers taking photos at Gillman's Point. In 30 minutes, we'll be there."

Only 30 more minutes and we'll be at the top of Africa? I can't believe it, wasn't so bad after all! For me, that is.

Chris and I are elated and turn downhill to look back at where we have come from. There's a little hill.

"Look at that!"

"That's Mawenzi!"

Africa's third highest peak is no longer majestically towering into the night sky seemingly touching the stars. Now we are. Have we really come that high? It's all just a matter of perspective.

"Let's go," Evance starts walking again.

"I can't," Jana remonstrates.

"Don't give up now. Only thirty more minutes."

Jana obeys.

With the end more measurably in sight, we get a renewed boost of energy, knowing that the struggle will soon be over.

Before long the skyline is turning red and blue in anticipation of the imminent sunrise. It's beautiful, auspicious and overwhelming all at the same time, immediately turning the cold endless night into a warmer new day. My spirits and energy levels couldn't be any higher. The remainder seems like a piece of cake to me. Our slow motion pace leaves me all the air I need.

Giovanni is leaving our path to the right and heading away from the group.

"Stay in line!" Evance calls after him.

Giovanni keeps moving. He must have finally gotten too frustrated with our slow progress and just wants to reach the top quickly, at his own pace.

"Giovanni, stop!" Evance shouts.

Giovanni turns around.

"It's dangerous," Evance implores him to come back.

"Noh, noh, jahst peeh," Giovanni's typical relaxed Italian voice finds its way back to us.

"And I thought he just went 'fuck that'," Chris utters his thoughts.

"Yes, me too!" I was thinking exactly the same, and we both break out into wholehearted laughter.

Finally, after this long night when everyone just seemed to be miserable, we can laugh again, about little things. Or perhaps this situation just gives us an excuse to laugh; perhaps we laugh more because we realize that we're not alone with our thoughts, that there's still someone thinking and feeling like us. How boring would this all be without Chris keeping me company!

"OK, but be careful with the stones," Evance lets Giovanni go off. He is a very fit and capable hiker, there's no need to worry too much about him.

The path becomes flatter and flatter. I'm getting impatient and would love to run ahead, but Jana is still fighting for each and every step, and we all slowly follow behind.

There is a random patch of glacier in the far distance to our right, on about the same level horizontally, and then in front of us . . . the volcanic caldera . . . and a wooden signboard.

That's it! There's nowhere further to go! That's the summit! I become euphoric.

By 5:50am, just in time for sunrise, the first of us reach Gillman's Point: our lead guide Evance, followed by Jana, Diego, myself, Chris and Giovanni. We've made it! I want to hug my friends and celebrate.

Jana walks straight to the Gillman's Point sign and broadly positions herself straight in front of it.

"Take a photo," she orders Diego to celebrate her achievement.

Her commanding tone and imperious demeanor surprise me.

Diego obliges.

I'm watching blankly, trying to process. "OK, let's just give her a second, and then we can all take a photo together," I remind myself to be patient and wait my turn, our turn.

"OK," Diego confirms that he completed the task and puts down the camera.

I guess Jana will now take a picture for him, and then we can all take one together.

"Water," she demands.

Diego doesn't react much.

"Where is my water?!" she repeats, without moving a single step away from the Gillman's Point signboard.

"I don't know where the porter is," Diego replies helplessly.

One of the guides or porters has been carrying their bag and thermos, but whoever it was isn't here yet.

"I want my water!" Jana shouts angrily, almost hysterically, completely ignorant of everyone else who might also want to take a photo in front of the sign that proves our accomplishment.

I'm dumbfounded. Never before have I seen her that egocentric and bossy, and I don't understand what's going on in her mind. Isn't this the time to finally be happy and cheerful together?

I don't understand that that bloody summit photo was the only vision that kept her going all night, that by now she's exhausted herself beyond reason, beyond any reason that I can comprehend.

An electrified cloud of negative emotions flares up inside me, threatening to thunder down on Jana and wash away my euphoria. Hurt, anger, impatience, blame and I don't even know what else — everything I've been trying to control and suppress for the past week. But most of all, I feel deeply hurt and rejected. I had asked Jana to join me on this trip so I wouldn't have to do it alone. Now we've reached our joint goal, but she doesn't even acknowledge my presence. The whole week she hasn't spoken to me, nor asked me to take a photo together. I thought this would change on the summit, but it doesn't.

Hurt turns into anger. This is not only her special moment, but also everyone else's. It's my special moment that I had been looking forward to for almost a year, but she is about to ruin it for me. I also feel impatient, impatient to have my photo taken, as if the sign would disappear if I don't do it quickly. And I feel blame, blame that she slowed me down all night, blame that I had to freeze for her.

I tried so hard to be considerate and understanding, not to be selfish myself, but I can't help it any longer.

"Don't be so bossy! Just go look for the summit porter yourself! Or ask Evance to help locate him. And move away from the bloody sign so others can also take a picture!" I want to shout at her but manage to keep my thoughts to myself.

This is not the same Jana I know from Zurich, and neither am I the same Alex that I've been until a week ago. Right now, while standing together side-by-side on this tiny spot on top of Africa, no more than two meters from each other, our minds couldn't be farther apart.

We are living through opposing worlds of emotions and our connecting mechanism suffers from lack of maintenance over the past week. Jana hasn't fueled hers to start with – so it seems to me – and thus I also stopped at some point to bother.

While I am overwhelmed by my ecstasy of feeling alive, longing to call out my joy and share my experience with a friend from home, Jana is overwhelmed by exhaustion and basic physical needs – oxygen and water.

Unable to reconnect our mental worlds that have drifted so far apart, I leave it to Evance, Diego and their summit porter to take care of her and focus my attention back to Chris.

"Let's take a photo," Chris and I agree.

"Could you please move a step so we can also take a picture?" I ask Jana as calmly as I can.

And she moves.

I immediately ban her from my consciousness. I can't allow her to spoil my moment.

Giovanni is standing aside, admiring the view.

"Come here, let's take a photo together," Chris and I call him over, and the three of us take photos together in celebration and memory of this very special moment. I'm so glad they are here with me. Thanks guys, I don't know what I would have done without you!

Chris, Giovanni and me at Gillman's Point

We look back down to where we started. An almost uniform greyish veil of morning dew covers the expansive lowlands, near and far, as far as our eyes can see. Only a black gentle elevation distinguishes itself against the grey backdrop. That's Mawenzi. It's so small by now that we can see beyond its peak into the far distance. A thin layer of orange and yellow is rising from behind the greyish veil, all the way from left to right. It indicates the edge of the horizon, where the earth seems to be falling off into its own curvature. Straight in front, behind Mawenzi, the intensity of the light blinds our eyes. The sun is just about to promise a new day.

▲ ▲ ▲

"Alex, can you help me take a photo?" Diego asks me.

Um, he needs me to take a photo for him? Hasn't Jana done that? I feel sorry for him, but still don't realize the ill state Jana must be in right now. I don't want to think of her.

"Yes, sure . . ."

And he also does the same for me.

By the time I fully realize what we have just accomplished, Eva, Lynn, Jeannette and Ravi are all here already.

Lynn is overwhelmed with tears of joy. She knew this was going to happen, she already told us beforehand. It reminds me about the moment when I saw the Taj Mahal for the first time with my own eyes, when I had tears of joy in my eyes.

The same night, one same special moment, yet we all experience it so differently. There's no single one reality, only the one we perceive with our own eyes, through our own lenses.

However, one thing almost all of us have in common: We are exuberant about our joint efforts and achievement, and hug each other. We have made it! We are on top of Africa!

Before long, Juli, Farrah and Stewart also arrive – all of us have made it! So Stewart did get back up and kept pushing through, against all odds, and has arrived so soon!

"Everyone is here now. We will take a break before we continue," Evance brings us back to reality.

"Oh, there is more to come?" Chris and I look at each other and laugh. Again we were thinking the same. We deluded ourselves into believing we had reached the summit already, even though I should have known better.

Well, it can't be that bad by the looks of it, with no visible further inclination in sight, only the rather flat rim of the crater. The Gillman's Point sign would tell the truth to those paying attention (I'm not) – we are at 5,685 meters (18,652ft), so still some 200 meters (700ft) of elevation ahead of us to Uhuru Peak, the real summit. Gillman's Point is only a sub-summit, the magic point at the lip of the crater that hikers need to reach in order to earn their certificate and be able to say that they've climbed Kilimanjaro. But we are all in for the real thing; stopping so short of the peak is not even worth a thought to us, nor to our guides.

I don't mind there is more to go, or perhaps I'm even excited that it's not over yet? This high altitude that gives others fatigue seems to have the opposite impact on me – I've never felt more alive before.

In our excitement, we haven't even taken off our backpacks yet. Now it feels good to finally lift the heavy weight from my shoulders for a short break.

"I want my water!" Jana keeps demanding in the background.

I ignore her, hurt by her distance towards me. "Go look for it and don't be so selfish," I am thinking to myself.

But that reminds me that it has also been a while since I had anything to drink, and so I unpack my thermos. Nobody else is drinking anything. Probably everyone's Nalgene bottles are completely frozen (or empty) by now. Thus I happily hand around my cup of hot water to my fellow hikers standing near me, who all gladly accept and take a few sips, other than Eva. I'm not sure whether she really doesn't want any or is simply too polite.

It makes me happy to share with others, but I can't get myself to offer it to Jana and Diego, who are standing a bit apart from us.

"They've got their own", I'm thinking.

I'm about to put the thermos away again.

"Alex, could we also have some water?" Diego's sweet, gentle voice surprises me.

What has he just said?

For a moment, I'm lost for words. They haven't spoken to me all week, they brought their own thermos, they gave all their stuff to someone else to carry while I was carrying the heavy weight on my own back and my shoulders are completely sore from it, yet now they have the cheek to ask for my water, because they are too lazy to take a few steps and find their own?!

Outrage, disgust, rebellion . . . – all negative emotions of this world are welling back up inside me.

I turn around to face Diego. He looks at me with soft innocent eyes. And then the worst of all emotions – guilt.

No, I can't allow that to happen, they can't just abuse me like that. I'm fighting an inner struggle, bigger than any physical struggle I've endured all night.

"Haven't you brought your own thermos?" I hear myself reply.

"I don't know where it is."

How convenient, to just ask me instead of locating their own! "I've carried it myself. Why should I share it?"[51]

"Not for me, for Jana," Diego replies compassionately.

He's won, makes me feel guilty more than I'd like to admit. Moved by his overwhelming sympathy and love for her, I give in and hand Jana a full cup of water.

She barely looks at me, takes the cup off me and starts drinking. No acknowledgement, no thank you.

I'm stunned and confused about her attitude and my own feelings. Amongst the mixture of hurt, frustration and anger, I hear a shameful voice blaming myself for not helping her out immediately. I'm telling myself there's nothing to be ashamed about. I'm right and she's wrong, obviously, everyone in their right mind would agree with me, I'm comforting myself.

But I'm not in my right mind, otherwise I would be realizing her very ill state, seriously dehydrated and short of oxygen. I can't see the obvious – how much the thin air and exhaustion is to blame for her behavior. What seems like a tough but doable marathon to me must feel like a torturing and close to impossible ironman triathlon to her. Only when writing this down I would realize that I was in a stronger position to see more clearly. Right now, I'm just lost in my own emotional fog.

"Get ready," Evance pushes us to get going again.

Other hikers are coming up and there is not a lot of space at Gillman's Point. Jana is still sipping the water. Everyone else already has their backpacks on again, ready to move. I am also keen to get going and don't want to have the others wait.

"Could you drink a bit faster?" I push Jana. Then I realize Diego is still standing next to her. "Or give it to Diego to finish," I suggest.

Rushed by me, Jana rapidly finishes it all to hand me back the cup. Still not hearing any thank you or acknowledgement, I store the thermos away and quickly get ready to continue. I'm oblivious that Diego might be as dehydrated as Jana and in need of water as much as everyone else. Only later I would realize and regret my omission to offer him some as well. For now, I immediately banish what just happened from my consciousness.

DAY 8 – ALL THE WAY UP

What's the point?

27 SEPTEMBER 2015

Gilman's Point (5,685m/18,652ft) to Uhuru Peak (5,895m/19,341ft)

Distance — elevation — time:
2km/1mi⇨ — 200m/700ft⇧ — 1 hour☺

As a group all together, we continue our hike along the brim of the crater, following it clockwise towards Stella Point. It's already bright daylight and there is not a single cloud in sight, only the intense bright blue sky. There's not much wind and it doesn't feel too cold. The weather couldn't be any better.

I'd love to say that the landscape looks stunning and beautiful, but it's really just barren and deserted. Probably it's nicer when there's snow.

The caldera looks like a big excavated field of sand and earth, with a diameter of roughly 2-3 kilometers (1-2mi).[52] A slope of sand and scree connects our path at the brim with the bottom of the caldera. One could probably run and slide down in few minutes . . . and struggle an hour to come back up.

But it doesn't matter to us how it looks, it's about knowing where we are and what we have accomplished.

I am in my element, energetic, intoxicated by a high of dopamine that's surely flushing through my veins right now. The path is rather flat and I feel like jumping and running, but we continue to walk very *pole pole*. Most are still fighting with the thin air to catch their breaths. My body takes control and my legs speed up.

"Alex, stay behind me," Evance reminds me to slow down.

It feels painfully slow to me. I lethargically shut off my willpower and focus on the person in front of me. Next time I look up again, I see that Chris somehow managed to escape. He is already walking far ahead of us. Lynn is also going her own pace, walking somewhere between Chris and us. The slow pace of our group feels like chains holding me back. I restrain myself and stay next to Evance. Chris disappears around a bend out of sight. That's too much for me to just observe passively. I also want to break loose and start walking my own pace, and so I do. For a few minutes, I feel free and liberated, doing my thing.

"Alex, wait," Evance calls me back again.

I know that it is his responsibility to lead us all up there safely. He already bears a huge burden on his shoulders to take care of Jana and everyone else. The last thing he needs right now is a crazy Austrian mountain goat. Thus I give in, fasten my chains again and stay next to him.

It takes us about 30 minutes from Gillman's Point to reach Stella Point, to cover a distance of only 750 meters (2,500ft)[53] and to gain another 70 meters (230ft) in elevation. To our left just before reaching Stella Point, we can see hikers coming up a steep slope of earth, sand and scree. For them, Stella Point is that magical threshold they need to reach in order to earn their climbing certificate.

"Evance, is this the Machame route?" I ask.

"Yes, the hikers from the Machame and Lemosho route come up here."

That's where our paths join, for the last kilometer to Uhuru Peak.

"We'll go down here," Evance points downhill. "See the white roof? That's our camp tonight."

There's a conglomeration of tents some three kilometers down the slope.

"You mean there?"

"No, further, in the trees."

"Ah, I see. Doesn't look too bad." Perhaps another five kilometers further down, though it's close to impossible to gauge distances up here.

"Yes, you can do it," Evance smiles at me. He knows the truth, while I don't have the slightest doubt that we would all make it there just fine.

Further behind the trees, where the mountain falls off into the lowlands, a layer of clouds blocks the view. In the far distance beyond the clouds, the landscape is still covered by a blurring layer of morning dew.

We all rest at Stella Point to wait again for our whole group to catch up before continuing onwards to Uhuru Peak. It feels so pleasantly warm in the morning sun that I even open my jackets.

"Alex, still got any of that water?" Chris looks a bit tired.

"Sure!"

"By any chance have you also still got any of those lovely snacks of yours?"

"Yes, heaps!"

This night would have been miserable without Chris. It makes me happy that I can finally give back something to him in return. Following my new habit, I also offer my snacks to our guides and summit porters.

"No thanks," Robert is the only one to reject, all others gladly accept.

"You don't like them?"

"I can't eat right now," he explains politely.

I'm not sure whether he doesn't like them, feels sick himself or simply is not hungry. But one thing I know for sure — without my mittens while messing around with the packaging, my fingers immediately turn biting cold again. The sun and my eight layers of clothes are deceiving; it's still freezing cold up here without any protection.

While also refueling my own energy with some water and a small bite, I see Jana and Diego taking pictures in front of the Stella Point sign. I want one too and hurry up to store away my stuff.

"Could anyone help me take a picture?" I ask aimlessly looking around our group.

Everyone is sitting. No one reacts. Surely they must have heard me? I am unable to understand that people simply don't have the energy left to grant me such a simple favor, wrongly expecting everybody else to be as enthusiastic as I am. Here I am at Stella Point and no one can help me take a photo?

Evance stands a bit apart. I resort to my guardian angel who always assists me.

"Sure," he immediately comes to help, with his bare fingers in the freezing cold.

"I'm sorry that I make you do this. Your fingers must be cold."

"Don't worry. That's what I'm here for."

▲ ▲ ▲

317

I look at the remaining path further along the southern brim of the crater with nothing but the intense blue sky beyond. Jana and Diego have already started to progress towards Uhuru Peak together with Skoba.

"Let's go!" I look at Evance.

"Yes, let's go!" he agrees.

Evance is as keen as me to keep going, and we call upon the rest of the group to get moving again.

The remaining 1,100 meters (3,600ft)[54] from Stella Point to Uhuru Peak appear to be very easy and almost flat, just following along the brim of the crater with a very gentle uphill incline. We'll be gaining another 140 meters (460ft) of elevation, so that would imply a gradient of just over 10%. I'm still in my element and my body would love to just run there, enjoying the crisp air. Surely it doesn't take more than five minutes.

I speed up. Nghh, my head spins, my lungs cry out. All oxygen is sucked from my brain as if I'd just walked into a vacuum, and that vacuum feels like a wall. Up to here, and no further. Something invisible pushes me back.

"Alex, stay here," Evance reminds me at the same time not to walk ahead.

I keep pace with him and the others for a few minutes, but soon turn impatient again with the slow progress.

"Evance, can I go ahead, just to where Jana and Diego are? Promise I will stay with Skoba."

"OK," he lets me go.

Off I rush at my own pace. Again I meet my invisible foe, the vacuum, and slow down to catch my breath, just to speed up again and repeat the same pattern. I just can't accept my limits. The effective oxygen up here is only half the amount at sea level, but I can't see it, hence my brain can't accept it.

Soon I catch up with Skoba, Jana and Diego, and walk next to them but no further, as promised. To our left, just some twenty meters down a gentle slope of sand and scree, a long wall of glacier rises a few meters into the air, seemingly out of nowhere. It's one of the few patchy remnants of the once mighty ice cap covering the entire top of Kilimanjaro. Settled in between the intensely bright equatorial sky and dry sand, it looks as if it didn't belong here, like a miracle.

Scientists agree that the glaciers on Kilimanjaro have retreated by about 85% compared to the surface they covered 100 years ago.[55] However, there has been confusion about the reasons for their disappearance. While ten years ago it was all blamed on global warming, deforestation at the lower slopes of Kilimanjaro has later on been brought into play.[56] Meanwhile, however, leading scientists have now shown that regional climate change is the main reason. In particular, moisture circulation patterns have changed due to the warming of the Indian Ocean, which may or may not be due to global warming.[57] There are also different estimates of when the glaciers will disappear completely, but most probably within decades it will be all gone.[58]

Glacier near Uhuru Peak

While I keep entertained taking photos of what our grandchildren won't get to see anymore, Evance and the remainder of our group are catching up with us. For a while, we all walk together, quietly but happily, slowly but steadily, just a few more steps towards the climax of our adventure, no more than a few hundred meters.

Next time I look up towards Uhuru Peak, Chris is already far ahead of us. He managed to escape again. Seeing him going his own pace, doing his own thing, I can't restrain myself any longer and follow his footsteps, finishing this last stretch at my own speed. With the end in sight, no one is calling me back this time. I walk at my own pace, yet this time I've learned the rules of the game. My legs and lungs walk in sync with each other, freeing my brain to focus on my surroundings and the sheer endless view into the far distance.

The lowlands expanding endlessly behind the glacier look worlds away, still covered by a pale greyish blue layer of morning dew that reflects the sky and blurs the landscape underneath. No landmark peeks through, no mountain breaks the monotony before the vast open plain meets the intense blue sky.

People have told me that up here one could see the curvature of the earth with one's own eyes. I zoom in and out of the thin white layer of atmosphere that marks the horizon like an endless straight line. Is it curved? I try, but it doesn't work for me. To my eyes, it still looks straight.

I take in the serene beauty of the mountaintop, the glaciers and the clear sky above. The mountaintop is beautiful not because of how it looks in isolation – no one comes here for all the sand and scree. It's beautiful because of the holistic view and experience, out of this world; because there's nowhere like here, unique; because I know where I am, a place that seemed out of reach just a year ago.

I feel extremely blessed. This is it, the highlight not only of the past week, but also of my entire year. I am about to accomplish a major goal, to complete my little pet project that seems so huge to me. I made it, and not only that – I had an amazing time along the way. I know I did well, both physically and mentally, far better than I'd ever expected. I'm so alive and couldn't feel any happier right now, taking these last steps towards the finish line.

I've left our group far behind me. In front, Chris's red jacket has disappeared from my view. He must have reached the peak where the path levels off. I can't see beyond the last hump. No human soul is in sight. I had mentally prepared for the crowds at the summit, yet here I have my last few meters to myself. There are no other hiking groups. It couldn't get any better.

All of a sudden, from one split second to the other, I long to share this special moment with someone special, a good friend, a family member, a partner-in-crime, someone from home. What's the point of it all? Why have I gone through all this effort? In the twinkling of an eye, my achievement over the past week and in particular the past ten hours has become meaningless to me in light of my solitude.

Brutally, without warning, a drowning sense of deep loneliness hits me, bursts from my heart to inundate my veins, like a ghost taking possession of my entire body from my center to the tips of my fingers and toes, so violently it makes my chest shake in convulsion. I sob uncontrollably. All the joy and enthusiasm I felt just moments ago have vanished without trace. I'm engulfed in an abyss of extreme sadness, so powerful, so much bigger than me, that I can't help but submit to my tears. I let it all out, sobbing my way towards the top of Africa. Ironically, I find relief in walking alone, knowing that no one can see nor hear me right now.

After a few minutes of uncontrolled sorrow, I see the Uhuru Peak sign come into view. There will be people there. I must control myself again. No one should see me like this. "You're not the only one who has come here alone. Get your act together! Don't be so unappreciative! Don't spoil this moment for yourself," I force my thoughts back on the positive.

I recall the fun we've had, remind myself of the people I've met, of the suffering that I've been spared, and of my luck to now have these last few meters entirely to myself. What more could I possibly have hoped for?

Busy controlling my feelings, I approach the finish line without being conscious of any physical efforts, just floating through my emotional cloud until I finally emerge on top again.

By the time I step onto the peak of my journey, I've recovered my positive self, but there still is an emotional void inside me. Reaching my goal doesn't make me happy. I am unable to experience that sense of achievement, satisfaction and accomplishment that should naturally follow my actions.

Chris is sitting on the ground leaning against a rock, alone, eyes closed. There is not a single other hiker here. And I thought this would be one of the busiest days of the entire year! Feelings aside, my body is still bursting with energy, and I'm longing to reconnect.

"What's up with you?" I walk over to Chris. How can he just sit there quietly in such a special moment? How can he close his eyes instead of opening them wide and soaking it all in?

He opens his eyes and briefly looks at me. "I'm tired."

"Really?"

"I'd just like to sleep," he closes his eyes again.

Seriously? Chris is tired?

Soon Lynn also arrives.

"Hey, we made it!" I shout at her in welcome.

"I'm smashed," she joins Chris straight on the floor.

"Me too," he opens his eyes briefly to welcome her.

The two of them understand each other, while I am lacking that connection. Oh guys, how is that possible, how can you just sit down at this special moment?! I would love to jump and celebrate, to share and rejoice the significance of the moment, but no one has the energy to celebrate with me. No congratulations, no hugs. Celebrating alone is no fun.

The guides had warned us that we wouldn't spend more than 5 to 20 minutes at Uhuru Peak due its tough conditions. Well, physically speaking, it couldn't be any better for me right now. I'm neither cold nor tired nor short of breath, and the weather couldn't be more favorable. Is it really possible that I'm the freak of nature this time round, the one odd outlier that will always be there by statistical probabilities? I don't know, but one thing I know for sure: While my body feels good being an outlier, my mind suffers from this lack of connection. I really wish I could celebrate with someone who feels like me, or that I could be as tired as everyone else.

All right, then I'll just have to focus on the view. Uhuru Peak is a patch of earth and sand, perhaps the size of a volleyball field, surrounded by boulders and stones. There are two wooden Uhuru Peak signboards. They were only erected in 2014, resembling the old wooden one that had been there all along but was replaced in 2012 by a sturdier green plastic sign. The plastic sign didn't look nice on photos and caused a series of complaints. The new *old* ones indeed look a lot nicer.

The *real* Uhuru Peak sign that replaces the original one faces west, at the opposite end of the path along the brim of the crater from Gillman's Point in the east. It directly welcomes each hiker:

"MOUNT KILIMANJARO.
CONGRATULATIONS.
YOU ARE NOW AT
UHURU PEAK. TANZANIA. 5895M/19341Ft AMSL. AFRICA'S
HIGHEST POINT.
WORLD'S HIGHEST FREE STANDING MOUNTAIN.
ONE OF WORLD'S LARGEST VOLCANOES.
WOLRD HERITAGE AND WONDER OF AFRICA."

The signboard conveniently sits amongst an assembly of knee-high boulders, perfect to sit on and for picture-taking. The park authorities did a good job. Behind the sign, the ground falls off into the western end of the caldera. It is possible to take photos in front of the sign with only the horizon and the sky in the background, or with a five-meter tall wall of glacier at the bottom of the caldera as its backdrop to the right. That's the Furtwängler glacier that you get to see close up if you opt for a route that includes an overnight stay at the so-called Crater Camp.

Standing directly at the signboard at the very peak, one has an unobstructed 360-degree view of the horizon. What a curiosity! Surely now I should be able to make out the curvature of the earth with my own eyes, as I had read so many times. I try hard, but it still doesn't work for me. Even though the horizon logically forms a circle around me, my brain interprets each individual snippet like a straight line. Perhaps I suffer from tunnel vision, or perhaps I foolishly allowed myself to be misled by stereotypically exaggerated stories of other reviewers?

I won't perpetuate the cliché, so let me quote what I will only find out later: You need to be at an elevation of 10,000 meters (almost 35,000 feet) in order to discern the curvature of the earth with your own eyes.[59] Everything else is wishful thinking. So if that's the fuel of your climbing motivation, you might as well save your energy and sip cocktails on a rooftop at the beach, looking out into the open ocean!

The second peak sign faces east, to one's left as one makes the final steps on Kilimanjaro's red carpet to reach the stage that only a few hundred thousand tourists have stepped onto before.[60] Looking at it from the front, it reads the same as the other sign. There used to be a big flag of Tanzania at its place, but the park authorities have put up a second peak sign instead, to provide more pristine photo opportunities for the rush of tourists in recent years. On popular days, apparently one has to queue to have one's photo taken.

To the left of this second signboard, I see our group slowly approaching the peak on the path along the brim of the crater that now seems almost flat. Behind the brim of the crater, Mawenzi still showcases the top of its crown, right under the morning sun, as if to remind us that it's still there, though no hiker who has come that far really cares any longer about its existence.

To the right of the sign, the ground gently slopes downhill towards the same wall of glacier that runs in parallel to the path and accompanies hikers on their last few hundred meters. The glacier reaches almost as far west as Uhuru Peak, where it suddenly stops and the ground seems to fall off into the lowlands far below.

Further to the west, a dark wide triangle sets itself apart within the monotonous layer of greyish blue morning dew that still shrouds the landscape. That can only be Mount Meru. It looks evenly shaped with a seemingly snow-clad top that I assume are white clouds in real, would that my eyes be stronger or the zoom of my phone camera more powerful.

Before long, Giovanni arrives, and shortly after Evance with most of our group. Finally we all hug and congratulate each other.

Soon Jana and Diego, accompanied by Skoba, also reach the finish line. We don't hug nor congratulate each other. An invisible barrier has come between us. Or perhaps they are just content celebrating between themselves and don't need anyone else to share their experience. I don't know, but this is not the way I thought it would be. Anyway, I can't change it right now and focus my attention on the amazing view and everyone else again.

While some people are exhausted, overall everyone seems to be doing fine, more or less. The atmosphere is cheerful and relaxed with relief that we've all made it.

Skoba happens to stand next to me.

"Could you help me take a photo?" I ask him.

"Of course."

I position myself in front of the signboard and smile into the camera. All of a sudden, out of nowhere, Chris grabs my waist and lifts me high into the air, just as he did at Lava Tower. I scream in surprise. So Chris is not that tired after all and still has enough energy left for his shenanigans?

"Hey, haha, I said you shouldn't do that." I scold him when he puts me down again. "It's bad for your back."

"No, you're not that heavy," he shrugs it off again. "Was going to spin you around again, but can't. The thin air really makes a difference. OK, I'll let you take your photos now."

"Um—"

Gone. He has already moved on to some other shenanigans, but has left me instantly feeling better, less freakish myself, and more connected again.

When done with my photos, I notice Stewart sitting on a rock. He must have arrived meanwhile. His facial expression speaks of exhaustion, testimony to the massive strength and iron willpower he had to summon up to make it that far. But now he has made it and we've all been witnesses of his miracle. Despite spine surgery two years ago and only having been walking again properly for a year, he has accomplished the seemingly impossible. And along the way, he has not only reached his own goal, but also provided a tremendous inspiration to others, and surely made his doctor very proud. I'm deeply impressed and walk up to him to express my congratulations.

Next to Stewart and some others who had to work so hard to get here, I feel like a fraud for celebrating my own achievement. I didn't have to work that hard and even enjoyed the process all along, except for that bloody hour between 2:30am and 3:30am, of course, when I thought I'd freeze to death and that the whole world had conspired against me. But that moment is long forgotten, and everything else seemed relatively easy compared to what I'd read and expected it to be like. Therefore, there's really not much for me to be proud of.

But my joy at feeling alive has returned and I'm not letting go of it so easily anymore. As everyone has arrived, I believe we should take that well-deserved group photo that we all wanted to have.

"Group photo," I call out and others immediately join in to draw everyone's attention.

We are quite a crowd all together: twelve hikers, six guides and two summit porters. Everyone has made it, and we are all here at the same time. Taking a summit photo all together is very special indeed.

In the other Kilimanjaro books I've read, no group managed to be at the summit together, either because some hikers couldn't make it at all, or because the first ones had to return due to the cold and thin air, unable to await everyone else to arrive.

Our guides and summit porters have made it possible for us to reach this aspirational goal together, and to take a summit group photo of us all. There is no way we could have made it without them. Now I feel deeply grateful that they made us walk as a group rather than allowing people like myself to rush ahead. Not only have they saved me from overexertion, which I probably would have brought upon myself without their constant reminder to slow down. More importantly, they have granted me the pleasure to enjoy and share this very special moment with our entire group. Without them, this achievement would have meant little to me. With them, it means everything.

Our group at Uhuru Peak

DAY 8 – HALF WAY DOWN

It's not about me

27 SEPTEMBER 2015

Uhuru Peak (5,895m/19,341ft)
to Millenium Camp (3,800m/12,600ft)
Distance — elevation — time:
8km/5mi⇨ — 2,100m/6,800ft⇩ — 3-7 hours☺

After the group photo, many can't wait to start their descent. I am reluctant to leave this very special place, the highlight of our journey, even though I've already spent some 30 minutes up here by now. Evance stands next to me. He looks weary and his eyes are all red.

"You look tired."

"Yes, I couldn't sleep yesterday, at School Hut. Can't sleep during the day."

As lead guide, he was carrying a huge responsibility on his shoulders, leading us all up here safely and making sure that no one gives up, despite the endless pleads for "no more" and "break". Surely that was a very difficult night for him, even though he would make it seem so easy, like an almost non-human hero who feels no cold, no pain, no thirst, no stress, no fatigue.

"You know your eyes are all red?"

"Yes, I feel sick up here."

Of course he would. He hasn't slept in more than 24 hours and, like all the guides, he hasn't drunk much since we left School Hut camp. I regret that I haven't offered him any water previously at Gillman's Point. Now it's all gone and I have nothing left for him.

"Can I offer you some medicine? I've got a lot . . ."

"Thanks, it's OK. Just need to descend a bit. Let's go."

"OK," I immediately agree because I know he needs at least one hiker to come along.

"Alex," Diego taps on my shoulder. "Could you help us take a photo?"

I smile apologetically at Evance.

"Of course," I'm happy to help take a photo of Diego and Jana together in front of the Uhuru Peak sign. Never mind that they haven't even acknowledged my presence so far, never mind that it would also have been nice to take a photo of the three of us together. It doesn't hurt that much anymore that they only talk to me when they need me; I've already regained control of my emotions.

As soon as I've completed my duty, I turn back to Evance. "Twende!" Off we go, or rather run. Evance's familiar *pole pole* pace instantly changes into a *haraka* (fast) rush. I like it. That's what I would call fun hiking. Finally I can walk as fast as I please and feel in my element again. *Pole pole* is only important on the way up for acclimatization. On the way down, there is no speed limit.

"Evance, you should come down with us runners. Then you will also get to the camp quickly."

"Yes, maybe I should."

I think he likes that idea.

Runners (or *sliders*) are those of us who prefer to go down quickly, skate-sliding downhill in the scree and sand. For those comfortable to keep our knees soft and rely on our heels to dig into the sand and catch us, that's the faster and easier way down. Others may not be able or comfortable to leverage the sand and prefer to go slowly, step by step. This will, however, make their descent almost as long and painful as their ascent.

On the way back down to Stella Point, I am amazed again by the beauty of everything that catches my eye and stop several times to take photos, capturing each and every view multiple times at the fear of leaving any memories behind. I know that Evance is keen to descend and I don't want to keep him back waiting for me. After repeatedly suggesting that he proceeds and doesn't need to wait for me, he finally agrees to leave me behind. He knows that I am in excellent condition and can take care of myself.

I take my time admiring the view and soaking it all in. The view extends all along the rim of the crater towards Gillman's Point at the far end, Stella Point half way through and a path leading down to the Crater Camp cutting diagonally through the crater rim. The ground alone could be described as an entirely uninteresting mixture of brown earth, boulders and stones, not worth much commentary or attention. Yet the sight into the far distance where the horizon meets the sky and the associated feeling of freedom and being alive converts the scenery into one of the most energizing views I've ever experienced.

While I can't get enough of what I'm seeing, Giovanni catches up with me. Like me, he is stunned by the view and takes many pictures, and he seems to be as energetic as I feel. I'm happy that I'm not the only outlier after all. Even though we don't talk much, simply walking together with him makes me feel more connected again.

When we reach Stella Point, Chris, Eva, Lynn, Jeannette and Farrah, together with Robert, Evance and Baraka, are already there, waiting for us.

The sun is shining strongly upon us, and our bodies have become hot underneath our many layers of clothing. It's time to strip off some of them. I take off my insulation jacket, merino jacket and waterproof pants. I also take out my chili-feet insoles and the useless supposedly self-heating toe warmers that are still glued to my socks. My feet have become hot and sweaty from the chili-feet that are delivering what they promised under a normal walking pace, just that now I don't need them anymore. What I need is space in my shoes so my toes won't feel too much pressure on the descent. Just as Christian from the outdoors store taught me, I make sure to tie my shoes tightly above the ankles for added downhill support. Finally, even though my calves are all sweaty from lack of airflow underneath my waterproof pants, I put my gaiters back on. We've got the dustiest stretch of the entire hike right ahead of us.

Under the sun, not only have our bodies become warm, but also our water supplies have melted again. We all busily rehydrate with soothing ice-cold water. Refreshed and liberated, I'm ready to get going again. "Do we need to wait for everyone?"

"No, let's go," Robert confirms what I hope to hear. On the way down, it doesn't make sense to walk as a group, so there's also no need to wait. "Alexy, Chris, Eva, Lynny, Farrah, Giovan – you come with Evance and me," he initiates part two of our summit adventure. "Jeannette – Baraka will stay with you. Take your time," for a more steady and stable step-by-step descent.

Robert goes first and we follow behind. At the beginning it is still quite stony and we go rather *pole pole*, but after few minutes the stones have mostly cleared in favor of a thick layer of sand and scree. Every step sinks in deeply and catches us softly. Instead of putting pressure on our toes, we can rely on our heels to dig into the sand and soften our falls. As anticipated, everyone triggers a thick layer of dust blowing up behind us. It is impossible to follow closely someone's footsteps, but better to leave at least a 20-meter distance.

Descending from Stella Point with view to Mawenzi

We take a couple of breaks along the way.

"Farrah, are you feeling any better?" I ask.

"Still dizzy, but the headache is getting better."

"Oh really?" Lynn comments, "I'm starting to feel my head now on the way down."

She has been fine all the way up. I heard that before from a friend, that she was fine all the way up but suffered on the way down. She was also taking Diamox, while her boyfriend without was fine both ways. I wonder whether Diamox has a role to play here? Yes, here we go again. I am still hunting for circumstantial evidence to support my theory, while others focus on what really matters, like rehydrating.

"Would you like some water?" Chris offers his supplies to Robert and Evance.

They shake their heads.

"Listen, I've got more than enough. I could pour it into a separate container for you."

But our guides still politely decline. They never decline when it comes to snacks, thus I complacently assume they are simply used to not drinking and indeed are not that thirsty. How can they stay hydrated like that? I don't know, but I'm feeling relieved. I kept blaming myself for not offering hot water to Evance earlier this morning. Now I know it wasn't such a big mistake after all; he simply would have rejected it in any case.

We head on. Eva, Lynn and Farrah prefer to go with a little more control and soon team up with Evance, while Chris, Giovanni and I run down as fast as we can, following Robert who is almost flying down the mountain, impossible for us to keep up with, and soon out of sight. It feels like skiing down a three or four kilometer long black world cup slope, and I love it. Finally I can go (or run, or fly) as fast as I like and no one would stop me. The deep sand gives us a treacherous feeling of security, but I wouldn't want to find out what kind of hard and edgy stones are hidden beneath if one stumbles.

We catch up with Robert sitting on a rock almost all the way down the scree slope, waiting for us. We also take a break. The sun has become very intense and our bodies are boiling. We strip off more layers. I take off my thick merino sweater and two long-sleeve merino shirts, only leaving on two rather thin shirts and my wind jacket.

"Alex, still got any of your snacks?" Chris asks me.

"Sure, not many, but finish them."

"Just a small piece, thanks."

"Robert, you want one?"

"No, thank you." He smiles politely.

"I've also still got heaps of nuts. Do you want any nuts?"

"Yes, nuts I like." His eyes open wider.

"Haha, got you. I knew you don't like my self-made snacks," I tease him.

Robert just smiles mischievously but is too polite to agree.

"Just take as many as you like," I hand him my bag of nuts and turn away back to my backpack to fix some stuff. From the side I notice that he is using hand sanitizer prior to opening the bag, and of course he wouldn't reach into the bag but pour whatever he likes into his palm. Wow, I am impressed by his focus on hygiene. Only now I realize that all our guides have been well groomed and shaved throughout the trip.

Jana told me about the bad body odor of their Sherpas when she went to the Everest Base Camp. We haven't had much of that on our hike so far, apart from only one exception that proves the rule. Considering we all haven't showered for over a week, this is surprising indeed . . . or perhaps we've gotten used to it and simply can't tell?

Evance and the girls pass us on a parallel path and soon disappear from our view around a corner at the bottom of the slope. Robert is still busy eating his big handful of nuts.

"Why don't you go ahead and follow them?" he suggests. "I will catch up with you."

"OK," with pleasure. As soon as he's said that, I launch into my downhill flight.

It's now around 10am in the morning and I start to feel my bladder. I've managed to avoid pulling down my trousers all night, by now for almost eleven hours since we started our summit ascent. Since my water supply has defrosted and I've been able to drink again from Stella Point onwards, I've been rehydrating quite substantially. Now I'm in trouble. There are no big rocks, no suitable hideaways. While I've lost almost all my shame on this trip, I still can't get myself to moonlight in bright daylight. The more urgent the pressure becomes, the faster I speed downhill in search of relief, leaving Chris and Giovanni far behind me.

At the end of the steep spree slope, where Evance and the girls have disappeared from our view around the corner, a circular assembly of big stones finally provides a rare hideaway opportunity.

Yuck! Leftover bits and pieces of toilet paper everywhere, and some even less pleasant leftovers that I immediately must look away from. Courtesy of prior hikers' bowel evacuations – ugh, phooey! That's what you get when you follow the busy routes. Things don't easily rot up here. Please don't leave toilet paper behind, be more considerate!

My shame and disgust have a quick fight, but the urgency of the situation settles their debate. The guys will soon catch up, I need to hurry up and my shame takes control. What a relief!

Chris catches up with me and we continue our descent together. Around the corner behind the rocky outcrop, there is a small camp with just a few tents. Moments ago, we could see into the far distance; now we can barely see a few meters ahead. We've left the sunshine behind and moved into the cloud zone. The sand and scree has turned into a stony slope. Within seconds, we seem to have entered a different world, as if that rock had represented a magic gateway.

After about 15 minutes alone, wondering whether we are on the right track, we find Evance and the girls sitting on the slope, waiting for us. We join them for a break. Everyone seems really tired. I would prefer to just keep moving and get it done with.

"Patience, Alex," I keep reminding myself.

Amidst the clouds and after hiking for 12 hours non-stop, it feels more like late afternoon rather than mid-morning.

Soon Giovanni and Robert also catch up. No one seems keen to move any further.

Just a few hundred meters beneath us, there is an agglomeration of some 100 tents in different colors. They are situated on a moderate slope of a rocky ridge facing towards us, surrounded by thick fog. This is Barafu Hut camp. It looks surreal, more like a Nepalese or South American mountain village than a hiking base camp.

The path leads straight through the camp to the top of the ridge, before it drops into the fog. Most of the tents are to the left of the path, on an inclination that looks too uncomfortable to sleep on. Memories from my two restless nights when I kept sliding downhill are immediately coming back. I wouldn't want to camp there.

We spot some tents that look like ours, including the orange/off-white sleeping tents as well as the black toilet tent, mess tent and cooking tent.

"These are ours, right?" everyone seems convinced.

However, Robert previously mentioned we would be sleeping at the third camp, and this is only the second camp. Neither can I locate the white roofs that Evance has pointed out to me in the morning from Stella Point.

"These must be the tents of another Ultimate Kilimanjaro group, perhaps the one following the Lemosho route," I state my logic.

Evance nods.

Everyone else ignores my comments. They don't want to believe the obvious. Going any further down the mountain just seems impossibly hard to them.

"Come on, these must be ours?" they urge Robert and Evance to confirm.

But both just keep a poker face. They previously pulled our legs on the hike suggesting that we would still have an hour to go and it turned out to be much shorter. We know they like to positively surprise us. Is this another such situation?

In their exhaustion, Chris and the girls choose to believe in the positive surprise.

"These are our tents."

"For sure."

"Yes, must be ours," everyone keeps saying out loud, reconfirming each other.

Evance just smiles, which strengthens their belief. They all cheer up and start getting excited about soon finishing our long hike for the day.

"I can't wait to sleep."

"Me neither."

"Finally!"

"Yay!"

Given the overall excitement that's not called back into restraint by our guides, I even start to believe it myself.

For the last 15 minutes' descent down to the camp, we scramble over huge flat stones looking like debris of damaged houses or bombed rock.

"Why do they break in such a smooth flat way?"

No one can give me the answer.

The whole scenery looks more like a mining area than a hiking track. Porters keep passing us walking uphill with huge bags on their heads.

"Isn't Barafu Hut the last big base camp?" I wonder. "Where are they all going?"

"For paragliding," Evance explains. "Seen the tents up there? That's where they camp before paragliding, so it's closer to hike up in the early morning."

"Wow, that's crazy!" But it also sounds fun.

"At least they don't have to walk back down," others comment.

We enter the campsite, and Evance continues to lead us straight on instead of turning left towards our familiar tents.

"Where are we going?" everyone asks him impatiently.

I already know the answer that the others still refuse to believe. This isn't our camp after all. I'm secretly relieved. It didn't look very comfortable, nor do I like its mass tourism feel.

Evance doesn't reply. Instead, he is talking into his radiophone, but there is no response. It sounds as if he is also waiting for more information. Robert has disappeared.

"What's going on?" we all demand to know.

But Evance won't say anything.

People are getting more and more impatient.

"You need the f . . . to let us know what's going on, can't just leave us in the f . . . ing dark like that," Chris demands with an unfamiliar harsh tone.

Huh, what's going on? He's been overwhelmingly appreciative and cheerful all week. What's just happened? How has our vibe retuned from friendly and positive all along to suddenly become so gloomy and loaded with tension? It feels as if someone had turned on the wrong movie. I guess everyone is just very, very tired.

"Eh, please, let's not spoil our good relationship towards the end of our hike," I'm silently begging everyone.

Evance receives a few broken radio messages.

"What's happening?" we all want to be updated.

"Stewart has a problem with his knee. He cannot walk any further."

"What happened? How bad is it?"

"I don't know, but he needs assistance."

"Oh no!"

"Terrible, man, that's too bad."

"I'm so sorry for him."

We're shocked.

"Yes. Also, we don't stay here. Sit down and have a rest before we continue to the next camp."

I'm sorry not only to hear about Stewart, but also for Robert and Evance. Have they made a mistake by coming down first with us stronger and fitter hikers, leaving the ones struggling more behind in the care of our assistant guides and summit porters?

Surely there have been very valid reasons for that. After all, not only Robert and Evance but also all the others are extremely capable and more than sufficiently strong to support us. Furthermore, we've come down with a ratio of two guides for six hikers, while the remainder of our group has one assistant guide or summit porter per hiker, meaning a ratio of 1:1 rather than 1:3.

But if Stewart had a bad accident, would they have to take the blame that they may not have cared or supported enough? I would not want this to overshadow their so far excellent performance and leave any of our group members with negative sentiments about them. Yikes!

The morale of our small and normally very strong group is at its lowest. Most simply lie down and close their eyes. I feel lost and disconnected again, unable to relate to their fatigue and exhaustion. "Why is everyone so overly negative? Cheer up guys! It's not that bad after all," I'm thinking to myself. "We've all made it to the summit, we are going to the third camp which is still closer than our original itinerary, and there's nothing we can do to help Stewart by being negative," I'm analyzing the situation for myself. "And we don't need to stay at this busy camp and hopefully get to sleep on even ground."

But I don't say anything. It doesn't seem my opinion would be appreciated right now. Instead, I use the time to browse through my summit pictures. I send one of myself at the summit to my dad to let him know that I made it up safely, in case my phone catches data reception somewhere on our way down.

After a few minutes, Robert reappears.

"What's happening?" everyone is wide awake again.

"We need to organize rescue porters for Stewart."

That doesn't sound good. "How bad is it? Was it an accident?"

"No accident. It's his knee. He'd already warned us he has a bad knee. Now it's too much. He can't walk any more, not even stand up by himself."[61]

"Ouch!" Being stretchered down is pretty much one of the worst things that could happen to someone on this mountain, especially with a bad back. Nevertheless, I'm relieved to hear that it was not an accident. There's nothing our guides could have done to prevent this.

Robert and Evance keep communicating on their radiophones. I assume they are talking both to our guides further up as well as trying to locate resources for Stewart's transportation.

"I need to stay up here to coordinate the rescue stretcher for Stewart," Robert explains almost apologetically for leaving us alone, "Evance will lead you down to the camp."

It's already 11:45am. Both Evance and I are keen to get moving again as fast as possible. The others agree there is no point dragging out our inevitable further descent any longer. Evance rushes ahead, and I follow him closely together with Giovanni, Chris and Lynn.

We pass a stretcher lying idly on the way. It's a simple wooden frame with handles sticking out at both ends for rescue porters to lift. A cream-colored linen-like fabric is stretched around the frame, for the wounded hiker to lie on. According to what I read, hikers would get strapped to the stretcher so they cannot fall off during the transport. The thought of being carried down on such a structure is certainly not pleasant.

The fog is getting thicker and thicker. While there is only one path down, Evance stops every now and then to wait for Eva and Farrah to catch up, making sure no one gets lost. They seem to be engaged in an entertaining conversation and prefer to take their time.

A bit further down, we come across several more stretchers lying idly near the path. This time the stretchers are made of a black metal frame with a wheel in the middle. I assume the wheel makes the descent easier for the porters, while at the same time even more bouncy and painful for the hiker. Flat stones and edgy boulders are scattered everywhere. The fog has become so thick we can't see more than ten meters. Everything looks grey and gloomy, like in a war zone.

Metal stretcher and foggy path below Barafu Hut

Chris walks off to the side. "Just keep going. I'll catch up."

We continue walking at a rather slow pace, but after several minutes he's still nowhere in sight. The fog is growing ever thicker.

"Evance, we'd better wait," I suggest. "What if he gets lost?"

We wait . . . and wait . . . and wait . . . Finally Chris reappears.

"We already thought you got lost!"

"I've got rid of my layers," he explains, "much better now." And somehow with his layers, his gloomy mood has disappeared as well. He is his smiling and cheerful self again.

We continue at quite a fast pace, soon realizing that Eva and Farrah have again fallen far behind.

"Why don't you all go ahead?" Evance suggests.

"It's not far, just further down this path. I'll wait for them. Sorry for that," he apologizes as if he were letting us down majorly.

"Not at all. Don't worry. It's not your fault." I feel sorry for him.

He hasn't done anything wrong and looks very tired. How does he manage to stay that considerate and caring? Surely he also just wants to get back down as fast as possible.

Chris, Giovanni, Lynn and I rush ahead at our maximum speed. I'm glad to be able to walk again at my own pace together with my three equally fast companions. The four of us make an excellent hiking team.

"Hey guys, remember when Stewart sat down on the way up to Gillman's Point?" Chris recalls.

"Sure."

"Did you hear his answer when Robert told him that he can sit, but only for five minutes?"

We shake our heads.

"Robert said: 'OK, you can sit, but only five minutes,' and Stewart . . ." Chris is laughing so hard that he struggles to talk at the same time. ". . . Stewart said . . . now listen to this . . . he said: 'I'll tell you when I'm ready.'"

His laughing is infectious. Imagining the conversation between Babu Stewart and Robert, we all get carried away in lightheaded laughter, so unrestrained that we need to stop walking, rolling over our shaking bellies while exhaustedly leaning against our hiking poles.

Chris repeats "I'll tell you when I'm ready," and we keep roaring as if the fog were loaded with laughing gas.

Stewart is Chris's big hero, and he's so impressed by his willpower for making it all the way up on his own, at his own terms. Little can we imagine, of course, Stewart's experience right now just a few kilometers further up, strapped in and bounced around on one of those one-wheeled stretchers just as we saw earlier, that would make the effort of his summit ascent pale in comparison to the ordeal of his descent. We just find this quote hilarious. "I'll tell you when I'm ready" instantly becomes our favorite one-liner of the entire trip.

We all love heroes, people who achieve the impossible, who stand up again and again to keep fighting against all odds, until they've reached the happy ending. Stewart is such an inspiration for us. He has proven wrong his doctor and everyone who thought that he couldn't or shouldn't do it. He has shown the world that no age and no spine injury can keep you from reaching the top of Africa. Perhaps we are simply exhilarated to be part of his story.

"Here's another quote," Lynn is laughing.

We all look at her and can't wait to hear her one-liner.

"When we went up to the base camp and everyone was exhausted, someone asked for a longer break: 'Evance, can we have a longer break this time?' You know what Evance replied?"

Everyone is already laughing before even hearing the answer.

"He said . . ." Lynn is wiping tears of laughter from her eyes, ". . . he said . . . 'OK, let's have a BIG SHORT break!'"

Evance knows how to fool us into believing we've got our way, being nice and tough at the same time. Again, we are roaring with laughter, craving for entertainment after the depressing past two hours.

The scenery is getting a bit greener again, some bushes here and there, and we're leaving the fog behind us. I love the change of atmosphere. Finally we've got our good spirits back, just as it used to be all week until mid-morning. I'm so glad we've left that gloomy vibe back up at Barafu Hut.

After about 15 minutes, and an increasingly greener landscape, the camp is still nowhere in sight. A porter passes us on his way up.

"My friend, how long is it to the next camp?" Chris asks him.

The porter looks at him skeptically, weighing his answer: "For me, 10 minutes . . . for you, 20 minutes."

Here we've got our third favorite quote, and we keep laughing almost all the way down about his witty and honest remark. This quote says it all about the true heroes of Kilimanjaro. It's not us *mzungus* (white foreigners), but the porters who bear all the heavy lifting. However, that porter also got it wrong and overestimated our capabilities. After 20 minutes, the camp is still nowhere in sight. We're getting bored.

"If you had a choice, which one would you go for first: shower, bed or food?" I ask for the sake of conversation.

"Bed!" the three of them agree.

"Really?" I probe.

"OK, no, shower first, then bed," they all correct.

"Um, shower first yes, but then lunch," I admit.

"I'm too tired to eat," three voices agree.

Here we go again; I've confirmed my voracious mountain cliché. I'm really looking forward to a hot soup, but not so much to sitting alone in the mess tent if everyone else goes to sleep. I'm not even planning to sleep at all this afternoon, but better keep that to myself. On the one hand, I'm simply not that tired, perhaps because I'm the only one who managed to get a good amount of sleep at our base camp both in the afternoon and in the evening, or perhaps because I'm still high from all the excitement. On the other hand, I'm keen to start writing down as much as I can remember of our summit adventure before my memory wanes.

However, while I've felt strong and energetic during the past 14 hours, I finally also start to feel my leg muscles and just want to get today's hiking marathon done with. My knees are also telling me that they have been supporting me for longer than they were built to do. When our camp finally comes in sight, I'm as happy and relieved as everyone else.

The camp is settled on a clearing behind a first line of trees that look rather dry and barren, their needles more brown than green. Just ahead of the camp and the tree line, there is a helicopter pad – a round earthen plot where the bushes have been removed and stones placed in a circular fashion to indicate its purpose.

"Have you seen that?"

"Yes, that's an awfully long way down from the summit for anyone who needs a helicopter evacuation."

"I wonder whether Stewart will get picked up there."

"Yes, probably . . ."

It's around 2pm, 30 minutes after we asked the passing porter and almost 15 hours since we left base camp, when we finally arrive amidst our familiar tents at Millenium Camp. All our cooks, waiters and porters immediately come to welcome us with their friendly smiles.

"Congratulations!" They shake our hands and pad our shoulders.

It feels like coming back home.

Chris, Giovanni and Lynn's porters show them to their tents. I feel lost and miss Liber who has been welcoming me with his broad smile and leading me to my tent all week. Right now he has way more important things to do, assisting other group members with their not so easy descent.

Which tent is mine? No one seems to know. Our waiter Crispin helps me check them all until we finally locate my bag and sleeping mat in the last tent that we open.

As soon as I've dropped my backpack, hot water is already waiting for our *shower*. I fill a little bowl and disappear into my tent, like everyone else.

Finally! I've been looking forward to this moment for the past hours – to strip off my remaining clothes and wipe the dust off my body.

"Lunch will be ready in a few minutes," Evance's voice informs me.

It's only ten minutes since I've crawled into my tent, and it feels as if I'd only just started my transformation back into a human being. "What's always this rush with lunch? Can't they give us more time?" I'm thinking slightly annoyed and stressed.

"I need more time," I shout back outside.

"I'm only letting you know," Evance replies gently. "Just come when you are ready."

I immediately regret my words. While we all have escaped into our tents to wash and rest, he continues working. Instead of showing our staff my deepest gratitude for having lunch ready so quickly for us, I've just given him a short unfriendly reply. Being tired is not a good excuse. There's still a long journey ahead of me before I've conquered all my emotions.

I try to speed up my washing to get ready for lunch. It is amazing how clean one can make oneself feel using tiny compressed towels and wet wipes; greasy hair and dirty finger nails aside.

It's relatively warm down here in the afternoon and my woolen beanie is as filthy as hell. Earthy dust is smeared all over its normally off white color. I need a new hair cover solution. My thin Buff that has so far been protecting my throat from the cold is my only option. It's probably as dirty as all my other clothes, just that its strong pink and blue colors nicely hide the truth. I squeeze it over my head to cover all my hair from my front and ears down to my shoulders. Easy. Not the most appealing look, but left without options I don't care any longer, provided that I don't need to provoke mass nausea with the true state of my hair. The mountain has helped me focus on more important things instead – eating, keeping warm, going to the bathroom, sleeping, and once these basic needs are satisfied, to build relationships with and enjoy the company of our fellow hikers and guides. That's why deodorant and my floral hair perfume that constantly I dump all over myself have become my favorite toiletries up here.

I expect to be alone in the mess tent for lunch. Surely everyone else is asleep by now. To my surprise, all six of us gather within few minutes – Chris, Giovanni and Lynn freshly *showered*, as well as Eva and Farrah straight from the hike.

"We made it!"

"Yay!"

"Congrats!"

On the table, we find our familiar pot of veggie soup, spaghetti egg frittata, grilled vegetarian sandwiches, and a big plate of fresh pineapple and orange slices. Since last night's dinner at 5:30pm, I've only eaten two cookies at the start of our summit hike and a piece of power snack early morning. The otherwise boring spaghetti egg frittata with an added twist of spicy curry ketchup sauce now tastes like a luxury meal, and the fresh pineapple slices like heaven on earth.

There's not much conversation going on. Everyone is too tired. We mostly comment on how sorry we are about what happened to Stewart, hoping that he will be fine. As soon as they have eaten, Chris, Giovanni and Lynn quickly head back to their tents. Thinking of the big mess of dusty clothes and toiletries that I have left behind spread all over my tent, I am not keen to rush back. Even though I need to sort it out sooner or later, taking my time to finish my tea seems way more appealing right now.

Eva and Farrah are not keen to move either. We awkwardly look at each other. It seems the two of them have formed a strong bond of friendship and built a special connection through the long descent. I feel like the third wheel, as if they hope to continue a conversation from before but can't do so in my presence. In reality, they are just really worried about Ravi and everyone else still up on the mountain. I hurry up with my tea, wish them a good rest and drag myself back into my tent.

The sun has meanwhile reappeared and made our tents feel nice and warm. I take my time to sort through all my mess, wrapping away my warm summit clothes and repacking my bags, leaving only the essentials that I will still need today and for our final descent tomorrow.

An inexplicably irrational flash of hope makes me try and clear the dust and dirt from my fingernails. In a lengthy process, I manage to reduce ten dark brown circles into ten patchy brown half-moons, but no further. The dirt seems to have become one with my dry skin around my nails. As soon as I touch anything – the tent floor, my bags, or my clothes – the circles of dirt return and the vanity of what I've just done strikes me as insane. It's a desperate never-ending struggle not worth fighting for.

While cleaning up, I hear the voices of the remainder of our group outside, including Stewart's, if I'm not mistaken. That's good, so however bad his knee, I hope the worst would be over now.

But then Farrah's concerned voice: "Where is Ravi? Is he OK?"

I can't hear any answer. With his twisted ankle, he surely doesn't have an easy time on this long way down.

▲ ▲ ▲

I hope to use the remaining afternoon to capture the past 40 hours in writing, knowing that I won't have a chance to get to it again until I start my safari in two days and concerned that my memory will fail me if I wait any longer. I'm keen to capture as much information as I can recall.

When I unlock my phone, to my surprise, I already find a reply from my dad to my summit photo: "We are proud of you." Apparently someone from my hometown in Austria also does guided tours on Kilimanjaro, and my dad has seen the same summit photo in our local newspaper this week. What a coincidence!

After such a long day, alone in my tent miles away from civilization, it feels particularly nice to receive his congratulatory message. I'd never thought about Kilimanjaro in terms of making anyone proud of me. When Lynn asked me this very question early on, whether my dad would be proud of me for doing Kili, I denied the possibility. Here we go – she was right after all.

Craving for some more connection, I also reply to my friend Rachael who had lent me her gear and sent me an encouraging message at the start of my trip:

"We did it! Your shirts kept me nice and warm on a freezing night."

"That's fantastic! What an achievement," she replies within seconds.

I smile just as I should have when I reached Uhuru Peak. In the end, our connections with family, friends and the people around us is all that matters.

Looking at my phone also makes me realize that my eyes haven't been sore all week as they used to be from staring at computer screens all the time. They really needed this break. And I had no problems whatsoever with my contact lenses or dry eyes as common in high altitudes. Seems I just got really lucky with all circumstances this time round. Even though summiting Kilimanjaro is nothing to be proud of for me, all the beneficial circumstances are to be appreciated and make me feel blessed.

Finally, I start typing my notes and get immersed in my memory, mentally reliving the past two days and losing myself in daydreaming.

"Hello-o? Dinner is ready," someone brings me back to the present.

How can that be? We've barely made it back up to our School Hut base camp in my written recollection. I check the time – it's close to 7pm. I'm not hungry yet, but my number one priority is to spend as much of the remaining time as possible with my new friends. Thus I put my phone down immediately.

Only now I realize that, with the sun almost down, it's become cold again. I deluded myself to believe that it would stay warm from now on, never mind that our camp is at 3,800 meters (12,600ft) of altitude, similar to all our prior non-base camps. We still have a long way to go tomorrow, but for now it's time for our last mountain evening together.

"Congratulations!" We all enter and welcome each other in the mess tent with the same one word.

Almost everyone is present, including Ravi. Only Stewart is missing.

"How is he doing?" we all want to know.

"He is OK, sleeping now," Juli explains.

"How will he get down tomorrow?"

"We don't know yet. Depends on how well he recovers overnight."

Let's hope for the best.

"People of this nation . . ." here comes Ravi again, but this time on a more serious note. He is doing well, considering what he's just been through with his twisted ankle. "I would like to take this opportunity to thank one of our group members who has displayed a heroic act of friendship last night, even though she didn't have to, and that's Eva. When I thought I couldn't go any further, she would stay with me and tell me that I could do it. I told her to leave me behind. She could have gone much faster. But she was persistent and wouldn't move from my side all the way up to the summit. If not for her, I would have turned around. I wouldn't have made it without her."

Wow! We all cheer and applaud her selfless display of friendship in a time when most others – not least myself – were busy with themselves and entangled with their own struggles.

Contrary to Ravi's beautiful story, our dinner that had us so excited on our first night on the mountain has become a boring routine affair. We all agree on one thing: While they do a great job with the cooking, it all starts tasting the same after a week of veggie soups and stews. Our taste buds have become a blur and the food has lost its appeal.

Typically, the tipping ceremony for the staff is performed on the last evening. However, our mood is tempered following Stewart's tough luck, the late arrival of several group members and our general state of exhaustion.

"Let's do it tomorrow morning instead," we all agree.

Chris already has a list of all our guides, cooks, waiters and porters, including how much each of them he had proposed, and our group had agreed, to tip. Now the money still needs to be collected from each of us and put into the right envelops – one for the guides and one for everyone else.

I help Chris count the money and sort out the numbers. What should have been a very simple task turns into a lengthy process of re-counting and recalculating – evidence that my mind is more exhausted from our lack of sleep than I would have admitted.

"Seventeen plus fifteen . . . what was that again?"

We need our phone calculators to double-check.

"OK, so here's fifty . . . hold on . . . how much did I just give you?"

"Eh?"

Giggle, giggle.

I start counting again.

Our sheer inability to think straight and memorize the simplest numbers has a surprisingly high entertainment factor, like a black comedy. I feel as if I'd just had a bottle of wine. No matter how tired, our humor is still wide awake.

When back in my tent, I try to keep writing down my memories, but by 9pm my exhaustion eventually takes control. Having dreaded my tent-night over the past week, I now fall asleep as soon as I close my eyes at last.

DAY 9

It's all about us

28 SEPTEMBER 2015

**Millenium Camp (3,800m/12,600ft)
to Mweka Gate (1,600m/5,400ft)**

Distance — elevation — time:
14km/11mi⇨ — 2,200m/7,200ft⇩ — 5-7 hours🕐

I wake up with our last day's sunrise on the mountain. My body feels fully recovered. I've slept like a baby for nine solid hours. Getting ready is quick and easy this morning, after over a week of optimizing my morning routine to perfection.

While I should be looking forward to finally getting off this mountain and having a shower, in my heart I don't want this trip to end. Today I want to savor every last moment.

It's another beautiful morning with lots of sunshine and a clear view back up to glacier-capped Kibo cone behind an olive-green line of trees and bushes, underneath a crystal clear morning sky. We are not the only ones active at these early morning hours. Ravenous birds are busily circling the nearby slopes, looking for their breakfast prey.

I run into Evance. He still looks tired.

"Good morning! How did you sleep?"

"Oh, not too much."

"Why not?"

"It was too loud. I lost my earplugs, kept hearing the porters talking."

"Oh no, I'm sorry to hear that! You must be looking forward to getting home, and to your three-week break before your next hike, right?"

We had already talked about that before.

"Yes, that's right."

I will miss my new friend.

Stewart is up as well.

"How are you? Seems you can walk again, that's great."

"Yes, but it's still painful. They will escort me down."

"Oh, I'm sorry to hear. I thought you might have organized a helicopter?"

"I tried yesterday, but impossible. They would have to fly one in from outside Tanzania and it would take ages to arrive."

"Oh really? I thought that's what we all got that insurance for," and I'm sure Stewart has the best possible insurance. "It's shocking, I mean, what would happen in an emergency?"

"Yes, I thought so too. Perhaps they just thought my case was not bad enough."

Only one way to find out what would happen in a life-threatening emergency, and I'm sure no one would want to be the reason.

Our breakfast this morning is the last meal we'll receive from our fabulous chef Mr. Delicious and his assistant Amani – some kind of fried roti bread, egg frittata, cucumber slices, sausages and porridge.

"No matter how good they cook," Chris mentions, "I'm really looking forward to my breakfast back home."

"Me too, to my cereals."

"Yes, and fresh yogurt."

"Yes! Yogurt and fresh berries"

"Fresh bread and real butter.

"Cappuccino with real milk."

Our fantasies are going wild.

Over breakfast, I'm helping Chris to collect the remaining tips. To make sure we haven't made any mistakes, Giovanni and Juli help us recount the two stacks for porters and guides. It all adds up as expected, but we are still short of the total required number. Seems we had not accounted for some staff members. As all of us have already chipped in more than 10% above the recommended tipping range, we agree that the gap needs to be rebalanced within the pool. Rerunning the numbers takes quite some time. Chris takes care and sorts it all out. I see him chip in some more from his own pocket.

"Don't do that. Why should you have to pay more? It's not fair."

"Doesn't add up otherwise," he shrugs. "We forgot to include the extra trip for the summit porters."

"But you didn't even use them!" I protest. "How about the people who actually used them contribute more?"

Chris looks at me apologetically and understandingly. No one comments on my suggestion.

"I will anyway give something also directly to my tent porter," some people add.

"Yes, I know, that's alright," Chris agrees with them.

Eh, why do people tip their tent porters directly? I thought the whole point of tipping in a group was not only to make it easier for us, but also to be fair to each crew member. If we leave it to each individual to tip their tent porters, then some will obviously be more generous than others, even though they may all have done the same good job. We all want to feel good by giving directly, but that's simply not fair to the porters.

The atmosphere is tense. I feel frustrated about the situation but don't say anything in order not to offend anyone. Chris looks torn between being generous to all crew members and being nice to all of us.

No one offers to help, as if to say: You screwed up the numbers, now you'd better sort it out. That's the thanks you get for volunteering for such tasks.

"OK, so how much are we still short?" I ask him.

"About 50. And we don't have any small change."

"Yes, I know, some people just handed me hundreds. OK, so here you've got another 20 from me," I contradict my own logic, "and the remainder will need to be rebalanced from within the pool, OK?"

"Perfect," somehow he manages to rebalance and make it all work. It would have been a disaster without him.

Our guides, waiters and cooks walk into the mess tent, cheerfully singing and passionately clapping their hands. Aw, I love their singing! It always makes me smile, that instinctive uncontrolled kind of smile like when one cuddles a super cute puppy.

Crispin is holding a cake. It is meticulously decorated like the one for Juli and Jana's anniversary, but this time covered in white icing with *"Hongera"* ("Congratulations") and *"5895m"* written in beautiful red and green letters. What a surprise!

We don't know what they sing, but it sounds like a congratulatory song. I can only make out the words *"wageni yetu"* ("our guests").

Their cheerful voices instantly energize and cast a good-humored spell on our entire group, all tension gone as if it never was. It inspires me to see and feel first-hand the big impact of their singing – such a simple act yet it makes us all so happy. It warms our hearts just as the morning sun warms our bodies, because we feel that it comes from their hearts and they truly mean to wish us well.

To me, listening to their unexpected singing is one of the best moments on the entire trip, and I think it's not only me – smiling eyes everywhere. Half of us participate by clapping our hands. The other half have immediately grabbed their cameras to take videos. This is a moment to be recovered forever.

"Yoo-hoo!"

"Whistle!"

"Hurrah!"

We all applaud exuberantly.

"Hip hip!"

"Robert!"

"On behalf of Ultimate Kilimanjaro, I would love to congratulate you for what you have done yesterday, because it wasn't easy for the average of your age – how tough it was – but it was all of you, a hundred percent, you made it to the summit. So, the chef, he didn't want to leave it as it is. He made a little surprise for you."

"Thank you!!!"

"This is a surprise from Mr. Chef, Mr. Delicious," Robert adds.

"Thank you!!!"

"We hand out this to Mr. Stewart on behalf of the group, and Stewart, he can pick who he wants to share with," Robert jokes.

"Haha, you'd better share with everybody!" Juli comments.

"Babu, baboo-oo yoh, babu, baboo-oo yoh . . ." our crew start singing again as Crispin places the cake in front of Stewart. What a celebration!

Stewart and Juli distribute pieces to each of us. It's a rich dark chocolate cake, yummy! No luxurious bakery in this world could make this taste any better than what Mr. Delicious has conjured up in his cooking tent on a simple gas flame without even the most basic kitchen equipment. It remains a mystery to me how they can do it.

After finishing our treat, we head outside for the tipping ceremony. Everyone is present, including all our porters. They have already assembled in a half circle facing downhill, with Kibo in the background. The stage couldn't be any more scenic.

Robert starts with a speech, but not just another congratulatory speech full of praise. "You've all become so close to us, like family," his words warm our hearts again. "We will miss you and remember you forever."

I'm sure he says something similar to every group, but it feels authentic, that he really means it. I feel like that about them. They've done so much for us, much more than just fulfilling their roles and treating us like clients. We've had so much fun together, exchanged our personal backgrounds, shared our experience, and become friends along the way. And more than that, by making us always walk in a group all the time, they helped all of us become friends with each other.

I mostly connected with others while hiking. Had I gone off at my own pace as initially I thought we all would, I would have missed out on Juli's inspirational story of how she traveled all of Africa on her own, on how Stewart became a successful property developer and led the HIV combat mission in Africa, on Jeannette's fascinating time living in Saudi Arabia, on . . . and on . . . and on.

Now it's up to Chris to make a speech on behalf of us hikers, and Robert translates for all the porters. Chris chooses his words wisely. He returns all the beautiful sentiments that Robert has shared with us and expresses our deepest gratitude for all of them:

"We've come here to climb a mountain, but what we have found is far bigger than that . . ." he restrains his tears, ". . . all of you, you are so much bigger than this mountain . . ."

I'm restraining my own tears.

". . . We are humbled by your strength, your work ethic, your friendship . . ."

Looking around, all of us share his emotions and most of us have wet eyes. I'm glad we have chosen Chris as our spokesperson. No one could have said it any better.

After another round of applause from all sides, Juli hands over the two envelopes. Mr. Delicious is supposed to receive the one on behalf of the guides. We are confused again, unsure which one to hand him and in which stack we've included our chef's tip. This tipping procedure, which should be a simple affair by normal standards, is posing an abnormal mental challenge to us. Our brains are still stuck in *pole pole* autopilot mode. So we'd better double-check, but it turns out to be all in order.

I hope at some point in time operators will find an easier way to deal with the tipping. If all operators simply paid a fair transparent salary and increased the tour price accordingly, that would make life a lot easier for everyone.

"Hip hip!"

"Robert!"

"These people," he's pointing to all the porters, "they have a couple of songs to sing to you as their appreciation. OK? . . . We have couple of songs . . ."

"*Malaika!*" Juli requests a song that I believe we haven't heard yet, at least it doesn't ring a bell to me. Of course Robert and all the porters readily have it in their repertoire. Little do I know that this is the most famous Swahili pop song of all times, from Kenya. It is about a man who can't marry the woman he loves, his angel ("*Malaika*"), because he can't afford to pay her bride price. It doesn't matter that I don't understand any of the words. With the slow pace and melancholic tune, I can still tell it's some kind of sad or romantic song.

Then it's getting faster-paced and cheerier with the two songs the words and melodies of which have become so familiar to all of us by now: *Kilimanjaro*, which tells of the very long mountain journey encircling us like a snake that wants to eat our meat; and of course the *Jambo* song, which welcomes us guests.[62]

I could listen to our guides and porters sing all day long, no matter what they sing. So much passion, so much joy! One doesn't find that easily in our Western societies. I'm sad it's the last time we will hear them, but at least this time I've remembered to record a video from beginning to end.[63] That way I will be able to enjoy it many more times. Surely it will cheer me up whenever I need an energy boost.

A round of yoo-hoos and thank-you's crowns their performance. "Asante sana!"

"So, now it is just Mr. Chris. You," Robert is looking at all of us, "will remain here because we . . ." he's looking for words, ". . . re-count those money . . ."

Giggle, giggle.

"Then we will shake hands . . ."

Laughter.

". . . The rest, just finalize your organizing of your daypack, then after a few minutes we will leave, OK?"

Chris, together with all our guides and the porters' representative, disappears into the mess tent to check and confirm the numbers.

Behind the tent, a thick layer of fleecy white cotton wool clouds gently covers the lower slopes and reaches all the way up to the first tree line behind our camp. The clouds are seemingly on an equal level with us.

"How nice would it be to jump right in and take a bath in their soft white foam?"

"It looks like on Jack's beanstalk," Lynn and I agree.

When Chris re-emerges, he is jumping excitedly and smiling broadly, keen to share with us what he has just witnessed: Big open eyes of our guides and the porters' representative speaking of their positive surprise at seeing the numbers; smiling glances furtively exchanged between them indicating that we've exceeded their expectations big time. This would become one of Chris's most memorable moments. It is great to know that we've made them happy and could give something back to them.

"You should have seen their eyes!" Chris is so overwhelmed when telling us about their reaction that he's almost got tears in his eyes.

▲ ▲ ▲

It's time to say goodbye to our porters. Only the guides and cooks will be coming with us on the bus back to Moshi. I shake Liber's hand again one last time. "Asante sana" – that's the only thing I've got for him right now, and I receive his broad smile in return.

Have I caught a hint of disappointment in his eyes? Does he expect a tip from me? Does he know that we have all tipped generously and he will be rewarded from our group tipping pot? Has he seen some of his colleagues getting tipped directly by other hikers? I feel bad, even though I know I haven't done anything wrong. He has been so wonderful to me. I hope he doesn't feel cheated.

"*Twende!*" "Let's go!"

People start walking. I can't locate my hiking poles which I'm sure were here just minutes ago.

"Anyone seen my poles?"

As soon as Robert realizes that something has gone amiss, he's back in charge again and helps me check with all the crew members. It doesn't take long to find out: "The porters escorting Stewart took them. They thought they were his."

"Ah OK, no problem." I start walking.

"We'll get them for you." Robert sends some porters down and motions me to stop.

"Thanks, no need. They can't be far. I'm sure we'll catch up with them soon."

"No, no, please wait." Robert makes sure that everything is correct and proper, that I am fully satisfied before leaving the camp.

Shortly after, Liber comes running uphill with my poles. One last time, he has been my silent hero.

Chris has been staying back with me and we quickly catch up with everyone else. Today, we escape the heath zone before the mid-morning-to-afternoon-clouds rule kicks in. At the same time, the thick layer of clouds beneath us keeps receding further and further down, always below us and covering the landscape underneath, but leaving us blessed with sunshine throughout our final descent.

As soon as we leave Millenium Camp, which is settled right at the edge between the alpine moorland and the first tree line, we find ourselves amidst a bushy kind of pine forest that's short enough not to block our view yet thick enough to turn the entire landscape green until it is submerged beneath the clouds. Indeed the growth is so thick and scrubby that you wouldn't voluntarily wander off to the sides of the path unless you really needed to, in which case, surely, it would provide a perfect hideaway.

Everyone is in good spirits and very talkative again today. We girls chat lightheartedly about love and relationships. Yes, so cliché but so true – we all love talking about that.

"So how come you are still single?" Farrah asks me, the only one without a partner.

"I guess I just haven't found Mr. Right yet."

"How about Chris? You seem to be getting along very well," Eva suggests.

"Yes indeed, he'd totally be the kind of guy I'd go for, but . . ." if there weren't always these buts. "Anyway, haha, we made a pact. If we're still single in thirty years, we'll meet up again."

"Aw guys," Eva is shaking her head, "if you like each other, why wait thirty years!"

She may be the youngest in our group, but is certainly not lacking in wisdom.

"First you need to know what you really want," Juli suggests. "Write it down. Then he will come into your life just like that when the time is right."

I like her thinking. She was already in her mid-forties when she met Stewart and look how happy they are together now! No need to rush.

"Farrah, you mentioned you are doing research at a university? Do you plan to go into academics?" I ask her.

"It's just a temporary assignment. I'm applying to get a project placement with MSF, but it's not easy."

"For a particular project? Or would you like to work with them long-term?"

"Well yes, I hope that once the connection is established it would be easier, and then I'd like to continue working with them."

"So that means working in developing countries and constantly moving?"

"Yes, I like traveling and I love helping people," her eyes sparkle as she talks about her work and passion. "I also do a lot of voluntary charity work . . ."

I find her very inspiring. Through her nursing career, she has been – and I'm sure will continue – living her dream, getting to travel and experience lots of different cultures along the way, while making the world a better place. I was brought up believing that eventually I would need to settle down, buy a house, and be happy ever after. Farrah is challenging my thinking. Isn't it much more important to have that sparkle in your eyes and do what you love?

"What's your next big plan after Kilimanjaro?" Ravi asks me.

I tell him about my ideas to start a business venture focused on providing support to working mothers, to make it easier for them to have a career and children at the same time.

"How would you make money?"

"It would initially have to be focused on wealthy clients who could afford such a service. There are plenty of them in Switzerland. They are used to having a financial relationship manager, it would be the family equivalent to that. Currently it's still mostly left to the woman to take care of all the family matters, even if she may be working in an as equally demanding job as the father."

"So you would be doing it for them?"

"Not me personally, I don't understand anything about kids, but yes, the company would. My idea is to provide a flexible way for stay-home mums or pensioners to earn additional income and do something meaningful, by pairing them up in a smart way."

Ravi is a good listener and asks the right questions.

"Sounds like you're up to something great. I wish you all the best for it."

I'm not so sure anymore that it's so great. Before I came here I was so motivated and thought this would be something meaningful. Now I find it pales and looks lofty next to the dedication of my fellow hikers, like Ravi.

"So how about you? Do you see yourself in the US long-term?"

"I'm happy with my current role, but if the right opportunity comes up, I'd definitely want to relocate and work again on the ground in the developing world."

Juli also gives me the pleasure of learning more about her. I find her such an amazing person, both joyful and energetic as well as humble and good-hearted throughout. While Juli is very modest in her self-description, she carries a treasure chest of life experience, compassion and inspirations waiting to be discovered. She has no need to boast about her great character and achievements: the most experienced and fearless traveler I've ever met; a tireless organizer and host of charity and political fundraising events; a caring person who doesn't prioritize herself but gets joy from giving and supporting others.

Only during our descent, I learn from Juli that she's also been a foster mum to two teenage boys from difficult family backgrounds, who only moved out two years ago.

"I can barely imagine how difficult that must have been."

"Sure, it wasn't always easy, but it was good. We gave them a home."

Juli is the kind of woman who would make a wonderful first lady, the kind of strong woman you find silently supporting successful men. I am already looking forward to reading her complete story, as well as Stewart's, in their memoirs that they are planning to write.

▲ ▲ ▲

It takes us about an hour to catch up with Stewart, who is being escorted by two porters, one to each side to give him shoulder support. However, he is still walking on his own feet. It's surprising how fast they've managed to move. Stewart doesn't say anything, gaze focused on the path, quietly suffering his pain. Surely he can't wait to get it over and done with.

The trees are now taller, partly covering our path to give us shade and gradually blocking our view afar. About ninety minutes into our hike, we reach Mweka Camp at about 3,000 meters (10,000ft) altitude. This would have been our second choice for last night's camp. The descent so far hasn't been too strenuous this morning, but would have been a nightmare to add on to yesterday's marathon hike.

"Guys, no need to offer this camp to hikers, it's too far away," Chris informs our guides and we all agree. "Everyone would just choose Millenium Camp instead."

From Mweka Camp onwards, we are back amidst a real pine forest of two-story tall trees and with fewer shrubs in between. Instead of blocking any opportunity for a private hideaway, the tree branches are now high above us and provide a welcome roof that almost entirely blocks the sun.

"Oh, here are those spooky trees again!" They are covered with whitish threads like angel hair on a Christmas tree, just like the ones we saw above Mti Mkubwa camp on our second morning.

"These are parasites," Evance explains.

"Do they harm the trees?"

"No, they are just there like that."

"Yes, I heard about them. They live in some kind of symbiotic relationship with the trees," Farrah comments. Botanists would probably recognize them as Spanish moss.

Just a few minutes after this curiosity, before we have time to even note any transition, we find ourselves back amidst a thick rain forest, so thick we can only see a few meters to the next bend of our path. In between talking and taking short uncoordinated breaks, our group is spreading out and we're losing count of who is where.

After another short pit stop, I find myself walking just with Chris who was waiting for me.

"Where is everyone?"

"No idea, I think Lynn and Evance went ahead. The others are still behind."

"Yes, I think Eva and Farrah took a break together with Ravi." He still feels his ankle, which – little do we suspect – would take five months to heal.

Skoba is with them. Giovanni is also somewhere nearby, but we have lost all the others. It doesn't really matter, there's only one way down and no one asks us any longer to go *pole pole*.

"Hey, when we reach the gate, we should have a cold beer to celebrate," Chris suggests.

"Yes, that sounds great! Let's get down quickly."

We pick up our pace in anticipation.

I stop to take a picture of a distinct tree with thin barren branches reaching straight up into the sky before they end in leaves that resemble artichokes with yellow flower buds on top. It looks like a flower that needs to grow meters tall in its fight for sunlight, the stalks of which becoming wooden in the process. Usually I wouldn't pay much attention, but I'm keen to capture as much as possible for this book.

"You take a great interest in these trees?" Chris notices my abnormal curiosity.

"Not really, but there's a reason for it."

I'm keen to own up to my book-writing idea. I want to finally let him know the true reason for my abnormal journaling throughout our trip, why I was always so keen to have my phone recharged with my solar panels. Yes I'm a freak but not that extreme after all, I'm not just reflecting for hours every day, as I alleged over the past week.

I explain myself and Chris is encouraging about my idea, but not surprised at all. Perhaps he already knew?

We run into Robert sitting at the side of the path.

"Here you are!" He's been waiting for us. "Please slow down. The others will be here soon. Skoba will walk together with you."

"Don't worry. We won't get lost." We only see cold beer ahead of us.

"I know, but these are the regulations," Robert explains. "You are not allowed to walk unaccompanied by a guide."

Giovanni, who as it turns out has only been a few steps behind us, keeps walking. He didn't understand. "Hey Giovanni!" we shout after him. "Robert says we have to wait and walk with a guide." The last thing we want is to get Robert into trouble, and thus we all dutifully wait for the others.

Skoba together with Eva, Ravi and Farrah catch up with us in no time, and we continue walking together while Robert heads back uphill. It doesn't take long until we lose sight of each other again, but this time Skoba follows Giovanni, Chris and myself closely.

Porters with heavy loads frequently pass us on their way up the mountain. We like greeting them with a casual *"jambo"* or *"mambo vipi"* to show our appreciation and recognition for their hard work. We've been greeting passing porters like that all week since Evance taught us some basic Swahili on our first day, but we haven't had a lot of porters actually come our way so far.

Every single porter would always greet us back with a friendly *"jambo"* or *"poa"*, and most of them would smile back at us sincerely. It's as if the concept of being unfriendly doesn't exist in this part of the world.

Having experienced yesterday how tough Kilimanjaro actually gets, Chris is overwhelmed by feelings of gratitude and now keeps calling out loudly "thank you" or *"asante sana"* to all the porters coming our way.

We have already seen them carry all kinds of things in totally non-ergonomic ways with crooked spines and diagonally bent heads, so it's hard to still shock us. At least we know the weight of their loads is controlled and limited to 20kg. But what comes up next is beyond imagination.

Two porters are transporting two of the big heavy metal stretchers back up the mountain, just like the ones we saw yesterday with a wheel in the middle. They carry one each lifted diagonally onto their shoulders, only with a blanket or sleeping bag in between the metal rods and their shoulders to soften the heavy pressure. As if these stretchers were made of aluminum, the porters walk with their heavy loads uphill still faster than a tourist hiker would. Only the sweat trickling down from their faces tells the truth of their tremendous physical toil.

"Would you like something to eat?" Chris asks them. "I've still got an energy bar somewhere."

I'm not sure they understand, but they immediately stop in anticipation, relieved to lift the stretchers off their shoulders for a short break.

"You guys are amazing. How much do these things weigh?"

They don't understand.

"How heavy?" Chris tries again.

"Fifty kilos," one of them replies.

"50kg! You guys are unreal!"

Chris can't believe what he's hearing. He is an orthotist and knows what human muscles are built for, certainly not for 50kg. I don't even have a concept of how heavy that is, but I know the park imposes a 20kg limit for porters. How come the limit does not apply to these rescue porters?

Porter carrying a heavy metal rescue stretcher (© Chris)

Chris scrabbles in his bag but struggles to locate his energy bar. Having raised the porters' expectations, we would feel sorry to disappoint them now.

"I've still got some nuts," that were intended for my lunch.

"Ah, great!" Chris sighs in relief.

I distribute a big handful to each porter.

"Asante sana," they hungrily dig in.

I also pour some for Skoba who has quietly been watching our scene. Meanwhile, Chris has also managed to locate his energy bar.

"Finally! Here you go," he hands it to the porters.

"Asante sana!" They thank us again with sparkling eyes and smiling faces, stuff the energy bar together with the remaining nuts into their pockets and dutifully continue speeding up the track. Within seconds, they have disappeared from our view.

Having seen how much they enjoy and appreciate the little things we can give to them makes us very happy. Sure, they didn't look as if they were going to starve, but it's the act that counts. Chris knows that already, that giving makes him happy. That's why he can't stop giving, like an addiction, but a good one for sure.

For me, it's a rather new sensation that I've only become so intensely aware of this week, and I'm overwhelmed by the change I'm experiencing within myself. Life becomes so much more enjoyable and meaningful when focusing on others. Should I ever get injured and need rescue, hopefully I will be able to remember the toil others are going through for me. Surely that will make my own suffering more bearable.

Meanwhile, Eva, Ravi and Farrah catch up with us again.

"Have you seen these porters?" Chris still can't believe what we just saw.

"Yes, I don't know how they do it," everyone agrees.

We come to a clearing where the footpath turns into a mud road. This is the closest a car could get to the mountain for emergencies.

"Do you think Stewart will get picked up here?" Chris asks.

"For sure, I'd hope so."

"Should we also wait and get a lift?" someone suggests.

"How much further is it?"

"Only twenty minutes," Skoba assures us.

"Look at that piece of art!" Chris points to a massive piece of wood with holes and remainders of branches or roots. "Let's take one last group photo!"

"Yay, group photo!" We all climb onto the tree trunk, like kids in the playground.

What's next? Some people don't want to walk any further. I don't want our walk to stop so soon. However, neither of us has a choice: "OK, let's get these last 20 minutes done with!"

And so we take our final steps along the dirt road to complete our hike. No one says much. I start to feel nostalgic and sad. This past week was so much fun. It has come to an end all too soon. I will miss these people, my new friends. I'm mentally replaying the past 48 hours and all that we've been through together. Looking at Giovanni walking directly ahead of me, I recall him singing the three words "*o sole mio*" on our summit hike, while everyone else seemed to be suffering and panting for air. It makes me laugh again.

"Hey Giovanni, could you sing 'o sole mio' for us?" I ask him as a joke, just for the sake of conversation.

Giovanni takes a deep breath, and, "Che bella cosa . . ." he starts to sing – who would have thought so! – with a loud and clear voice the full lines of the song, taking all of us by big surprise. Chris pulls out his video camera and Giovanni keeps walking and singing, every now and then looking into the camera like a super star, while we are all crouching in laughter behind his back.

The more we laugh, the louder he sings for the fun of the moment and the sake of our entertainment. I love his self-confidence and ability to laugh about himself. Finally, Giovanni pauses, takes another deep breath, lifts his arm and head, and looks straight into the camera for his grand finale, just like a big tenor.

"Sta nfro . . ." he manages to sing so loud he can probably be heard 100 meters up the mountain, but then makes the big mistake to look at all of us. Seeing our grins, he can't help but succumb to his own joke and joins us in hearty laughter, just two syllables short of the climax.

Sheer delight! Big applause for this unexpected performance! When I had already thought the trip was over, Giovanni has given all of us yet another great moment to remember.

▲ ▲ ▲

We reach our final gate, Mweka Gate, around 2pm. The gate sign welcomes us with

"CONGRATULATIONS!"

in big letters. At the visitor center, we register our names one last time in the official Kilimanjaro National Park logbook, this time in the so-called Coming Down Registration Book to record our completed hike.

Behind the registration counter, there is a small meadow. Lynn is already here, lying in her thick down jacket in the direct sun. It's at least 28 degrees Celsius. She is completely pale despite the heat.

"How's your headache?" I ask her.

"Still there."

"Oh no, and have you also caught a cold? Because it's really hot actually."

"Yes, I think so. And my tummy is quite upset."

"Sorry to hear that. So that's why you went down so quickly."

"Yes, it was really awkward. Every five minutes I had to ask Evance for a break to go off to the side. He must think I'm crazy." She hasn't lost her humor yet.

"Ah, I can imagine how awkward, but I'm sure Evance is used to that. It must happen all the time."

Lynn has been one of our strongest hikers, making it up to the summit without problems. Unfortunately, getting sick on Kilimanjaro, "that's normal" as our guides would say, no matter how fit you are. It requires a lot of luck to be spared any troubles.

"Coke, water, beer?" a local woman asks. There is no official store, but they know what tourists want and how to make money.

"Sure!"

She wanders off and comes back with three bottles of Kilimanjaro beer. We were so much looking forward to celebrate with cold beer, but now we give up after a few sips. It's lukewarm. Yuck, horrible, what a disappointment!

I quench my thirst from my water bladder instead, but also find the taste of my remineralization tablets in the warm water overpoweringly stale. I have been content with it for over a week. Now it almost makes me sick.

While we are digesting our disappointment, Jana and Diego have also arrived, soon to be followed by Stewart and Juli. Stewart's tired and exhausted face tells of the ordeal he's just been through. Unfortunately there are no chairs or benches, just the flat meadow. We all just accept the situation.

Not Chris: "Wait, I'll get you something to sit on."

Within no time, he has found a bucket. I'm impressed by his initiative. He wants to help and goes out of his way to find a solution, which wasn't that difficult after all but still too hard for myself to even contemplate.

Most people are quick to sit down on the meadow and take off their hiking boots.

"Ah, that feels so much better!"

"Yeah, great, isn't it?" they all agree.

I would also like to take my boots off, but I'm conscious that my feet may stink like rotten cheese. How embarrassing to possibly release that stench! If there's one thing I wish I had brought more of, it's a fresh pair of socks for every single day. I only brought three pairs of merino socks and despite all the good reports I had read about them, they still stink after a day of hiking and sweating, just like normal socks. Phooey!

"Shoe wash? You want shoe wash?" another local woman asks.

Juli and Stewart go for it, and after a few minutes they miraculously get back their brand-new boots. There are no traces left of all the dust and dirt that still cover mine. Wonderful! If I just wasn't too chicken to take them off.

Stewart has meanwhile lain down flat on the grass, relaxing his strained knees. Chris takes the opportunity to use his orthopedic expert skills to pull his legs and give him just the right stretches. Ouch, it looks painful to everyone else, but Steward's relaxed and savoring face testifies that Chris knows exactly what he's doing.

It's quiet. No one talks. Most people have their eyes closed. Their smiling faces tell me that they are enjoying the sunshine; that they are happy about their achievement but also happy that it's over; and that they are looking forward to going home or to their onward journey.

While I'm just sitting quietly observing everyone else, a dark fog builds up out of nowhere and clouds my mood. I was so happy all day until few minutes ago, now I just feel sad, disillusioned and disconnected. Sad because it's all over now and our group will soon go different ways again, because I felt so alive this past week and I'm afraid of losing this feeling. Disillusioned because I thought reaching the summit would make me happy yet I'm unable to enjoy my achievement, because I've been spared all the sufferings that others have been going through. Disconnected because everyone seems smashed and happy that it's over, because I still feel full of energy waiting to be consumed but I can't share this feeling.

When Chris is done with Stewart's massage, he sits down next to me.

"What's up with you?" he senses my downcast mood.

I tell him how I feel, randomly, without logic. ". . . You know I even cried on those last steps to the summit . . . I mean, what's the point of it all?"

"I felt the same," he says. "Would be so much better to share the experience with a partner. It's half the fun doing it alone."

"Yes, but it's not just that. I just can't feel happy about reaching the summit. It was too easy. I mean sure it was one of the hardest things I'd ever done, but I thought I would have to give my every last bit of energy for it, like others did, but I could have given more."

"Maybe you just need a bigger challenge, like Everest or one of the other 8,000-meter mountains."

"Oh no, I read all about it. It's too dangerous. You never know if you will make it back down alive. I wouldn't want to risk my life. That's also why I didn't go for the Western Breach route, you know, where Evance told us the American tourists died two weeks ago? I also wanted to do that route initially. But anyway, assume I do Everest and all goes well, I make it up and down safely – what's the point? Just to be all alone up there and feel lonely again?"

"That's right."

In between breaks of silence in our conversation, Chris jumps up to stretch and readjust Stewart's legs.

"I'll show you something," he pulls out his phone when he sits back down. "Look at that," Chris shows me photos of smiling kids. "This is from the Gaza zone."

I know he does voluntary prosthetics work there. Prosthetics – it sounds so clinical to me, because I have no concept of what it really means. Now it's becoming real in front of my eyes.

"See how beautiful these kids are? They all lost a limb during the war."

There's a cute girl with long curly hair.

"Isn't she gorgeous? I've made her arm." Chris beams all over his face as he shows me his work. "Look at that video." A boy walks carefully hand in hand with Chris. The boy smiles in disbelief with big open eyes, like my little niece in front of the Christmas tree. "He's taking his first steps. I've made him a beautiful leg."

I'm in awe. It's so wonderful I almost have tears in my eyes, like magic. It's not just prosthetics, not just charity. Chris describes each limb like a piece of art, each crafted specifically for one particular kid, so it would feel comfortable and become one with their bodies. It's like the ultimate fusion of passion and skill, of body and soul, of heart and mind; all with a clear need and purpose in mind. Like many others in our group, Chris has found his calling and is living his dream, finding meaning and joy in helping others.

"Wow!" I'm so humbled I don't even know what to say to give justice to all this. "I wish I could have such a positive impact on society."

"What's your next big thing after Kilimanjaro?" Chris asks me.

"Ah, remember that idea I told you about supporting working mothers? I'll work on that," but I don't really like talking about it anymore, especially after seeing what Chris has just shown me. All the passion I felt for it until a week ago is gone. It sounds so ironic and vain that I'm trying to do good by helping well-off people with their luxury society problems. "And first I need to get that book out of the way," I mumble for the sake of conversation, unaware that it would keep me busy well into the next year and turn out to be the most reflective exercise I've ever undertaken.

"Oh yes, of course," Chris acknowledges my plans.

"You know, I feel really bad about my life right now, after what you've just shown me and compared to the good work all of you are doing." I'm thinking of Juli, Jeannette, Ravi, Farrah, Stewart, the girl from the Philippines stationed as a nurse in Liberia whom we met on the first day, the Canadian hiker from MSF we met at Bristol Cottages . . .

"Tell me more about your life in Switzerland. You said you are in M&A. What exactly do you do?" Chris is determined to cheer me up.

"Ha, that's the worst part of it all! You know M&A people don't have a good reputation anyway, but it gets even worse," I'm laughing ironically. "I'm focused on banks. So in Switzerland that's all private banks, I mean the banks that serve the rich people, because they've all got their money there. What I mean to say is that by doing M&A for private banks, in essence, what I do for a living is to help rich people become even richer. Pretty bad, huh?"

"Oh no, not at all. Society needs that as well. These people are entrepreneurs, no? And they need someone to manage their finances, so then again they can invest it into good projects."

I like how Chris sees it all so clearly and focuses on the positive.

"Yes sure, that's how I've always explained it to myself. Don't get me wrong, I believe in efficient markets and how it makes life better for all of us . . . but still . . . it's just not the same." It won't give me the sparkle that I've just seen in Chris's eyes and it won't make me feel as alive as I've felt this past week. Now I know what it means to feel alive and this feeling is just about to slip through my fingers again. How can I possibly not feel depressed right now?

"Let's go for a walk," Chris won't give up easily. He's determined to entertain and cheer me up.

"You're crazy. Where do you want to walk to?"

"Let's walk back up the track towards Jeannette, to keep her company on her final path."

"OK." That sounds like a good enough excuse, and I like the idea of spending some more time quietly with Chris prior to going our separate ways again tomorrow. Everyone else must be thinking that we are completely nuts. How could we possibly want to voluntarily move again after what we've been through over the past 48 hours?

We make our way back to the gate.

"Where are you going?" Robert comes running after us. What kind of mischief could we be up to next?

"Don't worry. We'll just go back up to meet Jeannette, no further."

"It's not allowed for you to go alone, these are the regulations," Robert patiently explains again.

"Don't worry. No one will see us; and Jeannette can't be far," we insist like misbehaving school children.

"OK," he relents, "then one of the guides will come with you." Robert calls out towards the other guides in Swahili.

"Oh no, don't worry." This is an offer we cannot accept. "We don't want to bother them again."

"But you can't go alone."

"Yes, it's OK, we won't go."

We agree to behave and return to our group. I find it oppressively quiet, just waiting and hanging around. No one talks. Should I use the time now to let them all know about this book?

"Hey guys, I need to confess something to you," I hijack their meditative silence. "There's a reason why I kept writing my journal all the time. I'm actually planning to write a book about this hike."

I look around. Most people still have their eyes closed or are looking somewhere else. Some look at me quizzically.

"It's because there's no book yet about the Northern Circuit route, so I had that idea . . ."

No reactions. I hate being in the center and holding a monologue without feedback.

". . . I'm sorry to only tell you now, I didn't want to mislead you, I tried to keep it objective and not to influence anyone."

"You mean so you can write about us?" Ravi asks jokingly, but I think I hear a hint of cynicism.

I understand; I would be pissed off if someone were writing about me without telling me.

"No, I mean our guides and the Ultimate Kilimanjaro people. I didn't want to influence their performance." I didn't even know I would be meeting and writing about all of you, this gave my book a completely new meaning, but I don't find the right words to let you know the concepts currently swirling around in my head. "I will send you all a draft so you can see what I've written about you and comment, and I will delete whatever you want . . . And if you like, you can include your own thoughts or whatever you want to say or comment . . . I don't want this to be my book but our book."

Not sure I actually said this last sentence or just thought it. Some people briefly comment and appreciate my efforts, but most remain silent. No questions, no discussion, no feedback.

"OK everyone, good news, Jeannette is here, we can leave." Robert's voice interrupts my train of thought. I didn't see him coming over. Everyone is putting their shoes back on and getting ready.

"Perhaps you could use pseudonyms rather than real names," Ravi suggests in passing. "And perhaps you can also send a draft to our guides for their review."

"Yes, good idea. Thank you, I'll do that." I'm relieved to get his feedback, a sign that he was paying attention and cares. What about everyone else? Are they simply too tired to even process what I've just said, or frustrated about involuntarily featuring in a book, or perhaps they already knew and this doesn't come as a surprise to them anymore?

I can't help feeling disappointed about the general lack of interest, or rather frustrated about my inability to clearly communicate my good intentions.

We make our way to the bus.

"Group photo!" someone shouts.

Yes, great idea! We all pose in front of the CONGRATULATIONS sign.

"*Jambo*," Robert starts singing unexpectedly, and we all join in instantly. This time we not only clap the rhythm, but we sing all together as loud as we can the song that we've all become so familiar with and will surely remember forever:

Jambo, jambo bwana. (Hello, hello Sir.)
Habari gani? Nzuri sana. (How are you? Very well.)
Wageni, mwakaribishwa. (Visitors, welcome.)
Kilimanjaro? Hakuna matata. (Kilimanjaro? No problem.)

What a heart-warming cheerful grand finale! Singing has such a special bonding and happiness effect. People here know that, and Robert knows how to leave us all with a wonderful last impression.

▲ ▲ ▲

We finally depart from Kilimanjaro around 3:30pm, much later than initially anticipated. I crawl into a window seat and Chris takes the seat next to me. I wonder whether he feels like me, trying to hold on to the last hours of our companionship as much as possible? Our one-hour bus ride back to Moshi is mostly quiet and eventless. We are all either exhausted or busy with our own thoughts.

I had booked the spa treatment, Jana's birthday present, for 6pm. "It might get too late, would be too stressful. Let's cancel it," we both have just agreed. The Lala Salama spa in Moshi had kindly agreed to provide two beauticians for us at out-of-office hours. I feel bad if they wait in vain, but I still can't connect to any mobile network. At least my data connection is working, better than I would have hoped for the past 24 hours on the southern side of the mountain, bombarding me with work emails that I've been trying to ignore. I send an email to Lala Salama, hoping that they will receive it on time.

Other than that, I spend most of the bus ride just looking out of the window and taking in all the impressions. The way back to Moshi from Mweka Gate is much greener than our initial drive to Londorossi Gate. We drive past banana plantations covered with lush green banana palm trees, interspersed with coffee plantations filled with green knee-high coffee bushes. There are women working on the fields in their colorful clothing, as well as children in school uniforms joining them in the fields. I wonder whether the children are just passing by to say hello, or whether they will they stay in the fields all afternoon.

We also drive past a gated compound where young soldiers dressed in uniforms are running on the earthen training court. "You see?" Samwel remembers our conversation about Tanzania's school system and military services. "A military school," he points out to me, evidence of the newly introduced mandatory military service.

"Hip hip."

We all listen, but are too tired or lazy or bored to respond to our drill.

"Tonight, you will all be staying at the Stella Maris hotel, except for Chris. He is booked at Bristol Cottages. So first we will drive to Bristol Cottages," Robert explains. "Some of you have your stuff there, you can pick it up, we say goodbye to Chris and then we drive to Stella Maris, which is maybe another 20 minutes' drive outside of town, OK?"

"Why am I the only one at Bristol Cottages? Can't you also rebook me to Stella Maris?" Chris requests. "I'm going to join you all anyway for dinner, but it would just be a lot easier," he comments to me.

"It's because Stella Maris was full, they had no more rooms. We'll try," Robert agrees, but it doesn't sound too promising.

At Bristol Cottages, there is a small shop around the corner and a bank office with an ATM opposite its entrance. Some people use the opportunity to quickly run small errands while others are getting hold of their items, and our guides are finding Chris's bag on the roof of our bus. All our bags are piled up there and fastened under a sheet of plastic; getting any single bag is not an easy task.

It feels good to retrieve our spare bags from the storage room, knowing that clean clothes are waiting for us inside, and our valuables were reliably stored in the hotel safe.

I also hope to buy some local coffee as souvenir presents for family and friends. In the store next to Bristol Cottages, they have various bags of coffee beans wrapped in organic cotton material with nice pictures of coffee fields in front of Kilimanjaro.

"How much are they?"

The small ones with perhaps no more than 100g start at ten dollars. That's crazy! I'd spend less than ten dollars for 500g of organic and Fairtrade certified Arabica coffee beans back home in Zurich, one of the most expensive places on earth. What a tourist rip-off!

"You don't want?" the shop assistant asks me.

"No thanks, I just wanted the local coffee, not the tourist version. You don't have any Africafe, no?"

"Sorry ma'am." Of course not. I'd better pick that up on the road during my upcoming safari.

Once everyone has picked up their stuff and completed their errands, we are all keen to head on quickly to Stella Maris.

"So you'll come join us for dinner, right?" I confirm with Chris.

"Yes, I'll see you all later for dinner."

I'm so glad that I don't need to say goodbye yet; that would be quite an emotional disaster. I don't want to deal with it, not yet.

Just five minutes into our drive, "We have good news," Robert confirms. "We were able to change the hotel booking for Mr. Chris. He will also be staying at Stella Maris, so you will all be together. We will organize a separate car for him." Again our guides have gone out of their way to make everyone happy, to allow our whole group to spend a final celebratory evening all together.

The traffic is bad and it takes us another half hour before we finally arrive at Stella Maris. As soon as we arrive, everyone is keen to get out of the bus quickly. We are now not used to sitting in such a confined space.

An African woman with round hips in colorful clothing welcomes us with a broad smile. Before I realize, she gives me a tight hug. "Congratulations! Welcome back! Welcome home!"

"Um . . . hello . . . thank you," I mumble in shock that anyone would want to come close to me after I haven't showered for over a week. After she has released me again, I come back to myself. "Haha, you shouldn't hug us. We must stink like hell."

"No no, no worries, you smell very nice," she smiles at me.

What a reception! She reminds me of everything I would associate with the concept of mama Africa – friendly, cheerful, fertile, multicolored and alive. She must be the manager of the hotel. Do I really not stink, or does she smell the half a bottle of floral spray that I have dumped onto myself over the course of the trip, or is she just being polite? I won't find out, people are too friendly here.

While our bags are unloaded and carried into the hotel lobby, the hotel staff offers us cool welcoming drinks. It doesn't take us long to empty the glasses. What are we supposed to do next? We haven't received any further instructions. After constantly being told for the past nine days what comes next, without the need to make any decisions on our own other than what concerns our most basic needs, I feel a bit confused. Should we go and check in, or should we wait outside to receive our climbing certificates and say goodbye to our guides?

"Alex, you can go check in," Evance clarifies my confusion as if he could read my mind, yet again always here when I need him. "Take your bags to your room. Then come back for the closing ceremony."

Awesome! I can't wait for this short escape opportunity.

"What's your name?" the receptionist asks and hands me the key with a broad friendly smile.

"Ah, so you are Alexandra," the manager overheard my name. "Your safari company called. The driver will come pick you up tomorrow morning at 8am."

"Great," one less item to worry about. This trip is teaching me yet another lesson – just relax and things will sort out by themselves, no need to always try and control everything. There is order within what looks like chaos.

"Which are your bags?" a young girl half my size asks me. I point them out for her. Surely she'll instruct a guy to carry them, but she starts grabbing them herself.

"No, no," I can't possibly have her carry my heavy bags upstairs.

"No problem," she insists, full of self-confidence.

"OK, how about you take this one." I point to my small bag.

"I can take all of them," she cheerfully tries to grab my big one.

I won't give in to this fight and hold on to it.

"You're too kind. Are you sure?" she smiles at me.

"Yeah sure, I've been climbing Kilimanjaro, would be a shame if I can't make it up these stairs!"

The room is lovely, much nicer than I expected. There are two single beds made of dark wood. Each bed has tall pillars upholding a wooden frame around which decorative mosquito nets have been nicely arranged. The beds are covered with colorful blankets. There also are a cozy rug and a bedside table in between the beds. Though simple and basic, the sight reminds me more of a royal chamber than a hikers' lodge.

Finally I can take off my hot boots and damp socks. What liberation! How nice to walk barefoot on the cool tiles!

The bathroom is rather basic, but after nine days on the mountain, it feels deluxe. I can't wait to use a proper clean flush toilet and to wash my hands under as much running water as I please. If there wasn't this bloody mirror above the basin and my urge to look – disaster! My mood is about to drop into the cellar but my ability to respond is at its highest after a week full of exercise in fresh air. My eyes instantly divert their glance, forming my own reality by banning anything unpleasant from my consciousness. That works like magic!

When I head back downstairs, Chris is about to check into his room, bags all over him.

"Hey, that was quick!"

"Wait, for you . . ." He hands me two bags of Arabica coffee beans, the same I denied myself earlier.

"Really, for me? You should keep them for yourself."

"You said you wanted to buy coffee, so I got you some. See you later," he follows the hotel staff along the corridor.

"Thank you!" I shout after him.

Wow, how nice! Chris really thinks of everything and won't miss any opportunity to make others happy. I feel like a birthday girl.

In the courtyard, everyone is looking at menus, and a waiter is taking notes.

"Alex, we are pre-ordering dinner."

"Oh great," what a luxury to order our own food choice! "For what time?"

"For 8pm."

"Perfect. That will leave enough time," I sigh cheerfully. "I think I'll need two hours to get ready."

"Really? What for?" Eva asks in astonishment.

"One hour to get my own body back in order and another hour to repack my stuff and do some washing for my safari."

I thought everyone would need some time, but Eva and Jeannette just frown at my vanity.

"That long?"

I wish I could also be faster and more flexible, but just thinking of my hair and finger nails . . .

"Oh yes, two hours, me too," our quiet Italian hiking pro interjects.

We all stare at Giovanni with his thick beard.

"Really?" Eva still can't believe why people would waste that much time in the bathroom.

"Yes," we both agree, and I smile in relief that at least one person understands.

But no one understands why I keep checking my phone. The Lala Salama spa hasn't replied to my email, and I feel bad about my last minute cancellation. Will they be waiting for me in vain? "Could you help me call this number?" I ask the receptionist. No one picks up the phone.

"No worries," the receptionist assures me, "I will send them an SMS."

Fast-forward one day, I will find their message in my inbox: "Thank you so much for letting us know. Sorry not to have replied sooner and sorry that you couldn't make it." I can't believe how incredibly friendly people are in this country, thanking me and apologizing even though I'm the one who has caused all the unnecessary trouble.

We are still waiting for the others to come back from their rooms prior to starting our closing ceremony.

"Robert, Evance, do you have a second?" I take the opportunity to pull them aside.

"Sure, what is it?"

I inform them about my book idea, and that of course I only have good things to say about them.

"Thank you!" They don't comment much, but they are very appreciative and their eyes sparkle.

We exchange contact details and I promise that I will be touch. Now I've got some positive pressure to see my plans through to completion and get this book published. I can't disappoint them. The story of all they have done for us over the past days, beyond words that could be summarized in a single sentence or paragraph, as well as the excellent performance of the entire Ultimate Kilimanjaro team, all our porters and in general everyone working on Kilimanjaro deserves to be told. Telling their story gives me an entirely new and way more important meaning to reaching the summit – it's not about me but for them.

"Hip hip!"

One last time we get to hear Robert's charming voice. Everyone has come back downstairs, other than Stewart.

"He's resting upstairs," Juli explains, "I'll represent him."

"So let's start our closing ceremony."

Surely this will be a quick signing and handing out of the certificates? But Robert gives us yet another unexpected warm speech.

"It wasn't easy . . . your achievement . . . you can be proud . . . we will miss you . . . on behalf of all the guides, we think about you like our family . . . *Hongera*! Congratulations!"

"Yay!"

"Thank you!"

"Asante sana!"

"Now I give you each your certificate. First is Mr. . . ." One-by-one, Robert calls up each one of us to hand over the certificate and gives us a congratulatory hug.

We all applaud and cheer for everyone, and help each other take photos of the certificate handover. So that's why it's called closing ceremony. It's a real ceremony after all!

Their efforts are amazing. From Stewart's surprise cake in the morning, via the grand speeches and singing at the tipping ceremony, to our last joint signing at the final gate, and now this last closing ceremony – it feels as if we've been celebrating all day. Whenever I thought it's all over now, yet another highlight took me by surprise.

Certificate ceremony (© Jeannette)

By the time the last person has been called up, it's already 5:30pm. We still need to wait for the Ultimate Kilimanjaro ground staff because they wish to obtain our direct feedback on the trip. I would like to sort out all my stuff prior to dinner, knowing that I'll have yet another early start in the morning. Where are they? I can't help getting impatient. Waiting just fifteen more minutes while so close to my shower feels like torture to me. Why can't they be on time?

"Just relax. That's Africa. Don't stress," I can see what others are thinking while I keep checking the time on my phone. I find a new message from my friend Nicole:

"Hey, all good? Are you done with your hike? Everything worked out well?"

It makes me smile. Wow, so she remembered and was thinking of me. Being so far away, her message works like an instant relaxation and happiness drug. Feeling connected works wonders – another lesson this trip has been teaching me.

An Ultimate Kilimanjaro van drives into the courtyard.

"Yay, finally!" We all get excited.

Smashed but happy hikers emerge, and we welcome them with a round of applause. They quickly disappear into the lobby, probably keen to check into their rooms. But no ground staff. They finally arrive around 5:45pm.

Our guides move away from our sitting area while the ground staff receive our feedback. They are friendly and professional, but their congratulations feel formal and detached to me. I don't know them and my loyalty is towards our mountain crew.

"Do you have any complaints?"

"No, it was perfect!"

"Any feedback whatsoever?"

"It couldn't have been any better! Our guides and everyone was amazing."

It's true. We truly feel that way. They have exceeded our wildest expectations. We couldn't possibly come up with any suggestions for improvement. But even if, I don't think I would tell them. It would feel like betraying our guides, our new friends. As Robert said at the beginning and half way through, if there's anything, don't wait until the end but let them know immediately. Surely they would have gone out of their way to appease even our most ridiculous prima donna requests.

The ground staff run through their checklist.

"How was the food?"

"Delicious!"

"It says here you always had a lot of leftovers sent back to the kitchen. Your chef was surprised. Did you not like his food?"

"Huh? No way!"

"We always finished everything."

I've certainly kept my voracious reputation till the end. Perhaps only the massive plates of potatoes or pasta or rice were too much for us.

"On some days we had late lunch just before dinner, maybe on those days."

"Yes, please tell him not to worry."

"Yes, please tell him it was perfect."

We all pour out our honest praise and assurances.

"OK, so now we will confirm your further travel arrangements." They tell everyone their pick-up times for their safari or airport transfers. "Alexandra. No further bookings with us. You are dismissed."

Yay, finally! By now it's 6:00pm. I can't wait to jump under the shower. Our guides surely must also be looking forward to getting home to their families and having a good rest. It's been a long day for us, but even more so for them. One by one, I thank each of our guides for everything, shake their hands and hug them goodbye.

"So you are really writing a book?" Robert asks me cautiously, incredulously, as if I might just have been pulling his leg, as if he's excited but doesn't dare to fully believe.

"Yes," I assure him lightheartedly, unaware that he has no benchmark to assess whether he can believe me. Perhaps others have said the same before, never to be heard of again? "No worries, I'll email you a draft as soon as I've got it."

His eyes light up. I've just made a promise and I know that I can't let them down.

"Evance, goodbye my friend! Thank you for everything."

"You've got my number, right?"

"Yes, I'll be in touch."

I am so relieved that I've got their contact details. It feels a lot better than saying goodbye forever. Somehow, I know I'll see them again.

▲ ▲ ▲

Within five minutes, I manage to convert my nice room into a big mess. My stuff is everywhere, all over the floor and dispersed on both beds, but I couldn't care less for now. Shower time! Finally, after nine days!

I only take off my head cover as I step into the shower and purposely avoid the mirror, manipulating my own reality. Never seen my greasy hair, thus it never was.

The water comes out trickling and won't heat up beyond lukewarm, just the way it would make me frustrated and complain under any other circumstances. Not here, not today. It just feels great to finally have running water again.

"The shower was boiling hot," people will comment over dinner, "almost burnt myself."

"Eh, really? What floor are you on?"

"First."

"Ah, I'm on the second, perhaps that's why," especially when the entire hotel is showering at the same time!

Nevertheless, I'm having the most extensive shower session of my entire life, starting with an endless pre-wash rinsing program. Grey-brownish water keeps splashing onto the shower floor. Only after several minutes does it finally turn clear. Obviously, and contrary to what I thought so far, the dust not only made its way in between my fingernails, but all over my skin and seems particularly glued to my hair – my next challenge. I need half a bottle of shampoo until there seems to be any impact, until finally I feel the familiar foamy texture in between my fingers. Mmmmm, that feels good! And never before have I rubbed my whole body so carefully from top to toe with soap, enjoying every single bit of the process. Some people say they like cleaning when things are dirty, because then they can see the difference. I never understood why that would cause someone to actually like cleaning, but now I'm getting a bit closer to that miracle.

Just in time, the water is going from lukewarm to cold and encourages me not to waste more than needed. Perfect, otherwise I would have stayed there until my skin became wrinkly, unaware that I will need that time to brush my hair. It's quite short, not even reaching my shoulder, and usually fixed in no time. Not today. My brush just won't move. What an entangled mess, half of it ending up on my brush.

Blow-drying my hair is another adventure. Within seconds, my hair-dryer drops silent, my bedside table lamp turns off, and with it the entire room goes darker than Kilimanjaro under moonlight. I try to fix the cables but can't make it work. I try the phone to call the reception but there's no signal. Only one solution – I scrabble about for some clothes and make my way downstairs.

The manager immediately walks back upstairs with me.

"Please don't get shocked when you see my room," I'm embarrassed. "It's a big mess."

"Don't worry," she must be used to that.

After a quick look at the cables, she immediately knows what's going on. I follow her to the fuse box in the corridor.

"Probably again one of the devices of the American guests," she comments, I guess because of voltage incompatibility issues. "So sorry for the inconvenience."

Phew, at least just a shortcut with a quick fix. It's full house right now with some 30 power-deprived travelers trying to recharge their devices. No surprise!

I continue getting my body back in order. After having felt really good about myself during the past week, completely ignorant and disinterested in the way I look, it's disturbing how this properly lit mirror in the bathroom is trying to make me conscious of all my imperfections. I notice how my nose sticks out like a fireball, distinguishing itself from the rest of my face with its partly reddish freshly sunburnt and partly dark brown past sunburnt patches, framed by white flakes of dry skin at the edges. I can't resist trying to hide its coloration under make-up. What a disaster, nature defeats my stupid attempt. Now it looks even flakier. Quick rewind. Like all week, I resort again to a thick layer of heavy cream instead. That feels better. What the heck – my group has seen me like this over the past week, there's no need to return to my civilized me just yet.

My second defeat comes when trying to clean my fingernails. Dirt and dust is so ingrained in what has turned to dry skin at the edges that I give up after ten minutes. I wish I had time for a proper manicure. Fortunately, my stuff is easier to fix than myself and I'm done just in time by 8pm, ready to relax and celebrate.

▲ ▲ ▲

I find Farrah alone downstairs.

"Where is everyone? I thought you'd all started with pre-dinner drinks already and I'm missing the fun."

"No, no one is here yet."

But within seconds, one after the other, they are all coming down the stairs.

"Dinnertime!"

"Let's have a drink!"

"I can't wait for a cold beer!"

Our goals are aligned. We may all be healthy outdoor enthusiasts, but we also know how to celebrate. And so our group is spending a wonderful last evening together.

Jana is back to her normal chatty and joking character. It's almost as if the mountain had completely changed her personality and has now released her from its spell, as it did with me on the opposite extreme. Diego is equally jovial, as if a huge weight has dropped from his shoulders. I'm glad to have my friends back; relieved to finally know for sure it was just the mountain and nothing between us.

Giovanni is telling me about his travel plans in Spanish and is good at guessing the meaning of my broken babbling in our common language.

Farrah is complaining about her sunburnt nose just like me.

Ravi gives us *people of this nation* yet another one of his preacher-like talks.

Eva is her usual casual and relaxed self.

Lynn has recovered a bit and is excited about her further travels to South Africa.

Juli is stunning everyone with her transformed looks in make-up, short skirt and high heels.

Only Stewart is missing, recovering from his ordeal on the long way down.

And when Farrah offers Jeannette a ginger tea, just as she did after every dinner on the mountain, Jeannette says it all about the spirit of our evening to come: "No thanks, keep your tea, I'll have gin and tonic."

Oh I will miss this bunch – random people with one shared passion for hiking thrown together to form a strong bond while reaching the top of Africa.

Most of all, I will miss Chris who has made me laugh so many times, taught me so many things and shared so many special moments with me. It's almost as if none of us wants this evening to end. We stay up late enjoying our companionship and rejoicing on our joint experience.

"Remember how you told me you felt lonely on the summit?" Chris recalls. "I felt the same, but you know what? We didn't do it alone."

"No, we did it together," and found a soul mate along the way.

Epilogue

Most of us meet again for breakfast the next morning, which has become a bit of a mental blur to me. I will remember that everyone is in a great mood, proud of their achievements and looking forward to their onward journeys or flying back home. I will remember Farrah's quizzical smile, one eyebrow raised, and the sparkling eyes on Eva's poker face as I walk to the breakfast table, making me wonder what they were just talking about. I will remember going overboard on the fresh fruit buffet and feeling spoilt. I will remember Juli being as energetic and cheerful as ever. She had risen early and had already visited the adjacent school for orphans and impoverished kids, which is funded by the Stella Maris hotel. I will remember the queasy feeling in my stomach when all too soon one after the other departs to get their day started. And I will remember Ravi's warm and heartfelt goodbye hug.

Chris has a late flight and stays back to keep me company while I'm waiting for Jana and Diego to get ready for our safari. My feelings are an overwhelming blur of happiness and sadness, clarity and confusion, excitement and vulnerability. When my friends are ready to leave, I feel my throat tightening so hard I am afraid any words of goodbye to Chris will end in tears. With all my energy, I manage to command my feelings and focus on gratitude instead, gratitude that I had these wonderful past nine days of feeling truly alive, gratitude that I met all these wonderful people, tremendous gratitude that I was even so fortunate to meet a soul mate while hiking Kilimanjaro and to share this very special experience with him. What more could I possibly ever have wished for? Indulging in my wonderful, almost dream-like memories of the past nine days, I would feel blessed and cheerful for the remainder of my trip, and many more weeks and months to come.

▲ ▲ ▲

I had set out to reach the top of Africa. More than finding contentment in my own endurance and achievement, I found happiness in making friends with my fellow hikers and our guides. I feel grateful for their friendship and openness, for sharing with me their life, work and travel experience, for giving me new inspirations, for reminding me about what's important in life, for showing me yet again that true happiness doesn't come from seeking my own pleasure but from giving and sharing with others.

I also found meaning in learning more about the working conditions of porters on Kilimanjaro. Hopefully, via this book, I am able to make a small contribution to help raise awareness, to encourage future hikers to pay attention to porters' treatment when selecting their tour operator. If at least one of you will book with a KPAP-certified partner company instead of a non-certified operator based on what I have written, my writing will not have been in vain.

Finally, our guides Robert, Evance, Skoba, Samwel, Estomee and Baraka, our cooks Mr. Delicious and Amani, our waiters Crispin and Sostenence, our toilet porter Dominick, our summit porters Liberat and Charles, and all our porters deserve a big praise again. Without them, none of us would have made it to the top, our trip wouldn't have been so enjoyable and smooth, and this book wouldn't have been written. They are the true heroes of Kilimanjaro.

▲ ▲ ▲

Dear reader, now it's your turn to reach for the sky. Let me conclude with a quote of Steve Jobs from Juli's email tagline, which has inspired me ever since I've returned back to my life that will never be the same again: "Your time is limited, so don't waste it living someone else's life. Don't let the noise of others' opinions drown out your own inner voice, and most important, have the courage to follow your heart and intuition."

APPENDIX

Expectations management

The economist, entrepreneur, and international development specialist Nat Ware explains in his TEDx talk how our happiness depends on our expectations. [64] We are unhappy when our expectations are not met, and we are happy when they are exceeded. Relating that to my Kilimanjaro experience, I can clearly see the truth. With the aim to help you find happiness in your own experience, I would like to give you some recommendations in this regard.

Making it to the top

I never doubted that I would make it to the top, but I expected that I would have to work hard for it and give all my last bit of energy. In reality, while it certainly was the most enduring effort I have ever undertaken, it didn't feel as if I had to give my best. Consequently, reaching the summit didn't make me happy. To the contrary, I felt like a fraud, as if I didn't have to work hard enough for it. Weeks and months have passed, but I am still not able to feel proud of it. On the other hand, some hikers may have struggled a lot more than they expected, hence they may have been unhappy for the opposite reason.

Please don't form expectations from my experience, or you may be setting yourself up for disappointment. Of course it's a tough hike. 99% of hikers will probably find this to be the most difficult physical challenge they've ever been through. Chances are high that you will find the summit hike like a super-marathon or triathlon, your heart rate constantly up and never catching enough breath, constantly fighting to your limit. And there is the risk that you may not reach the summit. A lot of things may go wrong, many of which are not in your control: The weather might be a lot worse, you may be very sensitive to altitude, and you might twist your ankle or catch a cold. Other things you can prepare and plan for to increase your chances, but they are no guarantees either. That's also why I've described the experience of my fellow hikers, not to put them down, but to give you as a reader a more comprehensive account of what might happen.

I suggest you don't come with a lot of expectations about reaching the summit, but you focus more on enjoying the journey along the way. There's a lot more to Kilimanjaro than the summit, which is – in my opinion – not that beautiful in any case.

Roughing it up

I expected that I would struggle with camping and not having access to a clean bathroom or running water, so my expectations were low. In reality, I found the roughness of camping not that difficult once I got the hang of it, and I even enjoyed it. Consequently, I felt extremely happy about the whole camping experience and how quickly I adapted to it. However, it may be different for you. In any case, as a bare minimum, I suggest you expect that you will feel cold, terribly cold, that you will struggle to sleep, for consecutive nights, and that you will have a sick stomach or cold at some point in time, perhaps even both. Then you will be happy for every morning filled with sunshine, for every hour of sleep, and for every day spent without feeling sick. The secret of happiness can be that simple!

Maintaining your friendships

I expected to become closer friends with my hiking buddies from back home. However, the opposite happened and that was a distressing experience, probably on both sides. Unfortunately this seems to be an experience made by many hikers. "Kilimanjaro breaks friends as easily as it breaks records." Henry Stedman comforts me in his Kilimanjaro trekking guide that it wasn't just us: "Different levels of stamina, different levels of desire to reach the top, different attitudes towards the porters and guides . . . on Kilimanjaro these things, for some reason, suddenly matter." I should have read his book before, not after the hike!

But it could have been a lot worse, as Henry nails it spot on: "Then there's the farting. It is a well-known fact that the regular breaking of wind is a sure sign that you are acclimatizing satisfactorily . . . Problems occur, of course, when two friends acclimatize at different rates: ie, the vociferous and joyful flatulence of Friend A is simply not appreciated by Friend B, who has a bad headache, insomnia and an ill-temper. Put the two parties together in a remote, confined space, such as that provided by a two-man tent on the slopes of a cold and lonely mountain, and you have an explosive cocktail that can blow apart even the strongest of friendships." And we didn't even share a tent!

For the sake of your relationship, no matter how well you know your friend, I would highly recommend not sharing a tent. Beware that your friendships will be severely tested. However, "the above is just one possible scenario," Henry gives hope to friends sharing similar physical conditions. "It may be that you adapt equally well/badly to the new conditions and can draw pleasure/comfort from each other accordingly." Let that be an unexpected upside and not your expectation at the outset.

Making new friends or connecting with your inner self

I expected that I would make new acquaintances as part of our hiking group, some easy going, others perhaps less easy to get along with. I also expected that we would all mostly do our own thing and go our own pace, as it seemed to be in all the other review books I read. In reality, we spent not only all meals but also the entire hike together. Each and every member of our group was wonderful, contributing their own very special strengths and characters to create an overwhelming and entirely unexpected bonding experience. We all became friends along the way. The process of meeting, getting to know and sharing the experience with my fellow hikers and new friends made me extremely happy, happier than I ever could have felt about any kind of physical achievement.

I suggest you come without any expectations whatsoever, yet with an open heart and the curiosity to get to know whoever you are lucky to meet on your journey. Perhaps it's a different experience altogether for you. Perhaps for you finding solitude and serenity with a lot of me-time to reconnect with your inner self is what you will find. Enjoy the process of finding out for yourself and discovering something entirely unexpected along the way.

Basic Kilimanjaro Swahili

English	*Swahili*

ESSENTIALS

Slow	Pole pole
Thank you (very much)	Asante (sana)
(Very) welcome	Karibu (sana)
Yes	Ndio
No	Hapana
Let's go!	Twende!
I'm sorry / excuse me!	Samahani!
OK!	Sawa!
Danger!	Hatari!
Great!	Nzuri!
I'm tired	Nimechoka
Water	Maji
Toilet	Choo
Hot	Moto
Cold	Baridi
Much	Mengi
Little	Kidogo
Fast	Haraka

GREETINGS

Hello	Jambo
How are you *[informal greeting]*	Habari
(Very) good *[response to habari]*	Nzuri (sana)

Hello *[to an older person; literally "I touch your feet"]*	Shikamoo
Fine *[response to shikamoo; literally "I acknowledge your respect"]*	Marahaba
What's up *[casual slang greeting]*	Mambo (vipi)
Cool *[response to mambo (vipi)]*	Poa
Crazy cool like a banana (in the fridge) *[reponse to mambo (vipi) if you feel particularly well]*	Poa kichizi kama ndizi (ndani ya friji)

ADDRESSING PEOPLE

Sir	Bwana
Madam; grandmother *[addressing a woman of older age]*	Bibi
Grandfather *[addressing a man of older age]*	Babu
Friend	Rafiki
Sister *[addressing a woman of similar age]*	Dada
Brother *[addressing a man of similar age]*	Kaka

OTHER

What is your name?	Jina lako nani?
My name is . . .	Jina langu ni . . .
Where are you from?	Unatoka wapi?
I'm from . . .	Natoka. . .
Naomba . . .	I need . . .
Naraka . . .	I want . . .
Congratulation	Hongera
European (white foreigner)	Mzungu
Strong like a lion	Nguvu kama simba

Quotes that made us laugh

Our chief guide Robert when asked whether we would receive hot water for washing again after our dusty bonus hike late afternoon: "No need for wash."

Our lead guide Evance when asked whether we could have a longer break: "OK, let's have a BIG SHORT break."

Our waiter commenting about a certain spicy dish: "It's not hot, it's a little spicy."

Eva on asking whether she didn't feel cold, wearing a thin top whilst the rest of us were bundled up in warm layers including beanies, sitting inside the mess tent: "It's hot here. I'm boiling all the time. I'm English!"

Robert when asked about the point of our completely unnecessary so-called bonus hike late afternoon after just completing our sixth day's trek: "You've come here to hike, right?"

Lynn cheerfully on asking her first thing in the morning how she was feeling after a few days' hiking and when most weren't sleeping well: "Jubilant!"

Robert briefing us about summit hike: "If you feel sick, you just puke one time . . . or four times . . . and you carry on. It's normal."

A passing porter when asked about the distance to the next camp: "For me, 10 minutes . . . for you, 20 minutes."

Unexpected things to expect on Kilimanjaro

Getting sick – cold, nausea, headache, upset stomach – that's normal, even for the most fit and sturdy.

Suffering from altitude sickness despite taking Diamox, or not suffering from it despite not taking Diamox.

Change of character (or revelation of true character?) – more extrovert due to excitement or completely introvert due to mental and physical challenge.

Dust and dirty fingernails – all the time and always again within seconds of cleaning.

Wearing your gaiters all the time even in sunshine – welcome to the land of sand and dust!

Losing temper or becoming unfriendly during the summit hike despite best intentions – due to physical exhaustion.

Change in taste – meat eaters loving veggie soup; coffee addicts hating coffee; non-South Africans loving porridge; non-pregnant people enjoying egg frittata on top of a Nutella bread.

Porters carrying more than 20kg walking twice as fast as you.

Rescue porters carrying stretchers weighing 50kg walking still faster than you.

Never getting exhausted on the way up (except summit day) due to the constant *pole pole* slow motion pace.

Getting exhausted on the way down when all guides seem to turn their *pole pole* into *haraka* or run as fast as you can.

Losing your shame – peeing next to others, not caring whether anyone hears you fart in the toilet tent or your own tent.

Asking your guides about the distance to the next camp or milestone, and finding out later that it was a huge over- or understatement.

Having cold feet despite sleeping with two pairs of thick socks, but getting warm feet when sleeping without socks.

Losing weight despite stuffing yourself like crazy, or gaining weight even though you didn't go overboard.

Finding a ghost on your night photo shot, hovering and watching over your camp while everyone is sleeping . . . or your fantasy going wild.

Either hating or loving your trip while people sharing exactly the same trip make the extreme opposite experience – there's no in between.

Forming new lasting friendships amongst your hiking group and/or realizing that people with whom you have booked your hike are not friends after all.

Falling in love – with the mountain; with the simple lifestyle focused on eating, sleeping, keeping warm and having a great time with the people around you, without caring a dime about how you look or what's happening in the world; with your guides' singing; or perhaps even in the most literal sense.

Acknowledgements

I would like to express my deepest gratitude to my fellow hikers on Kilimanjaro. Thank you for making our adventure so enjoyable, for your friendship and comradeship, for sharing your experience and wisdom with me, for bearing with me when I may have been overly excited, talkative or loud while some of you may have preferred a more quiet and meditative experience. Each of you contributed to making this trip so special. Most of all, thank you for simply being there and sharing this experience with me. It would have meant little without you. I will often look at our joint summit photo and think back with very fond memories of each of you: Chris, Diego, Eva, Giovanni, Juli, Lynn, Jeannette, Jana, Ravindra, Farrah, Stewart – thank you.

In particular, I am tremendously grateful to Chris for sharing this experience with me. You made this trip special for me. Feeling our connection gave an entirely new and unexpected meaning to my adventure. I can't find the right words to give justice to how grateful I am, but I trust you know what I mean without the need to articulate, and that silent understanding captures it all. Thank you.

Furthermore, I am grateful to Jeannette for her intriguing foreword; to Juli for inspiring me to follow my heart and intuition; to Stewart for his generous review quote; to Jana and Diego for sharing with me their side of the story and to everyone else for their encouragements, perspectives and clarifications; to Jana for her helpful editing comments; and to Chris, Giovanni, Lynn, Jeannette and Ravi for allowing me to reproduce their photos.

I am also deeply grateful to the entire Ultimate Kilimanjaro team for making this possible and for providing such a smooth and flawless service. Thank you Shawn for patiently answering all and each of my myriad of questions in record time. Most importantly, I would like to express my highest appreciation for the tremendous work and efforts of our entire hiking crew. You made sure that we all made it to the top and safely down again. But to me, making it to the top was secondary, something I had taken as a given. What blew my mind was the way you treated us and made us feel, more like friends and family rather than the kind of annoying clients that definitely at times we were.

A special thank you to our chief guide Robert, our lead guide Evance as well as our supporting guides Baraka, Estomee, Hapygod and Samwel. You were always friendly and supportive, yet serious and firm when we needed a bit of a mental push for our own good. You prioritized our health and safety, you set the pace to make sure we could all make it to the top, you offered us your friendship and shared with us your experience, you made us laugh many times, you sang for us with all your passion and joy, and you made us walk as a group fostering the connection and friendship amongst us. Thank you.

I would also like to mention our summit porters Liberat and Charles. You accompanied us to the top carrying some of our heavy bags all the way up and staying behind to support our group members on their difficult way back down. Without you, some of us may not have made it to the top and we wouldn't have been able to share this special moment together as a group at Uhuru Peak. Thank you.

In order to give us strength and energy, we relied on the nutritious meals prepared for us by our skillful chef Justine (Mr. Delicious) and his assistant cook Amani, served by our two waiters Crispin and Sostenence. Not only was the food nutritious, fresh and plentiful, it was also extremely tasty. I will never forget your warm smiles and cheerful singing and dancing when you came into our mess tent twice unexpectedly with a delicious congratulatory cake, giving us all a very special moment. Thank you.

Last but not least, I would like to thank those people who did the heavy lifting and carried our personal equipment, tents and food, who fetched our water, who packed out tents after we left camp, overtook us swiftly on the way and made sure everything was set up again by the time we arrived, just like fairies. On top of that, they would welcome us with a warm smile and heartfelt congratulations when we arrived at the camp, after they had actually done all the work and deserved the praise. Albert, Alfred, Augustion, Calvin, Cosmas, David, Deo, Elias, Eliasa, Elibariki, Elisamehe, Elisante, Emanuel C., Emanuel M., Erasto, Ezekiel, Godfrey, Gudlack, Hamidu, Martin, Mashaka, Melkyori, Meshack, Michael, Ojungu, Omary, Peter, Ramadhani, Richard, Severine, Tumaini – thank you.

One of our porters deserves a special mention – our toilet porter Dominick. He would not only carry our portable plastic toilet and always set up the toilet tent for us, but also keep it clean and empty our waste. Thank you Dominick.

Prior to my hike, I met with the Kilimanjaro Porters Assistance Project (KPAP) team. I would like to thank them for welcoming me so warmly and in particular the KPAP Program Manager Karen Valenti for taking the time to explain to me the porter treatment situation, the background of KPAP and the wonderful work that the KPAP team are doing. Thank you.

During my trip preparations, I had to organize a lot of equipment, clothing and accessories. In that context, Christian of SportXX deserves a special mention. You patiently and expertly advised me on buying my hiking boots and other gear. The boots were perfect, the state-of-the art hiking poles attracted quite some attention, and also everything else worked like a charm. Thank you.

In order to gather enough energy to see my little project through from the beginning to the end, I am grateful to my family and friends in Zurich who had to bear with me throughout 2015 and the bigger part of 2016, constantly hijacking our conversation topics to tell them about my latest discoveries and developments regarding Kilimanjaro and this book. Thank you for always listening to me and giving me the opportunity to share my excitement with someone, at the risk of boring you to death.

In particular, I would like to thank Nicole for sharing with me her passion for extreme travels; for constantly keeping me on track and making sure I actually finish this book; for proofreading and providing valuable suggestions.

I would also like to say a special thanks to Rachael for lending me her hiking gear and sharing her expert hiking insights with me. More importantly, thank you for pushing me to aim higher; for being a constant sounding board throughout my creative process; for convincing me to have the book properly edited; and for asking your mum to be such a great editor for me.

Hence, I am greatly indebted to Rachael's mum Raewyn for volunteering to proofread and edit this book. Your valuable comments and suggestions, the result of your overwhelming endurance and long hours dedicated to this book, have not only made me sound less like a German speaker, but more importantly helped me downsize from the volume of an impossible epic to the length of a barely manageable trilogy. Through your work, *Kilimanjaro Uncovered* has become a lot more readable. My stubbornness is to blame for remaining excesses.

Finally, I would also like to thank my parents for bearing with me while I went off the grid into the unknown and made you worry. I hope now you can see that my trip was not dangerous and that you will be more at ease during my next adventure. Tour d'Afrique 2017 – here I come!

About the author

Alexandra is a passionate traveler and explorer. Born in Austria and currently living in Switzerland, Tanbai is her pseudonym as a hobby writer. It is Mandarin Chinese and derived from the combination of the first character for Tanzania (坦, pronounced *tǎn*) as well as her Chinese surname (白, pronounced *bái*). Incidentally, the two characters in combination (坦白, pronounced *tǎnbái*) have the meaning of being frank and honest, perhaps to the degree of confessing. And that's what Alexandra also hopes to reflect in her writing, an authentic account of her experience including innermost feelings and emotions, positive and negative, strong and vulnerable alike. Via her writing, she hopes to foster mutual understanding and thereby provide her tiny little contribution to making this world a better place.

Kilimanjaro Uncovered is Alexandra's first publication. It started with a simple idea – to provide a review of a little-known hiking route as well as helpful preparatory information that she found lacking in other Kilimanjaro literature. It ended with an extraordinary story of a truly life-changing experience – written in real time while the author was unaware of being the subject of transformation. On Kilimanjaro, Alexandra found what no book could have prepared her for: herself. One year down the path, Alexandra's life changes couldn't be more profound – from a career in corporate finance into founding a social enterprise; from being a hopeless city chic scared of a week in the wild into a hopeful adventurer scared of a life in the city; from being intimidated by her first travel to Africa into planning to cycle all the way from Cairo to Cape Town. All because of Kilimanjaro, a simple idea and the courage to follow her intuition.

There's only one constant, and that's change. But there will be many more stories, and they remain to be written. Follow @AlexandraTanbai on Twitter to stay tuned.

Notes and references

[1] Henry Stedman's Kilimanjaro Trekking Guide mentions 57,456 climbers in 2011/12 as per official KINAPA statistics. Most recently, AllAfrica refers to over 60,000 visitors in an article of June 2016 (allafrica.com/stories/201606060064.html).

[2] My operator also quotes an estimate of about ten tourist deaths per year, but confirmed this is based on hearsay only as there is no official data.

[3] Source: *Climbing Kilimanjaro*, video production by CCTV (2016).

[4] Source: Swiss Statistics.

[5] Source: Swiss Alpine Club

[6] Source: Ultimate Kilimanjaro.

[7] Source: Climate System Research Center, UMass Amherst Department of Geosciences, Doug Hardy et al. (2008).

[8] Sources: Kilimanjaro National Park, Ultimate Kilimanjaro.

[9] Source: www.climbkilimanjaroguide.com.

[10] Source: Ultimate Kilimanjaro.

[11] According to Google Maps, the distance between Crater Camp and Uhuru Peak is 650m.

[12] Source: Wikipedia.

[13] Source: www.westernbreach.co.uk.

[14] If Crater Camp tempts you, you are looking for a group tour and budget is not a concern, check out Thomson Safaris. I will only learn about them on Kilimanjaro. They offer the Crater Camp via Uhuru Peak as part of their so-called 10-day Grand Traverse. If I ever hike Kilimanjaro a second time, I would be tempted to try their tour for an even more extreme experience, even though it would break my new record of most expensive vacation ever that I'm establishing this time round. However, as a Kilimanjaro first timer, I would only recommend it if you already have high altitude experience and evidence to believe that your body handles altitude well. For most hikers, it would be an absolute nightmare to stay up near the peak for another night after summiting.

[15] Source: Ultimate Kilimanjaro as per Kilimanjaro National Park data reported in 2006. I was not able to locate the original source of information or any more up-to-date data. The same source also reports an average success rate across all routes of 45% (as of 2006). As there has been an increase in the average route length following more awareness of the role of acclimatization, the average success rate most likely has gone up significantly over the past ten years.

[16] Source: www.mountkilimanjaroguide.com.

[17] Once on Kilimanjaro, I will be told that the route is not that new after all but has been in existence for a long time. However, it hadn't been advertised for group tours and only offered in private arrangements.

[18] It also joins again with the Lemosho and/or Shira Route (different variations exist) on the fourth night at Moir Hut, but the hiking routes getting there are different.

[19] Source: summitpost.org.

[20] According to the travelhealthpro.org.uk and fitfortravel.nhs.uk websites (both recommended by the UK government for travel health advice), no antimalarials are 100% effective. However, my tropics specialist doctor later suggested that I wouldn't need to worry about a malaria infection when taking Malarone which in her opinion could be considered a safe 100% protection when taken correctly.

[21] Source: www.climbmountkilimanjaro.com.

[22] Source: www.mountainexplorers.org.

[23] At the time of writing, 2013 was the last year for which KPAP published data on their website (www.kiliporters.org).

[24] Source: Gane and Marshall.

[25] Source: *The truth about Porters Treatment on Mount Kilimanjaro*, video by Peal Deakin (2012).

[26] Source: www.ultimatekilimanjaro.com/blog/should-i-use-supplemental-oxygen-on-kilimanjaro/.

[27] Sources: www.amperordirect.com/pc/help-pulse-oximeter/z-pulse-oximeter-limitations.html, amga.com, www.ncbi.nlm.nih.gov/pubmed/21718156.

[28] We found modern toilet facilities at Shira 2 and Millenium Camp, but none of the other camps along the Northern Circuit route.

[29] Source: wafe-technology.ch.

[30] Malarone is the common trade name for atovaquone/proguanil. Generics might be available in your country at your time of reading.

[31] Lariam is the common trade name for mefloquine. Generics might be available in your country at your time of reading.

[32] I got lucky and would not notice any side effects from Malarone.

[33] Sources: www.webmd.com/drugs/2/drug-6753/diamox-oral/details#uses, www.drugs.com/mtm/diamox.html, www.medicinenet.com/acetazolamide-oral/article.htm, www.traveldoctor.co.uk/altitude.htm.

[34] In hindsight, I should have known better because several articles have been written about KPAP and its volunteer manager Karen Valenti, e.g.: www.mcclatchydc.com/news/nation-world/world/article24722476.html, www.ibtimes.com/everest-sherpas-boycott-climbing-season-porters-kilimanjaro-work-less-1577402, newspapers.bc.edu/cgi-bin/bostonsh?a=d&d=bcheights20110411-01.2.37.

[35]Sources: www.webmd.com/drugs/2/drug-6753/diamox-oral/details#uses, www.drugs.com/mtm/diamox.html, www.medicinenet.com/acetazolamide-oral/article.htm, www.traveldoctor.co.uk/altitude.htm and many more.

[36] For more information about Diamox, please refer to the expert advice provided by the Everest Base Camp Medical Clinic at www.basecampmd.com/expguide/diamox.shtml.

[37] Ravi kindly clarified afterwards that he advised people to keep taking both anti-malarial drugs and Diamox, and that he also advised on the best way to prevent malaria by continuing to take their anti-malarial drugs both before and after the malaria zone. He considers malaria a substantial risk. Only in the context if people really had concerns about co-administration of both anti-malarial drugs and Diamox and needed to choose one over the other, he would consider AMS the higher risk.

[38] Sources: www.lonelyplanet.com/tanzania/health, www.tripadvisor.com/ShowTopic-g293747-i9226-k8563158-Anti_Malaria_Treatments_pros_cons-Tanzania.html.

[39] In hindsight, I understand why our operator didn't bother to take note of our insurance details. Hiking Kilimanjaro is no more dangerous than hiking in the Swiss Alps, and I wouldn't even think of taking any such measures when going off for a weekend hike at home. It's rather a perceived risk and would make tourists feel more comfortable to know someone has their insurance details, rather than a meaningful likelihood that it would ever be required and accessed by the operator (versus the hiker being sufficiently conscious to do so).

[40] Different reputable sources quote different elevation indications for the same camps. For example, Ultimate Kilimanjaro and other websites base their quotes on Henry Stedman's Kilimanjaro guidebook, which however is different to the indications of the official park signs. Throughout this book, quotes are based on the elevation indications stated by the official park signs, if any, and based on Ultimate Kilimanjaro's website otherwise.

[41] Sources: news.trust.org//item/?map=deforestation-fuels-temperature-hikes-around-mt-kilimanjaro, www.reuters.com/article/us-climate-tanzania-kilimanjaro-idUSTRE5B72AQ20091208.

[42] Source: mellowswanafrica.org/reforest-tanzania/.

[43] Source: www.unep.org/dewa/Portals/67/pdf/kili_forest.pdf.

[44] At the time of our hike, there was still little known and Evance's information was based on hearsay. In fact, one tourist (not two) lost his live. His name was Scott Dinsmore (American, 33 years old). He was hiking with his wife who escaped without serious injuries. A National Geographic article by James Balog as an eyewitness provides a shocking account of this tragic incident and the dangers of the Western Breach: www.nationalgeographic.com/adventure/activities/climbing/kilimanjaro-breach-climbing-death/.

According to local sources, the tour operator was Destination Tanzania Safaris. That operator advertises the Western Breach route on its website. I sent them an inquiry, which remains unanswered as of publication.

[45] Source: www.ncbi.nlm.nih.gov/pubmed/16355646.

[46] Source: www.thomsontreks.com/blog/kilimanjaro-lava-tower/.

[47] Source: en.wikipedia.org/wiki/Volcanic_plug.

[48] Upon return, I found the price of the 10-day Grand Traverse quoted as US$7,890 on the Thomson Safaris website. Their itinerary looks interesting, approaching the mountain from the west, crossing on the northern side all the way over to Mawenzi Tarn in the east, and finally an overnight stay at Crater Camp after summiting Uhuru Peak. According to their Strategic Development Director, their seemingly high price is justified by their longer route including a safari acclimatization day prior to the start of the hike, the fact that they offer Crater Camp which means that they also need to pay more to the porters who carry the tents and limited equipment all the way up to the summit, their luxurious equipment, and their outstanding staff and porters treatment. As confirmed by KPAP, they are not only a partner organization but also one of the organization's founding members and have been dedicating significant efforts to establish ethical industry practices and treat their own staff significantly better than the minimum standards. KPAP would also point out to me that Thomson Safaris have a greater number of porters to support their climbs in order to give the climber a special experience. Furthermore, they are known for their exceptional safety precautions and always have a separate "medical porter" who is at the rear end of the crew with all of the specialized medical equipment. In KPAP's opinion, they are a 5-star climbing company in their services and this is reflected in the number of crew as well as their prices.

Regarding their 10-day Grand Traverse route, I also asked Thomson Safaris whether ascending all the way up to Moir Hut at c. 4,200m / 13,600ft already on day 2 isn't really bad for altitude acclimatization. They argue that such altitude can still be handled very well by most hikers, especially because the route they follow is not too steep, gaining altitude only slowly. They claim to have a summit success rate of 98%, which is in line with the success rate advertised by Ultimate Kilimanjaro for the Northern Circuit route.

[49] Thomson Safaris doesn't provide showers on group tours, but they could be booked as an extra feature on a private tour if absolutely required. However, they would discourage it due to the environmental impact, the need to carry water requiring the labor of at least two more porters, as well as the temperature in general being too cold to enjoy a shower in the first place.

[50] You will find the photo in color and bigger resolution at www.kilimanjaro-uncovered.com/spookiest-kilimanjaro-night-shot/.

[51] While I remember the summit experience very vividly, I cannot remember saying "I've carried it myself. Why should I share it?" Diego seems confident that I said that, thus I have included it giving him the benefit of doubt.

[52] Source: volcano.oregonstate.edu/kilimanjaro.

[53] Different sources provide different estimates; throughout this book I base distance indications on the Google Maps route planner.

[54] Different sources provide different estimates; throughout this book I base distance indications on the Google Maps route planner.

[55] Source: www.the-cryosphere.net/7/419/2013/tc-7-419-2013.pdf.

[56] Source: www.skepticalscience.com/mount-kilimanjaro-snow.htm.

[57] Source: www.thomasmoelg.info/factsheet_kili.pdf.

[58] Source: www.livescience.com/41930-kilimanjaro-glaciers-shrinking.html.

[59] Source: thulescientific.com/Lynch Curvature 2008.pdf.

[60] There are no official statistics on how many hikers have summited Kilimanjaro. Based on my own rough estimate, considering that Kilimanjaro has only become popular over the past 20 years, with perhaps initially some 10,000 and now up to 30,000 summits a year (maximum, based on average success rates and considering that some hikers stop at Gillman's or Stella Point), I assume that no more than 500,000 tourists have summited Uhuru Peak to date.

[61] In fact it was not Stewart's knee but his SI (sacroiliac) joint that would make his descent an ordeal.

[62] You fill find the full lyrics of the *Kilimanjaro* and *Jambo* songs at www.thomsontreks.com/blog/jambo-song-on-kilimanjaro/. The *Jambo* song is an adaptation of the most well-known Kenyan pop song among foreigners, which sings about *"Kenya yetu"* (our Kenya) instead of Kilimanjaro (source: en.wikipedia.org/wiki/Jambo_Bwana).

[63] You will find the full video including lyrics and translations at www.youtube.com/watch?v=ugg01Me-2R4.

[64] Source: tedxtalks.ted.com/video/Why-we-re-unhappy-the-expectati.

Printed in Poland
by Amazon Fulfillment
Poland Sp. z o.o., Wrocław